T0212377

Lecture Notes in Artificial Intelligence   **12336**

Subseries of Lecture Notes in Computer Science

More information about this series at http://www.springer.com/series/1244

Andrey Ronzhin · Gerhard Rigoll ·
Roman Meshcheryakov (Eds.)

Interactive Collaborative Robotics

5th International Conference, ICR 2020
St Petersburg, Russia, October 7–9, 2020
Proceedings

 Springer

Editors
Andrey Ronzhin 🆔
St. Petersburg Federal Research Center
of the Russian Academy of Sciences
St. Petersburg, Russia

Roman Meshcheryakov 🆔
Institute of Control Sciences
of the Russian Academy of Sciences
Moscow, Russia

Gerhard Rigoll 🆔
Technical University of Munich
Munich, Germany

ISSN 0302-9743   ISSN 1611-3349   (electronic)
Lecture Notes in Artificial Intelligence
ISBN 978-3-030-60336-6   ISBN 978-3-030-60337-3   (eBook)
https://doi.org/10.1007/978-3-030-60337-3

LNCS Sublibrary: SL7 – Artificial Intelligence

This Springer imprint is published by the registered company Springer Nature Switzerland AG
The registered company address is: Gewerbestrasse 11, 6330 Cham, Switzerland

ICR 2020 Preface

The 5th International Conference on Interactive Collaborative Robotics (ICR 2020) was organized as a satellite event of the 22nd International Conference on Speech and Computer (SPECOM 2020) by the St. Petersburg Institute for Informatics and Automation of the Russian Academy of Sciences (SPIIRAS, St. Petersburg, Russia) and the Technical University of Munich (TUM, Munich, Germany). In July 2020, SPIIRAS incorporated five other research institutions, but has now been transformed into the St. Petersburg Federal Research Center of the Russian Academy of Sciences (SPC RAS).

ICR 2020 was organized as a virtual conference in the online format during October 7–9, 2020. Challenges of human-robot interaction, robot control and behavior in social robotics and collaborative robotics, as well as applied robotic and cyber-physical systems were mainly discussed at the conference.

During the conference an invited talk "A Concept for a Human-Robot Collaboration Workspace using Proximity Sensors" was given by Prof. Ilshat Mamaev (Karlsruhe Institute of Technology, Germany).

Due to the COVID-19 global pandemic, for the first time, ICR 2020 was organized as a fully virtual conference. The virtual conference, in the online format by Zoom had a number of advantages including: an increased number of participants because listeners could take part without any fees, essentially reduced registration fees for authors of the presented papers, no costs for travel and accommodation, a paperless green conference with only electronic proceedings, free access to video presentations after the conference, comfortable home conditions, etc.

This volume contains a collection of 31 papers presented at the conference, which were thoroughly reviewed by members of the Program Committee consisting of more than 20 top specialists in the conference topic areas. Theoretical and more general contributions were presented in common (plenary) sessions. Problem-oriented sessions as well as panel discussions then brought together specialists in limited problem areas with the aim of exchanging knowledge and skills resulting from research projects of all kinds.

Last but not least, we would like to express our gratitude to the authors for providing their papers on time, to the members of the conference reviewing team and Program Committee for their careful reviews and paper selection, and to the editors for their hard work preparing this volume. Special thanks are due to the members of the Local Organizing Committee for their tireless effort and enthusiasm during the conference organization. We hope that you benefitted from the event and that you also enjoyed the social program prepared by the members of the Organizing Committee.

October 2020

Andrey Ronzhin
Gerhard Rigoll
Roman Meshcheryakov

Organization

The ICR 2020 conference was organized by the St. Petersburg Institute for Informatics and Automation of the Russian Academy of Sciences (SPIIRAS, St. Petersburg, Russia) in cooperation with the Technical University of Munich (TUM, Munich, Germany). The conference website is located at: http://www.specom.nw.ru/icr2020/.

Program Committee

Roman Meshcheryakov (Co-chair), Russia
Gerhard Rigoll (Co-chair), Germany
Andrey Ronzhin (Co-chair), Russia
Andres Annuk, Estonia
Christos Antonopoulos, Greece
Branislav Borovac, Serbia
Oleg Darintsev, Russia
Ivan Ermolov, Russia
Rinat Galin, Russia
Oliver Jokisch, Germany
Igor Kalyaev, Russia
Alexey Kashevnik, Russia
Dongheui Lee, Germany
Evgeni Magid, Russia
Vladimir Pavlovskiy, Russia
Viacheslav Pshikhopov, Russia
Mirko Rakovic, Serbia
José Rosado, Portugal
Hooman Samani, Taiwan
Jesus Savage, Mexico
Anton Saveliev, Russia
Evgeny Shandarov, Russia
Lev Stankevich, Russia
Tilo Strutz, Germany
Sergey Yatsun, Russia
Zeynep Yucel, Japan
Milos Zelezny, Czech Republic
Lyudmila Zinchenko, Russia

Organizing Committee

Andrey Ronzhin (Chair)
Anton Saveliev
Dmitry Ryumin
Natalia Kashina
Ekaterina Miroshnikova
Margarita Avstriyskaya
Natalia Dormidontova
Dmitriy Levonevskiy

Contents

A Concept for a HRC Workspace Using Proximity Sensors

Ilshat Mamaev[1(✉)], Hosam Alagi[1], Gergely Sóti[1], and Björn Hein[1,2]

[1] IAR-IPR, Karlsruhe Institute of Technology, Karlsruhe, Germany
{ilshat.mamaev,hosam.alagi,gergely.soti,bjoern.hein}@kit.edu
[2] Karlsruhe University of Applied Sciences, Karlsruhe, Germany

Abstract. Human-Robot Collaboration (HRC) poses new challenges for robotic perception systems. This paper proposes a concept for HRC workspace augmented with capacitive proximity sensors and present methods for camera-less multi-human/multi-object detection, localization, and tracking based on proximity feedback. A gamified HRC experiment realizing shell-game is designed for evaluation purposes. Experimental results performed in the presented HRC setup verify that the proposed methods are able to detect, localize, and track objects using only the Capacitive Proximity Sensors (CPS) feedback.

Keywords: Human-Robot Collaboration · Capacitive proximity sensing · Object detection · Localization and tracking

1 Introduction

Collaborative robots can complement human capabilities and push forward automation in previously exclusively manual production lines. In this way, monotonous or physically demanding work steps can be laid out to robots, which would relieve the employees' burden and maintain consistent high quality. In robotics, optical sensors like cameras and laser scanners are traditionally used for perception and safety. However, they are prone to challenges in divergent light conditions, limited focal range, highly reflective or transparent surfaces, etc.

In this paper, we propose a concept for a versatile Human-Robot Collaborative (HRC) workspace using multi-modal sensors and a collaborative robot. Due to the nature of HRC, the joint effort of such a human-robot team implies proximity and close collaboration between the robot and the human. To augment the system sensor capabilities and compensate drawbacks of optical sensors, we introduce Capacitive Proximity Sensors (CPS) into the HRC concept and propose methods for camera-less multi human/object detection, localization, and tracking. Finally, we evaluate the proposed concept against gamified HRC scenario, where human is playing a shell-game in the HRC workspace with a robot.

© Springer Nature Switzerland AG 2020
A. Ronzhin et al. (Eds.): ICR 2020, LNAI 12336, pp. 1–12, 2020.
https://doi.org/10.1007/978-3-030-60337-3_1

2   State of the Art

2.1   Human-Robot Collaboration

While human entering into the workspace of a robot is considered an emergency in classical industrial robotics, there are new research fields of Human-Robot Interaction (HRI) and Human-Robot Collaboration (HRC) where robots are expected to work side by side with humans. The difference between HRI and sub-setted HRC is the necessity of joint effort for the collaboration (e.g., handshake), whereas interaction entails "only" acting on someone or something else (e.g., commanding the robot to move) [6]. Collaborative systems without safety fences have been introduced in normative document ISO 10218-2 [1], proposing more relaxed and flexible safeguarding solutions. Consequently, the ISO/TS15066 [2] permitted the contact between humans and robots and proposed 4 modes for collaborative operation: safety-rated monitored stop, hand-guiding operation, speed and separation monitoring, and power and force limiting. In this paper, we mainly focus on the Speed and Separation Monitoring (SSM) in HRC tasks, where user tracking and object detection/localization is of utmost importance for safe and robust collaborative operation. We address the high level human and robot collaboration as it is categorized in a feasibility study of the United States Consortium for Automotive Research (USCAR) [12]. It is characterized by fully automated and sensor-based robot motion while a human is in the working space of the robot. Such scenarios could include multiple humans and multiple robots, which increases the potential of blind spots in the perception.

2.2   Sensors

One of the main challenges in monitoring HRI/HRC is optical occlusion, which may occur when robots or humans in action obstruct the field of view of globally installed perception systems, such as cameras, laser scanners or radar sensors.

Traditionally, optical sensors are widely used in robotic applications, e.g., safety laser scanners for safeguarding operational space, stereo- and ToF-cameras for visual perception in robotic manipulation tasks.

Sadrfaridpour and Wang [11] presented a framework for a collaborative assembly task, where the worker's hand was tracked using Phase-Space system with active markers. Based on the pose of the hand, the paths of the robot end-effector from and to the shared workspace were adapted, showing the reduction in the human workload while maintaining the overall performance.

In industrial robotics, the sensor of choice for safety is the LIDAR (Light Detection and Ranging) [5], which uses reflections from the human body for operator presence detection [13]. Nevertheless, optical systems are susceptible to light and weather conditions, visual occlusions in the scene, problems in close range situations due to focal length or bi-static configuration of emitter and receiver [4].

Unlike vision-based systems, radio technology can detect occluded targets and can work in different light conditions. Rampa et al. [10] propose an approach for safe HRC using device-free radio localization. The wireless system is used to detect and localize humans in multi-robot collaborative environments by analyzing the fluctuations of radio-frequency electromagnetic waves in dense wireless networks. Radar systems can be beneficial to optical ones in harsh conditions and occluded spaces, however, they are prone to electromagnetic interference and lack of accuracy.

Overall, a well designed global perception system would solve the detection and localization problem in some HRC scenarios, however, with the drawback being expensive and complex. Furthermore, for close and intensive interactive tasks, a gapless perception of the robot's near-field is essential.

To address these challenges, we propose a concept for an HRC workspace with capacitive proximity sensors integrated into the worktable. The sensor system is capable of detecting, localizing as well as tracking multi-objects.

3   Concept

3.1   HRC Workspace

We present a concept for HRC scenarios including moving humans and collaborative robots. The usage of collaborative robots ensures the Power and Force Limiting operation due to reactive control strategies and torque feedback [7]. As the human is closely interacting with the robot to complete a task, the shared workspace must be continuously monitored. By integrating proximity sensors inside the table both under the tabletop and on the sides, we can detect operator proximity to the collaborative workspace and localize objects on the table without using a camera. Human detection and tracking is beneficial for collaborative operations with speed and separation monitoring.

Figure 1 illustrates the model of the HRC workspace and highlights the different workspaces:

- robot operating space: the room where the robot joint movements take place (in contrast to robot workspace - set of all reachable endpoint positions);
- human workspace: the room where a human can perform tasks
- collaborative space: room inside the robot operation space where robotic system and a human can perform tasks either jointly or concurrently (TS15066, 3.3);

3.2   Capacitive Sensing

By driving an electrode (electrically conductive part) with an alternating electrical potential, an alternating electrical field is generated between this electrode and objects in its environment and build a *capacitor*; an alternating current flow through this capacitor can be then measured at the driver. As long the environment is static, the current flow is constant. While moving objects influence the electrical field configuration (field lines) and thus the current flow. These changes correspond to the objects' material, size, and relative position to the electrode.

Figure 2 shows our implementation of a capacitive sensing system that has been presented in a previous work [3]. A signal generator drives *eight* electrodes sequentially while the current flow is determined over a shunt resistor R. A microcontroller μC synchronizes the multiplexer M and the analog-digital-convector ADC and calculates the amplitude of the current of each electrode. The sensing electrodes E_s are shielded with driven electrode E_g in order to eliminate parasitic effects. The presented system is modular and can be scaled up to form a large sensing area with higher spatial resolution.

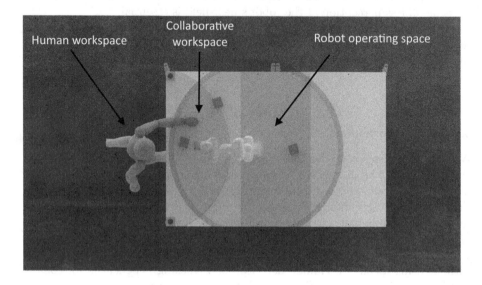

Fig. 1. CAD model of the HRC workspace.

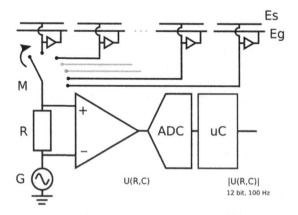

Fig. 2. Capacitive sensor module - Measurement circuit.

4   Implementation

4.1   Hardware Setup

Capacitive Sensor Array. The developed capacitive sensors are modular and highly scalable. Over an *Inter-Integrated Circuit* bus *(I2C)* multiple sensor modules are addressable as slaves. The number of the slaves depends on the electrical capabilities of the I2C bus such as the capacitive load and the data rate; it can reach 123 slaves in case of 7-Bit I2C-addresses. The exciter signals of the modules are synchronized to eliminate the self-influence (Fig. 3).

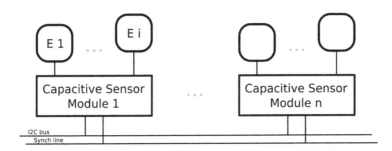

Fig. 3. Capacitive proximity sensor system. Multiple capacitive sensor modules can be networked over an I2C bus and a synchronization line. The number of the modules n depends on the capabilities of the I2C bus and can be up to 123.

We have built and integrated two sensor arrays with different electrode sizes deepening on the required perception.

Sensor Array for Tracking Hands and Objects. The array covers an area of 76×24 cm^2 and consist of 96 measurement points (electrodes) and is driven by 12 sensor modules, as shown in Fig. 4. The electrodes are round shaped with a diameter of 4 cm, providing a measurement range of 10 cm.

Sensor Array for Tracking Workers. The sensors are mounted inside the table at each wall, as shown in Fig. 5. The electrodes for a strip with dimensions 1×24 with the size of 10×10 cm^2 each are driven by 3 modules. They provide a measurement range of 15 cm.

Both arrays are interfaced with a *ROS* driver, which can configure and read out the sensor modules over a *COM port*. The association of the electrode positions to a specific geometry is done in further *ROS*-nodes, which includes the geometric description of the arrays.

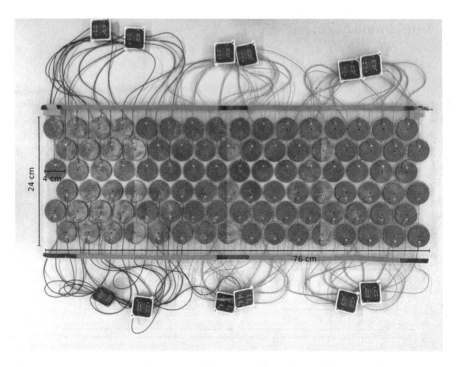

Fig. 4. Capacitive Sensor array 6 × 16 driven by 12 modules. Each electrode has a round shape with a diameter of 4 cm, providing a measurement range of 10 cm.

Fig. 5. Capacitive Sensor array 1 × 24 driven by 3 modules. Each electrode has the size of 10 × 10 cm² a measurement range of 15 cm.

4.2   Software Methods

Interaction Detection. Data from the sensor arrays can be used to detect whether a user is interacting with the table. Since the CPS values caused by the proximity of a human user are significantly larger than values caused by inanimate objects, a threshold can be applied to the difference of two consecutively received raw CPS data to differentiate whether the user is currently acting in the shared workspace or not.

Object Detection and Localization. Two methods from image processing were applied to localize multi objects, wherever they appear, at the side of the table (human) or on the table (workers hands and objects).

The *Connected Component Labeling* algorithm is used to identify multi detection and returns multi objects depending on a prior knowledge, e.g. the minimum projection area. The appearance duration of an object is also considered to filter out the noise, which is as follows:

$$\begin{cases} object, & if\ C_i > \tau_c \\ Noise, Otherwise \end{cases},\qquad(1)$$

where C_i is the component area of ith detected object, and τ_c is the threshold value.

A more sophisticated algorithm *k-means* is applied to localize k objects. It uses the locations of the CPS weighted with their sensor values to determine the centroids of k clusters. These can then be refined if additional information of the objects is available.

Multi-object Tracking. Object tracking can be divided into two phases as follows: object detection and object tracking. For object detection the data collected from the sensor arrays – 1×8 and 6×16 – is treated as a one-dimensional and a two-dimension image respectively. This allows us to apply methods from computer vision to detect moving objects in the proximity of the worktable.

First we apply *background subtraction* by calculating the initial offset of the sensor data and subtracting it from the sensor data stream. This can be expressed as follows:

$$BS_t(x) = \begin{cases} 0,\ if\,(I_t(x) - B(x)) < \tau_{BS} \\ 1,\ if\,(I_t(x) - B(x)) \geq \tau_{BS} \end{cases},\qquad(2)$$

where $I_t(x)$ is the input sensor values at step t, $BS(x)$ is the background signals and τ_{BS} is the threshold value. After this process, we assign the areas, where an object exists, to 1, and other areas to 0. In this way, the sensor values are changed into a binary vector. We then apply the *Connected Component Labeling* algorithm taking the binary vector/matrix as an input; the output is a symbolic vector/matrix, where the labels are assigned, identifying the unique connected component.

In the second phase the objects are tracked using *Kalman-Filter*. This was successfully evaluated in previous works [8,9]. The same number of trackers as the detected objects are deployed in order to estimate the object's state. Each Kalman-Filter tracker is configured as follows:

$$\begin{aligned} x_k &= Ax_{k-1} + \omega_k \\ z_k &= Hx_k + v_k, \end{aligned}\qquad(3)$$

where ω_k and v_k are the Gaussian noise with corresponding error covariances Q_k and R_k.

In the case of multiple object tracking, we obtain several measurements through detection. In order to assign the correct measurement to the corresponding object tracker, we use the method *Intersection over Union (IoU)* that describes the similarity of the sample sets.

The cost of assignment is described in Eq. (4). The smaller the cost is, the higher probability of the assignment being true.

$$Cost = \begin{cases} 1 - IoU, & if\ IoU > \tau \\ 1 + punishCost, & others \end{cases}, \tag{4}$$

where τ is the similarity threshold, and the IoU is then calculated with (5),

$$IoU = \frac{area(A \bigcap B)}{area(A \bigcup B)}, \tag{5}$$

where A represents the detected objects area and B represents the predicted objects area.

We obtain a $M * N$ cost matrix, where M represents the tracker's number, and N the measurement's. This way, the assignment problem turns into a cost minimization problem, which is then solved with the *Hungarian algorithm*.

5   HRC Experiment

To evaluate the setup, we designed an interaction scenario based on the shell-game. In this game, an operator shuffles three shells, one with a ball placed beneath, and a player has to guess which shell hides the ball. In our case, the operator would be the human, and the player would be the robot. The shells are ceramic espresso cups, and the ball is replaced by an aluminum disk that fits under the cup.

The rules of the shell-game are the following:

– There are always exactly two shells and one ball (disc) on the table.
– The shells and disc always have to be inside the sensor-area indicated by LEDs.
– Only game-relevant items should be in the field of vision of the camera (collaboration table, robot, shells, disc, player's hands).
– The operator has to wait for *idle* state (indicated by green pulsating lights) to start the game.
– The operator has to shuffle the shells and disc while in *observe* state. After shuffling, the disc has to be below one of the shells.
– The operator has to wait for the robot to pick the shell hiding the disc while in *grab* state (indicated by pulsating yellow lights).
– The operator should not interact with the table, shells and the robot if *grab* state is indicated by the LEDs.

If the player follows the rules, the collaboration table will not enter *stop* state (indicated by pulsating blue lights).

The human-robot collaboration table and the shell-game experiment were implemented using the Robot Operating System (ROS). ROS is an open-source, meta-operating system that abstracts processes as nodes in a graph. These processes communicate via the ROS infrastructure: messages, services, and actions. ROS enables operating system functions like hardware abstraction, low-level device control, and package management for robots. It also provides tools and libraries for obtaining, building, writing, and running code across multiple computers.

5.1   Shell-Game: System Architecture

The nodes used to implement the shell-game interact as follows (see Fig. 6):

- **CPS node:** provides raw sensor data and their offsets to the CPS wrapper node.
- **CPS geometry tools node:** pairs raw sensor data and sensor locations.
- **CPS wrapper node:** processes raw sensor data and data from the CPS geometry tools node. It detects movement and determines grasp positions.
- **LED node:** controls the color and dimming of the LEDs.
- **LED wrapper node:** implements the light patterns depending on the state of the shell-game.
- **Robot controller node:** controls robot movement via the *libfranka* interface provided by FRANKA EMIKA.
- **Collaboration table node:** implements the state machine of the shell-game, by using the CPS wrapper, LED wrapper, and robot controller nodes.

To detect user interaction in the CPS wrapper node, the method described in Sect. 4.2 is used with a threshold of 2 (empirically derived). For determining the grasp position of the shell hiding the ball, k-means is used (see Sect. 4.2). Additionally to the basic clustering method, the centroids are refined by averaging the sensor locations, weighted with their sensor values within a radius of 4 cm around the original centroids. To select the shell hiding the ball, the sensor values, within a radius of 4 cm around the refined centroids, are averaged. The location with the maximum average sensor value is used as grasp position if the said value is greater than a threshold (0.14, empirically derived). Otherwise, there is no valid grasp position.

Finite State Machine. The robot can be in four states during the shell-game. State transitions are controlled based on interaction detection of the CPS wrapper node (see Fig. 7). The four states are as follows:

- **idle** - the robot is in the home position and does nothing; a transition is made to *observe* state whenever the sensors indicate movement. The *idle* state is indicated by green pulsating lights on the LEDs.
- **observe** - the robot is in a home position and does nothing; after the sensors signal that there is no more movement, the position of the winning shell is

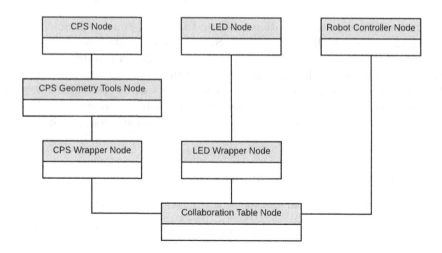

Fig. 6. ROS nodes controlling the shell-game.

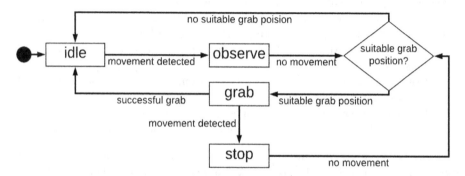

Fig. 7. States and state transitions during the shell game.

determined based on the sensor data. If no suitable position is found, the state changes to *idle*, if there is one, the state changes to *grab*. The *observe* state is indicated by green blinking lights on the LEDs.

- **grab** - the robot moves to the grasp position, and grabs the cup. It lifts the cup to show whether the disc is beneath. After putting the cup back down, the robot goes back to the home position, and the state changes to *idle*. During grasping, whenever the sensors indicate movement, robot movement is stopped and the state changes to *stop*. After the state changes back to *grab*, the grasp position is estimated again if the cup was not grasped yet, and the movement continues. The *grab* state is indicated by pulsating yellow lights on the LEDs.
- **stop** - the robot stops its movement completely; a transition is made to *grab* state, whenever the sensors indicate no more movement. The *stop* state is indicated by blue blinking lights on the LEDs.

6   Results and Conclusion

This paper describes the preliminary results of employing capacitive proximity sensors for multi-human/object detection, localization, and tracking without a camera in the HRC setup. The sensors were integrated into the table and can measure the capacitive fluctuations of the EMF. The proposed object detection method is based upon *Connected Component Labeling* algorithm and allows multi-object detection based on proximity feedback. For the object localization, we also propose to use *k-means clustering*. The object tracking is built upon the object detection method and *Kalman-Filter* for tracking, while the multi-object tracking is achieved using *Hungarian Algorithm*.

To evaluate the HRC setup, we asked 10 participants to play the shell-game. Out of 115 games, the correct shell hiding the ball was identified 114 times. Of these 114 times, the shell was grasped 110 times correctly. The 4 unsuccessful grasp attempts were caused by collisions with the other shell, as they were too close to each other, or the robot tried to grasp the cup by its handle. There were several instances where the user interacted with the table while the robot was moving. All these invalid interactions were detected correctly, and the robot movement was stopped automatically. Experimental tests in a real collaborative environment show that the proposed methods are able to correctly detect, localize and track human and object positions. Overall, capacitive proximity sensing technology offers beneficial modality for close distance and intensive interaction tasks for gapless perception. However, the capacitive measurement principle has a strong material dependency.

In further studies, we plan to evaluate the performance of CPS in different HRC scenarios and investigate hybrid sensory systems, where CPS augment optical systems in order to combine sensor feedback and compensate for the drawbacks of both sides. Additionally, deep learning approaches for material recognition using capacitive feedback has to be evaluated, which could be the key element for solving the material dependency problem.

References

1. ISO 10218–2: Robots and robotic devices - Safety requirements for industrial robots - Part 2: Robot systems and integration (2011)
2. ISO/TS 15066: Robots and robotic devices - Collaborative robots (2016)
3. Alagi, H., Navarro, S.E., Mende, M., Hein, B.: A versatile and modular capacitive tactile proximity sensor. In: 2016 IEEE Haptics Symposium (HAPTICS), pp. 290–296, April 2016. https://doi.org/10.1109/HAPTICS.2016.7463192
4. Alenyà, G., Foix, S., Torras, C.: ToF cameras for active vision in robotics. Sen. Actuat. A Phys. **218**, 10–22 (2014). https://doi.org/10.1016/j.sna.2014.07.014, https://linkinghub.elsevier.com/retrieve/pii/S0924424714003458
5. Behroozpour, B., Sandborn, P.A.M., Wu, M.C., Boser, B.E.: Lidar system architectures and circuits. IEEE Commun. Mag. **55**(10), 135–142 (2017). https://doi.org/10.1109/MCOM.2017.1700030. conference Name: IEEE Communications Magazine

6. Grosz, B.J.: Collaborative systems. In: AAAI-94 Presidential Address, p. 19 (1996)
7. Haddadin, S., Albu-Schaffer, A., De Luca, A., Hirzinger, G.: Collision detection and reaction: a contribution to safe physical human-robot interaction. In: 2008 IEEE/RSJ International Conference on Intelligent Robots and Systems, pp. 3356–3363, September 2008. https://doi.org/10.1109/IROS.2008.4650764, iSSN: 2153-0866
8. Huang, S., Alagi, H., Hein, B.: Model-based multiple object tracking using capacitive proximity sensors. In: 2nd Full-day Workshop on Progress in Ergonomic Physical Human-Robot Collaboration. p. 3. Macau, China (2019). wS-Paper
9. Navarro, S.E., et al.: Methods for safe human-robot-interaction using capacitive tactile proximity sensors. In: 2013 IEEE/RSJ International Conference on Intelligent Robots and Systems, pp. 1149–1154, November 2013. https://doi.org/10.1109/IROS.2013.6696495
10. Rampa, V., Vicentini, F., Savazzi, S., Pedrocchi, N., Ioppolo, M., Giussani, M.: Safe human-robot cooperation through sensor-less radio localization. In: 2014 12th IEEE International Conference on Industrial Informatics (INDIN), pp. 683–689, July 2014. https://doi.org/10.1109/INDIN.2014.6945596, ISSN: 2378-363X
11. Sadrfaridpour, B., Wang, Y.: Collaborative assembly in hybrid manufacturing cells: an integrated framework for human-robot interaction. IEEE Trans. Autom. Sci. Eng. **15**(3), 1178–1192 (2018). https://doi.org/10.1109/TASE.2017.2748386
12. Shi, J., Jimmerson, G., Pearson, T., Menassa, R.: Levels of human and robot collaboration for automotive manufacturing. In: Proceedings of the Workshop on Performance Metrics for Intelligent Systems. PerMIS 2012, pp. 95–100 Association for Computing Machinery, College Park, Maryland, March 2012. https://doi.org/10.1145/2393091.2393111, https://doi.org/10.1145/2393091.2393111
13. Taipalus, T., Ahtiainen, J.: Human detection and tracking with knee-high mobile 2D LIDAR. In: 2011 IEEE International Conference on Robotics and Biomimetics, pp. 1672–1677, December 2011. https://doi.org/10.1109/ROBIO.2011.6181529

Approach to Obstacle Localization for Robot Navigation in Agricultural Territories

Egor Aksamentov$^{(\boxtimes)}$ (ID), Marina Astapova (ID), and Elizaveta Usina (ID)

St. Petersburg Institute for Informatics and Automation of the Russian Academy of Sciences, 39, 14th Line, 199178 St. Petersburg, Russia
Egor.aksamentov.96@mail.ru

Abstract. Search and localization of obstacles is one of the main tasks in path planning for robotic systems. In this paper, an approach to obstacle localization for robot navigation in agricultural territories is proposed. The developed approach is based on a combination of calculation of Normalized Difference Vegetation Index (NDVI) and artificial neural network (ANN). The NDVI is used to detect obstacles: buildings, stones, garbage and the Convolutional Neural Network (CNN) is intended to search other obstacles: trees and vegetation. This separation allowed to reduce the amount of data necessary for CNN training to one data class. The result of the presented approach is a binary map, which shows passable and non-passable areas for robots. The total accuracy of obstacle detection using proposed approach ranges from 56 to 90% of the whole area, occupied by obstacles, on image.

Keywords: Multispectral image · Navigation of robotic system · Mask R-CNN · NDVI

1 Introduction

Navigation of robotic systems (RS) is one of the main tasks in robotics. This task includes several subtasks: search and localization of obstacles, RS localization and path planning [1, 2]. Search and localization of obstacles serve to solve the subtasks of path planning and path adjustment to ensure the RS movement in agricultural territories. For path planning, the system must know site sketch with the impassable areas marked on it. These can be static objects, for example, trees, marshy areas or ravines. Due to large area of agricultural territories, orthophotomap is used to represent all terrain features in detail. Orthophotomap can be obtained using satellite images or unmanned aerial vehicle (UAV) image stitching [3]. Images obtained with UAVs, in comparison with satellite images, have higher detail, in addition, satellite images can become outdated, while UAV images show the situation at a given moment.

When the RS moves, any objects can represent some sort of obstacle: stone, pillar, garbage, as well as vegetation. The objective of this paper is to develop an approach to the obstacle localization of on a map, by combining the CNN output and Normalized Difference Vegetation Index (NDVI) calculation.

A. Ronzhin et al. (Eds.): ICR 2020, LNAI 12336, pp. 13–20, 2020.
https://doi.org/10.1007/978-3-030-60337-3_2

2 Related Work

In addition to conventional RGB cameras, multispectral and hyperspectral cameras are also used to expand the amount of data on terrain features [4]. Images obtained using such cameras represent a map in different spectra. Using multispectral images, the NDVI index can be calculated [5, 6]. The NDVI index allows to detect genotype of plants and types of obstacles. The range of the index varies from −1 to 1. For buildings, NDVI are less than −0.2, for vegetation more than −0.25, for water less than −0.37 and for bare soil from −0.28 to −0.2 [7]. The accuracy of terrain NDVI calculation depends directly on image quality. For example, due to weather conditions, some UAV images may be of poor quality, so camera calibration is required prior to each capture [8].

For robot navigation based on the resulting orthophotomap, it is necessary to localize areas where static obstacles are situated. A popular approach to classification of objects in images is CNN. CNNs are used for pattern recognition in images and identification of object types [9]. In [10] authors proposed a forest classification method based on CNN and images obtained from the Sentinel-2 satellite. The method consists of four main stages: determining the forest type, extracting the characteristics of an optical image, extracting an image element from a satellite image, and classifying objects in the image using the CNN classifier. The accuracy of classification was 97%.

The authors of [11] used UAV images and deep neural networks to search for tobacco plants. They developed an algorithm consisting of three stages: 1) identification of regions where tobacco can grow, 2) search for tobacco plants, using the NA in the selected regions, after which post-processing is performed to separate tobacco specimens from other plants. As a result, the use of ANN allowed achieving a classification accuracy of 93%.

The authors of [12] used ANN to classify plant cultures in UAV images. A hybrid ANN HistNN was proposed for simultaneously evaluation both the color and texture of plant. The resulting hybrid ANN classifies plants with an accuracy of 90%, which is 10% more accurate than ANN based on texture or color only.

NDVI are mainly used in agricultural domain to monitor vegetation, soil condition estimation, etc. This paper discusses the use of the NDVI to search for obstacles in agricultural areas for RS navigation. Using the NDVI, both plant objects and non-plant objects can be classified. It is clear that the robot will move in irregular agricultural terrain, therefore all non-plant objects can be considered as obstacles. Since the can move on grass easily, not all types of vegetation will be obstacles. NDVI is intended for quantitative estimation of condition of the agricultural territory; its main purpose is to determine healthy and diseased vegetation; therefore, it is likely that this method cannot be used to classify healthy plants relative to each other. In this case, we propose to use CNN to search for plant obstacles. Using CNN, you can localize areas of objects in the image without using NDVI. However, it is very difficult to collect such a data set for CNN training, which would guarantee a complete classification of all objects, detected on agricultural territory. Therefore, to localize obstacles, we propose to combine the output of CNN and the NDVI calculation.

3   NDVI Calculation

The agricultural area, considered in this paper, contains different natural and artificial obstacles, such as trees, shrubs, grass, buildings. NDVI allows to distinguish areas with vegetation from other surface types, for example, houses, bare soil, water bodies. NDVI is calculated as [5]:

$$NDVI = \frac{NIR - RED}{NIR + RED},$$

where RED – reflection in the red range of the spectrum, NIR – reflection in the near-infrared spectrum. Let us denote types of objects, treated as obstacles. Non-vegetative types include objects such as buildings, fences, stones, and various rubbish, while vegetative ones include trees and shrubs. Since the robot will move along agricultural land without roads, we will assume that the roads also belong to a non-vegetative type of obstacles.

For a more convenient presentation, the calculated NDVI in the image is represented by a set of colors. One of the most common kinds of color maps is "red-green" one, where green indicates vegetation and red indicates non-vegetative objects [13]. Figure 1 shows an example of NDVI calculation for agricultural areas.

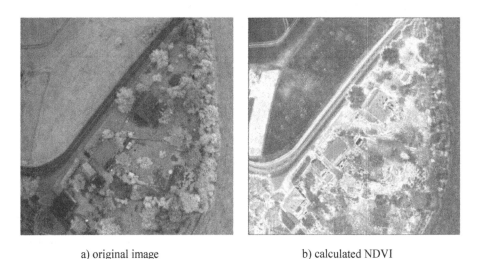

a) original image   b) calculated NDVI

Fig. 1. NDVI calculation example. (Color figure online)

In red in Fig. 1b, all non-vegetative objects are highlighted, and green - vegetative objects. This example shows that NDVI allows to accurately distinguish all plant objects from non-plant, which in the framework of this study are obstacles. It should be noted that the calculated NDVI for vegetation, in particular for trees, is equal to the index value obtained for grass. However, grass is not an obstacle for RS movement, unlike trees, which are obviously dangerous. Thus, it becomes necessary to introduce additional methods for vegetative object localization.

4   Mask R-CNN Training

In earlier research it was revealed that trees and shrubs are obstacles of a vegetative type and only their crown is visible while UAV shooting. Since the outward crown of trees from bushes differs only in size, it was decided to combine them into one class - "trees". Mask R-CNN [14] was selected for "trees" detection. Mask R-CNN is distinguished by the automatic generation of the mask of the detected object, which allows to accurately determine its outlines.

The pre-trained MS COCO model was used to train CNN [15] MS COCO is a large-scale dataset containing more than 80 classes trained on more than 200 thousand labeled images. In addition to the mask of the detected object, this model also builds a frame around the object and classifies it. The output of the Mask R-CNN for detecting trees is shown in Fig. 2.

Fig. 2. Mask R-CNN output.

For training, 700 photographs were used, 625 of which were used for training and validation and 75 for testing. Training took place over 250 eras. The accuracy of Mask R-CNN on the test data set was 63.3%. Relatively low accuracy is associated with a small amount of training data, since its marking is a cumbersome task, especially with fuzzy outlined objects. For example, in [16], Mask R-CNN is used to reveal buildings on image in the building search task. The authors used a total of 3, 500 images for training and achieved the accuracy only 71%. Thus, a significant increase in the data set size will improve the quality of the CNN.

5 The Combination of Mask R-CNN Output with NDVI Calculation

Since the considered methods for obstacle detection are not effective as standalone approaches, to solve the problem of finding obstacles for RS navigation in agricultural terrain, we propose to combine calculated NDVI with CNN output. As NDVI does not allow to accurately determine all vegetative objects which are hazardous to RS, we propose to use NDVI to localize all non-vegetative objects. CNN will be used to detect vegetative objects. The obstacle localization algorithm for the RS is presented in Fig. 3.

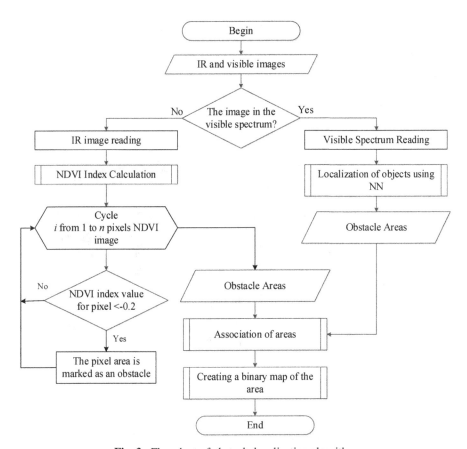

Fig. 3. Flowchart of obstacle localization algorithm.

The input of the algorithm (see Fig. 3) is infrared and near infrared images, as well as RGB, obtained using the UAV. For multispectral images, the NDVI is calculated. Vegetative and non-vegetative areas are distinguished based on the obtained NDVI. Simultaneously, CNN network searches for trees on the RGB image. Areas where trees were found, as well as non-vegetative areas are treated as dangerous.

The motion of the robot in such areas is prohibited. As a result, all the obtained information allows us to present the map of the area as a binary image, where black spots indicate possible obstacles, and white areas where RS movement is allowed. The output of such workflow is presented in Fig. 4.

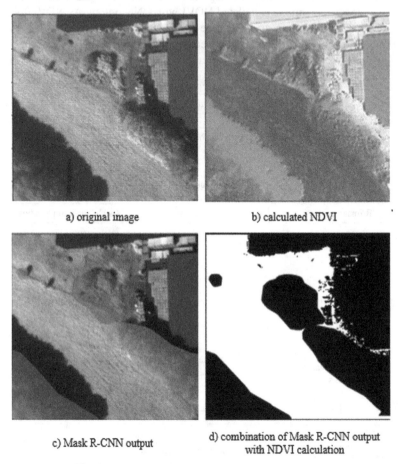

a) original image   b) calculated NDVI

c) Mask R-CNN output   d) combination of Mask R-CNN output
with NDVI calculation

Fig. 4. The intermediate results of proposed algorithm.

To quantify the performance of the approach, the area of obstacles found using various methods was calculated. 25 images were manually labeled for it. In each image, vegetative and non-vegetative obstacles were marked. In order to determine the percentage of the territory with obstacles relative to free territory, the ratio of the total area with obstacles to the entire image area was calculated. The obtained data were taken as a reference set. Then, for the initial images, each method was individually applied for obstacle searching: non-vegetative objects were recognized using the NDVI, vegetative objects using CNN. Both types of obstacles were classified using the developed app-roach. The area of obstacles found by each method was compared with the reference values. The results are presented in Fig. 5.

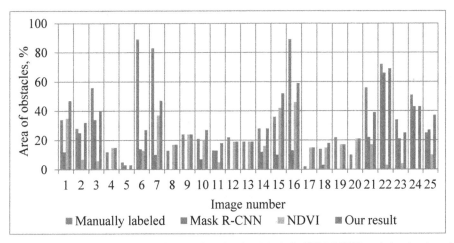

Fig. 5. Comparison of the obstacle area found using Mask R-CNN, NDVI and the developed approach with manual marking.

If only non-vegetative objects are located on the image, then the obtained values using the NDVI are similar to the reference values for the same images. If there are only trees in the image, the CNN determines them with an accuracy of 63.3%. It is worth noting that to increase the speed of finding obstacles, it is advisable to use no single images, but the orthophotomap with both vegetative and non-vegetative obstacles. In this case, the values of the found area occupied by various types of obstacles, using the developed approach, are closest to the standard in comparison with the previously considered individual methods. Using the NDVI allowed to determine an average of 39% of the total area of obstacles, with Mask R-CNN 49%, and the developed approach on average provides detection of 88% of the total area of all obstacles. The advantage of the developed approach is the ability to localize obstacles without generating a large training data set. Nevertheless, there may be areas with dry or burnt vegetation are present in the area under consideration, where the calculated NDVI may be equal to the values of non-vegetative areas.

6   Conclusion

In this paper, an approach to the obstacle localization for robot navigation in agricultural territories is proposed. The essence of the approach is to divide obstacles into vegetative and non-vegetative. This separation allowed to select the methods that are best suited for the detection of objects of a particular type. NDVI was used to search for non-vegetative obstacles, and MASK R-CNN for vegetative ones. The output is a binary map with passable and non-passable areas. This approach allowed to reduce the number of classes of objects that need to be detected by ANN and, as a result, significantly reduce the amount of training data. The developed approach can be used in territories with many objects of various classes. Using NDVI allows to not train the CNN to classify each individual object. The proposed approach on average provides localization of 88% of all obstacles in the image. Further research will focus on the use of hyperspectral images to localize obstacles, which will allow to analyze a wider range of spectra and improve the developed approach.

References

1. Kostjukov, V.A., Medvedev, M.Y., Pshikhopov, V.K.: Optimization of mobile robot movement on a plane with finite number of repeller sources. SPIIRAS Proc. **19**(1), 43–78 (2020). https://doi.org/10.15622/10.15622/sp.2020.19.1.2
2. Lavrenov, R.O., Magid, E.A., Matsuno, F., Svinin, M.M., Suthakorn, J.: Artificial intelligence. Knowledge and data engineering. SPIIRAS Proc. **18**(1), 57–84 (2019). https://doi.org/10.15622/sp.18.1.57-84
3. Tchernykh, V., Beck, M., Janschek, K.: Optical flow navigation for an outdoor UAV using a wide angle mono camera and DEM matching. IFAC Proc. Vol. **39**(16), 590–595 (2006)
4. Ross, M.: NDVI vegetation analysis using UAV imagery. Bachelor's thesis in Mathematical Information Technology (2019)
5. Modi, A.K., Das, P.: Multispectral imaging camera sensing to evaluate vegetation index from UAV. Methodology **16**(29), 12 (2019)
6. Xu, R., Li, C., Paterson, A.H.: Multispectral imaging and unmanned aerial systems for cotton plant phenotyping. PLoS ONE **14**(2), e0205083 (2019)
7. Murcko, J.: Object-based classification for estimation of built-up density within urban environment. Environmental Sciences, Technische Universität Dresden (2017). http://cartographymaster.eu/wp-content/theses/2017_Murcko_Thesis.pdf
8. Steven, M.D., et al.: Intercalibration of vegetation indices from different sensor systems. Remote Sens. Environ. **88**(4), 412–422 (2003)
9. Zhang, L., Zhang, L., Du, B.: Deep learning for remote sensing data: a technical tutorial on the state of the art. IEEE Geosci. Remote Sens. Mag. **4**(2), 22–40 (2016)
10. Miranda, E., Mutiara, A.B., Ernastuti, W.C.W.: Forest classification method based on convolutional neural networks and Sentinel-2 satellite imagery. Int. J. Fuzzy Logic Intell. Syst. **19**(4), 272–282 (2019)
11. Fan, Z., Lu, J., Gong, M., Xie, H., Goodman, E.D.: Automatic tobacco plant detection in UAV images via deep neural networks. IEEE J. Sel. Top. Appl. Earth Observat. Remote Sens. **11**(3), 876–887 (2018)
12. Rebetez, J., et al.: Augmenting a convolutional neural network with local histograms-a case study in crop classification from high-resolution UAV imagery. In: ESANN, April 2016
13. Genik, W.: Case Study: wild Oat control efficiency using UAV imagery – Green Aero Tech (2015). https://www.greenaerotech.com/case-study-wild-oatcontrol-efficiency-using-uav-imagery. accessed 15 May 2020
14. He, K., Gkioxari, G., Dollár, P., Girshick, R.: Mask R-CNN. In: Proceedings of the IEEE International Conference on Computer Vision, pp. 2961–2969 (2017)
15. Lin, T.-Y., et al.: Microsoft COCO: common objects in context. In: Fleet, D., Pajdla, T., Schiele, B., Tuytelaars, T. (eds.) ECCV 2014. LNCS, vol. 8693, pp. 740–755. Springer, Cham (2014). https://doi.org/10.1007/978-3-319-10602-1_48
16. Zhao, K., Kang, J., Jung, J., Sohn, G.: Building extraction from satellite images using mask R-CNN with building boundary regularization. In: CVPR Workshops, pp. 247–251 (2018)

Person-Following Algorithm Based on Laser Range Finder and Monocular Camera Data Fusion for a Wheeled Autonomous Mobile Robot

Elvira Chebotareva[1]($\boxtimes$)(iD), Ramil Safin[1](iD), Kuo-Hsien Hsia[2](iD),
Alexander Carballo[3](iD), and Evgeni Magid[1](iD)

[1] Laboratory of Intelligent Robotic Systems (LIRS), Intelligent Robotics Department, Higher Institute for Information Technology and Intelligent Systems, Kazan Federal University, Kazan, Russian Federation
elvira.chebotareva@kpfu.ru,safin.ramil@it.kfu.ru
https://kpfu.ru/erobotics

[2] Department of Electrical Engineering, National Yunlin University of Science and Technology, Douliu, Taiwan
khhsia@yuntech.edu.tw

[3] Institute of Innovation for Future Society, Nagoya University, Nagoya, Japan
alexander@g.sp.m.is.nagoya-u.ac.jp

Abstract. Reliable human following is one of the key capabilities of service and personal assisting robots. This paper presents a novel person tracking and following approach for autonomous mobile robots that are equipped with a 2D laser rangefinder (LRF) and a monocular camera. The proposed method does not impose restrictions on a person's clothes, does not require a head or an upper body to be within a camera field of view and is suitable for low height indoor robots as well. The algorithm is based on a metric that takes into an account parameters obtained directly from LRF and monocular camera data. The algorithm was implemented and tested in the Gazebo simulator. Next, it was integrated into a control system of the TIAGo Base mobile robot and successfully validated in university environment experiments with real people. In addition, this paper proposes a new criterion of algorithm performance estimation, which is a function of false positives number and traveled distances by a person and by a robot. Further this criterion is used to compare performance of the proposed method with the Multiple Instance Learning (MIL) tracker in simulated and in real world environments.

Keywords: Mobile robot · Human tracking · Human following algorithm · Laser range finder · Monocular camera · Multisensor tracking · Accuracy score · ROS · Gazebo

1 Introduction

Person-following algorithms are used by various types of service robots, including robotic suitcases, cargo robots, autonomous wheelchairs [33], shopping robots

© Springer Nature Switzerland AG 2020
A. Ronzhin et al. (Eds.): ICR 2020, LNAI 12336, pp. 21–33, 2020.
https://doi.org/10.1007/978-3-030-60337-3_3

[14], rescue robots [26,28], and others [31]. A person-following robot simultaneously deals with three problems: a self-localization, followed person coordinates
detection (and tracking) and path planning [21]. A significant variety of works
on person-following algorithms for autonomous mobile robots, which were proposed in the past decades, could be roughly divided into laser range finder (LRF)
based approaches, camera-based approaches and mixed approaches [13].

Mobile robots are often equipped with a 2D LRF. While these on-board
LRFs are generally employed for simultaneous localization and mapping (SLAM)
tasks [34], they could be also utilized for tracking of a target person's legs position. Major LRF-based human tracking solutions employ a geometric approach
assuming that human legs or body have a specific shape and geometric parameters [16,27,35] or apply well-established machine learning techniques [4,12,24].
Yet, the assumption that person clothes allow distinguishing two separate legs
in LRF data is not applicable when clothes completely cover legs, e.g., a person
wearing a skirt or a long overcoat. Moreover, while LRF-based tracking is mainly
successful in large open spaces, they often fail distinguishing human legs from
other obstacles in a cluttered environment. Multidimensional LRF data based
approaches could significantly improve accuracy of human detection, position
estimation and tracking [8]. Alternatively, a 3D LiDAR could be used to track
objects in 3D space [20,36], but it is important to emphasize that these sensors
are quite expensive.

Additional visual sensors, such as mono cameras, stereo cameras, and 360°
cameras, are used to increase person-detection and tracking reliability [32]. In [30]
authors applied skeleton tracking by Microsoft Kinect SDK and an auxiliary
tracker, which utilized Camshift algorithm. In [15] a mobile robot used an RGB-
D camera based simple 2D tracker of a human. In [23] an RGB-D camera based
framework for a human following robot combined deep learning and variational
Bayesian techniques. A stereo vision based CNN tracker for a person-following
robot was proposed in [10]. In [18] a person-following robot used a monocular
camera for a person tracking and identification. However, if a robot has a low
height, then a human head and upper body are not always contained in a camera's field of view. This makes visual person detection and tracking difficult. To
increase a person identification and tracking reliability, it is advisable to jointly
use a LRF and a camera. A person-following algorithm in [19] fused data of
a LRF and a panoramic camera. In [17] authors suggested a person tracking
and following algorithm for a mobile robot, which was equipped by a right-side
monocular camera and a frontal LRF.

This paper presents a human following algorithm for an autonomous person-
following mobile robot of a low height. The algorithm is based on a LRF and a
monocular camera data fusion. We implemented and tested our approach with
the PAL Robotics TIAGo Base [29] wheeled differential drive robot. The robot
has a cylindrical shape with 54 cm diameter and 30 cm height. Relatively small
dimensions allow the robot to traverse environments of various types, including
cluttered office rooms [6]. In addition to original Hokuyo URG-04LX-UG1 LRF
[1], which is located in the front of the robot at 10 cm height from a floor level, we

equipped the TIAGo Base with a monocular Web camera of 640×480 resolution. The camera was placed on the top of the robot, in its front, at a height of 40 cm from the floor level. The person-following algorithm was initially validated in the Gazebo simulator [3,22] and then in a real world indoor environment.

2   Human Tracking and Following

2.1   Human Tracking

To successfully follow a person, a robot needs to track him/her continuously and to be capable of searching and identifying the person in case of loss. Our algorithm simultaneously tracks a person in two 2D images: the first image is constructed from LRF data and the second is a monocular camera image. Using LRF data we constructed a 2D image of 500×500 pixels, which contains LRF distance readings toward environment obstacles. Closely located pixels that corresponded to occupied locations (a static or a dynamic obstacle, including a human) were connected with straight lines. Figures 1a, b show examples of LRF-based images with a person in front of the TIAGo Base robot: a person in trousers with clearly distinguished legs (Fig. 1a) and a person in a skirt (Fig. 1b).

Our previous work [9] compared five popular trackers of OpenCV library: KCF, TLD, Median Flow, MOSSE and MIL [5]. They were compared in a virtual world of the Gazebo simulator for a person tracking task using LRF data. MIL [5] tracker demonstrated less false positives and a longer path length of successful tracking (without loosing a tracked person) than the other four approaches. However, it should be emphasized that a common disadvantage of all five trackers was a large number of false positives when a person approached any virtual obstacles including walls, furniture or other people. Therefore, to successfully track a person in LRF data, a tracker should be capable to distinguish a person from another object within the LRF data. Combining strong features of LRF-based and camera-based tracking we could obtain better tracking results. Yet, to combine these data, a person should simultaneously appear within a camera and an LRF field of view, which allows (at least partial) matching of LRF-based and camera-based images. This paper proposes a new method of LRF and camera data fusion that elicits a more precise human tracking and following.

Both in virtual experiments within the Gazebo environment and real world experiments with TIAGo Base robot we use the following notations in this paper:

- LRF_{img} is $n \times n$ pixel binary image, which is constructed using LRF data;
- LRF_p is $d \times d$ pixel fragment of LRF_{img} that contains a person (exhaustive target person data within LRF_{img} image, which could reflect the entire person or only a part of his/her body);
- C_{img} is an image from a camera;
- C_p is a fragment of C_{img} that corresponds to LRF_p fragment (i.e., the person).

Our method requires at least $n = 500$ and $d = 75$, which were obtained empirically. In this case, 500×500 pixel image LRF_{img} corresponds to a square pattern that reflects virtual or real world data within 5×5 m^2 square. When tracking starts we save the first C_p as a sample image S and keep updating C_p variable with time. If a person is simultaneously within a camera and an LRF fields of view, a new value of C_p is obtained and compared with S. In addition to tracking the target person within LRF data we track the person in camera data using an independent tracker. C_τ denotes an image of the person, which is obtained using the independent tracker. Figure 1c demonstrates examples of images LRF_p, C_p, C_τ and S.

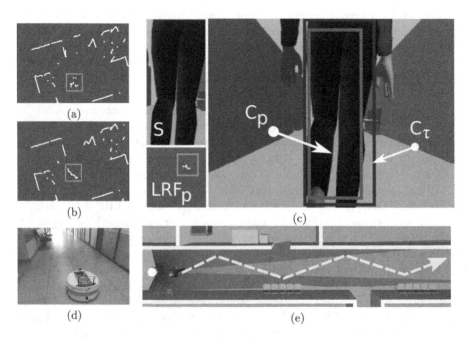

Fig. 1. (a) LRF data based 2D image. Black pixels correspond to empty or unknown (due to an occlusion) space, white pixels correspond to visible obstacles. The red dot denotes the TIAGo Base robot position. Legs of a person in trousers form two curves (inside the green square). (b) LRF data based 2D image. A person in a long skirt forms the single curve (inside the green square). (c) Examples of LRF_p, C_p, C_τ, S images in the Gazebo virtual experiments. (d) Real world experiments with the TIAGo Base robot inside the 2-nd Study Building of KFU, 35 Kremlevskaya street, Kazan. (e) A person trajectory in virtual experiments in Gazebo. (Color figure online)

A person is displayed in LRF_p (LRF data based) image as a set of points and there is a particular C_p (monocular camera data based) image that corresponds to LRF_p. The idea of our method is based on the construction of an abstract metric space. The points of this space are ordered pairs of the form (LRF_p, C_p). The tracked person is associated with some point (LRF_p, C_p) of this metric space at each moment. We introduce a feature system for each pair (LRF_p, C_p). At the initialization time images LRF_p and C_p correspond to a target person.

To determine a position of a person at the next moment, we construct a metric, which allows us to compare objects within the LRF and camera field of view with the initial sample.

We denote a correlation coefficient of normalized histograms of C_p and S as $corr(C_p, S)$. $LRF_p(x, y)$ denotes a pixel value at (x, y) cell of an image, where x and y are integer numbers so that $0 \leq x, y \leq d - 1$. $LRF_p(x, y)$ takes a value of 0 for an empty cell and 1 for a cell with an obstacle, which could be a person or another object (in Fig. 1a black pixels are assumed to be an empty space, white pixels correspond to visible obstacles). Thus LRF_p image could be viewed as a matrix with zeros and ones. We process LRF_p matrix in a such way that each column of a resulting matrix LRF_p^N has at most one nonzero element. The convention is to keep only the lowest index element if several nonzero elements appear in the column. Next, using LRF_p^N matrix, we construct function $f(x)$ on the set $[0, d - 1]$. The value of $f(x)$ is a row number of a nonzero element of column x and is zero if $LRF_p(x, Y) = 0$ for all $Y \in [0, d - 1]$.

Consider an abstract space M whose elements are ordered pairs (LRF_p, C_p). Let $P = P(LRF_p, C_p)$ be a point of this space. Using a set of $\{n_i\}, i = [0..7]$ functions for each point of space M we describe a target human appearance using a number of mathematical features of his/her shape as follows:

- $n_0(P)$ denotes function $f(x)$, which is constructed for point P (its LRF_p part) by the method described above;
- $n_1(P)$ denotes a number of local minima of $f(x)$;
- $n_2(P)$ denotes a number of discontinuity points of $f(x)$;
- $n_3(P)$ denotes a cardinality of a set of points at which $f(x) \neq 0$;
- $n_4(P)$ denotes a *height* of a tracked curve in terms of columns of LRF_p image $n_4(P) = |\max f(x) - \min f(x)|$;
- $n_5(P)$ denotes an indicator function that allows detecting whether LRF_p image contains a straight line as follows:

$$n_5(P) = \begin{cases} 0 & if |corr(x, f(x))| < \sigma_1 \\ 1 & if |corr(x, f(x))| \geq \sigma_1 \end{cases}, \tag{1}$$

where $corr(x, f(x))$ is a linear correlation coefficient of x and $f(x)$, σ_1 is an empirically established threshold value, which was set to 0.9. $n_5(P)$ allows reducing probability of false positives on walls and other objects with flat vertical surfaces;
- $n_6(P_0, P)$ denotes a result of comparing C_p image and the one that is obtained by an independent tracker

$$n_6(P_0, P) = |corr(C_{p_0}, C_\tau) - corr(C_p, C_\tau)|, \tag{2}$$

where $P_0(LRF_{p_0}, C_{p_0})$, $P(LRF_p, C_p) \in M$; $C_{p_0}, C_p \subset C_{img}$ and $C_{p_0} \neq \varnothing$, $C_p \neq \varnothing$; C_τ was previously defined as an image of the person, which is obtained by the independent tracker.

– $n_7(P_0, P)$ denotes a result of comparing C_p image with the initial sample of the human image

$$n_7(P_0, P) = \begin{cases} 0, & if\ corr(C_{p_0}, C_p) \geq \sigma_2 \\ 1, & if\ corr(C_{p_0}, C_p) < \sigma_2 \end{cases}, \tag{3}$$

where σ_2 is an empirically established threshold value, which was set to 0.8 in our experiments.

For space M we set the following metric for measuring a distance between two distinct points P_0 and P_1:

$$\rho(P_0, P_1) = \lambda_0 \max |n_0(P_0) - n_0(P_1)| \\ + \sum_{i=1}^{5} \lambda_i |n_i(P_0) - n_i(P_1)| + \sum_{i=6}^{7} \lambda_i n_i(P_0, P_1), \tag{4}$$

where $\lambda_i > 0$ are weighting coefficients that allow to adjust metric in Eq. (4) sensitivity to particular parameters. In our experiments all values $\{\lambda_0, .., \lambda_7\}$ were set to 1 and a research of their correlation and selection is left as a part of our future work.

Using metric defined by Eq. (4) we constructed a tracker that fuses LRF and monocular camera data. At an initial moment of time a target person is the closest object to a robot, which allows setting P as a set of a sample image S of the target person and the corresponding n_i, $i = [0..7]$. Next, at each step the algorithm could find point P_0, which is the closest one to P.

As an independent tracker that provides image C_τ we used the MIL tracker [5]. To eliminate the problem of loss and false positives by the MIL tracker, we re-initialize it with a newly obtained target person image every time when $\rho(P, P_0) < \sigma_\tau$ holds. Here σ_τ is an empirically established threshold value, which is set to 7 in our experiments.

2.2   Person-Following Algorithm

Using the above described tracker a robot can determine a position and coordinates of a person. The next task is to plan a path from current robot position S_{loc} to local target T_{loc}, which is located in a close vicinity of a person, at a safe distance from him/her [25]. Points S_{loc} and T_{loc} are selected in a robot centered system of coordinates, and thus S_{loc} is the origin (0,0) of the robot centered system. If a straight line (S_{loc}, T_{loc}) intersects an obstacle, the algorithm applies a local planner, e.g., the ROS *move_base* package. Upon reaching T_{loc}, the algorithm sets S_{loc} to T_{loc}, defines new T_{loc} and plans a path to new T_{loc}.

The person-following algorithm is presented in Algorithm 1. At a start, a person stands in front of a robot and the robot determines local to LRF coordinates $\widetilde{\Psi}$ of a nearest object using LRF. These coordinates correspond to $P(LRF_p(\widetilde{\Psi}), C_p(\widetilde{\Psi}))$ point of space M. We assume that $LRF_p(\widetilde{\Psi})$ and $C_p(\widetilde{\Psi})$ images always contain an image of the person. To determine coordinates of the person at the next moment, we build an array of 100 points Ψ_i (i=1..100), located no farther than Euclidean distance ε (empirically selected as $\varepsilon = d$) from a previous position of the person. The selection of 100 points is an empirically defined trade-off between accuracy and execution time. This array corresponds to array of points $P_i(LRF_p(\Psi_i), C_p(\Psi_i))$. First, we fix a minimum value $\rho(P, P_i)$ as P_0 point; then we select a point with index i that has a minimal value $\rho(P, P_i)$ within the array. If $\rho(P, P_i) < \theta$ (empirically selected as $\theta = 34$ based on an analysis of a set of virtual pilot experiments), then the robot moves to point Ψ_i; otherwise the robot begins searching for a person. During the search, the robot compares all detected objects with the person using Eq. (4).

Algorithm 1. Person-following algorithm

1: Get LRF_{img} and C_{img} images

2: Find nearest object coordinates $\widetilde{\Psi}$

3: $P := (LRF_p(\widetilde{\Psi}), C_p(\widetilde{\Psi}))$

4: $\Psi_{prev} := \widetilde{\Psi}$

5: Initialize tracker for C_τ

6: **while not** "Return command" **do**

7:   Update $LRF_{img}, C_{img}, C_\tau$

8:   $P_0 := (LRF_p(\Psi_{prev}), C_p(\Psi_{prev}))$

9:   $min_\rho := \rho(P, P_0)$

10:   **for all** $|\Psi_i - \Psi_{prev}| < \varepsilon$ **do**

11:   $P_i := (LRF_p(\Psi_i), C_p(\Psi_i)$

12:   **if** $\rho(P, P_i) < min_\rho$ **then**

13:   $min_\rho := \rho(P, P_i)$

14:   $\Psi_{goal} := \Psi_{min}$

15:   **end if**

16:   **end for**

17:   **if** $min_\rho < \theta$ **then**

18:   **if** $min_\rho < \sigma_\tau$ **then**

19:   Initialize tracker for C_τ

20:   **end if**

21:   Move to $T_{loc}(\Psi_{goal})$

22:   $\Psi_{prev} := \Psi_{goal}$

23:   **else**

24:   Run person search procedure

25:   **end if**

26: **end while**

---

3   Experiments

This section describes experimental work with TIAGo Base robot in the Gazebo simulator virtual environment and in real world environment.

3.1   Simulation in Gazebo

For real world experiments, we used a corridor of the 2-nd study building of
Kazan Federal University (Fig. 1d). A part of the corridor and one room of the
Laboratory of Intelligent Robotic Systems (LIRS) were modelled in the Gazebo
simulator for virtual experiments (Fig. 1e). Algorithm 1 was implemented in
the Gazebo simulator using the TIAGo Base robot simulation packages [2]. A
38 m piecewise linear trajectory of a target person (Fig. 1e) was used in 400
virtual experiments in the Gazebo simulation (Fig. 2a). Figure 2b demonstrates
LRF_{img}, LRF_p, C_{img}, C_p and C_τ that correspond to the particular frame of
Fig. 2a.

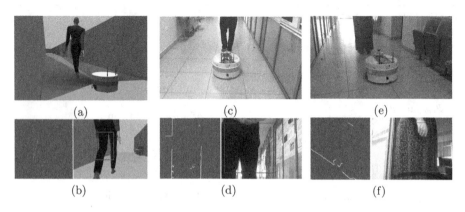

Fig. 2. (a) The Gazebo simulation frame of Algorithm 1. (b) Tracking a person using
LRF (left) and camera (right) data in the Gazebo. On the left: LRF_{img} image with
LRF_p area denoted with the red square. On the right: C_{img} image with C_p area (inside
the red rectangle) and C_τ area (inside the blue rectangle). (c) TIAGo Base follows a
person in pants. (d) Tracking the person in the pants using LRF (left) and camera
(right) data. In the left image the target person is in the red square" (e) TIAGo Base
follows a person in a long dress that covers legs. (f) Tracking the person in the long
dress using LRF (left) and camera (right) data. In the left image the target person is
in the red square. (Color figure online)

In our previous work [9], we attempted tracking a straight line walking human
in LRF data with KCF, TLD, Median Flow, MOSSE and MIL trackers. Their
performance comparison demonstrated a clear superiority of the MIL tracker.
Therefore in this work the MIL tracker was selected as an independent tracker
(within Algorithm 1) as well as the only competitor for Algorithm 1 evaluation.
We used standard parameters of the MIL tracker of the OpenCV library: a
radius for gathering positive instances during init – 3, a search window size – 25,
negative samples to use during init – 65, radius for gathering positive instances
during tracking – 4, positive samples to use during tracking – 100000, negative
samples to use during tracking – 65, features – 250.

We evaluate the accuracy of person-following algorithms according to an average traveled distance, tracker false positives, and an average person speed. On a false positive occurrence, we stopped the experiment and measured a distance traveled by the robot. For algorithm performance evaluation, the following accuracy score was used:

$$\mu = \frac{1}{2}\left(1 + \frac{\sum_i l_i}{\sum_i L_i} - \frac{N_f}{N}\right), \mu \in [0, 1], \tag{5}$$

where N_f is a number of false positives, l_i is a distance traveled by a person in i-th experiment, L_i is the person's path length, N is a total number of experiments. The four aforementioned values correspond to an entire set of experiments for an algorithm with a particular human walking speed. The ratio $\sum_i l_i / \sum_i L_i$ allows evaluating whether a robot succeeded to complete an entire path without losing the person. The ratio N_f/N reflects an average number of false positives per experiment. The parameter μ reaches its maximum of $\mu = 1$ if the robot succeeded to follow the person along the entire path ($\sum_i l_i = \sum_i L_i$) and there were no false positives ($N_f = 0$). The minimum possible value is $\mu = 0$ if the robot did not start (i.e., immediately lost the human at the start and thus $\sum_i l_i = 0$) and each test was featured with a false positive ($N_f = N$).

A pedestrian walking speed depends on several factors including a person age [7] and environment conditions [11]. Taking into account that the maximum speed of the TIAGo Base robot is only $1\,\mathrm{m/s}$, we tested the algorithms for two human walking speeds of 0.5 and $0.9\,\mathrm{m/s}$. Table 1 presents virtual experimental results in the Gazebo simulation for MIL tracker and for Algorithm 1 (denoted as Alg1). Both algorithms were tested at $0.5\,\mathrm{m/s}$ and $0.9\,\mathrm{m/s}$ walking speed of a human with 100 runs for each speed.

In total, we conducted 400 virtual experiments. In each experiment, a person walked along a corridor according to the preplanned route (Fig. 1e). The route length in each experiment was $38\,\mathrm{m}$. When a false positive was detected, the experiment stopped and the total distance traveled by the robot was measured at this point. MIL tracker demonstrated 41 false positives within 100 experiments at a speed of $0.5\,\mathrm{m/s}$ and 49 false positives within 100 experiments at a speed of $0.9\,\mathrm{m/s}$. Algorithm 1 did not provide any false positives within 100 experiments both at $0.5\,\mathrm{m/s}$ and $0.9\,\mathrm{m/s}$ speed. The total accuracy score was calculated with Eq. (5). For MIL tracker the score was 0.67 at $0.5\,\mathrm{m/s}$ and 0.57 at $0.9\,\mathrm{m/s}$, while Algorithm 1 demonstrated maximal possible accuracy score (of 1) at both speeds due to a monocular camera and LRF data fusion approach.

3.2   Experiments in a Real World Environment

A set of real world experiments was conducted in the environment that served as a source for Gazebo environment modelling (Fig. 1d). One male and one female participated in real world experiments. The male wore black trousers (Fig. 2c, 2d) and the female tested one pair of trousers and 2 different long one-piece garments (Fig. 2e, 2f). We asked the experiment participants to stand at a short distance

Table 1. Experimental results in the Gazebo simulation and in real environment for MIL tracker and for Algorithm 1 (denoted as Algorithm 1).

Environment	Simulation				Real world	
Tracker	MIL	MIL	Alg1	Alg1	MIL	Alg1
Average human walking speed, m/s	0.5	0.9	0.5	0.9	0.5	0.5
Average distance traveled by robot, m	28.2	24.1	38	38	19.1	28.9
Total false positives number	41	49	0	0	14	0
Number of experiments	100	100	100	100	30	30
Total accuracy score	0.67	0.57	1	1	0.59	0.89

from the robot (between 20 cm and 1.8 m) and slowly walk a distance of 30 m. If the tracker lost a person the robot stopped moving.

Our experiments demonstrated a stable behavior of Algorithm 1 regardless of having clothes that completely cover human legs or allow to distinguish two separate legs. Figure 2c demonstrates an experiment of following a person in trousers that allow distinguish two legs. Figure 2e shows an experiment of following a person in a long dress that does not allow distinguish two legs. Figures 2d, f show examples of areas LRF_{img}, LRF_p, C_{img}, C_p and C_τ for people in different clothes. The same experiments were conducted for the MIL tracker.

Table 1 also presents the results of 30 real world experiments. In these experiments the robot speed was set to 0.5 m/s. Total accuracy score was calculated using Eq. (5). Algorithm 1 demonstrated significantly better results of $\mu = 0.89$ than the MIL approach with $\mu = 0.59$. Moreover, while the MIL approach had false positives almost in 50% of the experiments, Algorithm 1 did not have any false positives in all 30 runs.

4   Conclusions and Future Work

In this paper, we presented a novel person tracking and following approach for autonomous mobile robots that are equipped with a 2D laser range finder (LRF) and a monocular camera. A LRF and a monocular camera data fusion improved a person tracking reliability for indoor environments. The proposed method does not impose restrictions on person's clothes and does not require a head or an upper body to be within a monocular camera field of view. This allows to employ our method for low height indoor robots. Our algorithm was implemented in the Gazebo simulator and validated with TIAGo Base mobile robot. In addition, we proposed a new algorithm performance estimation criterion as a total accuracy score, which is a function of false positives number and traveled distance by a person and by a robot. The algorithm performance was compared with the MIL tracker performance using the proposed accuracy score in the Gazebo simulation and in real world experiments with the TIAGo Base robot and demonstrated significantly better results than the MIL tracker.

In this work, the algorithms were tested only in static environments with a single walking person in a scene. As a part of our future work, we plan to extend our algorithm to the case of multiple static and dynamic objects in a scene, to increase a number of participants and clothing variety in real world experiments and to validate the algorithm at a broad variety of human walking speeds.

Acknowledgements. The reported study was funded by the Russian Foundation for Basic Research (RFBR) according to the research project No. 19-58-70002. Special thanks to PAL Robotics for their kind professional support with TIAGo Base robot software and hardware related issues.

References

1. PMB-2 technical specifications. http://pal-robotics.com/wp-content/uploads/2016/07/PMB-2-Datasheet.pdf
2. Tiago base. http://wiki.ros.org/Robots/PMB-2
3. Abbyasov, B., Lavrenov, R., Zakiev, A., Yakovlev, K., Svinin, M., Magid, E.: Automatic tool for gazebo world construction: from a grayscale image to a 3D solid model. In: International Conference on Robotics and Automation (ICRA), pp. 7226–7232 (2020)
4. Arras, K.O., et al.: Range-based people detection and tracking for socially enabled service robots. In: Prassler, E., et al. (eds.) Towards Service Robots for Everyday Environments, pp. 235–280. Springer, Heidelberg (2012). https://doi.org/10.1007/978-3-642-25116-0_18
5. Babenko, B., Yang, M., Belongie, S.: Visual tracking with online multiple instance learning. In: Conference on Computer Vision and Pattern Recognition, pp. 983–990. IEEE (2009)
6. Bereznikov, D., Zakiev, A.: Network failure detection and autonomous return for PMB-2 mobile robot. In: International Conference on Artificial Life and Robotics (ICAROB 2020), pp. 444–447 (2020)
7. Bohannon, R.: Comfortable and maximum walking speed of adults aged 20–79 years: Reference values and determinants. Age Ageing **26**(1), 15–19 (1997)
8. Carballo, A., Ohya, A., Yuta, S.: Reliable people detection using range and intensity data from multiple layers of laser range finders on a mobile robot. Int. J. Soc. Robot. **3**, 167–186 (2011)
9. Chebotareva, E., Hsia, K.H., Yakovlev, K., Magid, E.: Laser rangefinder and monocular camera data fusion for human-following algorithm by PMB-2 mobile robot in simulated Gazebo environment. Smart Innovation, Syst. Technol. **187** (2020)
10. Chen, B.X., Sahdev, R., Tsotsos, J.K.: Integrating stereo vision with a CNN tracker for a person-following robot. In: Liu, M., Chen, H., Vincze, M. (eds.) ICVS 2017. LNCS, vol. 10528, pp. 300–313. Springer, Cham (2017). https://doi.org/10.1007/978-3-319-68345-4_27
11. Franĕk, M.: Environmental factors influencing pedestrian walking speed. Percept. Mot. Skills **116**(3), 992–1019 (2013)

12. Guerrero-Higueras, Á.M., et al.: Tracking people in a mobile robot from 2D LIDAR scans using full convolutional neural networks for security in cluttered environments. Front. Neurorobot. **12** (2018)
13. Islam, M.J., Hong, J., Sattar, J.: Person-following by autonomous robots: a categorical overview. The Int. J. Robot. Res. **38**(14), 1581–1618 (2019)
14. Islam, M.M., Lam, A., Fukuda, H., Kobayashi, Y., Kuno, Y.: An intelligent shopping support robot: understanding shopping behavior from 2D skeleton data using GRU network. ROBOMECH J. **6**(1), 1–10 (2019). https://doi.org/10.1186/s40648-019-0150-1
15. Jiang, S., Li, L., Hang, M., Kuc, T.: An adaptive 2D tracking approach for person following robot. In: International Symposium on Computer Science and Intelligent Controls, pp. 147–151 (2017)
16. Kawarazaki, N., et al.: Development of human following mobile robot system using laser range scanner. Procedia Comput. Sci. **76**, 455–460 (2015)
17. Kim, H., et al.: Sensor fusion-based human tracking using particle filter and data mapping analysis in in/outdoor environment. In: International Conference on Ubiquitous Robots and Ambient Intelligence, pp. 741–744 (2013)
18. Koide, K., et al.: Monocular person tracking and identification with on-line deep feature selection for person following robots. Robot. Auton. Syst. **124** (2020)
19. Kristou, M., et al.: Target person identification and following based on omnidirectional camera and LRF data fusion. In: International Conference on Robot & Human Interactive Communication, pp. 419–424. IEEE (2011)
20. Lang, A., Vora, S., Caesar, H., Zhou, L., Yang, J., Beijbom, O.: Pointpillars: fast encoders for object detection from point clouds. In: Conference on Computer Vision and Pattern Recognition, pp. 12689–12697 (2019)
21. Lavrenov, R., Matsuno, F., Magid, E.: Modified spline-based navigation: guaranteed safety for obstacle avoidance. In: Ronzhin, A., Rigoll, G., Meshcheryakov, R. (eds.) ICR 2017. LNCS (LNAI), vol. 10459, pp. 123–133. Springer, Cham (2017). https://doi.org/10.1007/978-3-319-66471-2_14
22. Lavrenov, R.O., Magid, E.A., Matsuno, F., Svinin, M.M., Suthakorn, J.: Development and implementation of spline-based path planning algorithm in ROS/gazebo environment. Trudy SPIIRAN **18**(1), 57–84 (2019)
23. Lee, B.J., et al.: Robust human following by deep Bayesian trajectory prediction for home service robots. In: International Conference on Robotics and Automation, pp. 7189–7195. IEEE (2018)
24. Leigh, A., et al.: Person tracking and following with 2D laser scanners. In: International Conference on Robotics and Automation, pp. 726–733. IEEE (2015)
25. Magid, E., Lavrenov, R., Khasianov, A.: Modified spline-based path planning for autonomous ground vehicle. ICINCO **2**, 132–141 (2017)
26. Moskvin, I., Lavrenov, R.: Modeling tracks and controller for servosila engineer robot. In: Ronzhin, A., Shishlakov, V. (eds.) Proceedings of 14th International Conference on Electromechanics and Robotics "Zavalishin's Readings". SIST, vol. 154, pp. 411–422. Springer, Singapore (2020). https://doi.org/10.1007/978-981-13-9267-2_33
27. Nakamori, Y., Hiroi, Y., Ito, A.: Multiple player detection and tracking method using a laser range finder for a robot that plays with human. ROBOMECH Journal **5**(1), 1–15 (2018). https://doi.org/10.1186/s40648-018-0122-x
28. Orita, Y., Fukao, T.: Robust human tracking of a crawler robot. J. Robot. Mechatron. **31**(2), 194–202 (2019)

29. Pages, J., Marchionni, L., Ferro, F.: Tiago: the modular robot that adapts to different research needs. In: International Workshop on Robot Modularity, IROS (2016)

30. Ren, Q., et al.: Real-time target tracking system for person-following robot. In: Chinese Control Conference, pp. 6160–6165 (2016)

31. Ronzhin, A., Saveliev, A., Basov, O., Solyonyj, S.: Conceptual model of cyberphysical environment based on collaborative work of distributed means and mobile robots. In: Ronzhin, A., Rigoll, G., Meshcheryakov, R. (eds.) ICR 2016. LNCS (LNAI), vol. 9812, pp. 32–39. Springer, Cham (2016). https://doi.org/10.1007/978-3-319-43955-6_5

32. Safin, R., Lavrenov, R., Tsoy, T., Svinin, M., Magid, E.: Real-time video server implementation for a mobile robot. In: 11th International Conference on Developments in eSystems Engineering (DeSE), pp. 180–185. IEEE (2018)

33. Sato, Y., et al.: A maneuverable robotic wheelchair able to move adaptively with a caregiver by considering the situation. In: International Conference on Robot & Human Interactive Communication, pp. 282–287. IEEE (2013)

34. Simakov, N., Lavrenov, R., Zakiev, A., Safin, R., Martínez-García, E.A.: Modeling USAR maps for the collection of information on the state of the environment. In: 2019 12th International Conference on Developments in eSystems Engineering (DeSE), pp. 918–923. IEEE (2019)

35. Sung, Y., Chung, W.: Hierarchical sample-based joint probabilistic data association filter for following human legs using a mobile robot in a cluttered environment. IEEE Trans. Hum. Mach. Syst. **46**(3), 340–349 (2015)

36. Yan, Y., Mao, Y., Li, B.: SECOND: sparsely embedded convolutional detection. Sensors **18**, 3337 (2018)

On the Problems of SLAM Simulation for Mobile Robots in the Arctic Conditions

Elvira Chebotareva[1]([envelope]) [iD], Tatyana Tsoy[1] [iD], Bulat Abbyasov[1] [iD],
Jamila Mustafina[2] [iD], Edgar A. Martinez-Garcia[3] [iD], Yang Bai[4] [iD],
and Mikhail Svinin[4] [iD]

[1] Laboratory of Intelligent Robotic Systems (LIRS), Intelligent Robotics
Department, Higher Institute for Information Technology and Intelligent Systems,
Kazan Federal University, Kazan, Russian Federation
elvira.chebotareva@kpfu.ru, tt@it.kfu.ru
https://kpfu.ru/erobotics
[2] Naberezhnye Chelny Institute, Kazan Federal University, Kazan, Russia
jamila0111@hotmail.com
[3] Laboratorio de Robotica, Institute Engineering and Technology, Universidad
Autonoma de Ciudad Juarez, Juarez, Mexico
edmartin@uacj.mx
[4] College of Information Science and Engineering, Ritsumeikan University,
Kyoto, Japan
{yangbai,svinin}@fc.ritsumei.ac.jp

Abstract. Autonomous robots in the Arctic cover a number of strategically important tasks, including climate research, reconnaissance, transportation, material delivery, search and rescue. These goals require adapting standard navigation, localization and mapping algorithms to the harsh Arctic conditions, which do not allow their straightforward usage. The paper describes main problems of using simultaneous localization and mapping (SLAM) algorithms in the Arctic region and formulate requirements for the Arctic landscape simulator. With regard to these requirements we constructed Arctic terrains in Gazebo simulator, which implemented three of the eight proposed Arctic features, and studied behavior of ROS implementations of GMapping, Hector SLAM, ORB-SLAM2 and RTAB-Map SLAM algorithms within the obtained terrains.

Keywords: SLAM · Arctic · ROS · Gazebo · Hector SLAM ·
ORB-SLAM2 · RTAB-Map

1 Introduction

Strategic needs of mastering the Far North and the Arctic region [1] require development of robotic systems and algorithms that could be utilized in the harsh Arctic conditions Unmanned ground (UGV) and aerial (UAV) vehicles as well as unmanned surface (USV) and underwater (UUV) vehicles could be employed to perform a wide variety of specialized tasks in the Arctic, including

© Springer Nature Switzerland AG 2020
A. Ronzhin et al. (Eds.): ICR 2020, LNAI 12336, pp. 34–44, 2020.
https://doi.org/10.1007/978-3-030-60337-3_4

resource exploration, monitoring, climate research, reconnaissance, transportation, material delivery, search and rescue operations, etc. [23,32]. At the same time, solving the problem of autonomous robot navigation [20] requires considering extreme climate and weather conditions of the Arctic region, taking into account low temperatures, precipitation, strong winds and a presence of snow and ice covers.

When moving toward practical applications of mobile robots within the Arctic region, potential problems with steady radio communication, GLONASS/ GPS availability and precision should be also considered. In the absence of a reliable GLONASS/GPS signal for navigation robots have to rely on data from inertial and visual onboard sensors, such as mono and stereo cameras. However, standard algorithms for visual localization and mapping usage are seriously constrained by a landscape uniformity and a negligibly small number of available feature points, as well as by a blurred horizon line. Despite individual attempts to solve this problem, there is still no qualitative algorithms for visual autonomous localization and navigation under the Far North and the Arctic conditions [11].

Effective development and testing of new algorithms for autonomous localization and navigation in the Arctic require numerous experiments. Therefore, a development of a realistic simulator that takes into account weather and climate features of the Arctic region and is suitable for virtual testing of algorithms for autonomous robot navigation becomes critical. While virtual experiments in a simulator could not substitute a real world validation, they might help to significantly reduce amount of algorithmic mistakes and discover various undesirable features prior to a high-cost testing in the Arctic region.

In this paper, we review existing problems of autonomous navigation in the Arctic and formulate requirements for virtual environments to be used for testing simultaneous localization and mapping algorithms (SLAM), which are intended for the Arctic region. With a help of our robot operating system (ROS) based software [9,19] we created a set of ROS/Gazebo environments that simulate uneven snowy landscapes and tested ROS implementations of GMapping, Hector SLAM, ORB-SLAM2 and RTAB-Map SLAM algorithms within the obtained terrains.

2 Problems of Visual SLAM in the Arctic

Mobile robots, both autonomous and semi-autonomous [35], face a number of challenges in severe Arctic environmental conditions. In the Arctic it is difficult to use radio systems for determining a current location of a UGV [31]. Failures of GLONASS/GPS signals receiving could be observed even at latitudes of 70° of the north latitude [26]. Short-wave communication systems are hampered by ionospheric and atmospheric noise [22,31]. Ultrashort waves are not liable to this interference, but their use is limited by a range of a direct geometric visibility. An absence of external reference systems for autonomous mobile robots in an unknown environment makes the problem of simultaneous localization and mapping (SLAM) [10,13] particularly prominent. Using SLAM, a mobile robot could build an environment map and simultaneously use this map to determine its current location. SLAM algorithms could utilize different types of onboard sensors, such as laser range finders, inertial sensors, various cameras and others. SLAM algorithms that use cameras, the so-called visual SLAM (vSLAM) [33], are particularly interesting and prospective.

Using standard SLAM algorithms in the Arctic is seriously complicated by rather troublesome natural conditions of the environment. The Arctic climatic conditions are characterized by extremely low temperatures. The coldest winter month is January with an average temperatures ranging from $-32...-36\,°C$ to $-45...-50\,°C$ [29]. Snow cover and precipitation impede LiDAR sensors use while glacier environments affect odometry as a UGV often stalls on snow and ice covers.

Predominant snow and ice covers also complicate visual navigation. Strong winds of up to $40\,m/s$ [22], blizzards and snowfalls frequently modify a terrain and hamper visibility. In winter, fogs are often observed over ice-free bays. Cracks in an ice cover complicate navigation and locomotion of a UGV. At low temperatures ice fogs [29] could be observed in anticyclones. Moreover, uniform snow and ice landscapes contain a very small number of feature points that could be utilized for visual orientation, while cloudiness makes the horizon line difficult to distinguish.

While moving, a UGV should to take into account a possible presence of deep cracks and holes in an ice surface, which may easily cause a robot loss [8]. Visual detection of such obstacles is hampered by the fact that they are often hidden under snow. Characteristics of the Arctic include long periods of a polar day, a twilight, and a polar night that require visual navigation to account for a natural lighting. A number of clear days per year varies from 20 to $46\,d$ [22]. This way, the best time that allows for visual navigation is the period after the end of the polar night from early March to the middle of May, when there is an improvement of weather conditions [22], while all other time periods cause a broad variety of problems. We summarize the following general problems of using SLAM in arctic conditions as follows:

1. Snow and ice cover complicate the use of odometry
2. Snowfalls and snowstorms produce noise for laser and visual sensors
3. Snow and fog reduce visibility of laser and visual sensors
4. The uniformity of a landscape, a predominance of a white color and clouds make it difficult to navigate
5. Dips and cracks that are hidden under snow complicate maneuverability of a robot; moreover, their visual detection and recognition is tricky

While there was a number of attempts to solve these issues in robot navigation within the Arctic, a comprehensive solution to these problems does not exist yet. Interesting examples of mobile robots that were specially designed for a field work in the Arctic and Antarctic conditions include Cool Robot [27,28], Frosrty Boy [2] and Yeti robots [21]. Cool Robot is a four-wheel drive autonomous solar-powered robot that was designed to support scientific summer campaigns in Antarctica and Greenland. Frosty Boy robot was developed

Fig. 1. (**a**) A snowy landscape. (**b**) Harris detector features. (**c**) FAST detector features.

Fig. 2. (**a**) The horizon line (red) with a clear sky. (**b**) Using Canny edge detector to image 2a. (**c**) The horizon line (red) with a cloudy sky. (**d**) Using Canny edge detector to image 2c. (Color figure online)

by Polar Research Equipment to work on hard and soft surfaces in polar conditions. The autonomous Yeti rover was created specially for conducting ground-penetrating radar (GPR) surveys in the polar ice.

Snow-covered landscapes are featured by a visual uniformity and a small number of feature points. Figure 1a demonstrates a photograph that was taken in January on the territory of Central Russia during the daytime. While the real Arctic environment has a significantly worse visual conditions (from the point of visual sensors), these images demonstrate complicacy of the task even under a less demanding environment conditions. Using Harris corner detector [16] to this image (Fig. 1b) and FAST detector [30] (Fig. 1c) provided points on the snow cover that are unstable under a different observation angle and might be frequently modified by strong winds.

With a small and unstable number of feature points a horizon line becomes an important guideline. However, in cloudy conditions, the horizon line becomes difficult to distinguish. Figures 2a and 2c show a real skyline of a snow-covered terrain. Figures 2b and 2d present the result of using Canny edge detector [12]. It is notable, that in the case of Figure 2b most of the horizon line was selected, while in Figure 2d the foreground contours were selected and only a barely noticeable part (of several pixels) of the real horizon line was selected. Though, in this case, the highlighted top edge may also be suitable for a robot orientation.

Williams in [34] proposed an approach for solving a problem of identifying a horizon line in images of a snowy terrain assuming that a trapezoid area directly in front of a camera is a snow. Edges were extracted from an image and each edge was approximated by a piecewise linear form. Lines that were shorter than

Fig. 3. (a) The Arctic terrain model constructed in Gazebo. (b) Husky robot in the simulated terrain.

a minimum threshold were removed in order to exclude noise. Remaining line segments were considered to (probably) belong to the horizon line. Applying a length of a segment and colors of an area above and below the segment as heuristic criteria, each segment received a particular weight. Next, the horizon line was constructed as follows. First, a segment with a highest weight was selected. Then it was connected with one of the nearest potential segments. A cost of connecting a seed segment to another candidate segment minus the candidate segment weight was compared to a cost of simply extending the seed segment along its current trajectory to an endpoint of the candidate segment [34].

3   Requirements for Simulators of the Arctic Conditions

Due to a geographic remoteness, harsh weather and climate conditions, a field testing of SLAM algorithms in the Arctic has an increased risk of losing a robot and requires additional costs. Therefore, it is important to create a realistic simulator of the Arctic conditions that could allow a preliminary assessment of algorithms. According to the above mentioned problems of using SLAM in the Arctic conditions, we formulated requirements for the simulator as follows.

The Arctic Terrain Features. The peculiarity of ice and snow cover is its roughness and a presence of cracks, many of which are hidden under snow. Therefore, a terrain simulator should be able to generate uneven surfaces with particular textures.

Weather. This includes illumination, cloudiness, a presence of wind and precipitation. The horizon allocating problem solution in [34] partially removes a necessity of cloud simulation, making clouds presence non critical. However, this doesn't solve a problem of a wind and precipitation since even in a clear weather the wind could cause a blizzard and impair visibility. Modeling of snow precipitation could be done by adding snow particles in a simulation or directly applying noise to sensory data; the later approach avoids visual effects and deals directly with the precipitation consequences.

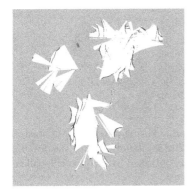 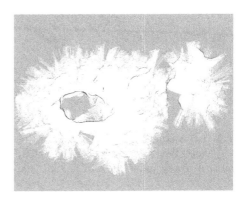

Fig. 4. A map obtained by Husky robot using (**a**) ROS GMapping package; (**b**) Hector SLAM package.

One of the most convenient ways to create and test robots in different environments is to use a popular Gazebo simulator, which is integrated with ROS [25]. Gazebo allows to accurately and effectively simulate robots in various conditions and to integrate a rather large set of existing robot models into virtual worlds with different environments. To simulate a terrain within Gazebo world, an arbitrary surface and its physical properties should be specified. Since a presence of specific relief is a mandatory requirement for the Arctic conditions simulation, a possibility of quick and convenient generation of such surfaces is an important task. We used an automatic tool [9,19] to generate such surfaces. This tool provides automatic filtering and maps an occupancy grid into Gazebo framework as a heightmap. Figure 3a shows an example of the Arctic landscape simulation that was generated by the tool.

4   Virtual Experiments in Gazebo

For virtual experiments we constructed a snow-covered landscape that was featured with small surface patches of a different height (which simulated underlying surface roughness) and white visual textures of different shades (which simulated snow and ice colors). The size of the constructed flat rough Arctic terrain was 320×320 m with a large mountain within, all being covered with snow. Figure 3a demonstrates an example of the landscape simulation in Gazebo. The experiments' goal was to compare the performance of popular ROS-based mapping methods in the virtual Arctic landscape.

In the experiments we used Clearpath Robotics Husky robot model [5], which was specially designed to work in difficult field conditions. It is worth mentioning that before running virtual experiments with Husky, we had tested the passability of the constructed Arctic terrain with several indoor robots, including TurtleBot [6]. In the virtual Arctic landscape the TurtleBot robot had rolled down from small slopes, stuck in mounds and pits, and could not move away

Fig. 5. (a) An image with feature points that was obtained using ORB-SLAM2 library. (b) A map that was obtained using ORB-SLAM2 library before losing the feature points. (c) An example of ORB-SLAM2 map that was obtained by erroneous localization.

from its starting point for any significant distance due to the virtual terrain roughness. At the same time, the Husky robot demonstrated a steady overcoming of the constructed terrain. Three cones marked the starting position of the Husky robot (Fig. 3b), and the robot was controlled in a teleoperation mode while the operator moved it from the starting point towards the mountain.

The first experiment run GMapping algorithm [14,15], which is a laser-based SLAM approach. The resulting map (Fig. 4a) that was constructed by GMapping package [3] was not suitable for navigating the robot. The experiment demonstrated that odometry could not be applied while navigating on rough Arctic surfaces.

Since a surface unevenness prevents effective use of odometry based algorithms, the second experiment employed Hector SLAM [17] to construct a map, which allows building a map without odometry data if the robot does not provide it. In the second experiment we moved Husky robot from the starting point, around the mountain and returned it to the starting point. Similarly to the first experiment, in addition to the snow mountain, small irregularities of the ground distorted information about obstacles' presence on the starting position. However, the robot was relatively correctly localized on the map. However, after the robot completed a loop around the mountain and moved away from it, the robot localized itself in a completely different (wrong) location of the map. Figure 4b demonstrates the resulting map that was built by Hector SLAM algorithm. A large gray area spot in the middle of the map was obtained when the robot moved from the starting position to the mountain and around the mountain. A small spot was obtained on the way back, when the robot moved away from the mountain towards the starting point and on the way back Hector SLAM stopped working correctly.

In the third experiment we used ORB-SLAM2 [24] library for visual SLAM. ORB-SLAM2 is a real-time SLAM library for monocular, stereo, and RGB-D cameras that calculates a camera path [4]. Within several attempts to construct a map, in all cases the robot succeeded to map only several first meters of a path, and then feature points were lost and localization errors occurred. Figure 5a presents a single frame with feature points. Figure 5b demonstrates a map that was obtained in one of the attempts, before losing feature points.

Fig. 6. (a) A loop closure obtained by RTAB-Map. (b) An example of an erroneous localization of RTAB-Map.

Figure 5c demonstrates an example of a map that was obtained in the case of an erroneous localization. Note that the nature of the feature points in Figure 5a resembles the situation, which we had previously encountered while detecting feature points in the image of a real snowy landscape (Fig. 1c).

In the fourth experiment, we used RTAB-Map ROS package based on Lidar and Visual SLAM [7, 18]. In this experiment, the robot walked around an area of $2500\,\text{m}^2$ and returned to the starting point. During the experiment, we observed the loop closure of the first loop (Fig. 6a), but on the second loop (with approximately the same trajectory) a localization error occurred (Fig. 6b) and the robot got lost.

Table 1. The features of the arctic terrain.

Feature description	Implemented
Uneven underlying surface	Yes
Holes and cracks hidden by snow	No
Wind	No
Precipitation	No
Landscape temporary changes due to weather conditions	No
Predominance of white color shades in a landscape	Yes
Lack of visual feature points	Yes
Fuzzy skyline	No

The robot failed to construct a satisfactory map in virtual experiments with all four SLAM approaches. The best results were obtained by RTAB-Map approach, which allowed to achieve a single loop closure. The virtual experiments demonstrated that an uneven landscape, a predominance of white shade colors, and a small number of feature points make popular SLAM methods impractical for the Arctic terrains. Table 1 summarizes the environment features that have a significant impact on SLAM algorithms in the Arctic conditions. The second column reflects those features, which were already integrated into our virtual environments at this stage of the project.

5   Conclusions

Autonomous robots in the Arctic cover a number of strategically important tasks, including climate research, reconnaissance, transportation, material delivery, search and rescue. These goals require adapting standard navigation, localization and mapping techniques to the harsh Arctic conditions, which do not allow their straightforward usage. This paper discussed main problems of using simultaneous localization and mapping (SLAM) algorithms in the Arctic region and formulated requirements for simulators of Arctic environments. Our ROS-based software was used to construct Arctic terrains in the Gazebo simulator, and three of the eight basic features of the Arctic conditions were implemented within these terrains. ROS implementations of GMapping, Hector SLAM, ORB-SLAM2 and RTAB-Map SLAM algorithms were tested within the constructed Arctic terrains in order to conclude on their applicability in the Arctic.

The results of the virtual experiments in Gazebo simulator demonstrated that the presence of uneven snow surface in the simulated environment significantly complicated the work of all four SLAM algorithms and none of them could construct a satisfactory map of the environment. Yet, based on Lidar and Visual SLAM approaches RTAB-Map algorithm performed slightly better than its counterparts. The virtual experiments demonstrated that existing popular SLAM methods failed in the Arctic conditions even for the virtual environment with only three typical features of the Arctic region being integrated into the terrain. Therefore, a proper simulation of the Arctic that would incorporate all requirements, which were listed in our paper, and new SLAM algorithms should be developed in order to ensure a possibility of autonomous mobile robot navigation in severe and demanding Arctic environment.

As a part of our ongoing work within this project, we gradually increase a number of the Arctic environment's features that were proposed in this paper. To develop a new SLAM algorithm for the Arctic we consider fussing data from multiple sources and defining new type of multi-source feature points.

Acknowledgements. The reported study was funded by the Russian Foundation for Basic Research (RFBR) according to the research project No. 19-58-70002. The sixth author acknowledges the support of the Japan Science and Technology Agency, the JST Strategic International Collaborative Research Program, Project No. 18065977.

References

1. The strategy for the development of the Arctic zone of the Russian Federation and national security up to 2020 (2013)
2. Frosty boy (2020). https://www.polarresearchequipment.com/specs
3. GMapping (2020). https://openslam-org.github.io/gmapping.html

4. ORB-SLAM2 - ROS Wiki (2020). http://wiki.ros.org/orb_slam2_ros
5. Robots/Husky - ROS Wiki (2020). http://wiki.ros.org/Robots/Husky
6. Robots/TurtleBot - ROS Wiki (2020). http://wiki.ros.org/Robots/TurtleBot
7. Rtabmap - ROS Wiki (2020). http://wiki.ros.org/rtabmap/
8. Alishev, N., Lavrenov, R., Hsia, K.H., Su, K.L., Magid, E.: Network failure detection and autonomous return algorithms for a crawler mobile robot navigation. In: 11th International Conference on Developments in eSystems Engineering (DeSE), pp. 169–174 (2018)
9. Abbyasov, B., Lavrenov, R., Zakiev, A., Magid, E.: Automatic tool for Gazebo world construction: from a grayscale image to a 3D solid model. In: IEEE International Conference on Robotics and Automation (ICRA), pp. 7226–7232 (2020)
10. Bailey, T., Durrant-Whyte, H.: Simultaneous localization and mapping (slam): Part II. IEEE Robot. Autom. Mag. **13**(3), 108–117 (2006)
11. Bokovoy, A., Yakovlev, K.: Enhancing semi-dense monocular VSLAM used for multi-rotor UAV navigation in indoor environment by fusing IMU data. In: International Conference on Artificial Life and Robotics (ICAROB), pp. 391–394 (2018)
12. Canny, J.: A computational approach to edge detection. IEEE Trans. Pattern Anal. Mach. Intell. **PAMI–8**(6), 679–698 (1986)
13. Durrant-Whyte, H., Bailey, T.: Simultaneous localization and mapping: Part I. IEEE Robot. Autom. Mag. **13**(2), 99–110 (2006)
14. Grisetti, G., Stachniss, C., Burgard, W.: Improved techniques for grid mapping with Rao-Blackwellized particle filters. Trans. Robot. **23**, 34–46 (2007)
15. Grisettiyz, G., Stachniss, C., Burgard, W.: Improving grid-based SLAM with Rao-Blackwellized particle filters by adaptive proposals and selective resampling. In: International Conference on Robotics and Automation, pp. 2432–2437 (2005)
16. Harris, C., Stephens, M.: A combined corner and edge detector. In: Proceedings of Fourth Alvey Vision Conference, pp. 147–151 (1988)
17. Kohlbrecher, S., Von Stryk, O., Meyer, J., Klingauf, U.: A flexible and scalable SLAM system with full 3D motion estimation. In: 2011 IEEE International Symposium on Safety, Security, and Rescue Robotics (SSRR), pp. 155–160, November 2011
18. Labbé, M., Michaud, F.: RTAB-Map as an open-source lidar and visual simultaneous localization and mapping library for large-scale and long-term online operation. J. Field Robot. **36**(2), 416–446 (2019)
19. Lavrenov, R., Zakiev, A., Magid, E.: Automatic mapping and filtering tool: from a sensor-based occupancy grid to a 3D Gazebo OCTOMAP. In: International Conference on Mechanical, System and Control Engineering (ICMSC), pp. 190–195 (2017)
20. Lavrenov, R., Matsuno, F., Magid, E.: Modified spline-based navigation: guaranteed safety for obstacle avoidance. In: Ronzhin, A., Rigoll, G., Meshcheryakov, R. (eds.) ICR 2017. LNCS (LNAI), vol. 10459, pp. 123–133. Springer, Cham (2017). https://doi.org/10.1007/978-3-319-66471-2_14
21. Lever, J., Delaney, A., Ray, L., Trautmann, E., Barna, L.: Autonomous GPR surveys using the polar rover. J. Field Robot. **30**, 194–215 (2013)
22. Molchanov, V., Akimov, V., Sokolov, Y.: Risks of emergency situations in Arctic zone of Russian Federation. FGU VNII GOCHS, Moscow (2011)
23. Moskvin, I., Lavrenov, R.: Modeling tracks and controller for servosila engineer robot. In: Ronzhin, A., Shishlakov, V. (eds.) Proceedings of 14th International Conference on Electromechanics and Robotics "Zavalishin's Readings". SIST, vol. 154, pp. 411–422. Springer, Singapore (2020). https://doi.org/10.1007/978-981-13-9267-2_33

24. Mur-Artal, R., Tardós, J.D.: ORB-SLAM2: an open-source SLAM system for monocular, stereo, and RGB-D cameras. IEEE Trans. Robot. **33**(5), 1255–1262 (2017)

25. Pashkin, A., Lavrenov, R., Zakiev, A., Svinin, M.: Pilot communication protocols for group of mobile robots in USAR scenarios. In: 12th International Conference on Developments in eSystems Engineering (DeSE), pp. 37–41 (2019)

26. Platonov, S., Buriak, T., Gorovoy, A., Bermishev, A., Lapshin, V.: Problems of navigation and high-precision positioning in Arctic and their solutions. Meas. World **7**, 3–9 (2014)

27. Ray, L., et al.: Autonomous rover for polar science support and remote sensing. In: Geoscience and Remote Sensing Symposium, pp. 4101–4104 (2014)

28. Ray, L., Lever, J., Streeter, A., Price, A.: Design and power management of a solar-powered "Cool Robot" for polar instrument networks: Research articles. J. Field Robot. **24**, 581–599 (2007)

29. Remenson, V., Timofeev, V., Shabalin, P.: The synoptic analysis of the peculiarities of the impact of atmospheric processes and weather-climate conditions on the activity of the state in the Arctic zone. In: Proceedings of the A.F. Mozhaysky Military Space Academy, vol. 651, pp. 130–138 (2016)

30. Rosten, E., Drummond, T.: Fusing points and lines for high performance tracking. In: Tenth IEEE International Conference on Computer Vision (ICCV 2005), vol. 1, pp. 1508–1515. Beijing, October 2005

31. Shadrin, B., Zachateyskiy, D., Dvoryanchikov, V.: Improving of data transferring effectiveness in communication systems operated in arctic regions. In: 4th International Conference on Radio Engineering, Electronics and Communication, pp. 98–105 (2017)

32. Simakov, N., Lavrenov, R., Zakiev, A., Safin, R., Martínez-García, E.A.: Modeling USAR maps for the collection of information on the state of the environment. In: 12th International Conference on Developments in eSystems Engineering (DeSE), pp. 918–923. IEEE (2019)

33. Taketomi, T., Uchiyama, H., Ikeda, S.: Visual SLAM algorithms: a survey from 2010 to 2016. IPSJ Trans. Comput. Vis. Appl. **9**, 16 (2017)

34. Williams, S.: Visual arctic navigation: techniques for autonomous agents in glacial environments (2011)

35. Zakiev, A., Tsoy, T., Magid, E.: Swarm robotics: remarks on terminology and classification. In: International Conference on Interactive Collaborative Robotics, pp. 291–300 (2018)

Data Exchange Method for Wireless UAV-Aided Communication in Sensor Systems and Robotic Devices

Alexander Denisov$^{(\boxtimes)}$ ⓘ, Aleksandra Shabanova ⓘ, and Oleg Sivchenko

St. Petersburg Institute for Informatics and Automation of the Russian Academy of Sciences, 39, 14th Line, 199178 St. Petersburg, Russia
sdenisov93@mail.ru

Abstract. This paper considers the problem of reliable connection maintenance among robotic devices, used in agriculture and operating autonomously in the wide area. For this, models of wireless data exchange between sensor systems and robotic devices were developed. To maintain seamless connection among robotic devices, radio modules, repeaters and gateways are proposed. Due to vastness of agricultural areas, the developed models of data exchange account for possible utilization of unmanned aerial vehicles as repeaters. Such solution allows to reduce the number of radio modules in use, as well leverage aerial vehicles efficiently. To ensure communication with land-based robotic devices with the aid of unmanned aerial vehicles a specific algorithm of radio module layout was developed, which implements the «tesselation» pattern. This algorithm also can be utilized to connect several standalone telecommunication networks, data exchange among which is affected using unmanned aerial vehicles.

Keywords: Unmanned aerial vehicles · LoRa · Agricultural Engineering · Data exchange · Path planning · Robotics · Networking · Telemetry

1 Introduction

Currently robotic devices are actively implemented in agriculture, as robotization of this domain would allow to relieve humans from farming chore, reduce loss of working time and increase productivity. Efficient performance of different workflows in husbandry and horticulture in vast agricultural areas requires autonomous operation of robotic devices. To achieve this, seamless inter-robot communication should be ensured, what is complicated because of territorial expanse.

Deployment of smart grid communication networks (SGCN) in urban areas became feasible because of accessibility of wired and wireless technologies there. But in rural areas these solutions are often precluded or too expensive, what complicates the implementation of such networks. As alternative to wired communication, LPWA networks (low power wide area) can be used, suitable for transfer of small data batches over large distances [1]. LPWA-networks are characterized by low-cost deployment, little energy consumption and greater distance of radio signaling, compared to other wireless

© Springer Nature Switzerland AG 2020
A. Ronzhin et al. (Eds.): ICR 2020, LNAI 12336, pp. 45–54, 2020.
https://doi.org/10.1007/978-3-030-60337-3_5

solutions (GPRS [2], ZigBee [3]) [4]. Possible topologies of LPWA-networks are: star topology, point-to-point topology, cluster tree topology and mesh topology as well, such as in context of the IQRF-technology [5].

One of the principally accessible LPWA-technologies is LoRa [5], characterized by low-cost radio modules, broad frequency band, secure data transfer protocol. LoRa also ensures robust communication between modules at distance up to 3 km. The LoRa architecture can be divided into a back-end and a front-end part. Back-end is implemented as a gateway server, receiving sensor data. Front-end consists of network gateway modules and endpoint device nodes [6].

LoRa can be used in establishment of sensor network for flood early warning system [7]. Level sensors were used to determine distance between sensor and water surface. LoRa technology enabled data transfer from sensor to single-board computer, which was publishing the warnings in social networks. Testing of the proposed system demonstrated lossless data transfer at distance of 500 m.

In [8] LoRa is used to implement navigation and localization of mobile robotic devices. As satellite navigation systems show insufficient precision (2–3 m) and high energy consumption, authors of this paper developed a navigation system for mobile robots for outdoor purposes; this system is based on wireless data transfer networks. This system consists of sensor nodes, which include LoRa-modules, sensors, satellite navigation unit and solar cells. Such structure of sensor nodes enables robot localization with high accuracy, as well low energy consumption due to solar cells. LoRa-modules enable transfer of data on robot position to user, as well data exchange with server.

Autonomous performance of mobile robotic devices can be implemented with programmable Radio Frequency beacons, which establish an Ad-Hoc network [9, 10]. Such Ad-Hoc networks enable localization and navigation of agricultural robots in open areas. Such network has no fixed architecture; therefore, it can be easily deployed in any area without additional tuning. To establish communication among network nodes, routing protocols Demand Reactive Protocol and Trace-Back Routing Protocol were used [9]. Testing of an Ad-Hoc network with six nodes showed, that the proposed solution enables path adjustment for robotic devices and fast performance. Generally, the networks, based on radio beacons, can be assembled of commodity hardware and are easily to deploy. Though, the protocols, being in use here, are less standardized compared to analogues (WiFi, LPWAN) [11].

For autonomous motion of mobile robots in agricultural areas, not covered by GPS signaling, Ad-Hoc network can be augmented by Bluetooth-like technologies [12, 13]. Application of Bluetooth enables to get rid of radio noise using adaptive frequency hopping strategy, AFHS. TAODV (time-slotted, ad hoc on-demand distance vector routing) can be used as routing protocol, which enables secure communication among robotic devices [12]. The key downside of the proposed solution is poor scalability, due to the limited threshold number of devices in pico-network, imposed by Bluetooth technology.

Ad-Hoc networks also can be useful in establishment of UAV-based flying sensor networks (UAV – unmanned aerial vehicles) [14, 15]. Flying sensor networks are a subset of Ubiquitous Sensor Networks, in which the UAV can act as a transient master node [16].

To ensure seamless connection for robotic devices in agriculture, models of wireless data exchange between sensor systems and robotic devices have to be developed. If direct radio communication between some modules is infeasible, repeaters should be used. As robotic devices operate in vast areas, UAV can act as repeaters in the locations, where stationary repeaters cannot be installed, what should be considered during development of such models.

2 Models of Wireless Data Exchange for Entities of Agricultural Facility

For formal representation of the seamless connection problem in context of robotic systems, conceptual model of data exchange for entities of agricultural facility was developed. This model includes robotic devices (RD), service area, request, entities, sensor framework and archive (see Fig. 1). Engineering components of an agricultural facility can be classified to the following main groups: 1) sensor systems, essentially the sets of sensors (sensing units), reading the changes of properties and parameters of the entity in question; 2) RS, performing the specified functions in the agricultural area, particularly, mobile robotic platforms (MRP) and UAV; 3) network for wireless data exchange (telemetry), consisting of gateway, radio modules and repeaters, sending data batches from sensor systems of RD to server and control signals backward.

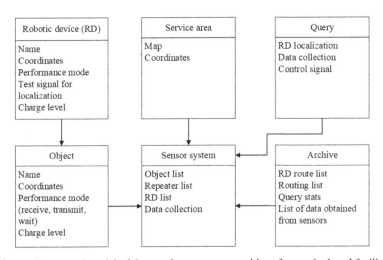

Fig. 1. Conceptual model of data exchange among entities of an agricultural facility.

It is assumed, that an extensive agricultural area is under consideration, where RDs operate and sensors are installed, together comprising a sensor system. Every mobile platform can move within its operational area only. Connection has to be established between RD and sensor system. For this radio modules, repeaters and gateways are utilized, which have to be installed in this area. There are some points, where the modules must be situated anyway; that's said, the modules must connect to the gateway and ensure coverage of operational areas of the MRPs. This paper considers the setting, where, due to domain-specific peculiarities, it is hardly feasible to distribute the repeaters across the whole operational area of the MRP. Therefore, it is proposed to use UAVs for data collection and transfer in some regions.

Data exchange between sensor system and server is affected via gateways. If the sensor data cannot be sent directly to the gateway, repeaters are utilized, embracing several radio modules. Then the repeater data are sent to the gateway, which aggregates the data from all repeaters, and further sent to server. The said elements establish a sensor complex. Structural diagram of the sensor complex is presented in Fig. 2.

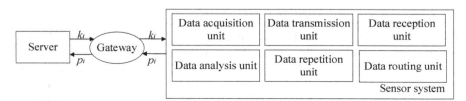

Fig. 2. Structural diagram of the sensor complex k_i – control signal, p_i – sensor data.

During modeling of LoRa-based interactions between RD and sensor system, the following assumptions were made. Suppose, the agricultural area in question, where the wireless data exchange between RD and sensor system has to be established, contains no obstacles, which could interrupt the radio signal.

Suppose, $D = \{d_1, d_2, \dots D_h, \dots, d_H\}$ is a set of radio modules, including repeaters, acting in the territory of the aggricultural facility, $R = \{r_1, r_2, \dots, r_n, \dots, r_N\}$ is a set of mobile RDs, $S = \{s_1, s_2, \dots, s_m, \dots, s_M\}$ –is a set of sensors, which transmit data, A are features of the agricultural area under consideration. Then, formal statement of interaction establishment problem between RD and sensor system can be formulated as follows: considering the known distribution of radio modules D and motion paths of RDs R within the area A, ensure transfer of data from sensor system entities S and RD R to one of the gateways B with coordinates B_{xy}, thereby maintaining data transfer speed at least at the threshold value L. The area A is described by the tuple of following components:

$$A = <F, B_{xy}, Q, W>, \tag{1}$$

where F is topological map of the agricultural area with specified coordinates of the points, where sensor system modules are installed, B_{xy} are gateway coordinates, Q are coordinates of data repeaters, W is path and schedule of data exchange for each of radio modules and repeaters.

Transfer of data batches p_i from each radio module or repeater to the gateway is described by the following tuple of parameters:

$$p_i = <Z_i, B_{xy}, X_i, C_i, V>, \tag{2}$$

where Z_i are coordinates of the transmitting radio module, i is number of the repeater in the chain of radio modules, X_i is data transmission delay from the i-th repeater, C_i

is number of repeater modules from the i-th module to the gateway, V is data exchange schedule.

Sensor complex, including the server, the gateway and the sensor system is characterized by the following tuple of parameters:

$$y = \ <Z_j, \ C_j, \ V, \ f_j, \ B_{xy}, \ RS_j, \ G_j, \ Q>, \tag{3}$$

where Z_j are coordinates of the j-th transmitting radio module, C_j is number of repeater modules from the j-th transmitting radio module to the gateway, V is data exchange schedule, f_j is actual operational mode of the j-th radio module, RS_j is motion speed of robotic devices, G_j are additional parameters (condition of the embedded engineering components, necessary for radio modules to function), Q is data on actual positions and operation mode of all service systems within the facility.

In the proposed model the actual operational mode of the module is selected from the following set:

$$f = \{f_a, f_b, f_c, f_d\}, \tag{4}$$

where f_a is sleep mode, f_b is transmitter mode, f_c is receiver mode, f_d is repeater mode.

The interaction of the sensor complex y_i with the server u consists in exposing of data E on sensor system entity or RD R:

$$E(u) = f(y, A, R). \tag{5}$$

For convenience all the aforementioned quantities and their values are presented in the Table 1.

Table 1. List of terms.

Term	Description
D	Set of radio modules, including repeaters
R	Set of mobile robotic devices
S	Set of sensor system components (sensors)
A	Description of serviced agricultural area
Z_i	Coordinates of repeater radio module
X_i	Data transmission delay
C_i	Count of repeater modules to gateway
V	Schedule of data reception and transmission
f_i	Current radio module performance mode
F	Topological map of the agricultural area
G_i	Additional parameters (level of charge in batteries and other embedded hardware), necessary for the radio module function
Q	Data of current position and performance modes of all service system within the facility
RS_i	Robotic device motion velocity
B_{xy}	Gateway coordinates
E	Data about object, obtained from sensors

3   Algorithm of Distribution of Repeater Modules

For transmission of data from MRD to server UAVs can be used, but before the data exchange the positions of land-based RDs must be defined. Therefore, the respective algorithm of UAV-aided MRD localization was developed. As land-based RD the mobile robotic platform was considered (see Fig. 3).

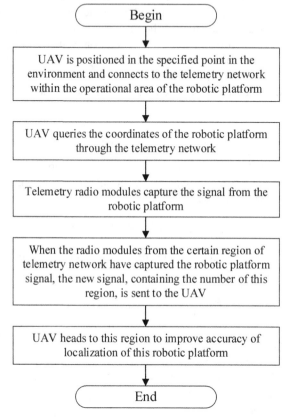

Fig. 3. Algorithm for UAV-aided localization of the robotic platform.

This algorithm allows to employ relatively few radio modules to ensure radio communication with robotic platforms, but, at the same time, it efficiently leverages the features of UAVs. To reduce the number of radio modules in use and ensure tighter interoperability between telemetry network and UAVs, an algorithm of radio module distribution within the operational area of the robotic platform is proposed (see Fig. 4). This core of this algorithm is the «tesselation» approach [17]. Thereby maximum acceptable module spacing is chosen, which allows for data transmission (e.g. 3 km for ESP-32 LoRa modules). This allows to minimize the number of modules on the path of the robotic platform in its operational environment.

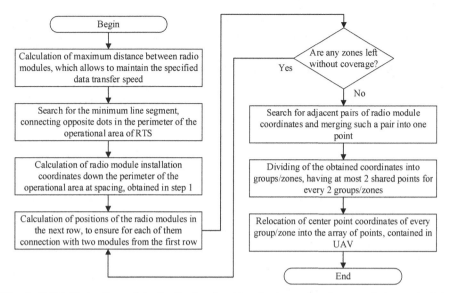

Fig. 4. UAV-aided radio module distribution algorithm, implementing the « tesselation » principle for complex terrains.

This algorithm assumes merging of closely adjacent repeaters into one point, what allows to reduce the number of radio modules in use and workload in the telemetry network, accordingly. Then the obtained radio module coordinates are classified into groups/zones in such manner, that every zone would have at most two shared modules with the adjacent groups. This enables maintain connection among the modules from different groups, hence, within the whole telemetry network. These groups are data collection areas for the UAVs. Therefore, due to minimum overlapping of groups with each other, no UAV makes redundant data captures from multiple modules. The results of application of the presented algorithm are shown in the Fig. 5.

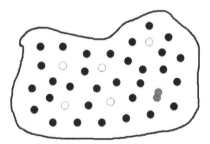

Fig. 5. Algorithm for radio module spacing in action. (Color figure online)

Figure 5 presents the operational area of the robotic platform. Black dots denote the points with radio modules, white dots denote the positions of UAVs for data collection, blue dots denote anticipated locations for the UAVs. The advantage of this algorithm is, that it requires less repeaters and data collection points compared to the «grid»-like algorithm [17]. In the first step of the «grid»-like algorithm an arbitrarily shaped region is sized to a rectangle, then intersection points between grid lines are calculated, and points with those coordinates are discarded, that do not fit into the operational area of the MRP. For radio module spacing algorithm in an arbitrarily shaped region, implementing the «tesselation» approach, 31 repeater and 6 data collection points are needed, whereas for the «grid»-like algorithm [17] – 35 repeaters and 9 points of data collection points for UAVs.

The algorithms, presented above, can be utilized for connection of several separate telemetry networks, data exchange among which is performed using UAVs. Therefore, several groups of radio modules and repeaters with a gateway are established. The data will be sent to this gateway, and UAVs will routinely capture this data from it and send it further to the master gateway server. This networking approach fits for groups of radio modules, that are installed far from the gateway server or in complex locations, where the installation and maintenance of the equipment is complicated. It is suboptimal to use a repeater chain in such cases. Such approach allows to reduce the number of radio modules in use, hence, decreasing the overheads for network deployment and operation. It also reduces workload in the network.

4 Conclusion

This paper considered the problem of seamless communication establishment among MRPs, operating in vast areas. Conceptual and set-theoretic models of data exchange for sensor complexes are proposed, ensuring on the given topological map of the serviced area the connection of the devices to the wireless network and their interoperation, based on the LoRa technology in the agricultural domain. Based on this model, the radio module distribution algorithm was developed, which ensures UAV-aided communication with land-based RS. Here the UAV acts as repeater, what allows to reduce the number of radio modules in action and efficiently leverage features of the UAVs. Reduced number of radio modules also provides for less noise, less collisions between data batches and simplification of scheduling, because radio wave interference decreases. Though, utilization of UAVs as repeaters complicates the layout and deployment of the network, as well increases the overheads for its maintenance.

Further research will be aimed to enhancing of the proposed models to automate their workflows and data exchange between robotic devices and distributed sensor networks. Additional noise immunity of radio modules is also among the key research objectives, as well working with batch collisions data, supplied to the recommender system for optimization of repeater layout and establishment of wireless networks in agricultural facilities [18–24].

Acknowledgements. This research is supported by the RFBR Project No. 18-58-76001 ERA_a.

References

1. Barriquello, C.H., Bernardon, D.P., Canha, L.N., e Silva, F.E.S., Porto, D.S., da Silveira Ramos, M.J.: Performance assessment of a low power wide area network in rural smart grids. In: 2017 52nd International Universities Power Engineering Conference (UPEC), pp. 1–4. IEEE (2017)
2. Ghribi, B., Logrippo, L.: Understanding GPRS: the GSM packet radio service. Comput. Netw. **34**(5), 763–779 (2000)
3. Wadhwa, L.K., Deshpande, R.S., Priye, V.: Extended shortcut tree routing for ZigBee based wireless sensor network. Ad Hoc Netw. **37**, 295–300 (2016)
4. Krasnov, P.A., Roslyakov, A.V.: Model of ZigBee wireless sensor network. In: Problems of Engineering and Technology of Telecommunications. Optical Technologies in Telecommunications, pp. 176–177 (2018)
5. LoRa Alliance. https://lora-alliance.org. Accessed 30 Apr 2020
6. Lavric, A., Popa, V.: Internet of things and LoRa™ low-power wide-area networks: a survey. In: 2017 International Symposium on Signals, Circuits and Systems (ISSCS), pp. 1–5. IEEE (2017)
7. Leon, E., Alberoni, C., Wister, M., Hernández-Nolasco, J.: flood early warning system by Twitter using LoRa. In: Multidisciplinary Digital Publishing Institute Proceedings, vol. 2, no. 19, 1213 p. (2018)
8. Magno, M., Rickli, S., Quack, J., Brunecker, O., Benini, L.: Combining LoRa and RTK to achieve a high precision self-sustaining geo-localization system. In: Proceedings of the 17th ACM/IEEE International Conference on Information Processing in Sensor Networks, pp. 160–161. IEEE (2018)
9. Rabie, T., Suleiman, S.: A novel wireless mesh network for indoor robotic navigation. In: 2016 5th International Conference on Electronic Devices, Systems and Applications (ICEDSA), pp. 1–4. IEEE (2016)
10. Konieczny, M., Pawłowicz, B., Potencki, J., Skoczylas, M.: Application of RFID technology in navigation of mobile robot. In: 2017 21st European Microelectronics and Packaging Conference (EMPC) & Exhibition, pp. 1–4. IEEE (2017)
11. Malandra, F., Sansò, B.: A Markov-modulated end-to-end delay analysis of large-scale RF mesh networks with time-slotted ALOHA and FHSS for smart grid applications. IEEE Trans. Wireless Commun. **17**(11), 7116–7127 (2018)
12. Nykorak, A., Hiromoto, R. E., Sachenko, A., Koval, V.: A wireless navigation system with no external positions. In: 2015 IEEE 8th International Conference on Intelligent Data Acquisition and Advanced Computing Systems: Technology and Applications (IDAACS), vol. 2, pp. 898–901. IEEE (2015)
13. Efremov, D.A., Roslyakov, A.V.: Network Calculus modeling of BLE sensor network. In: Optical Technologies in Telecommunications, pp. 154–156 (2018)
14. Koucheryavy, A.E., et al.: Flying sensor networks. Elektrosvyaz **9**, 2–5 (2014)
15. Koucheryavy, A.E., Vladyko, A.G., Kirichek, R.V.: Theoretical and practical directions of research in the field of flying sensor networks. Elektrosvyaz (7), 9 (2015)
16. Vyrelkin, A.D., Koucheryavy, A.E., Prokopyev, A.V.: The study of the possibility of using an unmanned aerial vehicle as a temporary head node of clusters of the ground sensor network. Inf. Technol. Telecommun. **1**, 27–34 (2015)
17. Denisov, A.V., et al.: Algorithms for radio beacon mesh network establishment for navigation of robotic systems in agriculture. Bull. MSTU Stankin **3**, 57–65 (2019)
18. Andreev, S.J., Tregubov, R.B., Mironov, A.E.: Problem of selecting communication channels bandwidth of transport network taking into account imbalance of various priority traffic. SPIIRAS Proc. **19**, 412–445 (2020). https://doi.org/10.15622/sp.2020.19.2.7

19. Meshcheryakov, R.V., Trefilov, P.M., Chekhov, A.V., Novoselskiy, A.K., Goncharova, E.: An application of swarm of quadcopters for searching operations. IFAC-PapersOnLine **2**(25), 14–18 (2019)

20. Zakiev, A., Shabalina, K., Tsoy, T., Magid, E.: Pilot virtual experiments on ArUco and ArTag systems comparison for fiducial marker rotation resistance. In: Ronzhin, A., Shishlakov, V. (eds.) Proceedings of 14th International Conference on Electromechanics and Robotics "Zavalishin's Readings". SIST, vol. 154, pp. 455–464. Springer, Singapore (2020). https://doi.org/10.1007/978-981-13-9267-2_37

21. Kopkin, E.V., Kobzarev, I.M.: Information Value Measure for Optimization of Flexible Diagnosis Programs of Technical Objects. SPIIRAS Proceedings. **18**, 1434–1461 (2019). https://doi.org/10.15622/sp.2019.18.6.1434-1461

22. Svinin, M., Goncharenko, I., Kryssanov, V., Magid, E.: Motion planning strategies in human control of non-rigid objects with internal degrees of freedom. Hum. Mov. Sci. **63**, 209–230 (2019)

23. Gradetsky, V., Ermolov, I., Knyazkov, M., Semenov, E., Lapin, B., Sobolnikov, S., Sukhanov, A.: Parameters identification in UGV group for virtual simulation of joint task. In: Ronzhin, A., Shishlakov, V. (eds.) Proceedings of 14th International Conference on Electromechanics and Robotics "Zavalishin's Readings". SIST, vol. 154, pp. 371–381. Springer, Singapore (2020). https://doi.org/10.1007/978-981-13-9267-2_30

24. Larkin, E., Bogomolov, A., Privalov, A., Antonov, M.: About one approach to robot control system simulation. In: Ronzhin, A., Rigoll, G., Meshcheryakov, R. (eds.) ICR 2018. LNCS (LNAI), vol. 11097, pp. 159–169. Springer, Cham (2018). https://doi.org/10.1007/978-3-319-99582-3_17

A Combination of Theta*, ORCA and Push and Rotate for Multi-agent Navigation

Stepan Dergachev[1,2]([✉]) [iD], Konstantin Yakovlev[1,2] [iD],
and Ryhor Prakapovich[3] [iD]

[1] National Research University Higher School of Economics, Moscow, Russia
sadergachev@edu.hse.ru, yakovlev@isa.ru
[2] Federal Research Center for Computer Science and Control of Russian
Academy of Sciences, Moscow, Russia
[3] United Institute of Informatics Problems of the National Academy
of Sciences of Belarus, Minsk, Belarus
rprakapovich@robotics.by

Abstract. We study the problem of multi-agent navigation in static environments when no centralized controller is present. Each agent is controlled individually and relies on three algorithmic components to achieve its goal while avoiding collisions with the other agents and the obstacles: *i*) individual path planning which is done by THETA* algorithm; *ii*) collision avoidance while path following which is performed by ORCA* algorithm; *iii*) locally-confined multi-agent path planning done by PUSH AND ROTATE algorithm. The latter component is crucial to avoid deadlocks in confined areas, such as narrow passages or doors. We describe how the suggested components interact and form a coherent navigation pipeline. We carry out an extensive empirical evaluation of this pipeline in simulation. The obtained results clearly demonstrate that the number of occurring deadlocks significantly decreases enabling more agents to reach their goals compared to techniques that rely on collision-avoidance only and do not include multi-agent path planning component.

Keywords: Multi-agent systems · Path planning · Collision avoidance · Multi-agent path finding · Navigation · ORCA · Push and rotate

1 Introduction

When a group of mobile agents, such as service robots or video game characters, operates in the shared environment one of the key challenges they face is arriving at their target locations while avoiding collisions with the obstacles and each other. In general two approaches to solve this problem, i.e. multi-agent navigation, can be identified: centralized and decentralized.

© Springer Nature Switzerland AG 2020
A. Ronzhin et al. (Eds.): ICR 2020, LNAI 12336, pp. 55–66, 2020.
https://doi.org/10.1007/978-3-030-60337-3_6

The centralized approaches rely on a central planner that constructs a joint multi-agent plan utilizing the full knowledge of the agents' states. When the plan is constructed each agent follows it and if the execution is perfect or near-perfect collisions are guaranteed not to happen. Centralized planning can be carried out in such a way that the joint plan is guaranteed to be optimal[1]. Non-optimal yet computationally efficient centralized planners do exist as well.

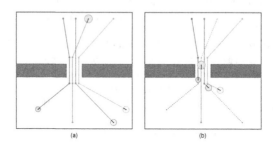

Fig. 1. An example of possible deadlock in the vicinity of narrow passage.

Decentralized approaches do not rely on the central planner. Instead each agent plans its trajectory individually and resolves conflicts at the execution stage, i.e. an agent reactively avoids collisions relying on the local observations and/or communication. Such approach naturally fits to numerous scenarios with heterogeneous agents, limited communication/visibility etc. It also scales well to large number of agents however it does not guarantee optimality. Moreover, no guarantees that each agent will reach its goal can be provided. The main reason for that is that each agent is egoistic in pursuing its goal this can lead to a deadlock. Consider a scenario shown on Fig. 1 when agents have to swap sides using a tight passage connecting the rooms. If they approach the passage nearly at the same time they will be stuck. For all of them to safely move through at least one of the agents has to step back and let other agent go. Thus, some form of cooperative behaviour (which is explicitly or implicitly centralized) is vital for accomplishing the mission.

In this work we present an algorithmic pipeline that combines decentralized and centralized approaches to multi-agent navigation. Within this pipeline each agent constructs and follows its path individually. When a pattern leading to potential deadlock is detected a locally-confined multi-agent path finding is invoked, i.e. agents that appear to be involved in a deadlock are identified and a joint safe plan for these agents is constructed. After executing this plan all involved agents switch back to the decentralized mode. We use THETA* [6], ORCA* [16], PUSH AND ROTATE [7] for individual path planing, local collision avoidance and multi-agent path finding respectively. Meanwhile, the suggested pipeline is not limited to these algorithms and other algorithmic components

---

[1] Typically, optimal centralized planers rely on the discretization of the workspace thus the solutions they provide are optimal w.r.t. the used space/time discretization.

may be used instead of the aforementioned methods as well. We extensively study the suggested approach in simulation and show that the suggested approach leads to much better results compared to fully decentralized method that does not utilize multi-agent path finding.

2 Related Work

The approaches to multi-agent navigation can be roughly divided into the two groups: centralized and decentralized [18]. The centralized approaches assume that a central planner is available that possess all the information about the agents and the environment and plans for a joint collision-free solution. Naive application of such search algorithms as A* [10], i.e. planning in the full joint configuration space, which is a cardinal product of the individual configuration spaces, is impractical as the search space grows exponentially in the number of agents. However there exist techniques that greatly reduce the search effort, such as subdimensional expansion [17], conflict-based search [12] to name a few. The latter technique is very popular nowadays and there exist a large variety of CBS planners that improve the performance of the original algorithm or extend it in numerous ways, e.g. in [3] a sub-optimal version of CBS is presented, the work [2] planning in continuous time is considered etc. All these algorithms are designed with the aim of minimizing cost of the result solution. At the same time, when large cost of the solution is acceptable one can use extremely fast polynomial algorithms, e.g. PUSH AND ROTATE [7]. Finally, a prioritized approach [4,19] is also a common choice in numerous cases. Prioritized planners are fast and typically provide solutions of reasonably low cost (very close to optimal in many cases). Their main drawback is that they are incomplete in general.

The decentralized approaches do not rely on the full knowledge of the agents' states and the environment and assume that each agent utilizes only the information available to it locally [9,18]. One of the common ways to solve multi-agent navigation problem under a decentralized setting is to plan individual paths for each agent, e.g. by a heuristic search algorithm such as DIJKSTRA [8], A* [10], THETA* [6], and then let all agent follow their paths. To avoid collisions algorithms of the ORCA-family are typically used [1,13,14,16]. Another techniques that rely on buffered Voronoi cells [21] or various reinforcement learning techniques [5,11] to avoid collisions can also be employed. In general decentralized approaches are prone to deadlocks and do not guarantee that each agent will reach its destination.

In this work we combine both decentralized and centralized methods into a coherent multi-agent navigation pipeline striving to combine the best of two worlds: flexibility and scalability of the decentralized navigation and completeness of the centralized planning.

3 Problem Statement

Consider a set of n agents moving through 2D workspace, $W \in \mathbb{R}^2$, composed of the free space and the obstacles: $W = W_{free} \cup O$. Each obstacle, $o \in O$, is a bounded subset in W. Every agent, i, is modelled as a disk of radius r_i. The state of an agent is defined by its position and velocity: $(\mathbf{p}_i, \mathbf{V}_i)$. The latter is bounded: $||\mathbf{V}_i|| \leq V_i^{max} \in \mathbb{R}^+$, i.e. maximum speed of each agent is given.

Let $T = 0, \Delta t, 2\Delta t, \dots$ be the discrete time ($\Delta t = const$). For the sake of simplicity assume that $\Delta t = 1$, thus the timeline is $T = 0, 1, 2, \dots$. At each moment of time an agent can either move or wait (the latter can be considered as moving with the velocity being zero). We neglect inertial effects and assume that an agent moves from one location to the other following a straight line defined by its current velocity. We also assume perfect localization and execution.

At each time step agent knows $i)$ its own position, $ii)$ positions of all the obstacles, $iii)$ states of the neighboring agents. The latter are the agents that are located withing a radius R_i. This radius models a communication range of an agent, i.e. we assume that an agent i can communicate with other neighboring agents and acquire any information from them. For the sake of exposition we will refer to this range as to the visibility range further on.

A spatio-temporal path for an agent is, formally, a mapping: $\pi : T \rightarrow W_{free}$. It can also be represented as a sequence of agent's locations at each time step: $\pi = \{\pi_0, \pi_1, \dots\}$. In this work we are interested in converging paths, i.e. paths by which an agent reaches a particular location and never moves away from it. This can be formulated as follows: $\exists k \in T : \pi_{k+t} = \pi_k \; \forall t > 1$.

The path for the agent i is valid w.r.t. velocity constraints and static obstacles *iff* the following conditions hold:

$$||\pi_{t+1} - \pi_t|| \leq V_i^{max} \Delta t, \; \forall t \in \overline{0, k-1}$$
$$\rho(\pi_t, o) > r_i, \; \forall o \in O, \; \forall t \in \overline{0, k},$$

where $\rho(\pi_t, o)$ stands for the distance to the closest obstacle.

Consider now the two paths for distinct agents: π^i, π^j. They are called conflict-free if they are valid and the agents following them never collide, that is:

$$||\pi_t^i - \pi_{t'}^j|| \leq r_i + r_j, \; \forall t \in \overline{0, k^i}, t' \in \overline{0, k^j}.$$

The set of paths $\Pi = \{\pi^1, \dots, \pi^n\}$, one for each agent, is conflict-free if any pair of paths forming this set is conflict-free.

The problem we are considering in this paper can now be formulated as follows. Given n start and goal locations at each time step for each agent choose a velocity s.t. the agent reaches the goal at some time step, the agent never collides with static obstacles and other agents, that is the resultant set of paths Π is conflict-free.

4   Method

Our approach relies on three algorithmic components: individual planning, path following with collision avoidance and locally-confined multi-agent path finding in case of potential deadlocks. We will now describe all these components.

4.1   Individual Path Finding

To find a valid path for an agent that avoids static obstacles we reduce path planning problem to graph search. We employ regular square grids [20] as the discretized workspace representation as they are easy-to-construct and informative graph models widely used for navigation purposes. To create a grid we tessellate the workspace into the square cells and mark each cell either blocked or traversable depending on whether this cell overlaps with any of the obstacle or not (see Fig. 2 on the right). To find a path on the grid we utilize THETA* [6] algorithm. It's a heuristic search algorithm of the A* family which augments the edge set of the graph on-the-fly by allowing any-angle moves, i.e. the moves between non-adjacent vertices, conditioned that such moves do not lead to the collisions with the obstacles. As a result, paths found by THETA* are typically shorter than the ones found by A* and contain less waypoints. The difference between these two types of paths is clearly visible on Fig. 2. Both THETA* and A* paths are collision-free, while the former contains 7 intermediate waypoints and the latter – only 2 of them.

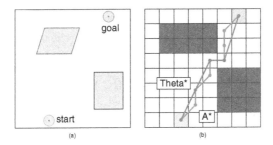

Fig. 2. Finding a path for an individual agent: a) the workspace of an agent; b) tesselation of the workspace into the grid and two paths on that grid: the one that was found by A* (in orange) and the one that was found by THETA* (in blue). We use THETA* paths in this work. (Color figure online)

4.2   Path Following with Collision Avoidance

Having the individual paths for all agent the considered multi-agent navigation problem can be naively solved as follows. At each time step an agent chooses such a velocity that it is directed towards the next waypoint on a path and its magnitude is maximal. In other words, agents move along the constructed paths as fast as they can without any temporal waits and spatial deviations. Obviously, such an approach leads to numerous collisions in practice. Instead, we rely on a more advanced method called Optimal Reciprocal Collision Avoidance (ORCA) [16]. This method is designed to move an agent safely towards its local goal (current waypoint of a path) by reactively adjusting the velocity profile at each timestep. When choosing a velocity ORCA relies on local observations: only other moving agents that are located within a visibility range and static obstacles are taken into account. We tie together individual path planning and path following with collision avoidance in the following fashion.

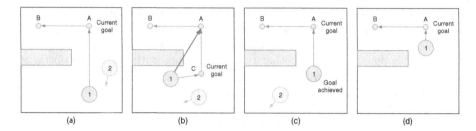

Fig. 3. Goal-setting for ORCA. (a) Waypoint A is the local goal of the agent 1. (b) The agent 1 deviates from the original trajectory in order to avoid collision with the agent 2, the line-of-sight to the local goal is lost, re-planning is triggered and the new waypoint, C, is added to the path, it becomes the current local goal. (c) C is reached, next local goal is A. (d) The agent safely moves towards A without any deviation as no other moving agents interfere with its plan.

The waypoints that comprise an individual path (the one found by THETA*) form a sequence of the local goals for ORCA and an agent always moves towards its current local goal until the latter is reached. When it happens next waypoint from the path becomes the local goal and ORCA is re-invoked. It is noteworthy, that when an agent moves to the current goal it may significantly deviate from the original path's segment (due to other moving agents forcing ORCA to do so). Thus, it may appear that the local goal can no longer be reached via the straight-line segment, which is a crucial condition for ORCA to operate appropriately. We detect such patterns and trigger re-planning from the current agent's position to the local goal with THETA*. New waypoints are added to sequence of the local goals as a result. The condition that there is a visible connection between any pair of waypoints now holds and ORCA continues. An illustration of the overall process is presented in Fig. 3.

4.3   Multi-agent Path Finding for Avoiding the Deadlocks

Path planning and collision avoidance mechanisms described so far can be attributed as non-cooperative, i.e. each agent pursues its own goal and does not take the goals of other agents into account. In general this can lead to deadlocks. A typical scenario when such a deadlock occurs is depicted on Fig. 4 on the left. Here all four agents have to come through the tight passage nearly at the same time. In such case ORCA is forced to set the velocity of each agent to zero to avoid the collisions. Thus, no agent is moving and a deadlock occurs. To avoid this we include a multi-agent path finding (MAPF) algorithm into the navigation pipeline with the aim of building a set of locally coordinated collision-free paths. Conceptually, when an agent detects a pattern that leads to a potential deadlock it switches to a coordinated path planning mode and forces its neighboring agents to do so. Upon entering this mode involved agents create a joint conflict-free plan and execute it. After they switch back to the independent execution mode.

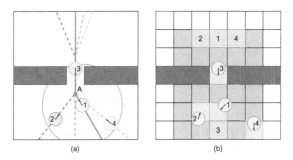

Fig. 4. Switching to coordinated mode. (a) Agent 1 detects its local goal, A, and 3 other agents within its visibility zone. (b) Based on the current positions and individual paths of agents 1–4 a local grid-map for multi-agent path-finding is identified as well as start and goal locations for each agent. (Color figure online)

Switching to the coordinated mode is triggered if both local goal A and k other agents appear in the visibility range of some agent (here k is the predefined threshold set up by the user). The latter forms a list of coordinated agents that include: itself, its neighboring agents and their neighboring agents as well. All these agents now share the information about their current states (positions and velocities) and individual paths with each other. Thus each agent constructs the same information model and uses it for operation, so no explicit centralized controller is introduced.

Based on the current positions of the agents, the boundaries of the area in which the joint collision-free plan will be built are estimated. This is done as follows. The minimum and maximum x- and y-positions across all agents are identified. These four coordinates define a square which is inflated by a visibility radius of the agent that has initiated switching to the coordinated mode. This square is translated to the grid which was originally used for the individual path planning. The resulting grid now becomes a local map for multi-agent path finding (it is depicted on Fig. 4b in grey). It might appear that two or more coordinated planning areas are separately constructed by different groups of agents close to each other. In this case those areas are combined into a single one and all agents become members of a single coordinated group.

After the grid map for multi-agent path finding is constructed each agent chooses its MAPF start and MAPF goal on that grid. The start cell is the one closest to the current location of the agent. If it coincides with the start of another agent or it is blocked by an obstacle a breadth-first search graph traversal is invoked from this cell to find a close un-blocked position which becomes a start.

Goal locations are identified in the similar way. First, a current local goal (path's waypoint) is identified. If it coincides with A the next waypoint is chosen. If the selected waypoint lies inside the planning area then the cell which contains it become the MAPF goal. If the waypoint is outside an area, i.e. at least its x- or y-coordinate is greater/less than the corresponding maximum/minimum values of the planning area, then this coordinate is replaced by the maximum or minimum value of the corresponding coordinate.

After the start and goal positions of the agents are fixed, an appropriate MAPF solver is invoked to obtain a solution, i.e. a set of sequences of moves between the grid cells and, possibly, wait actions, – one sequence per each agent. For the sake of simplicity we assume that all MAPF actions, i.e. move and wait, are of the uniform duration. This duration is chosen in such a way that the constraints on the agents' maximum moving speed are not violated. In this work we utilize PUSH AND ROTATE [7] for multi-agent path planning algorithm as it is very fast and scales well to large number of agents. We did not choose an optimal solver, such as CBS [12], because of its high computational budget. Using a prioritized planner is also not an option as prioritized MAPF solvers do not guarantee completeness.

When a MAPF problem is solved each agent starts moving towards its chosen MAPF-start position on a grid (with ORCA collision avoidance activated). When all agents are at their start positions synchronous execution of the plan begins. At this stage no collisions are guaranteed to happen (assuming perfect execution) so ORCA is not used. When all agent reach their MAPF-goals they switch back to the individual mode, i.e. continue path following to their next waypoint on a global path with ORCA as described in previous section.

In case some agent, i, which is not involved in the plan execution, gets inside the boundaries of the planning area and interferes with the coordinated agents, i.e. this agent appears in any coordinated agent's visibility range, the execution of the coordinated plan is stopped, the agent i is added to the list of coordinated agents and the plan is recomputed.

Similarly, if an agent i, which is involved in the plan execution, gets inside into the visibility zone of an agent j, which is also involved in the execution of plan, but belongs to another group of coordinated agents, then these two coordinated groups are merged and re-planning is triggered.

5   Experimental Evaluation

The proposed method was implemented in C++[2] and its experimental evaluation was carried out on a laptop running macOS 10.14.6 based on Intel Core i5-8259U (2.3 GHz) CPU and with 16 GB of RAM.

We used two types of grid maps, i.e. the maps composed of the free/blocked cells, for the experiments (see Fig. 5). First, we generated maps that were comprised of two open areas (rooms) separated by a wall with tight passages (doors)

---

[2] https://github.com/PathPlanning/ORCA-algorithm/tree/Deadlocks

in it. The number of passages varied from 1 to 4, thus 4 different maps of that type were generated in total. The overall size of each map was 64 × 64. We refer to these maps as to the gaps maps. Second, we took two maps from the *MovingAI* [15] benchmark. They represent indoor environments composed of numerous rooms connected by passages. The first map of that type has a size of 64 × 64 and was comprised of 16 rooms (9 of them of the size 15 × 15, 1 – 14 and the rest – 14 × 15 or 15 × 14). The size of the second map was 32 × 32 and it was composed of the 64 rooms of the size 3 × 3. The latter two maps, referred to as rooms further on, are depicted on Fig. 5b–c.

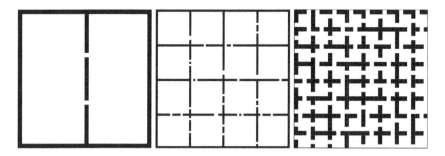

Fig. 5. Maps used for experimental evaluation. (a) Map comprised of two rooms connected by narrow passages. (b) and (c) Maps of the indoor environment composed of numerous rooms connected by narrow passages.

Start/goal locations on each map were generated as follows. For the gaps maps we always generated half of the start/goal locations in the left open area and the other half in the right one. So, to accomplish the mission, agents have to navigate between the two areas via the passages in the wall. For the rooms maps we picked start/goal locations randomly. For each map we created 250 different scenarios. Each scenario is a list of 40 start/goal locations for the agents. While testing the scenarios were used in the following fashion. First, we invoke the algorithm on 5 (first) start/goal pairs of a scenario, then we increased this number by 5 and invoke the algorithm again and so on until the number of agents reaches 40. At this time the scenario was considered to be processed and we moved to the next one.

We compared the suggested approach, referred to as ORCA*+P&R, to the one that does not utilize deadlock detection and multi-agent path finding, referred to as ORCA*. For both versions we set the radius of each agent to be equal to 0.3 of the cell size. We also introduced an additional 0.19 safe-buffer for individual path finding and collision avoidance. For ORCA*+P&R the number of neighbours for an agent required to switch to the coordinated mode was set to $k = 3$.

At each run the maximum number of simulation steps was limited to 12 800. If by that time the agents fail to reach their goals, i.e. at least one agent was not on its target position or at least one agent collided with another agent or static obstacle, the run was considered to be *failure*. If all agents managed to safely reach their goals the run was acknowledged as *success*. The main metric that we were interested in was the *success rate* i.e. the percentage of tasks that result with *success* out of all tasks attempted to be solved.

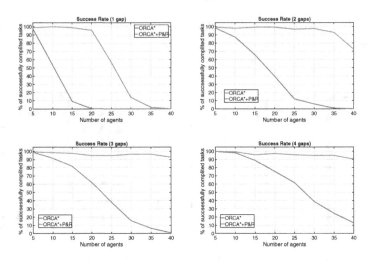

Fig. 6. Success rate for **gaps** maps.

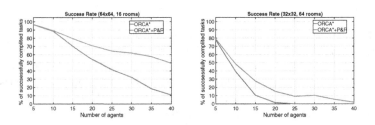

Fig. 7. Success rate for **rooms** maps.

Success rates for ORCA*+P&R and ORCA* are shown on Figs. 6 and 7. As one can see the selected environments are very challenging for ORCA* and its success rate is very low for large number of agents on all the maps. The most challenging environments are the one with 1 passage on a **gaps** map and the one with 64 rooms on **rooms** map. As expected on all maps ORCA*+P&R successfully solved profoundly more instances compared to the baseline. For example, for the challenging **gaps** map with 1 passage the success rate for ORCA*+P&R was 95% for 20 agents while the one for ORCA* was 0%. The difference in success rate for **rooms** maps is also clearly visible but less pronounced. We hypothesise that the main reason for that, as well as the reason for ORCA*+P&R

not to achieve 100% success in general, is the imposed time limit. The plans created by the PUSH AND ROTATE algorithm may have contained numerous actions and that prevented the agents to reach their goals before the timestep limit exhausted. One of the possible solutions to avoid this will be substituting PUSH AND ROTATE to another MAPF solver which creates plans containing less actions. However the solvers that are explicitly aimed at minimizing duration of the plan have much higher computational budget, so finding a right substitution is a challenging task for future research.

Overall, the results of the experiments clearly show that adding a locally-confined multi-agent path finding into the navigation pipeline significantly increase the chance that all agents will reach their goal locations and mission, thus, be accomplished.

6   Conclusion

In this paper we have studied a multi-agent navigation problem and suggested a decentralized approach that supplements the individual path planning and collision avoidance with the deadlock detection and multi-agent path finding. We implemented the proposed navigation pipeline and compared it the to the baseline, showing that adding the aformentioned components significantly increases the chances of agents safely arriving to the target destinations even in the congested environments with tight passages. An appealing direction of future work is the advancement of the deadlock detection procedure by making it less ad-hoc, as well as experimenting with different multi-agent path finding algorithms. Another direction for future research is evaluating the suggested approach on real robots.

Acknowledgements. The reported study was funded by RFBR and BRFBR, project number 20-57-00011. We would also like to thank Ilya Ivanashev for his implementation of PUSH AND ROTATE.

References

1. Alonso-Mora, J., Breitenmoser, A., Rufli, M., Beardsley, P., Siegwart, R.: Optimal reciprocal collision avoidance for multiple non-holonomic robots. In: Martinoli, A., et al. (eds.) Distributed Autonomous Robotic Systems, pp. 203–216. Springer, Heidelberg (2013). https://doi.org/10.1007/978-3-642-32723-0_15
2. Andreychuk, A., Yakovlev, K., Atzmon, D., Stern, R.: Multi-agent pathfinding with continuous time. In: Proceedings of the 28th International Joint Conference on Artificial Intelligence (IJCAI 2019), pp. 39–45 (2019)
3. Barer, M., Sharon, G., Stern, R., Felner, A.: Suboptimal variants of the conflict-based search algorithm for the multi-agent pathfinding problem. In: Proceedings of the 7th International Symposium on Combinatorial Search (SoCS 2014), vol. 263, pp. 961–962 (2014)
4. Čáp, M., Novák, P., Kleiner, A., Selecký, M.: Prioritized planning algorithms for trajectory coordination of multiple mobile robots. IEEE Trans. Autom. Sci. Eng. **12**(3), 835–849 (2015)

5. Chen, Y.F., Liu, M., Everett, M., How, J.P.: Decentralized non-communicating multiagent collision avoidance with deep reinforcement learning. In: Proceedings of the 2017 IEEE International Conference on Robotics and Automation (ICRA 2017), pp. 285–292 (2017)
6. Daniel, K., Nash, A., Koenig, S., Felner, A.: Theta*: any-angle path planning on grids. J. Artifi. Intell. Res. **39**, 533–579 (2010)
7. De Wilde, B., Ter Mors, A.W., Witteveen, C.: Push and rotate: a complete multi-agent pathfinding algorithm. J. Artif. Intell. Res. **51**, 443–492 (2014)
8. Dijkstra, E.W., et al.: A note on two problems in connexion with graphs. Numer. Math. **1**(1), 269–271 (1959)
9. Dimarogonas, D.V., Kyriakopoulos, K.J.: Decentralized navigation functions for multiple robotic agents with limited sensing capabilities. J. Intell. Rob. Syst. **48**(3), 411–433 (2007)
10. Hart, P.E., Nilsson, N.J., Raphael, B.: A formal basis for the heuristic determination of minimum cost paths. IEEE Trans. Syst. Sci. Cybern. **4**(2), 100–107 (1968)
11. Long, P., Fanl, T., Liao, X., Liu, W., Zhang, H., Pan, J.: Towards optimally decentralized multi-robot collision avoidance via deep reinforcement learning. In: Proceedings of the 2018 IEEE International Conference on Robotics and Automation (ICRA 2018), pp. 6252–6259 (2018)
12. Sharon, G., Stern, R., Felner, A., Sturtevant, N.R.: Conflict-based search for optimal multi-agent pathfinding. Artif. Intell. **219**, 40–66 (2015)
13. Snape, J., Guy, S.J., Van Den Berg, J., Manocha, D.: Smooth coordination and navigation for multiple differential-drive robots. In: Khatib, O., Kumar, V., Sukhatme, G. (eds.) Experimental Robotics, pp. 601–613. Springer, Heidelberg (2014)
14. Snape, J., Van Den Berg, J., Guy, S.J., Manocha, D.: Smooth and collision-free navigation for multiple robots under differential-drive constraints. In: Proceedings of the 2010 IEEE/RSJ International Conference on Intelligent Robots and Systems (IROS 2010), pp. 4584–4589 (2010)
15. Stern, R., et al.: Multi-agent pathfinding: Definitions, variants, and benchmarks. In: Proceedings of the 12th International Symposium on Combinatorial Search (SoCS 2019), pp. 151–158 (2019)
16. Van Den Berg, J., Guy, S.J., Lin, M., Manocha, D.: Reciprocal n-body collision avoidance. In: Pradalier, C., Siegwart, R., Hirzinger, G. (eds.) Robotics Research, vol. 70, pp. 3–19. Springer, Heidelberg (2011). https://doi.org/10.1007/978-3-642-19457-3_1
17. Wagner, G., Choset, H.: Subdimensional expansion for multirobot path planning. Artif. Intell. **219**, 1–24 (2015)
18. Xuan, P., Lesser, V.: Multi-agent policies: from centralized ones to decentralized ones. In: Proceedings of the 1st International Joint Conference on Autonomous Agents and Multiagent Systems (AAMAS 2002) : Part 3, pp. 1098–1105 (2002)
19. Yakovlev, K., Andreychuk, A., Vorobyev, V.: Prioritized multi-agent path finding for differential drive robots. In: Proceedings of the 2019 European Conference on Mobile Robots (ECMR 2019), pp. 1–6 (2019)
20. Yap, P.: Grid-based path-finding. In: Cohen, R., Spencer, B. (eds.) AI 2002. LNCS (LNAI), vol. 2338, pp. 44–55. Springer, Heidelberg (2002). https://doi.org/10.1007/3-540-47922-8_4
21. Zhou, D., Wang, Z., Bandyopadhyay, S., Schwager, M.: Fast, on-line collision avoidance for dynamic vehicles using buffered voronoi cells. IEEE Robot. Autom. Lett. **2**(2), 1047–1054 (2017)

Evaluation of Image Synthesis for Automotive Purposes

Václav Diviš$^{(\boxtimes)}$ (iD) and Marek Hrúz (iD)

Faculty of Applied Sciences, University of West Bohemia, Pilsen, Czechia
divisvaclav@gmail.com
https://fav.zcu.cz/en/

Abstract. The aim of this article is to evaluate a state of the art image synthesis carried out via Generative Adversarial Networks (conditional Wasserstein GAN and Self Attention GAN) on a traffic signs dataset. For the experiment, we focused on generating images with a 64×64-pixel resolution as well as on the GAN's ability to capture structural and geometric patterns. Four different GAN architectures were trained in order to highlight the difficulties of the training, such as collapse mode, vanishing gradient and resulting image fidelity. The Frechent Inception Distance is compared with other state of the art results. The importance of evaluating on automotive datasets as well as additional wishes for further improvements are addressed at the end of this article.

Keywords: Generative Adversarial Networks · Image dataset extension · BigGAN · SAGAN · WGAN · Traffic signs dataset

1 Introduction

Image synthesis became an important field of study with various use cases, such as data augmentation [2], data manipulation [27], adversarial training, text to image [22], or image to image translation [28]. Dataset extension (e.g. image to image translation - where different weather and lighting conditions are applied to the original dataset) can be especially useful for the automotive industry. Generative Adversarial Networks (GANs) are one class of implicit generative models, the task of which is to train themselves by means of indirectly sampling data from their parametrized distribution. GANs [10] comprise two networks (as can be seen in Fig. 1), a Generator (G) and a Discriminator (D), working in adversary mode, constantly pushing the performance of each other. The G tries to generate fake images as close as possible to the originals and fool the Discriminator, whereas the Discriminator is learning to distinguish fake images from the real ones. Despite many attempts to stabilize the training [3,11,16, 17,25], the fine-tuning of hyper-parameters and a careful choice of the GAN's architecture are still necessary.

© Springer Nature Switzerland AG 2020
A. Ronzhin et al. (Eds.): ICR 2020, LNAI 12336, pp. 67–77, 2020.
https://doi.org/10.1007/978-3-030-60337-3_7

The aim of our experiment can be divided as follows:

- On our own dataset of traffic signs, we will evaluate the performance of State of the Art (SotA) GAN architectures with the newest improvements.
- We will evaluate the generated image fidelity and compare the calculated FID.
- We will briefly mention the concept of future dataset extension as a possible machine learning standard.
- We will open-source our code and sample of one-sign dataset on GitHub [1]

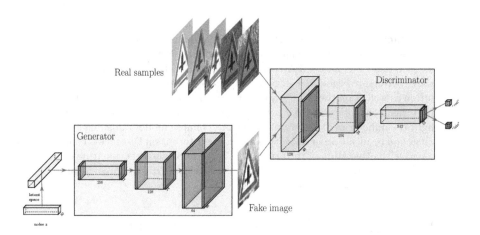

Fig. 1. Example of a GAN training framework. Starting from the left, a noise is sampled and passed to the G which synthesizes a false image and sends it to the Discriminator. The Discriminator takes a generated image and compares it to the genuine image: its task is to learn how to distinguish between them, while the G should generate fake images the Discriminator is incapable of distinguishing.

2   Methods Overview

While supervised learning techniques with Convolutional Neural Networks (CNNs) have shown in the last few years excellent results in mapping the input space X into the output space Y, unsupervised learning has received less attention and the community still struggles with many key aspects of training and evaluating methods. Contrary to supervised learning, the aim of unsupervised learning is to find the underlying hidden structure within the represented data without using any labeled data.

One of the unsupervised learning models is the GAN [10]. The goal of GANs is to generate new samples based on the input data distribution. GANs are learning to estimate density through a min-max game of two players. The Discriminator

---

[1] https://github.com/VincieD/TrafficSign_GAN_Benchmark.

(D), which is in most cases a CNN, is trained to recognize the difference between the original image and the one created by the Generator (G). Its goal is to maximize its win. In parallel, the task of the G is to generate images as close as possible to the originals, so that the D does not recognize the difference. Its goal is to minimize its loss. Both networks are trained jointly so as to find the Nash equilibrium of the min-max game, as depicted in Eq. 1.

$$\min_{G} \max_{D} V(D, G) = E_{x \sim Pdata(x)}[log D(x)] + E_{z \sim Pz(z)}[log(1 - D(G(z)))]. \quad (1)$$

The original training of GAN mainly suffers from learning instability or from its inability to capture structural and geometric features. Consequently, the GANs architecture has evolved into deep convolutional GAN [20], then into SaGAN [26] and finally into SotA BigGAN [6] with ResNet blocks [13]. Radford et al. [25] pointed out that these architectures can lead to a stable training, irrespective of the dataset. They suggested three improvements, which helped stabilize the training significantly. First of all, pooling functions (such as Max pooling) should be replaced by convolution layers with stride $= 2$, which allows the network to prioritize its own spatial down-sampling. Secondly, fully connected layers, which were connected on the top of the convolutional features, should be removed. Finally, batch norm layers [15] should be used in the D as well as in the G.

Additionally, Self-Attention GAN [26] allows the network to learn long-range dependencies, improving the resulting fidelity of the images. It is recommended that the Self-Attention layer, which encapsulates the weighting of feature maps, should be applied in both the D and the G.

Further improvements were achieved in BigGAN [6] by demonstrating that scaling up the batch size and the number of parameters will decrease the brittleness of the training. New and existing techniques were implemented, particularly the spectral normalization [17] and label conditioning (original idea from CGAN [16]) with a truncation trick. In addition, the relation between the latent space and the image resolution was defined. Most of these architectural details were adopted and used in this work.

Fig. 2. Example of signs included and excluded from the training-set. It is obvious that the quality of some signs is insufficient.

Whereas the first research groups were constantly improving the GAN architecture, the second line of research focused on improving the objective function or on different methods of constraining the D through penalties. The aim of GANs is to minimize the distance between the generated distribution and the real data distribution i.e. to learn the real data distribution via learning the probability density. The original GAN tries to minimize KL divergence between $P_{data}(x)$ and $P_z(z)$. Arjovsky et al., who came out with Wasserstein GAN (WGAN) [3], claim that in common cases, the model manifold and the true distribution support have a negligible intersection, which means that the KL distance is not defined (or simply infinite). As a solution, a random noise term covering the whole spectrum of examples is added to the model distribution, resulting in blurred images as a side-effect.

The WGAN article provides a comprehensive comparison of popular probability distances to Earth Mover (EM) distance, resulting in a new WGAN standard. WGAN with gradient penalty (WGAN-GP) [11] improves the optimization process with a gradient penalty of the Critic (C) to enforce the Lipschitz constraint. This leads to a new objective function as can be seen in Eq. 2.

$$L = E_{x \sim P_{data}(x)}[log D(x)] + E_{z \sim P_z(z)}[log(1 - D(G(z)))]$$
$$+ \lambda E_{\hat{x} \sim P_{data}(x)}[(\|\nabla_{\hat{x}} D(x)\|_2 - 1)^2], \tag{2}$$

where the penalty coefficient λ empirically results in 10. As stated in the original WGAN-GP work: it is good to avoid Batch Norm (BN) for the critic (Discriminator). BN creates a correlation between the samples in the same batch. It impacts the effectiveness of the gradient penalty, which was confirmed by experiments.

A research on high-resolution image synthesis with focus on image fidelity was carried out by Google [6]. The main outcomes were:

- In order to counteract the training instability, the spectral normalization should be used in both the D and the G.
- Scaling up to a certain level of model and batch size improves the fidelity of the generated images and allows training models up to 512 × 512 resolution.
- Modified ResNet blocks shall be used instead of combining UPSAMPL, CONV and BATCH layers.
- Latent vector z should be split and concatenated with shared class embedding, which is linearly projected to each BatchNorm in every ResNet block.
- A more comprehensive research was conducted on tuning hyper-parameters and describing side-effects. Leading to the conclusion of using an Adam optimizer with a different learning rate for the D and the G.

3   The Experiment Setup

3.1   Training Dataset

Our GAN models were trained on a traffic sign dataset, which contains 84 classes (types of signs) for a total of 30104 images. We did not pre-process the images, except for scaling them to 64 × 64 resolution and normalizing the individual color channels to $\langle -1.0, 1.0 \rangle$. We excluded from the training the following types of signs (according to Czech notation): G1, G2, G3, G4, G5, I1, IJ4b, IP1a, IP1b, IP4a, IP9, X1, X2, X3, Z4a, Z4b, Z4c, Z4e, Z5d, Z9, for their quality was inadequate. We also excluded the types of signs for which the quantity was below 100 pieces. An example of adequate and excluded signs can be seen in Fig. 2.

3.2 GAN Architecture

Throughout the experiment, we tried out four GAN models implemented from scratch in Keras [8], while using TensorFlow [1] as a backend and one in PyTorch [19]. We evaluated the training stability, convergence speed and image fidelity. For one model, LeakyRelu and Swish were used as activation function.

3.3 Model 1: Conditional WGAN-GP with Relu

WGAN was taken as basic model, with gradient penalty and label embedding done in the first dense layer of critic and G. The Relu activation function was used and all weights were initialized from a normal distribution with zero mean and standard deviation 0.02. The gradient penalty for the critic was set to 10 and the amount of critics chosen to be 2, for no significant changes were observed within a range of (1–6). The Fig. 3 depicts the architecture of this basic model without label embedding.

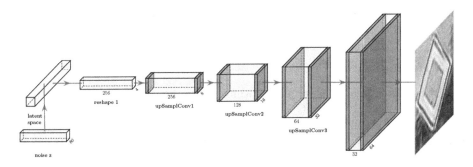

Fig. 3. Architecture of Model 1: with UpSampling layer (orange) RelU as activation function and batchnorm applied after convolutional layer (blue). (Colour figure online)

3.4 Model 2: Conditional WGAN-GP Swish

For Model 2 and 3 only the delta changes to the Model 1 will be outlined. The activation function implemented in G and D was a self-gated activation function (called Swish) [21]. Swish is a form of sigmoid, but its amplitude is scaled by the input tensor x. The notation of Swish is: $\phi = x\sigma(\beta x)$, where β is a constant or trainable parameter. Theoretical background was provided by Hayou et al. [12]

with the clear results that Swish can propagate the processed information more effectively than ReLU and it does not suffer from the vanishing gradient problem. To our best knowledge, we are the first to evaluate the fidelity of synthesized images generated by GAN with Swish activation function in G and D.

3.5 Model 3: Conditional WGAN with LeakyRelu and Self-attention Layer

Since the experiment with Swish activation function did not show any improvement (see Sect. 4), we changed it to leakyRelu. Because the self-attention layer has the ability to capture long-distance dependencies, we experimented with two settings. In the Model 3a, the self-attention layer was added between the 3rd and 4th layers of G and between the 2nd and 3rd layers of C. In the Model 3b, we moved the SA-block one layer deeper within G, resulting in a 32×32-pixel resolution with 32 channels, and one layer earlier for C.

3.6 Model 4 - Conditional GAN with ResNet Blocks, Spectral Normalization and Self-attention Layer

The Model 4 was built based on the "officially unofficial" (see the Authors Page) implementation of GAN from gitHub [7] and enhanced code, so that we could generate 1,000 samples every 100th iteration. Inspired by [6], we set the size of the latent space to 80, since in our case the training images were half the size of those generated via the official BigGAN (128×128). The Self-attention layer remained untouched and after 5,000 iterations, the Exponential Moving Average (EMA) weights update was turned on.

3.7 Training Setup

In all the experiments, the applied optimizer was Adam. We set $lr = 5 \cdot 10^{-5}$ for G and $lr = 2 \cdot 10^{-4}$ for C/D. β_1 was set to 0.0 and the β_2 was lowered to 0.7, to prevent stability issues as described in [25]. Apart from Adam, RMSprop with learning rate $lr = 5 \cdot 10^{-5}$ was working in most cases as well. The training was applied to a mini-batch size of 128 for 10,000 iterations. D and C loss were logged and every 100th iteration, 1,000 random samples of synthesized images were generated for later statistics observation.

4   Experiment Results

4.1 Training Instability

We can confirm that increasing the batch size in combination with batch norm layers and Xavier initialization [9] improves the training stability. Additionally, the loss fluctuation can be lowered by applying a gradient penalty on C. An important aspect, resulting from the training observation, was the bias initialization. We applied normal distribution with mean = 0.5 to every CONV and

DENSE layer. This helped stabilize the training convergence, which we posit is due to the fact that within the first hundreds of iterations, less neurons were biased towards the negative side (Relu can lead to a phenomenon known as "dead neurons" and to collapse mode).

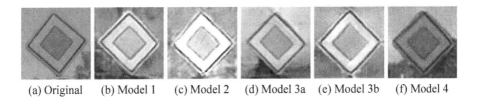

(a) Original   (b) Model 1   (c) Model 2   (d) Model 3a   (e) Model 3b   (f) Model 4

Fig. 4. Example of synthetically generated "Priority Road" sign, which was chosen arbitrarily. The first image on the left is the original one, taken randomly from the dataset. The rest of the images, on the right, are generated via different architectures after 10,000 iterations. The visually best results were achieved by Model 3a with Self-Attention GAN, Model 4 with ResNet blocks and spectral normalization and by Model 1 without Self-Attention layers or any training improvements.

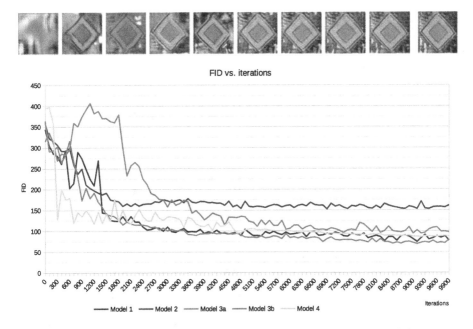

Fig. 5. In order to evaluate the image fidelity, the FID was calculated from 1,000 images generated every 100th iteration (see above for examples of those images). Since we applied EMA after 5,000th iterations, the FID does not decrease significantly. Consequently, the difference between generated images is subtle (visible are only changes of surrounding ambient, since the correct shape and structure of the sign was captured).

4.2   Evaluation Phase

Many articles have been dedicated to finding good evaluation metrics of GAN performance [5,14,25]. We decided to calculate a Fréchet Inception Distance (FID), since it can be derived directly from both original and generated images. Apart from FID, the Inception Score (IS) can be calculated as well. IS encapsulates the image fidelity which correlates well with human judgment [24] as well as the image variance. However, as mentioned in [4], in order to calculate the IS, the Inception v3 Network pre-trained on ImageNet is used. Furthermore, according to [23], calculating the IS on a dataset other than ImageNet could result in non-plausible results. FID will therefore be the chosen evaluating metric.

In order to calculate the FID, the extracted features from the Inception Network serve as input for building a data distribution. $X_g \sim \mathcal{N}(\mu_g, \Sigma_g)$ and $X_r \sim \mathcal{N}(\mu_r, \Sigma_r)$ are the 2048-dimensional activations of the Inception-v3 pool3

Fig. 6. Examples of high-fidelity samples of Model 4, after 10,000 iterations

Fig. 7. Examples of low-fidelity samples of Model 4, after 10,000 iterations. Samples' distortion and blurriness was presumably caused by lower number of training images.

layer for real and generated samples respectively. As can be seen in Eq. 3, FID expresses in numbers the difference between generated and real samples statistics assuming that their distribution is Gaussian-wise.

$$FID = ||\mu_r - \mu_g||^2 + \text{Tr}(\Sigma_r + \Sigma_g - 2(\Sigma_r\Sigma_g)^{1/2}) \tag{3}$$

Since training and evaluating GANs is computationally exhaustive, our deeper focus was laid on Models 3a and 4. We trained both models for 100,000 iterations and computed FID, resulting in 60.3 for Model 3a and 45.2 for Model 4. The FID achieved by bigGAN 64 × 64 on ImageNet [18] is 15.82 (Fig. 5).

5   Conclusion

We began this article by introducing GANs, as well as the main successes and difficulties of training and image synthesis. Building on recent improvements and fine-tuning processes, we have achieved stable training settings and architecture, as described in Sect. 3. Subsequently, the fidelity of the generated images increased. It is important to state that the resulting fidelity of 64 × 64-pixel images is satisfying, considering the quality of the original training-set Figs. 4, 6 and 7. Four different architectures were evaluated by calculating the Fréchet Inception Distance (FID). The best results were achieved with an architecture consisting of ResNet and spectral normalization layers (Model 4) 6 and by a simple 5-layer deep GAN with Self-Attention layer (Model 3a). It is noticeable that the fidelity of the generated images generally improved less after around 6,000 iterations. Since the visual representation of signs was designed to not be ambiguous, all four models captured the underlying structure well. Moreover, there is a very small difference in FID between Model 1, Model 3a, 3b and Model 4. By designing Model 2, we were hoping to increase the training stability and the visual quality of the generated images; but it turned out that a simple difference in activation function, on an already highly-generalized image synthesis task is not essential in order to capture the data probability density. Throughout this experiment, we encountered many difficulties in setting up the hyper-parameters while building our model from scratch. It became obvious that the trade-off between Generator and Discriminator optimization process is crucial. We can only confirm that the training setup described in BigGAN delivers the wished training stability as well as an outstanding image fidelity, but it comes at the cost of training duration (a 100,000-iteration training with the size of the batch equal to 128, deployed on one GTX 1080 10 GB RAM, takes approximately 10 days).

Acknowledgements. The work has been supported by the grant of the University of West Bohemia, project No. SGS-2019-027. Access to computing and storage facilities owned by parties and projects contributing to the National Grid Infrastructure Meta-Centrum provided under the programme "Projects of Large Research, Development, and Innovations Infrastructures" (CESNET LM2015042), is greatly appreciated.

References

1. Abadi, M., et al.: Tensorflow: large-scale machine learning on heterogeneous systems. software available from tensorflow.org (2015). http://tensorflow.org/
2. Antoniou, A., Storkey, A., Edwards, H.: Data augmentation generative adversarial networks. arXiv preprint arXiv:1711.04340 (2017)
3. Arjovsky, M., Chintala, S., Bottou, L.: Wasserstein gan. arXiv preprint arXiv:1701.07875 (2017)
4. Barratt, S., Sharma, R.: A note on the inception score (2018)
5. Borji, A.: Pros and cons of gan evaluation measures. Comput. Vis. Image Underst. **179**, 41–65 (2019)
6. Brock, A., Donahue, J., Simonyan, K.: Large scale gan training for high fidelity natural image synthesis. arXiv preprint arXiv:1809.11096 (2018)
7. Brock, A.: The author's officially unofficial pytorch biggan implementation, September 2019. https://github.com/ajbrock/BigGAN-PyTorch
8. Chollet, F., et al.: Keras (2015). https://keras.io
9. Glorot, X., Bengio, Y.: Understanding the difficulty of training deep feedforward neural networks. In: In Proceedings of the International Conference on Artificial Intelligence and Statistics (AISTATS'10). Society for Artificial Intelligence and Statistics (2010)
10. Goodfellow, I., et al.: Generative adversarial nets. In: Ghahramani, Z., Welling, M., Cortes, C., Lawrence, N.D., Weinberger, K.Q. (eds.) Advances in Neural Information Processing Systems 27, pp. 2672–2680. Curran Associates, Inc. (2014). http://papers.nips.cc/paper/5423-generative-adversarial-nets.pdf
11. Gulrajani, I., Ahmed, F., Arjovsky, M., Dumoulin, V., Courville, A.C.: Improved training of wasserstein gans. In: Guyon, I., Luxburg, U.V., et al. (eds.) Advances in Neural Information Processing Systems 30, pp. 5767–5777. Curran Associates, Inc. (2017). http://papers.nips.cc/paper/7159-improved-training-of-wasserstein-gans.pdf

12. Hayou, S., Doucet, A., Rousseau, J.: On the selection of initialization and activation function for deep neural networks. arXiv preprint arXiv:1805.08266 (2018)
13. He, K., Zhang, X., Ren, S., Sun, J.: Deep residual learning for image recognition. CoRR abs/1512.03385 (2015). http://arxiv.org/abs/1512.03385
14. Heusel, M., Ramsauer, H., Unterthiner, T., Nessler, B., Hochreiter, S.: Gans trained by a two time-scale update rule converge to a local nash equilibrium. In: Advances in Neural Information Processing Systems, pp. 6626–6637 (2017)
15. Ioffe, S., Szegedy, C.: Batch normalization: accelerating deep network training by reducing internal covariate shift. arXiv preprint arXiv:1502.03167 (2015)
16. Mirza, M., Osindero, S.: Conditional generative adversarial nets. CoRR abs/1411.1784 (2014). http://arxiv.org/abs/1411.1784
17. Miyato, T., Kataoka, T., Koyama, M., Yoshida, Y.: Spectral normalization for generative adversarial networks. arXiv preprint arXiv:1802.05957 (2018)
18. Paperswithcode: Image generation on imagenet 64x64, September 2019. https://paperswithcode.com/sota/image-generation-on-imagenet-64x64
19. Paszke, A., et al.: Automatic differentiation in PyTorch. In: NIPS Autodiff Workshop (2017)
20. Radford, A., Metz, L., Chintala, S.: Unsupervised representation learning with deep convolutional generative adversarial networks. arXiv preprint arXiv:1511.06434 (2015)
21. Ramachandran, P., Zoph, B., Le, Q.V.: Searching for activation functions. arXiv preprint arXiv:1710.05941 (2017)
22. Reed, S., Akata, Z., Yan, X., Logeswaran, L., Schiele, B., Lee, H.: Generative adversarial text to image synthesis. arXiv preprint arXiv:1605.05396 (2016)
23. Rosca, M., Lakshminarayanan, B., Warde-Farley, D., Mohamed, S.: Variational approaches for auto-encoding generative adversarial networks. arXiv preprint arXiv:1706.04987 (2017)
24. Salimans, T., Goodfellow, I., Zaremba, W., Cheung, V., Radford, A., Chen, X.: Improved techniques for training gans. In: Advances in neural information processing systems, pp. 2234–2242 (2016)
25. Salimans, T., Goodfellow, I.J., Zaremba, W., Cheung, V., Radford, A., Chen, X.: Improved techniques for training gans. CoRR abs/1606.03498 (2016). http://arxiv.org/abs/1606.03498
26. Zhang, H., Goodfellow, I., Metaxas, D., Odena, A.: Self-attention generative adversarial networks. arXiv preprint arXiv:1805.08318 (2018)
27. Zhang, H., Sindagi, V., Patel, V.M.: Image de-raining using a conditional generative adversarial network. arXiv preprint arXiv:1701.05957 (2017)
28. Zhu, J., Park, T., Isola, P., Efros, A.A.: Unpaired image-to-image translation using cycle-consistent adversarial networks. CoRR abs/1703.10593 (2017). http://arxiv.org/abs/1703.10593

Collision Detection in the Work of Collaborative Robots Using an Intelligent System

Dmitriy Dobrynin[1,2(✉)]

[1] Russian State University for the Humanities, Moscow, Russia
rabota51@mail.ru
[2] Federal Research Centre "Informatics and Management" RAS, Moscow, Russia

Abstract. This paper describes an approach to applying the JSM method for automatic recognition of collision situations when working with collaborative robots. The approach uses the description of situations in the form of a set of primitives that determine the position of a person in the work space and allow you to distinguish a person from surrounding objects. An intelligent JSM system requires training that can be realized in real time. In the course of experiments, the efficiency of the proposed approach was confirmed and estimates of the collision detection time were made.

Keywords: Safety robot behavior · Human-robot collaboration · Machine learning · JSM-method

1 Introduction

Collaborative robots have appeared relatively recently, but are already widely used in industry. HCR (human-robot collaboration) is a fairly young concept, but it is very actively developing and has already found application in many enterprises. A collaborative robot is a robot created to work together with a human, designed so that it does not endanger a nearby employee. Their use makes it possible to facilitate heavy operations for moving goods that were previously performed by people, or to replace people in simple monotonous operations for assembly and packaging [1].

The main difference between collaborative robots and industrial robots of previous generations is the ability to work together with people, which means either continuous tracking of a person in the robot's working field, or a rapid stop of the robot when it collides with obstacles (for example, a person). To do this, the robot always has special sensors to ensure its safety-optical, motion sensors, feedback sensors. An important task when building a control system for such robots is to predict early situations when it will be necessary to quickly stop or change the trajectories of robot elements.

To date, the safety of collaborative robots is mainly provided by passive means. For example, standard ISO 10218-1/5.10.5 & ISO/TS 15066 defines safe collaboration by limiting power and effort [2]:

© Springer Nature Switzerland AG 2020
A. Ronzhin et al. (Eds.): ICR 2020, LNAI 12336, pp. 78–88, 2020.
https://doi.org/10.1007/978-3-030-60337-3_8

- reducing risks by limiting possible mechanical impacts;
- taking into account the work, tool, workspace, and task;
- taking into account predictable transient and quasi-static contact situations (risk analysis);
- protective steps in the event when the boundary criteria is exceeded.

This is achieved by reducing the speed of the robot, reducing the mass of the moving parts of the robot, limiting the torques of the drives, special geometry and "protective pillows", safely designed working tools, designed with the safety requirements of control schemes, ergonomics of workplaces, and so on.

To date, it is not yet possible to solve the problem of excluding robot and human collisions, but the potential for human injuries in connection with possible collisions, even if they occurred, has been reduced.

In the future, it is planned to ensure safe collaboration by monitoring speed and spatial separation (ISO 10218-1/5/10.4 & ISO/TS 15066):

- reducing risks by ensuring effective separation distance;
- trip zones/dynamic distance selection;
- choosing distances based on risk analysis results, taking into account the robot, tool, workspace, and task;
- controlled emergency stops based on safety considerations in case of violation of safe "borders" (taking into account the robot's reaction time and stop time).

The problem of maintaining a safe distance between a human and a robot is not completely solved, and it is very difficult to ensure its solution in a dynamically changing working environment.

An important task when building a control system for such robots is to predict early dangerous situations when it is necessary to quickly stop or change the trajectories of robot elements. To solve this problem, it is advisable to use artificial intelligence technologies [3]. An overview of collision detection methods for collaborative robots is given in [4]. The most well-known AI technology is deep neural networks.

This is how [5] describes a neural network for detecting collisions. The conventional framework detects collisions by estimating collision monitoring signals with a particular type of observer, which is followed by collision decision processes. This results in unavoidable tradeoff between sensitivity to collisions and robustness to false alarms. Authors designed a deep neural network model to learn robot collision signals and recognize any occurrence of a collision. This data-driven approach unifies feature extraction from high-dimensional signals and the decision processes. CollisionNet eliminates heuristic and cumbersome nature of the traditional decision processes, showing high detection performance and generalization capability in real time.

We will use a classifier based on the JSM method [6, 7]. The abbreviation for JSM stands for John Stuart Mill. The method is named after the British philosopher of the XIX century, whose ideas are the basis of the method. JSM - method of automatic hypothesis generation [8] is a theory of automated reasoning and a way of presenting knowledge for solving forecasting problems in conditions of incomplete information.

The JSM method was used to solve many problems of machine learning - medical diagnostics, determining the carcinogenicity and mutagenicity of chemical compounds, sociological research, and building intelligent robot control systems [6, 8, 9]. The use of the JSM method for evaluating the collision of a robot and a human is a new development of the author in this field and is still formal. The theoretical development, experiments and computer system were developed by the author. This article describes the formal setting of the problem and performs experiments to test the method on the layout.

2 Statement of Problem

When a collaborative robot and a human work together, a dangerous situation is a collision between a robot and a human. Let's consider a formal statement of the problem for determining the collision. To detect collisions using the JSM method, you must present this situation as a finite set of attributes [9]. These attributes can be: the visible object belongs to a certain area of space, the object's color characteristics, the object's shape characteristics, the speed of movement, and so on. The object in this case is a person, and the attributes determine its position in space and allow you to distinguish it from the surrounding objects.

To determine the position of a person in the working environment of a robot, it is necessary to have sensors that can determine the spatial position of the person's body and hands. The highest accuracy is provided by 2D and 3D laser scanners. One solution is to use kinect-type surround-vision cameras that are safe for the eyes. However, processing a depth map obtained from a 3D camera is a complex task and requires a lot of computing resources. Acceptable accuracy is the use of two or more video cameras positioned so as to obtain two perpendicular projections. One camera provides a flat image, and two or more cameras allow you to get multiple projections (Fig. 1).

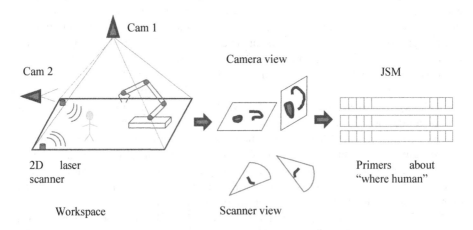

Fig. 1. The presentation of workspace.

To get a set of features from an image, you need to process information from the laser scanners and video cameras. When processing an image, areas where a person can be located are highlighted. The area sizes are selected based on the safe distances between the robot and the human. Areas may partially overlap with each other.

The image from the video camera is divided into zones, each of which is a separate primitive. Since the size of the zones can be chosen large enough, the total number of them is small. To search for a person in the zone, additional processing of the frame is required – for example, by the color or shape of objects [10–14]. These methods are well developed and are not considered in this paper.

For a 2D laser scanner, zones are also allocated by range and angle. Each zone where the scanner detected an obstacle is a separate primitive.

The set of all primitives for a visible scene with a known localization area forms a single JSM example. The information processing process is shown in Fig. 2. The JSM system for the current set of features determines which areas of the work zone a person or parts of his body is located in. Knowing the coordinates of the robot parts, you can determine whether there is a risk of a collision between a robot and a human.

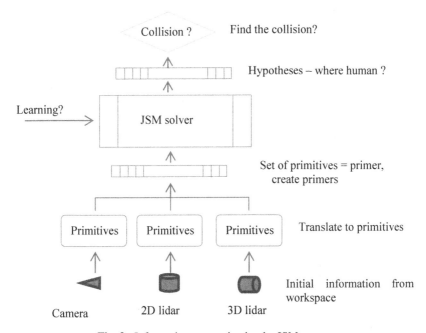

Fig. 2. Information processing by the JSM system.

An important feature of the proposed approach is the ease of combining multiple sensors into a single system. It is known that heterogeneous sensors do not agree well with each other. Another aspect of reliability is the redundancy of the number of sensors in case of failure of some of them. All this leads to a sharp complication of the management system and an increase in its cost. If the cost of a collaborative robot control system is very high, then the scope of its application is narrowed. The proposed approach makes it possible to resolve this contradiction. Using a trainable intelligent system allows you to use an excessive number of sensors and at the same time not increase the cost of the control system.

Another aspect is the accuracy of determining the position of a person in the robot's workspace. It is generally believed that the more accurately the measurement system determines the position of a person or their limbs, the better. However, the more accurate the measurements, the longer it takes, and the more expensive the system as a whole is. In this statement of the problem of determining the position of a person, a different principle is used. The intelligent control system must ensure safe operation (avoid collisions) with the minimum possible accuracy requirements. This reduces the reaction time and reduces the cost of the system as a whole.

3   JSM-System Training

To form the decisive rules of the JSM system, it is necessary to train it. In contrast to neural networks and genetic algorithms, learning a JSM system is a fairly fast process. To get a single decision rule, you must provide the system with several examples that will be used to generate the rule. A JSM system can get a decision rule from at least two examples. The maximum number of examples is limited by computational complexity, since rules are common parts of examples and all possible intersections must be obtained to create them. This operation has exponential complexity, which leads to a rapid increase in the time spent on execution.

In training mode, an external coordinate system – the so-called "teacher" - is used to generate training examples. The external system determines the coordinates of the object and decides which localization area the current position of the object can be attributed to. A single training example defines the set of primitives and their corresponding localization area. This example is checked for uniqueness and entered by the JSM system in the fact database. After entering each new example in the set of training examples, a hypothesis search is performed. The resulting hypotheses may be subject to additional restrictions, such as a ban on counterexamples, where a positive hypothesis should not be embedded in negative examples, and Vice versa. These restrictions are determined by the JSM method used [5].

The training process of the JSM system itself looks like this:

- the external coordinate system determines the position of the person and decides which areas of localization it belongs to at the moment. Information from the surveillance system is converted into a set of primitives. All this information is fed to the JSM-system, and the so-called "training example" is formed, which the JSM-system enters into the database of facts. If there is already such an example in this database of facts, nothing happens;
- if a new training example appears that was not previously found in the fact database, then it is passed to the JSM-solver, who uses it to form a new hypothesis. If the resulting hypothesis meets the consistency criteria, it is added to the hypothesis database;
- updating the database of facts and getting new hypotheses is performed as long as the training mode is running.

The criterion for completing training may be the fact that the hypothesis base will no longer be replenished. This means that no new information is received at the input of the training system. After the end of the training mode, the JSM-system has a set of hypotheses that are later used for the operation of the trained control system.

Note that since the information from different sensors is given to the same type of primitive, there is no difference for the JSM system whether the primitive was obtained from laser sensor or by complex processing of a frame from a video camera. Thus, it is possible to combine information from various sensors, which is achieved as if in a natural way, without excessive complexity of control algorithms. As the number of sensors increases, the processing time increases linearly. An important feature of the JSM system is the ability to explain how a particular result was obtained. Note that when using neural networks, all dependencies are hidden within the network and it is difficult to assess the effect of a particular sensor on the overall result. Since the JSM system can explain the process of obtaining a solution, it is possible to evaluate the contribution of each sensor. This allows you to minimize the number of sensors, thereby reducing the total cost of the system. At the same time, performance also increases, as the total amount of information processed is reduced.

4   JSM System Working Mode

In working mode, the JSM system analyzes information from sensors, receives a set of primitives found for the current scene, from which a test example is formed (Fig. 3).

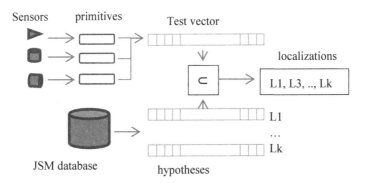

Fig. 3. Information processing in working mode.

The test example is a set, each element of which corresponds to a single primitive. The number of primitives corresponds to the number of zones for all sensors used and can be quite large.

The JSM system has a database in which hypotheses about localization were entered during training. One hypothesis corresponds to an elementary localization domain and contains primitives that were saved during the training stage.

The decision for a test vector is made by checking the embedding of all hypotheses from the database in this vector. To do this, use the operation of adding sets. If a hypothesis is embedded in the test vector for the current scene, the object is assumed to be located in the localization region of this hypothesis.

Combining all the found localization areas gives the position of the person in the workspace. Based on this information, you can assess the risk of collision between robot and human parts.

In the JSM operating mode, the system has a high speed, because the addition operation on sets is performed very quickly. Practice shows that the main time is taken by the algorithm for pre-processing information – getting primitives from the source information. Therefore, to increase the performance of the entire system, you need to speed up these algorithms.

To more accurately determine the position of human body parts in the workspace, it is necessary to reduce the size of the zones where the presence of a person is detected. The minimum size of zones is determined by the ability of video cameras, laser sensors, and computing power when searching for primitives. The main goal is to determine the possibility of a collision, not to accurately calculate the coordinates of a part of the human body. Therefore, a strong reduction in the size of the zone is not appropriate.

5   Experiments

A stand was built for experimental testing (Fig. 4a). The HD camera on a tripod looks down at the working field of 76 × 58 cm and gives an image of 1024 × 768 points. The image from the camera is slightly distorted because a short-focus lens is used (Fig. 4b). To the left of the working field is a side view camera, which gives an image of 1920 × 1080 pixels.

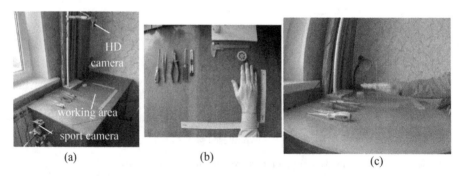

(a)   (b)   (c)

Fig. 4. a) general view of the stand; b) top view of the camera; c) side view of the camera.

For the stand, an action camera was used as a side view camera. Due to the wide-angle lens, the camera produces large distortions, which can be seen at the edges of the image (Fig. 4c). For the method used, the image distortion that cameras contribute does not play a significant role.

A human hand with clothing elements was used as a recognizable object. The area where the human hand was localized was set by the distances from the center of the working field (Fig. 4b) and the specified height above the table surface (Fig. 4c). The measurement step was 5 cm.

Two layers (5 and 10 cm) were used above the field surface. Each layer had 7 localization areas (-15 cm, -10 cm, -5 cm, 0 cm, 5 cm, 10 cm, 15 cm). The total number of regions was 14 units. During learning, images were taken from the top and side for each hand position. The images were saved as separate files.

To select objects by color, the auxiliary JSM system was previously learning using the following algorithm:

- the frame was divided into 32 vertical areas and 32 horizontal areas;
- in manual mode, you specified which areas contain the target object-separately for the person's hand, separately for the item of clothing;
- the JSM system was learning. The common color components for each point is finding. At the same time, the dimension of each color for a point was lowered from 8 bits to 5 bits. Thus, each of the colors (RGB) fell into one of the 32 intervals. The obtained hypotheses were stored in a separate database.

The number of areas that the workspace is divided into was selected based on the size of the target object. The minimum requirements are that the object image contains more than 10 areas. For splitting into 32×32 areas with a working field size of 76×58 cm, one area has a size of 2.38×1.81 cm. This size of the area provides more than 20 coatings for the side view and more than 30 coatings for the top view. The increase in area size leads to an increase in performance, but the simultaneous decrease of accuracy. Reducing the size of the region increases the precision but leads to slower performance. In general, you need to match the size of the area to the size of the target object in order to find the optimal accuracy/performance ratio.

The selection of objects on target frames was performed using the following algorithm:

- the frame was divided into 32 vertical areas and 32 horizontal areas. The total number of areas was 1024 elements. For the top view and side view, the total number of areas was 2048 elements;
- target objects were searched automatically for each area using a trained JSM system. Experiments have shown that the 50% threshold works well - half of the area points must have the color that belongs to the target objects. In Fig. 5b, green rectangles show the result of recognizing a person's hand, and purple rectangles show the result of recognizing clothing;
- for the specified localization area, the areas where the target object is found are defined. These areas make up a set of features that define the JSM-an example for this localization area. Several examples were used for one localization area (from 2 to 4);
- after production all the JSM examples, a hypothesis search is performed by intersecting (searching for common parts) a set of features. The resulting hypotheses are recorded in the localization database.

The resulting localization hypotheses were used to determine the position of an unknown object. After splitting the area and selecting objects by color, a search was

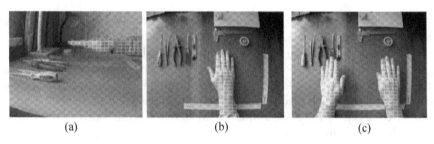

(a)   (b)   (c)

Fig. 5. a) recognizing areas for the side view; b) recognition of a single object; c) recognition of two objects. (Color figure online)

performed to include hypotheses from the localization database in the set of found features for an unknown object. If the hypothesis is including in an unknown object, it is considered to belong to this area. If none of the hypotheses is nested, then the position of the unknown object is considered uncertain.

The JSM-system was learning using one human hand (Fig. 5 a, b). Experiments have shown that the system successfully recognizes localization for two hands (Fig. 5b). In this case, each hand is considered a separate object and they can be distinguished from each other.

As a result of experiments, it turned out that external lighting strongly affects the color recognition procedure. The use of natural light results in large color fluctuations when the light changes. You can solve this problem by using artificial lighting. Another problem found during the experiments is the shading of background objects. When a person's hand moves, it obscures objects located on the table. Since background objects were not recognized in these experiments, shading was not so critical.

To determine the coordinates of a person's hand, a measuring system external to video cameras was used. We used rulers to determine the offset from the center of the field and a pin to set the height. This system is quite rough, so the measurement step was chosen quite large – 5 cm. In addition, there were difficulties in ensuring repeatability of measurement results. If you have a robot manipulator, you can use its coordinate system to set the position of the human hand.

Video cameras used to capture images produced image distortion due to the use of short-focus and wide-angle lenses. Image distortion was quite strong (especially on the side view camera), but this did not affect the accuracy of localization. The reason is that an external coordinate measurement system is used that is independent of video cameras, and during system training, the camera field is bound to this coordinate system. The only requirement was to maintain the position of the cameras for the duration of the experiments.

For experiments, a computer with an Intel Core i5 CPU 3.2 Ghz, 16 GB RAM was used. During the experiments, the performance was evaluated (Table 1).

From Table 1 you can see that the main processing time is spent on pre-processing the frame. Note that these procedures can be optimized and parallelized, which will reduce the overall processing time. An effective way to increase performance is to reduce the frame size.

Table 1. Experimental result.

Learning	
Top view, 1024 × 768 pixels, 32 × 32 areas processing a single frame	15.45 ms
Side view, 1920 × 1080 pixels, 32 × 32 areas processing a single frame	40.7 ms
The calculation hypotheses	10.6 ms
Total training time (4 examples)	260 ms
Position recognition	
Top view, 1024 × 768 pixels, 32 × 32 areas processing a single frame	15.45 ms
Side view, 1920 × 1080 pixels, 32 × 32 areas processing a single frame	40.7 ms
Hypothesis testing	2.1 ms
Localization position of one example	58.25 ms

Localization of an object's position consists of frame processing and hypothesis testing. The execution time of this operation is weakly dependent on the number of hypotheses. In the experiments conducted, localization was performed in 60 ms (16 times per second), which is a good result.

Experiments on a simple layout have shown that using standard video cameras, the problem of determining the collision of a human hand and a robot is solved in real time. The intelligent JSM system is also trained in real time. If we compare the training time with neural networks [4], the result is very good.

6 Conclusion

The author hopes that the proposed approach will allow using existing sensors to determine the position of a person in the working area of a collaborative robot. The use of an intelligent JSM system makes it easy to organize the learning process. Small computing resources are sufficient for the JSM system to work. The main computing power is consumed by algorithms for selecting features from the scene image. This makes it possible to use inexpensive equipment to create a control system for a collaborative robot.

An interesting feature of the JSM method is the ability to "explain" the results obtained. Each hypothesis about the causes, in our case, contains a set of necessary primitives sufficient to describe the scene. Hypothesis analysis allows you to determine which primitives and related input processing methods are sufficient to describe the scene, and which are redundant. This makes it possible to purposefully improve methods for processing video information.

Experiments on human hand localization have shown that this method can be used to determine the position of a person in the robot's working area. The possibility of real-time training of JSM system and the short time of collision detection show the promise of this approach.

References

1. Vysocky, A., Novak, P.: Human–robot collaboration in industry. MM Sci. J. **9**(2), 903–906 (2016)
2. IEEE Robotics and Automation Society (RAS). Robots and robotic devices—Safety requirements for industrial robots. Part 1: Robots, IEEE Std 10218-1-2011, pp. 1–43 (2011)
3. Gat, E.: Artificial Intelligence and Mobile Robots, pp. 195–210. MIT Press (1998)
4. Haddadin, S., de Luca, A., Albu-Schaffer, A.: Robot collisions: a survey on detection isolation and identification. IEEE Trans. Robot. **33**(6), 1292–1312 (2017)
5. Anvaripour, M., Saif, M.: Collision detection for human-robot interaction in an industrial setting using force myography and a deep learning approach. In: 2019 IEEE International Conference on Systems Man and Cybernetics (SMC), pp. 2149–2154 (2019)
6. Dobrynin, D.A.: Dynamic JSM-method in the problem of intelligent robot control. In: Tenth National Conference on Artificial Intelligence CII-2006, vol. 2 (2006)
7. Finn, V.K. (ed.): Automatic Generation of Hypotheses in Intelligent Systems. Book House "LIBROKOM", Moscow (2009). 528 p.
8. Finn, V.K.: Plausible Reasoning in JSM Type Intelligent Systems. Results of Science and Technology. Series "Informatics", vol. 15 (1991)
9. Dobrynin, D.A.: The problem of localization of an unmanned vehicle using the JSM method. In: Proceedings of the seminar Fifth All-Russian Scientific and Practical Seminar "Unmanned Vehicles with Artificial Intelligence Elements" (BTS-AI-2019), pp. 48–55 (2019)
10. Lemaignan, S., Ros, R., Msenlechner, L.: ORO, a knowledge management platform for cognitive architectures in robotics. In: Conference on IEEE/RSJ International Intelligent Robots and Systems (IROS), pp. 3548–3553 (2010)
11. Tenorth, M., Perzylo, A., Lafrenz, R.: Representation and exchange of knowledge about actions, objects, and environments in the roboearth framework. IEEE Trans. Autom. Sci. Eng. **10**, 643–651 (2013)
12. Stenmark, M., Malec, J.: Knowledge-based instruction of manipulation tasks for industrial robotics. Robot. Comput. Integr. Manuf. **33**, 56–67 (2015)
13. Oord, A.V.D., Kalchbrenner, N., Kavukcuoglu, K.: Pixel recurrent neural networks (2016)
14. Schou, C., Madsen, O.L.: A plug and produce framework for industrial collaborative robots. Int. J. Adv. Robot. Syst. **14**, 1–10 (2017)

Method of Formation of Reference Movement Speed of Working Tool of Multilink Manipulator

Vladimir Filaretov[1,2] (ID), Anton Gubankov[1,2] (ID), and Igor Gornostaev[1,3(✉)] (ID)

[1] Institute of Automation and Control Processes, Vladivostok 690041, Russia
gornostaev_iv@mail.ru
[2] Far Eastern Federal University, Vladivostok 690091, Russia
[3] Institute of Automation and Control Processes, Vladivostok 690091, Russia

Abstract. The solution of task of increasing the productivity of robotic systems containing multilink manipulators is presented in this paper. Their actuators have power limitations. To solve this task, a method has been developed for automatic formation of extremely high reference speeds of their working tools. This method allows to maintain a set dynamic control accuracy, taking into account interactions between all degrees of freedom of these manipulators and restrictions on input signals of their electric drives. The created method consists in calculating the maximum allowable speed of the working tool of the manipulator. A system for forming the speed of the working tool of the manipulator with three rotational degrees of freedom was synthesized based on the proposed method. These degrees of freedom are actuated by DC motors. This manipulator can move working tools along arbitrary smooth spatial trajectories formed using third-order parametric splines. This method provides significant increasing of the reference speed of the working tools due to continuous operation of at least one of the manipulator actuator near the saturation zone of its power amplifier without entering it. At the same time, the system speed was increased without reducing dynamic accuracy. The created method can be used to generate the extremely high reference speed of the working tools of manipulators with any kinematic schemes and various numbers of degrees of freedom.

Keywords: Multilink manipulator · Limitation · Speed formation · High accuracy · Reference signals

1 Introduction

Increasing a speed of technological operations (TO) by multilink manipulators (MM) is associated with an increase in torque effects between their degrees of freedom (DoF). This, as shown in [1], leads to a significant growth in the control signals from self-tuning regulators compensating the interactions. As a result, one or several actuators of the MM will enter the saturation mode, when their working tools (WT) can deviate from prescribed trajectories, causing emergencies.

The traditional and most common approach to solving a task of forming the reference movement speed of the MM WT is use of speed profiles [2], which determine the

© Springer Nature Switzerland AG 2020
A. Ronzhin et al. (Eds.): ICR 2020, LNAI 12336, pp. 89–98, 2020.
https://doi.org/10.1007/978-3-030-60337-3_9

dependence of this speed on time. This approach is simple to implement, but assume setting the speed based on the most loaded operating modes of the MM, which leads to its significant decreasing even in favorable working conditions.

Approaches to setting the optimal speed of movement of MM WT are described in [3–9]. These approaches allow consider restrictions on the movement speed of each MM DoF [3–7], accelerations [3–8], and even on derivatives of these accelerations [3–5, 9]. A common disadvantage of these approaches is need to set restrictions on the speeds and accelerations, which can significantly change, taking into account interactions between all DoF. But the tasks of determining the variable values of these restrictions are not solved in these articles, reducing applicability of the described methods.

In paper [10] algorithms of optimal and quasi-optimal (in terms of speed) contour control of MM are proposed. The algorithms allow to set limits on control torques in actuators. But their application in practice makes control systems (CS) work in high-frequency switching mode with all disadvantages of this mode.

In [11, 12] methods for automatic formation the references movement speeds of the MM WT considering, respectively, dynamic errors of their spatial displacements and the values of input voltages and anchor currents of all MM actuators are presented. A common disadvantage of these methods is that they only indirectly allow to take into account the saturation of input of power amplifiers and MM actuators. As a result, for their use it is necessary in advance to carry out multiple simulations of the MM WT movement for each specific trajectory, adjusting the parameters of the synthesized CS.

In [13] a method for calculating the extremely high reference speed of the WT movement with taking into account the limitations of input voltages of MM actuators is presented. The disadvantage of this method is that its application area is limited only by 2-DoF manipulators. Also the paper proposes a method for specifying spatial trajectories, which in practice is not convenient.

Thus, the analysis shows that the task of high-speed movement control of the MM WT, taking into account restrictions on the control signals, is still far from its effective solution.

2   Task Definition

The main aim of the work is to create a method of automatic formation the extremely high MM WT movement speed along spline trajectories, at which the required dynamic control accuracy is maintained and MM actuators work permanently in the linear zone without saturation mode.

3   Description of the Control Object

An MM with the PUMA kinematic scheme is considered below, but the generality of the solved task is also preserved for manipulators with other kinematic schemes. The influence of the orienting DoF located near the WT will be neglected, since their force and torques effects on the other DoF are negligible. In addition, we assume that all MM actuators operate in a linear zone, when their CS provide the required dynamic accuracy and the MM generalized coordinates q_i differ little from their references values q_i^*.

This allows to neglect the detailed description of the regulators without disturbing the operability of the proposed method.

Actuators of the MM are DC motors with permanent magnets. The equations of electric and mechanical chains of the i-th electric drive for small values of inductance of anchor chain, as well as viscous and dry friction, have the form:

$$\begin{cases} R_i I_i + K_{\omega i} i_{pi} \dot{q}_i = K_{yi} U_i, \\ M_{Di} = K_{Mi} I_i = J_{Ei} i_{pi} \ddot{q}_i + P_i / i_{pi}, \end{cases} \quad (1)$$

where $i = \overline{1,3}$ is number of the i-th DoF; q_i, $\dot{q}_i$, $\ddot{q}_i$ are, respectively, the values of generalized coordinates of the MM, as well as their speeds and accelerations; R_i are active resistances of anchor chains of electric motors; J_{Ei} are total inertia moments of their rotors and inertia moments of reducer rotating parts reduced to them; i_{pi} are reducer ratios; K_{Mi} and $K_{\omega i}$ are torque and voltage constants; K_{yi}, U_i are gain constants of power amplifiers of electric motors and voltage at their inputs; I_i is anchor currents of electric motors; M_{Di} is torque created by i-th electric motor; P_i external moments on output shaft of reducer. This moments P_i has following view:

$$P_i = H_i \ddot{q}_i + h_i \dot{q}_i + M_i, \quad (2)$$

where H_i is component of inertial properties of corresponding part of the manipulator; h_i is moment component proportional to $\dot{q}_i$; M_i is moment effect on i-th joint of the manipulator, taking into account gravitational forces and interactions of its DoF.

Considering (1) and (2) the equation of a loaded electric drive in the i-th DoF of the manipulator can be written:

$$R_i(H_i + J_{Ei} i_{pi}^2)\ddot{q}_i + (R_i h_i + K_{Mi} K_{\omega i} i_{pi}^2)\dot{q}_i + R_i M_i = K_{Mi} K_{yi} i_{pi} U_i. \quad (3)$$

Expression (3) will be used to create a method for automatic formation of the extremely high movement speed of the MM WT.

4 Description of Equation of Motion of the MM WT

The movement of the MM WT at the extremely high speed will be ensured if at least one of its actuators will operate at the limit of its power, taking into account the current load, rotating at extremely high speed and acceleration near a non-linear distortion zone of power amplifier, but not enter it. As a result, with the synchronous control of other MM actuators, it will be possible to provide an extremely high variable speed v of the WT movement along any smooth spatial trajectories in the Cartesian coordinate system (CS) $Oxyz$ associated with the MM base.

Equation (3) describes dependence of the generalized speed $\dot{q}_i$ and acceleration $\ddot{q}_i$ of the electric drive on its input voltage U_i at the current values H_i, h_i, M_i. But taking into account kinematics of the MM and current position of its WT on the trajectory, it would be desirable to rewrite it so that the equation describes the dependence of the velocity v and the acceleration $\dot{v}$ of the WT movement on U_i. The value U_i for one of the MM drives is set equal to maximum permissible. Then it is possible to obtain the law of change of limit values of v and $\dot{v}$. However, it is difficult to form dependences of v and $\dot{v}$ on all current values U_i for arbitrary spatial movement of the MM WT, since it will be necessary to determine in real time all variable parameters q_i, $\dot{q}_i$ and $\ddot{q}_i$. Therefore, it is proposed to apply an approximate method for calculating references values v^* and $\dot{v}^*$ when WT moving along trajectories. For this purpose, in Eq. (3) references values q_i^* $\dot{q}_i^*$ and $\ddot{q}_i^*$ are used instead of signals q_i, $\dot{q}_i$ and $\ddot{q}_i$. These references and real signals are approximately equal if all MM electric drives operate in linear zone and their tracking control systems provide them high dynamic control accuracy. Therewith the reference movement trajectory of the MM WT should be defined by smooth parametric splines.

As a result, in order to establish the dependence of v^* and $\dot{v}^*$ on corresponding limit values U_i, the references values of the generalized velocities $\dot{q}_i^*$ and accelerations $\ddot{q}_i^*$, as will be shown below, must be expressed, respectively, through the reference values v^* and $\dot{v}^*$ of the WT movement.

For the indicated transformation of Eq. (3), in the beginning it is necessary to obtain analytical dependences of $\dot{q}_i^*$ and $\ddot{q}_i^*$ on v^* and $\dot{v}^*$. For this, it is necessary to define a law of change of generalized coordinates q_i^* when moving the tool-center-point (TCP) along trajectories described by the specified splines [14], passing through set of given points, and to differentiate it twice in time.

Figure 1 shows the movement trajectory of the MM WT, consisting of a set of parametric third order Bezier splines [14]. The movement along the k-th spline begins at point $P_{k,0}$, where value of parameter $\tau = 0$, and ends at point $P_{k,3}$, where $\tau = 1$, and points $P_{k,1}$ and $P_{k,2}$ determine a shape of the spline curve.

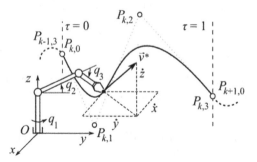

Fig. 1. Reference trajectory of movement of the MM WT.

Each k-th spline, being part of the reference trajectory of the WT movement, is defined by parametric polynomials of third order [15]:

$$
\begin{bmatrix} x \\ y \\ z \end{bmatrix} = \begin{bmatrix} A_{x,k} & B_{x,k} & C_{x,k} & D_{x,k} \\ A_{y,k} & B_{y,k} & C_{y,k} & D_{y,k} \\ A_{z,k} & B_{z,k} & C_{z,k} & D_{z,k} \end{bmatrix} \begin{bmatrix} \tau^3 \\ \tau^2 \\ \tau \\ 1 \end{bmatrix},
\tag{4}
$$

where $A_{x,k}$, $A_{y,k}$, $A_{z,k}$, $B_{x,k}$, $B_{y,k}$, $B_{z,k}$, $C_{x,k}$, $C_{y,k}$, $C_{z,k}$, $D_{x,k}$, $D_{y,k}$, $D_{z,k}$ are coefficients of the k-th spline for corresponding degrees of the parameter $\tau \in [0,1]$, determined by coordinates of the points $P_{k,0}$, $P_{k,1}$, $P_{k,2}$, $P_{k,3}$.

In this case, the law of change of generalized coordinates q_i^* when the TCP moves along the k-th spline (4) can be described by a system of three nonlinear equations [2] and formed on basis of analytical solution of inverse kinematics (IK) problem:

$$q_i^*(t) = f_i(x(\tau(t)), \, y(\tau(t)), \, z(\tau(t))), \tag{5}$$

where $x(\tau(t))$, $y(\tau(t))$ and $z(\tau(t))$ are variable in time coordinates of the TCP defined by parametric third order Bezier splines in the $Oxyz$ CS; t is time (for compactness of recording it is omitted below).

In order to obtain expressions for $\dot{q}_i^*$ и $\ddot{q}_i^*$ in the functions v^* and $\dot{v}^*$, we first differentiate expression (5) in time [13]. As a result, we will have:

$$\dot{q}_i^* = \left(\frac{\partial f_i}{\partial x}\frac{\partial x}{\partial \tau} + \frac{\partial f_i}{\partial y}\frac{\partial y}{\partial \tau} + \frac{\partial f_i}{\partial z}\frac{\partial z}{\partial \tau}\right)\frac{d\tau}{dt}. \tag{6}$$

Expression (4) will be differentiated in t to obtain the derivatives $\partial x/\partial \tau$, $\partial y/\partial \tau$, $\partial z/\partial \tau$. As a result:

$$\begin{bmatrix} \dot{x} \\ \dot{y} \\ \dot{z} \end{bmatrix} = \begin{bmatrix} 3A_{x,k} & 2B_{x,k} & C_{x,k} \\ 3A_{y,k} & 2B_{y,k} & C_{y,k} \\ 3A_{z,k} & 2B_{z,k} & C_{z,k} \end{bmatrix} \begin{bmatrix} \tau^2 \\ \tau \\ 1 \end{bmatrix} \frac{d\tau}{dt} = \begin{bmatrix} F_x \\ F_y \\ F_z \end{bmatrix} \frac{d\tau}{dt}, \tag{7}$$

where $3A_{x,k}\tau^2 + 2B_{x,k}\tau + C_{x,k} = \partial x/\partial \tau = F_x$, $3A_{y,k}\tau^2 + 2B_{y,k}\tau + C_{y,k} = \partial y/\partial \tau = F_y$, $3A_{z,k}\tau^2 + 2B_{z,k}\tau + C_{z,k} = \partial z/\partial \tau = F_z$.

Since $v^* = \sqrt{\dot{x}^2 + \dot{y}^2 + \dot{z}^2}$, then taking into account (7) we can write $v^* = d\tau/dt\sqrt{F_x^2 + F_y^2 + F_z^2}$ and, consequently, [15]

$$\frac{d\tau}{dt} = \frac{v^*}{\sqrt{F_x^2 + F_y^2 + F_z^2}}. \tag{8}$$

Taking into account (7) and (8), expression (6) can be rewritten in the form:

$$\dot{q}_i^* = \begin{bmatrix} \frac{\partial f_i}{\partial x} & \frac{\partial f_i}{\partial y} & \frac{\partial f_i}{\partial z} \end{bmatrix} \begin{bmatrix} F_x \\ F_y \\ F_z \end{bmatrix} \frac{v^*}{\sqrt{F_x^2 + F_y^2 + F_z^2}} = \mathbf{g}_i \mathbf{a} v^*, \tag{9}$$

where $\mathbf{g}_i = \begin{bmatrix} \partial f_i/\partial x & \partial f_i/\partial y & \partial f_i/\partial z \end{bmatrix}$ is row vector of first derivatives; $\mathbf{a} = [F_x \, F_y \, F_z]^T/(F_x^2 \, F_y^2 \, F_z^2)^{1/2}$ is unit vector coinciding with direction of the velocity vector $\vec{v}^* = \mathbf{a}v^* = [\dot{x} \, \dot{y} \, \dot{z}]^T$ in the CS $Oxyz$.

On basis of (9), one can write:

$$\ddot{q}_i^* = \dot{\mathbf{g}}_i \mathbf{a} v^* + \mathbf{g}_i \dot{\mathbf{a}} v^* + \mathbf{g}_i \mathbf{a} \dot{v}^* = \mathbf{g}_i \mathbf{a} \dot{v}^* + (\mathbf{a}^T \mathbf{G}_i \mathbf{a} v^* + \mathbf{g}_i \dot{\mathbf{a}}) v^*, \tag{10}$$

where $\dot{\mathbf{g}}_i = \begin{bmatrix} \frac{\partial^2 f_i}{\partial x^2}\dot{x} + \frac{\partial^2 f_i}{\partial x \partial y}\dot{y} + \frac{\partial^2 f_i}{\partial x \partial z}\dot{z} \\ \frac{\partial^2 f_i}{\partial x \partial y}\dot{x} + \frac{\partial^2 f_i}{\partial y^2}\dot{y} + \frac{\partial^2 f_i}{\partial y \partial z}\dot{z} \\ \frac{\partial^2 f_i}{\partial x \partial z}\dot{x} + \frac{\partial^2 f_i}{\partial y \partial z}\dot{y} + \frac{\partial^2 f_i}{\partial z^2}\dot{z} \end{bmatrix}^{\mathrm{T}} = (\begin{bmatrix} \frac{\partial^2 f_i}{\partial x^2} & \frac{\partial^2 f_i}{\partial x \partial y} & \frac{\partial^2 f_i}{\partial x \partial z} \\ \frac{\partial^2 f_i}{\partial x \partial y} & \frac{\partial^2 f_i}{\partial y^2} & \frac{\partial^2 f_i}{\partial y \partial z} \\ \frac{\partial^2 f_i}{\partial x \partial z} & \frac{\partial^2 f_i}{\partial y \partial z} & \frac{\partial^2 f_i}{\partial z^2} \end{bmatrix} \mathbf{a})^{\mathrm{T}} v^* = \mathbf{a}^{\mathrm{T}} \mathbf{G}_i v^*;$

$$\dot{\mathbf{a}} = \frac{1}{\sqrt{F_x^2 + F_y^2 + F_z^2}} \begin{bmatrix} \frac{\partial F_x}{\partial \tau} \\ \frac{\partial F_y}{\partial \tau} \\ \frac{\partial F_z}{\partial \tau} \end{bmatrix} \frac{d\tau}{dt} + \begin{bmatrix} F_x \\ F_y \\ F_z \end{bmatrix} \frac{d}{dt}(\frac{1}{\sqrt{F_x^2 + F_y^2 + F_z^2}}); \tag{11}$$

$\mathbf{G}_i$ is symmetric matrix of second derivatives.
Considering that:

$$\frac{d}{dt}(\frac{1}{\sqrt{F_x^2 + F_y^2 + F_z^2}}) = -\frac{F_x W_x + F_y W_y + F_z W_z}{(F_x^2 + F_y^2 + F_z^2)^{3/2}}\frac{d\tau}{dt},$$

where $W_x = \partial^2 x/\partial \tau^2 = 2(3A_{x,k}\tau + B_{x,k}), W_y = \partial^2 y/\partial \tau^2 = 2(3A_{y,k}\tau + B_{y,k}), W_z = \partial^2 z/\partial \tau^2 = 2(3A_{z,k}\tau + B_{z,k})$, expression (11) can be rewritten first as:

$$\dot{\mathbf{a}} = \frac{1}{\sqrt{F_x^2 + F_y^2 + F_z^2}} \begin{bmatrix} W_x \\ W_y \\ W_z \end{bmatrix} \frac{d\tau}{dt} - \begin{bmatrix} F_x \\ F_y \\ F_z \end{bmatrix} \frac{F_x W_x + F_y W_y + F_z W_z}{(F_x^2 + F_y^2 + F_z^2)^{3/2}}\frac{d\tau}{dt},$$

and after substituting $d\tau/dt$ (8) in the form:

$$\dot{\mathbf{a}} = (\begin{bmatrix} W_x \\ W_y \\ W_z \end{bmatrix} - \begin{bmatrix} F_x \\ F_y \\ F_z \end{bmatrix} \frac{F_x W_x + F_y W_y + F_z W_z}{F_x^2 + F_y^2 + F_z^2})\frac{v^*}{F_x^2 + F_y^2 + F_z^2} = \tilde{\mathbf{a}}v^*. \tag{12}$$

Considering (12) expression (10) can be rewritten as:

$$\ddot{q}_i^* = \mathbf{g}_i \mathbf{a}\dot{v}^* + (\mathbf{a}^{\mathrm{T}}\mathbf{G}_i\mathbf{a} + \mathbf{g}_i\tilde{\mathbf{a}})v^{*2}, \tag{13}$$

where the terms $\mathbf{a}^{\mathrm{T}}\mathbf{G}_i\mathbf{a}$, $\mathbf{g}_i\tilde{\mathbf{a}}$ and $\mathbf{g}_i\mathbf{a}$, after performing the corresponding matrix operations, become scalars.

Since q_i, $\dot{q}_i$ and $\ddot{q}_i$ included in H_i, h_i and M_i it is necessary to replace them in (2) with the corresponding references values q_i^*, $\dot{q}_i^*$, $\ddot{q}_i^*$. As a result, we obtain references components

$$H_i^*(q_j^*), \; i < j,$$
$$h_i^*(q_j^*, \dot{q}_j^*) = \sum_{j=1}^{3}(s_{j,i}(q_j^*)\dot{q}_j^*), \; i < j, \tag{14}$$

$$M_i^*(q^*, \dot{q}_j^*, \ddot{q}_j^*) = s_{4,i}(q^*) + \sum_{j=1}^{3}(s_{j+4,i}(q^*)\ddot{q}_j^* + s_{j+7,i}(q^*)\dot{q}_j^{*2}), \tag{15}$$

where $i = \overline{1,3}, j = \overline{1,3}, I \neq j; q^* = [q_1^* \ q_2^* \ q_3^*]^T$ is vector of generalized coordinates; $s_{j,I}$ are functions of references coordinates, some of which are equal to zero. The indices of all $s_{j,I}$ in (14) and (15) are chosen so that for each i-th DoF at $j = \overline{1,3}$ all possible functions $s_{j,I}$ will be designated. The first three $s_{j,I}$ at various generalized speeds $\dot{q}_j^*$ in (14), the fourth $s_{4,I}$ (component of gravitational forces) in (15) and the remaining six for various $\ddot{q}_j^*$ and $\dot{q}_j^{*2}$ in (15).

After substituting the components H_i^*, h_i^* (14) and M_i^* (15) in (3), we obtain

$$R_i(H_i^* + J_{Ei}i_{pi}^2)\ddot{q}_i^* + (R_i \sum_{j=1}^{3} (s_{j,i}\dot{q}_j^*) + K_{Mi}K_{\omega i}i_{pi}^2)\dot{q}_i^*$$

$$+ R_i(s_{4,i} + \sum_{j=1}^{3} (s_{j+4,i}\ddot{q}_j^* + s_{j+7,i}\dot{q}_j^{*2})) = K_{Mi}K_{yi}i_{pi}U_i, \quad i \neq j. \tag{16}$$

Replacing $\dot{q}_i^*$ and $\ddot{q}_i^*$ in Eq. (16) and using (9) and (13), one can write

$$\dot{v}^* a_i + v^{*2} b_i + v^* c_i + d_i = 0, \ i \neq j. \tag{17}$$

where $a_i = [R_i((H_i^* + J_{Ei}i_{pi}^2)\mathbf{g}_i\mathbf{a} + \sum_{j=1}^{3} (s_{j+4,i}\mathbf{g}_j)\mathbf{a})]$, $b_i = [R_i((H_i^* + J_{Ei}i_{pi}^2)(\mathbf{a}^T\mathbf{G}_i\mathbf{a} + \mathbf{g}_i\tilde{\mathbf{a}}) + \sum_{j=1}^{3} ((s_{j,i}\mathbf{g}_j)\mathbf{a}\mathbf{g}_i\mathbf{a} + s_{j+4,i}(\mathbf{a}^T\mathbf{G}_j\mathbf{a} + \mathbf{g}_j\tilde{\mathbf{a}}) + s_{j+7,i}(\mathbf{g}_j\mathbf{a})^2))]$, $c_i = K_{Mi}K_{\omega i}i_{pi}^2\mathbf{g}_i\mathbf{a}$, $d_i = R_i s_{4,i} - K_{Mi}K_{yi}i_{pi}U_i, \ i \neq j$

In first order nonlinear differential Eqs. (17) instead of U_i $(i = \overline{1,3})$ one can substitute their maximum permissible values, at which any of the MM electric drives will be in a near saturated mode. Solving these equations, it is possible to determine the maximum permissible value v^*.

5 Results of Simulation

In process of study of the developed system the movement of the 3-DoF MM (see Fig. 1) along the smooth trajectory shown in Fig. 2 was reviewed. This trajectory is represented by a sinusoid with an amplitude 0.23 m, located at an angle 45° to the horizontal plane. The MM base is located at the beginning of $Oxyz$ CS.

The electric drives of the considering MM have the following parameters: $R_i = 0.5$ Ohm, $K_{Mi} = 0.04$ Nm/A, $K_{\omega i} = 0.04$ Vs/rad, $K_{yi} = 1$, $J_{Ei} = 10^{-3}$ kg m^2, $i_{pi} = 100$ $(i = \overline{1,3})$. The nominal inertia moment $J_{nom\,I}$ of shaft of the i-th electric drive and rotating parts of the reducer used in the self-turning law [1] is 10^{-4} kg m^2. The lengths of the MM links are $l_1 = l_2 = l_3 = 0.5$ m, the masses of these links are $m_1 = 25$ kg, $m_2 = m_3 = 15$ kg and the load weight $m_g = 5$ kg. The inertia moments J_{si} and J_{ni} of the i-th MM links relative to their longitudinal axes and axes passing through mass centers and perpendicular to their longitudinal axes are, respectively, $J_{s1} = 0.1$ kg m^2, $J_{s2} = 0.007$ kg m^2, $J_{s3} = 0.005$ kgm^2, $J_{n2} = 0.55$ kg m^2, $J_{n3} = 0.31$ kg m^2. The typical PID controllers described by the equations $U = k_p \varepsilon + k_I \int \varepsilon dt + k_d \dot{\varepsilon}$, were: $k_p = 1883$, $k_I = 130$, $k_d = 140$, where ε is the control error of the corresponding electric drive. Limitations of linear zone of the signals U_i of all electric drives are ± 22.5 V. The limit value of the signal U_i, used in (17), is ± 20 V.

The WT was moved along the smooth trajectory (see Fig. 2), which consisted of 4 parametric splines (4), from point 1 to point 2. From the graphs it can be seen that the references values of all generalized coordinates q_i^* (see Fig. 3) varied smoothly, and the reference speed v^* was continuously adjusted, constantly providing alternating operation of one of the electric drives (see Fig. 4a) in a near saturated mode. At the same time, an increase in v^* occurred in parts of the trajectory with a small curvature, and a decrease – when the WT approaches to areas with a large curvature. The deviation D of the MM WT (see Fig. 3) from the reference trajectory did not exceed the set value 0.6 mm. It's possible to reduce the deviation D by replacing the standard controllers with better regulators [1].

If the WT moves without speed turning at constant value $v^* = 0.4$ m/s, at which all actuators only approach the boundary of linear zone without saturation, then the average speed of the WT decreases by approximately 1.9 times. Behavior of U_i of all MM electric drives with this limit constant speed v^* are shown in Fig. 4b.

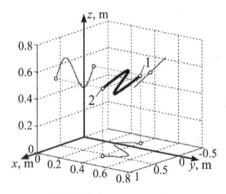

Fig. 2. Reference trajectory.

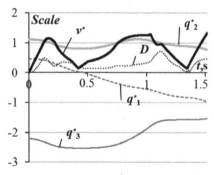

Fig. 3. Behavior of q_i^*, v^* and D (scale $q_i^* = 1$ rad; $v^* = 1$ m/s; $D = 1$ mm).

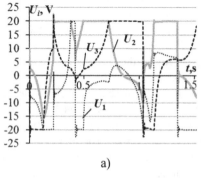

a)   b)

Fig. 4. Behavior of U_i.

The results of simulation the operation of the created system will be considered in more detail below. Figure 3 shows that the smoothness of change in v^* is lost at some instants of time (for example, see timepoints 0.45 s and 1.4 s). This is due to neglect of inductance in the anchor chains of the MM electric drives (see Eqs. (3)). This assumption allowed significantly reduce computational complexity when calculating the current value v^* in the created method. However, in real electric drives the inductance exists and, as shown by studies, with an increase in its value, it is possible for some MM electric drives to exit the linear zone of their operation. To eliminate this situation, the value U_i in (17) should be reduced. As a result, the speed v^* will decrease slightly, but productivity of the synthesized system will still remain more than 1.8 times higher than productivity of the system with the constant limit value v^* while maintaining high accuracy.

Also, for comparison, the operation of analogous system [12], providing the formation of v^* depending on the current values of U_i and I_i ($i = \overline{1, 3}$), measured during the movement of the MM WT, will be considered (see Fig. 5 and 6). It is shown in these figures that a similar behavior of v^* was obtained, and the electric drives also worked alternately in a pre-saturated mode after 0.25 s. The advantage of this system is its simplicity of realization, but it requires repeated simulations to adjust its parameters.

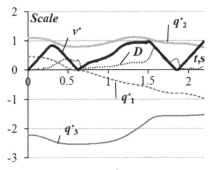

Fig. 5. Behavior of q_i^*, v^* and D (scale $q_i^* = $ 1 rad; $v^* = 1$ m/s; $D = 1$ mm).   **Fig. 6.** Behavior of U_i.

Comparison of productivity of the system [12] with the one described in this paper shows 20–30% advantage of the new method. At the same time, the accuracy of these systems (see Fig. 3 and 5) is on the same level.

6 Conclusion

A new method of automatic formation of the extremely high (variable) reference speed of the WT of various MM along the trajectories defined by third-order parametric splines is considered in the article. This speed ensures permanent operation of at least one MM electric drive in the near saturated mode (in the linear zone of operation of all used electric drives). At the same time, a continuous high dynamic control accuracy is maintained.

Acknowledgements. This work was supported by the Russian Foundation for Basic Research (№ 20-38-70161, 20-08-00701).

References

1. Filaretov, V.F., Gubankov, A.S.: Adaptive speed control system for end effectors of multilink manipulators. In: IEEE International Conference on Industrial Engineering, Applications and Manufacturing, pp. 1–5 (2017)
2. Craig, J.J.: Introduction to Robotics. Mechanics and Control. Pearson, London (2005). 408 p.
3. Valente, A., Baraldo, S., Carpanzano, E.: Smooth trajectory generation for industrial robots performing high precision assembly processes. CIRP Ann. – Manuf. Technol. **66**(1), 17–20 (2017)
4. Besset, P., Bearee, R.: FIR filter-based online jerk-constrained trajectory generation. Control Eng. Pract. **66**, 169–180 (2017)
5. Haschke, R., Weitnauer, E., Ritter, H.: On-line planning of time-optimal, jerk-limited trajectories. In: IEEE/RSJ International Conference on Intelligent Robots and Systems, pp. 3248–3253 (2008)
6. Shen, P., Zhang, X., Fang, Y.: Real-time acceleration-continuous path-constrained trajectory planning with built-in tradability between cruise and time-optimal motions, pp. 1–12. ArXiv (2018)
7. Somlo, J.: Robotised manufacturing process optimisation. In: RAAD 1997 Conference (1997)
8. Bobrow, J.E., Dubowsky, S., Gibson, J.S.: Time-optimal control of robotic manipulators along specified paths. Int. J. Robot. Res. **4**(3), 3–17 (1985)
9. Soon, Y.J., Yun, J.C., PooGyeon, P., Seung, G.Ch.: Jerk limited velocity profile generation for high speed industrial robot trajectories. IFAC Proc. Vol. **38**(1), 595–600 (2005)
10. Kalaykov, I., Iliev, B.: Time-optimal sliding mode control of robot manipulator. In: IEEE International Conference on Industrial Electronics, Control and Instrumentation, pp. 265–270 (2000)
11. Filaretov, V.F., Yukhimets, D.A.: A method for forming program control for velocity regime of motion of underwater vehicles along arbitrary spatial trajectories with given dynamic accuracy. J. Comput. Syst. Sci. Int. **50**(4), 673–682 (2011)
12. Filaretov, V.F., Gubankov, A.S.: Adaptive speed control system for end effectors of multilink manipulators. In: Proceedings of 2017 International Conference on Industrial Engineering, Applications and Manufacturing (ICIEAM), pp. 1–5 (2017)
13. Filaretov, V., Gubankov, A.: Synthesis of adaptive control system for formation of program speed of multilink manipulator. In: Tan, H. (eds.) Informatics in Control, Automation and Robotics. LNEE, vol. 132, pp. 347–350. Springer, Heidelberg (2011). https://doi.org/10.1007/978-3-642-25899-2_47
14. Rogers, D.F., Adams, J.A.: Mathematical Elements for Computer Graphics. McGraw-Hill, New York City (1976). 239 p.
15. Filaretov, V.F., Gubankov, A.S., Gornostaev, I.V.: The formation of motion laws for mechatronics objects along the paths with the desired speed. In: Proceedings of the International Conference on Computer, Control, Informatics and Its Applications, pp. 93–96 (2016)

Distributing Tasks in Multi-agent Robotic System for Human-Robot Interaction Applications

Rinat Galin$^{(\boxtimes)}$ (iD), Roman Meshcheryakov (iD), and Saniya Kamesheva (iD)

V.A. Trapeznikov Institute of Control Sciences of Russian Academy of Sciences, Moscow 117997, Russian Federation
rinat.r.galin@yandex.ru

Abstract. Human-robot interaction become a trend in robotics and happen in a wide range of situations. This research paper describes human and collaborative robots interaction behind traditional paradigms for robots in a shared workspace. This research shows that humans and robots distributing task in collaborative interaction of multi-agent robotic system. Different methods for distributing tasks on global and local levels in multi-agent robotic system analyzed as part of research work. Characteristics of tasks distribution algorithms are considered. The particle swarm algorithm for task distribution presented as an example.

Keywords: Multi-agent system · Collaboration · Human-robot interaction · Model · Safety-oriented behavior

1 Introduction

The process of robotic solutions integration into modern production automation become an integral of technological stage. Complex and monotonous work processes of human operators moved to automated process of robotic solutions. Robots and humans work hand by hand to complete a common tasks. This process called human-robot interaction (HRI). Human-robot interaction over the period of its development has evolved from the process of repeating actions after a human to the interaction of a human with an intelligent robot – an intelligent partner [1].

It is worth noting that HRI has undergone a number of changes that have led to the ability to establish the interaction process in collaboration. There is no need to build barriers around modern robots that work in a shared workspace. The presence of a variety of sensors and sensors in robotic solutions made it possible to make the process safe and controlled [2–4]. Such process in which a robot has safely interacts with a human is called collaborative process and robots – collaborative robots (cobots). These robotic solutions are subject to special safety requirements that regulated by international standards and specifications [5–8]. It is not just about the presence of robotic assistants with a variety of different sensors that allow to control the speed of movement, the angle of rotation or the presence of technical vision systems. First, it is necessary to ensure a safe working area [9, 10].

© Springer Nature Switzerland AG 2020
A. Ronzhin et al. (Eds.): ICR 2020, LNAI 12336, pp. 99–106, 2020.
https://doi.org/10.1007/978-3-030-60337-3_10

Collaborative robotic solutions are a new stage in the development of interactive robotics. This is a new working environment for a human in collaboration with a robot. Thus, new types of multi-agent systems involving robots are being form. Such systems called multi-agent robotic systems [11]. A human interact with the system as an intelligent agent and a partner. Such system called a multi-agent ergatic control system for a collaborative robot. It could consist of various types of robotic solutions and the structure of which allows exchanging information among themselves and providing interaction. Each agent has information about the actions and plans of the other agents [12].

With the expansion of the functionality of robotic solutions and the introduction of collaborative robots into production processes, a logical question how to make the process of interaction between a human and a robot more effective. The authors propose to consider the distribution of tasks between robots and humans in a multi-agent robotic system using the example of collaborative robotics.

2   Multi-agent System of Human and Collaborative Robot Type

An ergatic control system for a collaborative robot is a system in which some operations performed by a robots and some by a human in a safe mode in a shared workspace. It is necessary to divide functions between human and robot with reasonable of automation of the robot's actions. The problem of cooperation between human and robot in a shared workspace sets the task of determining the functions that should be transfer to the robot due to its functional efficiency, and which should remain with the human due to its unique ability to perceive the environment and make decisions in emergencies.

The main components of the functional scheme of a multi-agent ergatic control system for a collaborative robot shown in Fig. 1. In this concept of collaboration, the ergatic robotic system can be extend by the concept of human operator and robot to the level of human-robot type. In addition to the human operator in a semi-automatic control system, a human is an intelligent agent on a parity with a collaborative robot in order to automate and optimize the process.

Human functioning in interaction based on comparing incoming signals with certain reference signals (the function of the Central nervous system) stored in memory, with subsequent decision-making, taking into account work experience and skills. The effectiveness of interaction at the human-robot level is ensured by an optimal and consistent distribution of functions in Sects. 1 and 2. Getting efficiency depends on solving the problem of engineering psychology and ergonomics. In presented multi-agent robotic system, the upper level is a control center with modules for communication, planning and information processing. This level can create new tasks for a group of intelligent agents in the system.

The work process in a shared workspace of ergatic robotic system is a combination of robot and human capabilities in an effort to reduce human labor costs during performing common tasks.

Conceptually, the human-robot interaction and the work process in ergatic robotic system could be classify into the following components: work time, workspace, interaction tasks, and collaboration [13–15] that presented in Fig. 2.

Work time in this concept defined as a time during HRI in a shared workspace. Each entity has a task that achieve jointly or separately. If there is a common time in

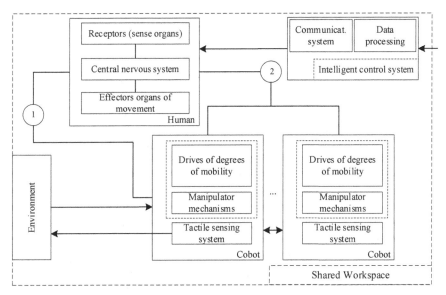

Fig. 1. Functional diagram of a multi-agent robotic control system.

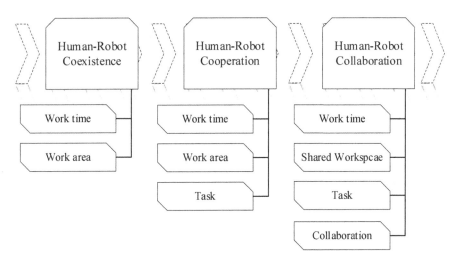

Fig. 2. Classification of Human-robot interaction.

a shared workspace then this interaction represents the coexistence of a human and a robot. If there is a common goal of interaction, entities can have different tasks, which characterizes their cooperation, and if there is a direct contact (for example, tactile or auditory) then this interaction can be described as a collaboration between a human and a robot.

3   Comparative Analysis of Methods for Distributing Tasks Between Intelligent Agents

There are various reasons that can affect the performance of the task in HRI. In this multi-agent robotic system (MARS), we consider collaborative robots that meet the requirements for safe interaction. However, the process of completing the task itself may be inefficient due to human factors. These factors may include human fatigue, its emotional state, and attitude to the robot [16, 17].

Correct tasks distribution allows to achieve optimal results with minimal time spent. Definitely, it is necessary to develop the structure of the MARS in such a way as to exclude conflict situations in the system that can lead to loss of time and harm to the human operator. Thus, the system needs to establish a communication link between agents.

There are two types of task distribution in MARS that possible to consider. These types include statistical and dynamic tasks distribution. First, organization of centralized control system for a collaborative robot. As shown in Fig. 1 the system supported by an intelligent control center. This allows adjusting the task completion process or changing the setting to complete a new task. However, we cannot exclude a decentralized management system, since all intelligent agents can participate in a multi-agent system and coordinate their actions.

Comparative analysis of the characteristics of various algorithms depending on the tasks presented in Table 1. These are tasks solved at the global distribution stage. On this level, the most efficient algorithm is the particle swarm optimization. This algorithm disclosed in work [18]. The particle swarm algorithm reflects the speed and finding the optimal solution.

Table 1. Comparative analysis of the characteristics of algorithms [18].

Method name	Time/dimension complexity	Best option for distribution	Convergence	Complexity of the algorithm model
Sorting method	−/−	+	+	+
Search algorithm	+/−	−	−	+
Linear programming	−/−	+	+	+
Ant colony optimization	−/+	+	+	−
Particle Swarm Optimization	+/+	+	+	+
Genetic algorithm	+/+	+	+	−

To distribute tasks at the local level in MARS an intelligent agents dynamically distribute tasks among themselves through negotiations. These methods include the protocol algorithm, auction algorithm, and game theory.

The contract protocol method is effective for dynamic task distribution, but it is largely dependent on the number of agents. The more agents there are, the less effective this method. The auction algorithm is flexible and allows for dynamic tasks distribution. The disadvantage is a poor global optimal solution associated with an increase in the number of agents. Game theory is the most appropriate method for distributing problems at the local level. The method consists of a process in which two or more agents participate with a specific strategy to achieve the goal. These agents act as system agents. The task of system agents is to perform the task effectively. Thus, at the local level, for safe and effective interaction between a human and a robot, it is advisable to use methods for solving tasks in game theory with active agents whose actions are mutually determined in relation to each other [18, 19].

4 Distributing Tasks in Multi-agent Robotic System

4.1 Task Definition

The definition for distributing tasks among intelligent agents is following. Let's assume that we are given a set of tasks for sorting objects of different sizes and colors. First, glance the task may seem simple and uncomplicated. However, as previously mentioned, many factors can affect the effective execution of the task. Therefore, intelligent agents will complement each other. There are set of $M = \{m_1, m_2 \ldots, m_k\}$ tasks. These tasks need to solve by intelligent agents of reviewed MARS. The set of $N = \{n_1, n_2 \ldots, n_p\}$ intelligent agents. The following matrices with dimension are specified $k \times p$: matrix emoluments $O = \{o_{ij}\}$, cost matrix $R = \{r_{ij}\}$, possibilities matrix $S = \{s_{ij}\}$, where o_{ij} – emolument for completing task i by an intelligent agent j. Next, r_{ij} – resources spent by the j intelligent agent to complete the task i and s_{ij} – opportunity j agent can perform the task i. $s_{ij} = \{0, 1\}, i = \{1, \ldots, k\}, j = \{1, \ldots, p\}$.

It is necessary to distribute tasks M among intelligent agents N to arrive maximum result $-Q = \sum_{j=1}^{p} \sum_{i=1}^{k} \left(s_{ij} * \left(o_{ij} - r_{ij}\right)\right)$. The distribution result need to be represented as an array. The size of the array corresponds to the number of distributed tasks. Each robot participating in the task distribution is an element of the array, and the sequential number of the element corresponds to the task number for the specified robot.

Next, consider a centralized method for distributing problems using the particle swarm algorithm.

4.2 MARS Centralized Task Distribution

Centralized task allocation used in global planning and is used in the control center block of the intelligent management system. Intelligent agents constantly repeat the task allocation procedure, due to possible failures in the execution of tasks.

The particle swarm algorithm is one of the bionic optimization methods [20–22]. This algorithm is iterative and has a sequence of steps. In relation to MARS, in the algorithm, the particle acts as the solution of the distribution problem, and the distance – the cost of performing tasks.

Particle Swarm Algorithm Steps. The following sequence of steps describes the algorithm.

- *Step 1.* Initializing a swarm of particles. Initially we assume a random location throughout the search area for the best solution.
- *Step 2.* Calculating the values of the target function. Search for the best local and global solution.
- *Step 3.* Adjusting the position of the particle in the pursuit of a better solution. A modified algorithm of the classical particle swarm algorithm is applied. Changes in the nature of particle motion and dynamic changes in the algorithm parameters.

$$w_i^{n+1} = w_i^n + a_1 \cdot rnd\,(0,\,1) \cdot \left(pb_i - x_i^n\right) + a_2 \cdot rnd\,(0,\,1) \cdot \left(lb_i - x_i^n\right);$$
$$x_i^{n+1} = x_i^n + w_i^{n+1},$$

w_i – current velocity of the i particle, x_i – its current position, a_1 and a_2 – weighting factors for local and global solutions; pb_i – best solution (local optimum), lb_i – the best solution among particles and its neighbors. It is worth noting that the classic version of the algorithm works faster, but has less effectiveness when increasing the number of agents in the system.

- *Step 4.* Checking the execution of the algorithm or the specified number of iterations. The search process end.

Involve of this algorithm is mainly due to its simplicity and a small number of parameters. Its result shows high accuracy and fast convergence of the algorithm.

5 Conclusions and Future Work

The prospect of human-robot interaction research is to obtain a synergistic effect from the joint process. Creating conditions for collaboration between human and robot will ensure the efficiency and productivity of technological processes by separating tasks and automating operations. Robots will become interactive and intelligent, and humans will be adapted to a life in which the robot is an integral component.

In the future work planned to test methods for distributing tasks on the example of a multi-agent robotic system with collaborative robots in real conditions. The centralized and decentralized methods described in this paper will be test on real conditions and the best option will be select in the comparative analysis in relation to the research task.

Acknowledgements. The reported study was partially funded by RFBR according to the research project № 19-08-00331.

References

1. Ermishin, K., Yuschenko, A: Collaborative mobile robots - a new stage of development of service robotics. J. Robot. Tech. Cybern. 3(12), 3–9 (2016)

2. Matheson, E.: Human-robot collaboration in manufacturing applications: a review. Robotics **8**(4), 100 (2019). https://doi.org/10.3390/robotics8040100

3. Galin, R., Meshcheryakov, R.: Review on human–robot interaction during collaboration in a shared workspace. In: Ronzhin, A., Rigoll, G., Meshcheryakov, R. (eds.) ICR 2019. LNCS (LNAI), vol. 11659, pp. 63–74. Springer, Cham (2019). https://doi.org/10.1007/978-3-030-26118-4_7

4. Villani, V., Pini, F., Leali, F., Secchi, C.: Survey on human–robot collaboration in industrial settings: safety, intuitive interfaces and applications. Mechatronics **55**, 248–266 (2018). https://doi.org/10.1016/j.mechatronics.2018.02.009

5. ISO 10218-1, 2:2011: Robots and robotic devices – Safety requirements for industrial robots – Part 1, 2: Robot systems and integration, Geneva (2011)

6. ISO: 12100:2010–11 Safety of machinery - General principles for design – Risk assessment and risk reduction. Standard, International Organization for Standardization (2013)

7. ISO/TC 299 Robotics – "ISO/TS 15066:2016 Robots and robotic devices – Collaborative robots". https://www.iso.org/standard/62996.html. Accessed 11 May 2020

8. Lazarte, M.: Robots and humans can work together with new ISO guidance. https://www.iso.org/news/2016/03/Ref2057.html. Accessed 13 May 2020

9. Galin, R.R., Meshcheryakov, R.V.: Human-robot interaction efficiency and human-robot collaboration. In: Kravets, A. (ed.) Robotics: Industry 4.0 Issues & New Intelligent Control Paradigms. SSDC, vol. 272, pp. 55–63. Springer, Cham (2020). https://doi.org/10.1007/978-3-030-37841-7_5

10. Kaiser, L., Schlotzhauer, A., Brandstötter, M.: Safety-related risks and opportunities of key design-aspects for industrial human-robot collaboration. In: Ronzhin, A., Rigoll, G., Meshcheryakov, R. (eds.) ICR 2018. LNCS (LNAI), vol. 11097, pp. 95–104. Springer, Cham (2018). https://doi.org/10.1007/978-3-319-99582-3_11

11. Vorotnikov, S., Ermishin, K., Nazarova, A., Yuschenko, A.: Multi-agent robotic systems in collaborative robotics. In: Ronzhin, A., Rigoll, G., Meshcheryakov, R. (eds.) ICR 2018. LNCS (LNAI), vol. 11097, pp. 270–279. Springer, Cham (2018). https://doi.org/10.1007/978-3-319-99582-3_28

12. Magrini, E., et al.: Human-robot coexistence and interaction in open industrial cells. Robot. Comput.-Integr. Manuf. **61**, 101846 (2020). https://doi.org/10.1016/j.rcim.2019.101846

13. Schmidtler, J., Knott, V., Hölzel, C., Bengler, K.: Human centered assistance applications for the working environment of the future. Occup. Ergon. **12**(3), 83–95 (2015)

14. Hoffman, G.: Evaluating fluency in human–robot collaboration. IEEE Trans. Hum.-Mach. Syst. 1–10 (2019). https://doi.org/10.1109/thms.2019.2904558

15. Lin, F., Hsu, J.Y.: Cooperation protocols in multi-agent robotic systems. Auton. Robots **4**, 175–198 (1997). https://doi.org/10.1023/a:1008813631823

16. Charalambous, G., et al.: Human-automation collaboration in manufacturing: identifying key implementation factors. In: ICMR 2013, pp. 301–306. Cranfield University, UK (2013)

17. Galin, R., et al.: Cobots and the benefits of their implementation in intelligent manufacturing. IOP Conf. Ser.: Mater. Sci. Eng. **862**, 032075 (2020). https://doi.org/10.1088/1757-899x/862/3/032075

18. Nazarova, A.V., Zhai, M.: Distributed solution of problems in multi agent robotic systems. In: Gorodetskiy, A.E., Tarasova, I.L. (eds.) Smart Electromechanical Systems. SSDC, vol. 174, pp. 107–124. Springer, Cham (2019). https://doi.org/10.1007/978-3-319-99759-9_9

19. Liu, C., Tomizuka, M.: Designing the robot behavior for safe human–robot interactions. In: Wang, Y., Zhang, F. (eds.) Trends in Control and Decision-Making for Human–Robot Collaboration Systems. SSDC, pp. 241–270. Springer, Cham (2017). https://doi.org/10.1007/978-3-319-40533-9_11

20. Kennedy, J., Eberhart, R.: Particle swarm optimization. In: IEEE International Conference on Neural Networks, pp. 1942–1948 (1995)

21. Wang, Y., Zeng, J.: A survey of a multi-objective particle swarm optimization algorithm. CAAI Trans. Intell. Syst. **5**(5), 377–384 (2010)
22. Azzouz, R., Bechikh, S., Ben Said, L.: Dynamic multi-objective optimization using evolutionary algorithms: a survey. In: Bechikh, S., Datta, R., Gupta, A. (eds.) Recent Advances in Evolutionary Multi-objective Optimization. ALO, vol. 20, pp. 31–70. Springer, Cham (2017). https://doi.org/10.1007/978-3-319-42978-6_2

A*-Based Path Planning Algorithm for Swarm Robotics

Valeriia Izhboldina$^{(\boxtimes)}$ ⓘ, Elizaveta Usinaⓘ, and Irina Vatamaniukⓘ

St. Petersburg Institute for Informatics and Automation of the Russian Academy of Sciences, 39, 14th Line, 199178 St. Petersburg, Russia
izhboldina.valeriia@gmail.com

Abstract. Currently path planning for a swarm of mobile robots is a relevant problem in the domain of robotics. Various approaches to its solution exist. One of such approaches comprises different methods of informed sampling, which boost the search process through direction of search frontier towards the target. This paper presents combination of such method with the simplified representation of the operational environment, specifically, cellular decomposition. The proposed method ensures transition of a robot swarm into the predefined formation in such manner, that during robot motion along the planned paths no collisions occurred. The experimentation was performed with groups of 5, 10, 15, 20, 25 and 30 robots in three different scenes. Upon experimentation it was revealed, that for a swarm of 30 robots in a complex scene the path computing time does not exceed 7 s.

Keywords: Swarm robotics · Path planning · Route map · Mobile robots · Group control

1 Introduction

Development of methods for solution of the path planning problem is relevant in the context of robot swarm. Efficient path planning allows to avoid potential collisions, as between individual robots, as between robots and obstacles [1–3]. Such method should meet the following requirements: easy implementation, flexibility in solving of various tasks, fitness to path planning in the environment with obstacles, and collision avoidance among the objects in the swarm. Efficiency evaluation for the path planning method, intended for utilization in the context of robot swarm, can be reduced to the analysis of aggregate path length of all robots [4], total time, spent for path computing and robot motion to target coordinates [5].

To solve the problem of path planning within a certain environment, it is possible to use relatively simple and efficient obstacle-avoidance methods based on cellular decomposition [6]. These methods assume partitioning of the robot's operational environment into some fixed-size cells aligned along the coordinate axes. For each cell the occupancy status is defined. If a cell contains an obstacle, it is considered occupied, else it is considered empty. The central coordinates of each cell are considered the graph vertices, whereas the transitions between the cells are considered to be the edges of this graph.

© Springer Nature Switzerland AG 2020
A. Ronzhin et al. (Eds.): ICR 2020, LNAI 12336, pp. 107–115, 2020.
https://doi.org/10.1007/978-3-030-60337-3_11

Therefore, instead of the initial complex model of the environment, its discrete representation is used, what simplifies the planning process [7]. Such approach allows to reduce the planning task in a complex environment to graph theory problems, for solution of which an extensive mathematical framework exists [8, 9].

The process of discovery of such a graph in the path, which maps to robot route, is a crucial step in path planning [10]. Often, to find the path of optimal length within the graph, informed path planning algorithms are used [11, 12]. Such algorithms are less time-consuming and computing-intensive, because they provide for search direction toward the target point [13]. A* is considered to be an efficient informed search algorithm [14, 15]. Algorithm A* combines two functions: distance estimation function (from start to target point) and cost function to reach the target point (heuristic function). This algorithm performs path search, directed toward the lowest-cost vertices, what reduces time, needed to compute paths [16].

Algorithm A* for a group of robots is put in practice in [17]. The authors of [17] engaged with reconfiguration of robots into predefined configurations in an obstacle-free environment. The approach, proposed in this paper, ensures the motion path planning for each robot in the swarm, excluding collisions with other robots. The proposed approach can be divided into two parts: 1) finding of optimal path for each robot, using the A* algorithm, whereby the degree of optimality is defined, depending on the length of the computed path or according to certain preset path cost criteria. 2) Establishment of the counting protocol: in such protocol a parameter α is assigned to each robot. The value of this parameter is passed to all robots, adjacent to current agent. If some robot blocks the path for the other robot, then the value of this parameter is incremented by 1, else it remains unchanged. Steady increase of the value of parameter α acts as a dead-end marker, preventing motion of other robots along the predefined paths. The considered method allows easily resolve the situations, where dead ends occur, but does not account for existing obstacles.

Many existing path planning methods for robot swarm rely on complex mathematical frameworks and do not account for obstacles on the map [18]. By combining the cell decomposition approach with the A* algorithm for a group of robots several advantages are achieved: simple implementation, easy extension in context of specific tasks, possibility of path planning in an environment with obstacles.

We are considering a scenario in which several robots of a swarm need to gather from random starting points into a formation of a certain geometric shape (predefined target points) for further joint task execution. For solution of the simultaneous group motion problem in a swarm of N robots in the environment with obstacles, it is necessary to compute for each robot the respective paths from starting coordinates to target coordinates in such a way, that excludes collisions among individual robots in the group. To that purpose this paper presents an algorithm of target coordinate allocation, which respects minimum distance from starting positions to target coordinates, and path planning algorithm A*, extended with the vertex check condition, what guarantees collision-free robot motion. The number of target coordinates can be other than the number of robots. To simplify the problem, let us assume that the number of robots in the group is the same as the number of target coordinates.

2   Principles of Algorithm A* Execution and Cost Function Calculation

To solve the problem, stated above, let us represent the operational environment of the robots as a grid with even-sized cells. The passing through each cell is associated with certain cost value; additionally, each cell can be «free» or «occupied». According to the algorithm for target coordinate allocation, each robot in the group obtains the destination point, which is the closest to it. Consider the graph, whose vertices are the central coordinates of cells in the grid, and edges correspond to the transitions between the cells. In this graph we need to find N paths from the vertices S, representing the starting coordinates, to the vertices T, representing the target coordinates.

The problem of path planning with algorithm A* consists in definition of cell sequence, the centers of which the robot passes within the minimum timeframe and without collisions with other robots and obstacles. The graph vertices can belong to the *Closed* list, *Open* list or outside of these lists. The *Open* list contains the vertices to be investigated, the *Closed* list contains already investigated vertices. Initially, both lists are empty. Every vertex has a parent vertex, i.e. the one, that has been investigated on previous iteration. Every vertex is also associated with certain cost value F defined according to the following expression:

$$F = G + H,$$

where G is the cost of reaching the target coordinate from the current point, following already established path, H is approximate cost of path from the starting point S to the current one. Estimation of H cost is a tentative length of the remained path, because it is actually unknown and depends on layout of obstacles in the scene. There are various ways to calculate the H cost. This paper employs one of the most common approaches of this kind – «reduced diagonal», based upon vertical and horizontal distances from the starting vertex S to the current one. We denote the terms of the equations as follows:

$$d_x = |x_C - x_S|$$
$$d_y = |y_C - y_S|$$

where (x_S, y_S), (x_C, y_C) are the coordinates of starting and target vertices respectively, hence, d_x, d_y – horizontal and vertical distance. Then the heuristic function H of this method is formulated as follows:

$$H = 1,4 \min (d_x, d_y) + 1,0(\max(d_x, d_y) - \min (d_x, d_y)).$$

Using heuristic rules, this algorithm estimates the remaining distance along the path, which generally represents an irregular line. After several iterations of recursive vertex processing, we obtain the map with cost values assigned to the cells and directions of decreasing cost among them. Proceeding from the start along these lines to the target, we obtain the path required.

3   Proposed Algorithm for A*-Based Path Planning

Based on algorithm A* for a single robot, paths for individual robots in the swarm can be planned. Under assumption, that all the robots will move simultaneously, the designed path should be planned in such manner, that it would ensure collision-free robot motion along these paths. Consider the robot collision problem in context of swarm motion and its solution via path planning before the motion begins. In this case, the constructed paths are pre-checked for collisions. The proposed approach contains the following steps: assigning target points to reduce the number of potential collisions as much as possible (Fig. 1) and finding a path for each robot with collision avoidance (Fig. 2).

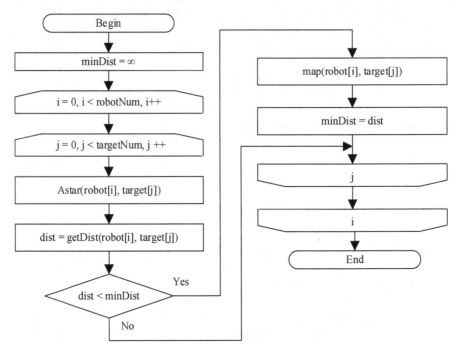

Fig. 1. Algorithm for assigning target points to the robots.

To assign the target positions to the group of robots we apply the algorithm, where each robot is assigned a destination point, which is the closest one to it. The algorithm receives as input the coordinates of robots and targets. The function *Astar(robot, target)* returns an array of dots, corresponding the path from start to target. Using the *getDist* function, for each robot the length of path between robot and target is computed and returned. Further the obtained length is compared with the preset minimum *minDist*. If it is smaller than *minDist*, then the current length is considered minimal and assigned to the actual robot. Then the relevant coordinate is deleted from the list. All steps of the algorithm are iterated for each robot. Hence, every robot is assigned the target, which is the closest to it. After this step, the path for each robot is constructed. The enhanced path planning algorithm, derived from A*, is presented in Fig. 2.

The developed algorithm works as follows. Firstly, the map of working area is segmented by a grid with predefined step. Two lists of vertices are composed: *Open* and *Closed*. The coordinate of starting point of the robot is added to the *Open* list, whereas the *Closed* list remains empty at this moment. Accessible vertices are looked up around

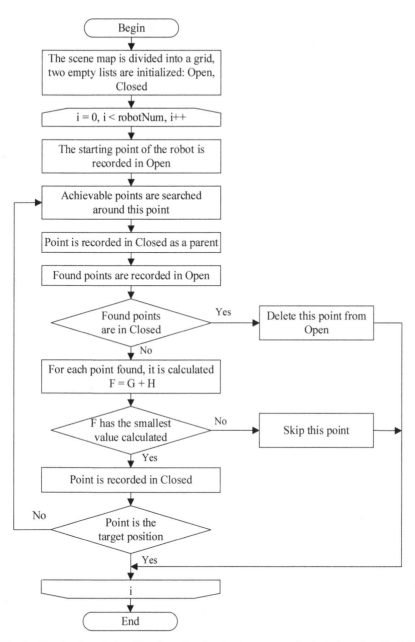

Fig. 2. The developed algorithm for path planning in a group of robots, based on the A*.

the point from the *Open* list. These vertices are added to *Open*, whereas the first point goes to the *Closed* list as the parent of the found ones. Further the check is performed against presence of the found vertices in the *Closed* list. Should some of the found vertices already be present in the *Closed* list, they are deleted from *Open* list. In the next step the cost F for each vertex is calculated, and the vertex with the least value F is included into *Closed*. Other vertices are omitted. Then, the found vertex with the least F is compared with the target point, and, if they are the same, the algorithm finishes. If the *Open* list is empty, and the target has not been reached, the respective path does not exist. Hence, the condition of check against the vertex under consideration in the *Closed* list allows to avoid situations, where paths of different robots are directed to the same vertices, what provides for collision avoidance among these robots.

4   Experiments

The purpose of the experiments consisted in "proof of concept" of the proposed method for groups of robots, with 5, 10, 15, 20, 25 and 30 devices in such group. The operational environment is represented as a scene of 100×100 points. The size of robot, as well the size of cell in the grid, laid over the scene, is equal to one point each. For each map (Fig. 3) and each set of robots 100 tests were performed to calculate average time, needed for path planning.

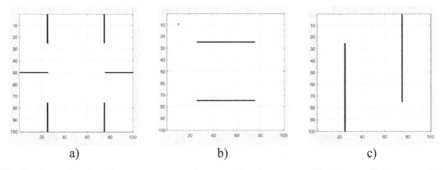

a)   b)   c)

Fig. 3. Operational environment maps under consideration: a) map №1, b) map №2, c) map №3.

In each test the robots obtain new starting coordinates in the environment. Resulting configuration in all tests is represented as a planar geometrical shape, consisting of dots and situated in the middle of the scene. The curve, showing the function of average time of path computation is depicted in the Fig. 4. A path construction example for 5 robots in map №1 is shown in Fig. 5.

The obtained experimental outcomes lead to conclusion, that for the map №1, where the obstacles do not hinder access to target positions, computation time in any group of robots does not exceed 1 s. In the group of 30 robots in the environment with obstacles, almost completely preventing access to the destination points, path computation time is 7 s. Such mapping approach is applicable for provisional path computation for a group of robots. The advantages of this approach are simplicity of implementation, possibility of extension in terms of the problems being solved, as well feasibility in low-power computing systems.

In the Fig. 5, the resulting configuration is composed of dots in the middle of the scene. All the robots in the group are numbered. The paths were computed in such

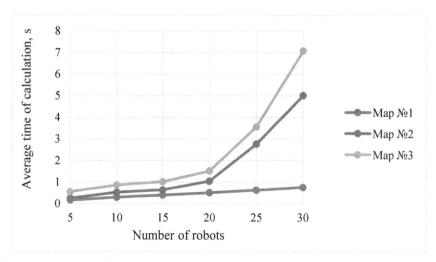

Fig. 4. Dependency of average time of computations from the number of robots in the group.

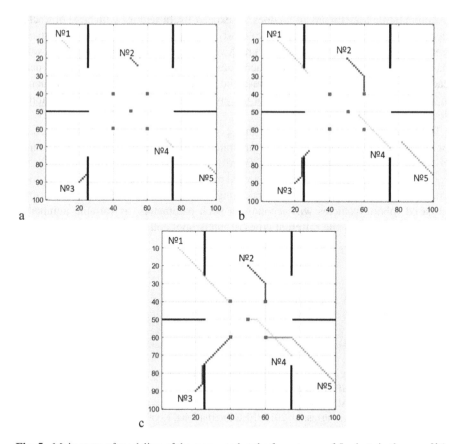

Fig. 5. Main steps of modeling of the computed paths for a group of 5 robots in the map №1.

manner, that the robot could bypass the obstacle along the path of optimal length (robot №3). As follows from the figures, intersection of paths of robots №4 and №5 caused no collisions between them, as at the moment of intersection, the robot №4 already was at a safe distance from the robot №5.

5 Discussion and Conclusion

In this paper a path planning approach for a swarm of robots was proposed. The setting under consideration is an environment with static obstacles. To simplify the representation of the operational environment, the cell decomposition method was chosen, consisting in overlaying of the grid on the working area. The proposed solution for robotic swarm path planning is based on two algorithms: 1) an algorithm for assignment of target coordinates to robots and 2) a modified A* algorithm, extended by the additional clause of graph vertex check, what prevents collisions among the robots.

Based on the developed approach, the motion of robots in groups of 5, 10, 15, 20, 25 and 30 robots was modeled in three different scenes. As follows from the experimental results, in the settings, where the obstacles do not prevent access to target points, the path computation time for any robot does not exceed 1 s. In settings with large obstacles, which prevent the access to target points almost completely, the time of path computation increases because of greater number of graph vertices to be considered. Here this value makes up 7 s. Such path routing approach does not require to compute the robot paths ahead of time. The advantages of the presented approach are simplicity of implementation, possibility of extension in terms of the problems being solved, as well feasibility in low-power computing systems.

The developed path planning algorithm can be used in conjunction with classical approaches to swarm control, as well as integrated into other reconfiguration algorithms. The authors expect that the best practical results will be obtained by combining the proposed algorithm with the method of virtual mutually repulsive forces between robots at small distances. Further research concerning path planning problem for a swarm of land-based robotic vehicles will account for such parameters, as variable number of targets, moving targets and different types of inter-robot collaboration.

References

1. Lee, G., Chong, N.Y., Christensen, H.: Tracking multiple moving targets with swarms of mobile robots. Intell. Serv. Robot. 3(2), 61–72 (2010). https://doi.org/10.1007/s11370-010-0059-2
2. Medvedev, M.Y., Kostjukov, V.A., Pshikhopov, V.K.: Optimization of mobile robot movement on a plane with finite number of repeller sources. SPIIRAS Proc. 19, 43–78 (2020)
3. Malyshev, A.A., Burgov, E.V.: Revisiting parameters of bioinspired behavior models in group foraging modeling. SPIIRAS Proc. 19, 79–103 (2020)
4. Banharnsakun, A., Achalakul, T., Batra, R.C.: Target finding and obstacle avoidance algorithm for microrobot swarms. In: 2012 IEEE International Conference on Systems, Man, and Cybernetics (SMC), pp. 1610–1615 (2012)

5. Kapanoglu, M., Alikalfa, M., Ozkan, M., Parlaktuna, O.: A pattern-based genetic algorithm for multi-robot coverage path planning minimizing completion time. J. Intell. Manuf. **23**(4), 1035–1045 (2012). https://doi.org/10.1007/s10845-010-0404-5
6. Afanasov, A.L.: Analysis of algorithms for avoiding obstacles and finding a path in an a priori uncertain environment for a mobile device. Quest. Sci. Educ. **17**(64) (2019)
7. Kazakov, K.A., Semenov, V.A.: Review of modern methods of traffic planning. In: Proceedings of ISP RAS, pp. 241–294 (2016)
8. Leow, W.Q.: Real time mobile robot route map plan. Doctoral dissertation, Tunku Abdul Rahman University College (2019)
9. Scholar, H.M.R., Gupta, P., Singh, G.: Path planning of an autonomous mobile robot with multiobjective functions. In: 2019 International Conference on Computing, Communication, and Intelligent Systems (ICCCIS), pp. 323–326 (2019)
10. Yu, J., LaValle, S.M.: Optimal multirobot path planning on graphs: complete algorithms and effective heuristics. IEEE Trans. Robot. **32**(5), 1163–1177 (2016)
11. Gammell, J.D., Barfoot, T.D., Srinivasa, S.S.: Informed sampling for asymptotically optimal path planning. IEEE Trans. Robot. **34**(4), 966–984 (2018)
12. Olofsson, J., Hendeby, G., Lauknes, T.R., Johansen, T.A.: Multi-agent informed path planning using the probability hypothesis density. Auton. Robots **44**(6), 913–925 (2020). https://doi.org/10.1007/s10514-020-09904-1
13. Gutiérrez, M.A., Manso, L.J., Núñez, P., Bustos, P.: Planning object informed search for robots in household environments. In: 2018 IEEE International Conference on Autonomous Robot Systems and Competitions (ICARSC), pp. 205–210 (2018)
14. Goyal, J.K., Nagla, K.S.: A new approach of path planning for mobile robots. In: 2014 International Conference on Advances in Computing, Communications and Informatics (ICACCI), pp. 863–867 (2014)
15. Yin, W., Yang, X.: A totally Astar-based multi-path algorithm for the recognition of reasonable route sets in vehicle navigation systems. Proc.-Soc. Behav. Sci. **96**, 1069–1078 (2013)
16. Guruji, A.K., Agarwal, H., Parsediya, D.K.: Time-efficient A* algorithm for robot path planning. Proc. Technol. **23**, 144–149 (2016)
17. Wang, H., Rubenstein, M.: Walk, stop, count, and swap: decentralized multi-agent path finding with theoretical guarantees. IEEE Robot. Autom. Lett. **5**(2), 1119–1126 (2020)
18. Vatamaniuk, I., Panina, G., Saveliev, A., Ronzhin, A.: Convex shape generation by robotic swarm. In: 2016 International Conference on Autonomous Robot Systems and Competitions (ICARSC), pp. 300–304 (2016)

Modeling of Human-Machine Interaction in an Industrial Exoskeleton Control System

Sergey Jatsun, Andrei Malchikov$^{(\boxtimes)}$, Oksana Loktionova, and Andrey Yatsun

Southwest State University, Kursk, Russia
teormeh@inbox.ru, zveroknnp@gmail.com

Abstract. The paper considers the urgent problem of human-machine interaction organizing when controlling the of industrial assistive exoskeleton suit links movement. A method that implements device's drives copy control, which ensures the operator and the exoskeleton movement synchronization is proposed. This method allows transfer the load from operator to exoskeleton mechanical frame, thereby facilitating the industrial workers manual labor. The article describes the human-machine interaction mathematical model and the results of the described system dynamics numerical modeling. The analysis of stiffness of the elastic suspension and controller coefficients influence of the on the assisting device control quality is carried out, and is made on the basis of complex criteria that take into account both positioning accuracy and device usage comfort.

Keywords: Industrial exoskeleton · Human-machine interaction · Control system · Mathematical modeling

1 Introduction

Industrial exoskeletons have already firmly taken their place in the manual labor automatization market [1–4]. This is due to the high efficiency of their use to facilitate the workers of various specialties labor when performing lifting, storage, holding and transfer of goods technological operations. Exoskeletal costumes can reduce fatigue, expand the workers functionality, reduce the probability of injury and the occupational diseases development. The most common exoskeleton constructive scheme is fixed on the body and allows operator to unload hands, compensate back and hip joint bending moments [5–7]. Typically, such devices use various mechanical energy storage devices – springs, dampers, link balances, etc.

In some cases, electromechanical or pneumatic drives are used to compensate the moment in hip or shoulder joints. Less common are devices equipped with full-sized legs that allow transfer the load from operator to supporting surface. Such devices have advantages, including high load capacity, static loads high efficiency, reliability and versatility [6, 7]. The disadvantage of this solution is the significantly greater weight of the device, limitation of mobility, the need for the device exact-tuning to the operator's parameters [8–10]. There are few full-sized exoskeletons equipped with electric drives and, as a rule, they are complicated and not universal. This is due to the complexity of the

© Springer Nature Switzerland AG 2020
A. Ronzhin et al. (Eds.): ICR 2020, LNAI 12336, pp. 116–125, 2020.
https://doi.org/10.1007/978-3-030-60337-3_12

exoskeleton and the operator movements synchronizing, the control systems construction that allows not only not to bother to the operator but also help with the technological operations performing.

Issues related to the study of man-machine interaction and the functioning of the lower limb exoskeleton are considered in the works of the authors [11, 12]. This work is the development of the models and methods described in the articles [13]. We propose the study of full-sized exoskeleton equipped with a copy control system (CCS) leg movement dynamic features, when moving on a movable base.

2   Mathematical Model of Exoskeleton with CCS Equipment

The use of the device hinges electric drives and CCS built on the principles of human-machine interaction, allows reduce the load on the operator, transferring all the payload to the power frame. In this case, the force necessary to bring the system into motion is constant and doesn't depend on the carried load weight.

The task of creating a CCS is complex and requires an integrated approach, therefore, that's why in this article we restrict ourselves to study of the movement of one exoskeleton leg on a movable base in the sagittal plane. The design diagram of the device is shown in Fig. 1.

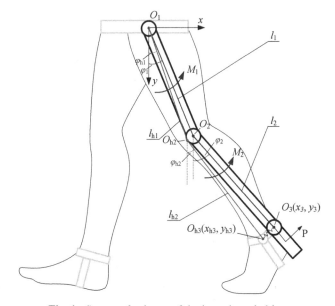

Fig. 1.   Structural scheme of the investigated object.

In this scheme: L_1, L_2 – femur and lower leg of the exoskeleton links respectively, L_{h1}, L_{h2} – the segments between the operator joints centers, respectively, between the knee joint O_{h2} and the ankle O_{h3} and knee and hip O_1. φ_1, φ_2 – absolute angles of the exoskeleton links rotation, $\varphi_{h1}, \varphi_{h2}$ – lower leg and thigh of the operator rotation angles.

We admit that the operator limb movement occurs under the influence of muscular forces and does not depend on the exoskeleton position. The exoskeleton links movement of occurs under the action of torques M_1, M_2 – developed by the exoskeleton drive system. The exoskeleton leg is fixed at a point O_1 that coincides with the origin of the fixed reference frame. The foot of the operator and the links of the exoskeleton are connected by means of a two-coordinate measuring cuff. The cuff contains elastic elements that determine the interaction force P.

The control task is reduced to the realization of the required interaction force provided by the synchronous movement of exoskeleton and limb units. To achieve this, the CCS a structural diagram of which is shown in Fig. 2 is proposed.

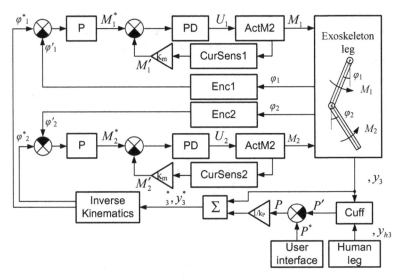

Fig. 2. Copy control system structural scheme.

The principle of control system operation is as follows. During moving, the operator's leg encounters the exoskeleton resistance, which is recorded by the elastic elements of the measuring cuff (Cuff). The measured force between the operator's foot and the exoskeleton P' is compared with the value P^* specified by the user. Further, the force value P is translated into the required deformation and is summed with the current coordinates of the point $O_3(x_3, y_3)$. Thus, if the desired force and current are equal, then the position of the point O_3 is saved. If the effort is different, then the links tend to occupy a position in which the error in effort will be zero. After determining the desired coordinates x_3^*, y_3^* sing the block IK (inverse kinematics) are formed the desired values of the links rotation angles φ_1^*, φ_2^*. Further, the desired values of the rotation angle are compared with the current values of the angles φ_1' and φ_2' measured by the encoders (Enc1, Enc2). Then, the obtained error values are transmitted to the torque control loops, where the feedback channels are implemented using current sensors (CurSens1, CurSens2) on the electric drive motors armature windings (ActM1, ActM2).

Such an implementation of the CCS can be described by the following equations:

$$U_i^k = k_{pM}\left(M_i^* - M_i'\right)_k + k_{dM}\left(\frac{\left(M_i^* - M_i'\right)_k - \left(M_i^* - M_i'\right)_{k-1}}{\Delta t}\right), \quad (1)$$

where $M_i^* = k_{p\phi}\left(\varphi_i^* - \varphi_i'\right)$ – i-th drive set torque, $M_i' = k_m I_i$ – i-th drive measured moment, k_{pM}, k_{dM} – the coefficients of the PD controller of the control loop by the moment, $k_{p\phi}$ – the loop angle P-controller coefficient, φ_i^* – desired rotation angle, φ_i' – the i-th link measured rotation angle, k_m – motor torque coefficient determined by motor and gearbox parameters, I_i – i-th drive anchor current.

φ_i^* is determined in solving the inverse kinematics problem in the following way:

$$\phi_1 = \begin{cases} arctng\left(\frac{y_3}{x_3}\right) + \arccos\left(\frac{l_1^2 - l_2^2 + \left(x_3^2 + y_3^2\right)}{2l_1\sqrt{x_3^2 + y_3^2}}\right) & \text{if } (x_3 > 0) \\ arctng\left(\frac{y_3}{x_3}\right) + \arccos\left(\frac{l_1^2 - l_2^2 + \left(x_3^2 + y_3^2\right)}{2l_1\sqrt{x_3^2 + y_3^2}}\right) - \pi & \text{if } (x_3 \le 0) \end{cases}, \quad (2)$$

$$\phi_2 = \phi_1 + \left(\pi + \arccos\left(\frac{l_1^2 + l_2^2 - \left(x_3^2 + y_3^2\right)}{2l_1 l_2}\right)\right). \quad (3)$$

Using Eqs. (2) and (3), the links rotation absolute angles when the point O_3 moves in the lower quadrants of the coordinate plane can be determined ($y_3 < 0$).

Next, let's consider in detail the method of obtaining the desired coordinates x_3^*, y_3^*.

The device shown in Fig. 3, consists of the following main parts: 1 – displacement sensor (horizontal), 2 – movable mounting base (horizontal), 3 – textile slings for attaching the limb, 4 – movable base (vertical), 5 – elastic elements of the cuff suspension. The displacement sensor (vertical) is located on the flip side and is not shown in Fig. 3.

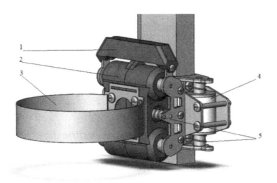

Fig. 3. Two-coordinate measuring cuff.

The cuff works as follows. When moving, the operator acts through textile straps of the cuff 3 on the measuring module, which consists of two movable springs, fixed with the help of springs 5, the bases 2 and 4, which move along the respective guides.

Displacements are recorded by appropriate sensors. The cuff mount is fixed to the link by means of a hinge. We assume that the cuff is always oriented in the same way, and the component forces are determined in absolute coordinates regardless of the position of the link. In fact, the position of the cuff will be determined by the orientation of the foot, which is not considered in this work. In practice, the cuff rotation angle relative to the link can be easily determined by a sensor placed in the hinge, after which the force components can be easily recounted, therefore this assumption is correct.

Further, considering the stiffness coefficients of the suspension springs (c_{3x}, c_{3y}) equal and measuring the relative displacement of the attachment point of the leg relative to the exoskeleton, we can determine the strength of the resistance to movement as follows:

$$P = \sqrt{P_x^2 + P_y^2} = \sqrt{c_{3x}(x_{h3} - x_3)^2 + c_{3y}(y_{h3} - y_3)^2}, \tag{4}$$

where P_x, P_y are the horizontal and vertical components of the force acting between the exoskeleton and the operator, respectively. The transition from displacement to force is necessary for the intuitiveness of setting the required force resistance or assisting during exoskeleton work.

In the general case, the user can set any value of force P^*, as a function of time, links rotation angle and other estimated system parameters. In [12], it was shown how this approach can be used to create an assisting effort that helps with walking. In the framework of this study, we will assume that the desired resistance force $P^* = 0$ the device should move in a way as to minimizing the movement resistance of the operator limb [12].

The next system's work stage is the calculation of the point O_3 required coordinates for implementation of a given force P, for this the inertial reference system projections on the axis followed by conversion into coordinates are determined:

$$x_3^* = x_3 + k_P P \sin(\gamma), \quad y_3^* = y_3 + k_P P \cos(\gamma), \tag{5}$$

where x_3, y_3 – are the current coordinates of the point O_3, and – is the angle of force application defined as:

$$\gamma = \arcsin\left(\frac{P_x}{\sqrt{P_x^2 + P_y^2}}\right). \tag{6}$$

Further, the angles x_3^*, y_3^* are transmitted to the electric drive regulators, where they are worked out by driving the exoskeleton leg links.

The driving action of the operator's legs, which can be represented by the trajectory of the point $O_{h3}(x_{h3}, y_{h3})$, acts as a driving influence initiating the movement of the exoskeleton during modeling. The method for specifying the trajectory of a point's motion based on a piecewise polynomial function is described in detail in other works of the authors. Here we show the final view of the point O_{h3} trajectory (Fig. 4).

To describe the movement of exoskeleton links under the action of torques, the differential equation will be used in the following form: $\mathbf{M}(q)\ddot{\mathbf{q}} + \mathbf{V}(q, \ddot{q}) + \mathbf{G}(q) = Q$.

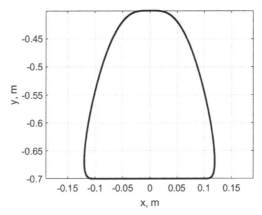

Fig. 4. The trajectory of the point O_{h3} during step described by the parameters: step width 0.2 m, step height 0.3 m.

In this equation, $\mathbf{M}(q)$ – is the inertia matrix, $\mathbf{V}(q, \dot{q})$ – is the vector of generalized inertia forces, $\mathbf{G}(q)$ – is the vector of gravity acting on the links.

$$\mathbf{M}(q) = \begin{bmatrix} \frac{m_1 l_1^2}{3} + m_2 l_1^2 & \frac{m_2}{2} l_1 l_2 \cos(\phi_1 - \phi_2) \\ \frac{m_2}{2} l_1 l_2 \cos(\phi_1 - \phi_2) & \frac{m_2 l_2^2}{3} \end{bmatrix}, \tag{7}$$

$$\mathbf{V}(q, \dot{q}) = \begin{bmatrix} \dot{\phi}_2^2 \frac{m_2}{2} l_1 l_2 \sin(\phi_1 - \phi_2) \\ \dot{\phi}_1^2 \frac{m_2}{2} l_1 l_2 \sin(\phi_1 - \phi_2) \end{bmatrix}, \quad \mathbf{G}(q) = \begin{bmatrix} -\left(m_2 + \frac{m_1}{2}\right) g l_1 \cos \phi_1 \\ -m_2 g \frac{l_2}{2} \cos \phi_2 \end{bmatrix}. \tag{8}$$

$\mathbf{Q}$ – vector of external forces acting on the mechanism:

$$\mathbf{Q} = \begin{bmatrix} M_1 - PL_1 \sin(\gamma - \phi_1) \\ M_2 - PL_2 \sin(\gamma - \phi_2) \end{bmatrix}. \tag{9}$$

Using the obtained equations, we can investigate the dynamics of the human-machine interaction of a person and an exoskeleton.

3   The Results of Numerical Simulation of the CCS

To implement this task, a modeling program was developed in the Matlab. The model parameters used in the simulation are shown in Table 1.

When evaluating the operation of the copying control system, two factors are important:

– the magnitude of the force that arises between the operator and the exoskeleton, it is important: both the integral assessment of the forces $P_I = \frac{1}{T} \int_0^T |P - P^*| dt$ and the limiting values of the force P_{MAX};

Table 1. Mathematical model parameters.

Parameter name	Designation	Value
First link length	L_1	0,44 m
Second link length	L_2	0,44 m
First link mass	m_1	8 kg
Second link mass	m_1	8 kg
Torque constant	k_m	13.9 Nm/A

- the magnitude of the executive link movement mismatch of the exoskeleton and the operator. Here, both the error in the angle $\varepsilon_i = \phi_{hi} - \phi_i$ for each link and the positioning error of the output link $\Delta_3 = \sqrt{(x_{h3} - x_3)^2 + (y_{h3} - y_3)^{-2}}$ can be estimated directly. Since the process is continuous but periodic, it is also convenient to present the error estimate in the form of an integral and maximum values:

$$\varepsilon_I = \frac{1}{T} \int_0^T |\varepsilon| dt, \tag{11}$$

$$\Delta_I = \frac{1}{T} \int_0^T |\Delta_3| dt. \tag{12}$$

Since an increase in stiffness on the one hand reduces the error, on the other hand, it increases the strength, we will try to introduce a complex criterion, with weight coefficients providing an equal contribution to the resulting graph.

Also, preliminary results showed (expected) that the errors in x and y behave the same, so it is proposed to make an estimate based on their vector sum. Thus, to assess the impact of customizable system parameters on the quality of the CCS, let's introduce a complex criterion:

$$In = In(\bar{a}) = \alpha_1 P_I + \alpha_2 P_{MAX} + \alpha_3 \varepsilon_I + \alpha_3 \Delta_I, \tag{13}$$

where α_1, α_2, α_3, α_4 – weight coefficients.

The parameters that determine the CCS nonlinear properties can be divided into unchanged, for example, masses, friction coefficients, etc. and variable, forming a vector $\bar{a} = (k_p, c_3)$. In the space of these parameters, we carry out a series of computational experiments to determine the response surface.

As the simulation results showed in Fig. 5, with an increase in stiffness (c_3), the force values increase at the attachment point of the exoskeleton to the operator's foot – which reduces the comfort of use, however, a decrease in stiffness leads to a decrease in positioning accuracy, which can be compensated by an increase in the controller proportional coefficient (k_p). To ensure the stability of the CCS and prevent the oscillatory nature of the movement of the links, it is necessary to use either mechanical damping structural elements or the introduction of a differential component of the regulator.

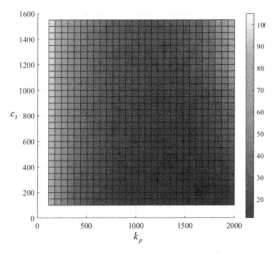

Fig. 5. The values of the complex criterion in the space of stiffness parameters and the CCS coefficient of proportionality.

In Fig. 6 shows the simulation results for $\bar{a} = (1500, 800)$ (such parameter values correspond good quality of the transient process according to Fig. 5 and can be provided technically).

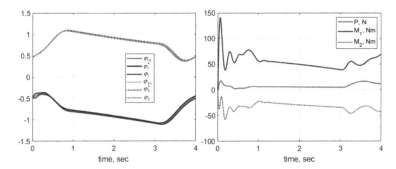

Fig. 6. Simulation results of exoskeleton links joint and operator limbs movement.

In Fig. 6, the following designations are adopted: φ_{1h}, φ_{2h} – angles of rotation, respectively, of the operator's femur and lower leg (rad), φ_1^*, φ_2^* – desired angles of rotation of the femoral link and the lower leg link (rad), φ_1, φ_2 – actual angles of rotation (rad), M_1, M_2 – actuators torques (Nm), P – the resulting force between humans leg and exoskeleton (N).

As the results of modeling the system showed, the positioning errors $\varepsilon_i = |\varphi_{ih} - \varphi_i|(i = 1, 2)$ does not exceed 2.9° for femur link and 0.35° for lower leg link, while the maximum force exerted by the exoskeleton P does not exceed 18 N. In this mode, the linear displacement of the elastic suspension is 22.5 mm, which is easily achievable in the design of the measuring cuff presented in the work.

4   Conclusions

The paper presents a mathematical model of human-machine interaction between the operator's legs and the links of an industrial exoskeleton equipped with a copying automatic control system. The structure of the control system is considered. Algorithms for calculating the driving actions for the device's motors are considered. The presented mathematical model allows study the collaborative functioning of the operator and exoskeleton, to optimize the regulator parameters and the design of the measuring cuff, for which a complex criterion was taken into account according to the values of the operator movement resistance forces and the accuracy of executive links positioning. The obtained results indicate the need to use a suspension with the lowest stiffness indicators, and to achieve the required accuracy due to the CCS regulator coefficients, however, in practice, the use of excessively soft elastic elements with a significant stroke is difficult, because it can cause discomfort for the user with others not considered in the framework work modes. Therefore, in each specific case, it is necessary to carry out numerical modeling and search for optimal controller parameters at acceptable stiffness values, for which we can use the method and quality criterion for the device proposed in the work functioning.

Acknowledgments. The work was supported by RFBR, research project № 19-08-00440, Andrei Malchikov was supported by the President grant, project MK-780.2020.8.

References

1. Young, A.J., Ferris, D.P.: State of the art and future directions for lower limb robotic exoskeletons. IEEE Trans. Neural Syst. Rehabil. Eng. **25**(2), 171–182 (2016)
2. Yamamoto, K., Hyodo, K., Ishii, M., Matsuo, T.: Development of power assisting suit for assisting nurse labor. JSME Int. J. Ser. C **45**(3), 703–711 (2002)
3. Anam, K., Al-Jumaily, A.A.: Active exoskeleton control systems: state of the art. Proc. Eng. **41**, 988–994 (2012)
4. Heo, P., et al.: Current hand exoskeleton technologies for rehabilitation and assistive engineering. Int. J. Precis. Eng. Manuf. **13**(5), 807–824 (2012). https://doi.org/10.1007/s12541-012-0107-2
5. Aguirre-Ollinger, G., Colgate, J.E., Peshkin, M.A., Goswami, A.: Active-impedance control of a lower-limb assistive exoskeleton. In: IEEE 10th International Conference on Rehabilitation Robotics, ICORR 2007, pp. 188–195. IEEE (2007)
6. Seo, K., et al.: Fully autonomous hip exoskeleton saves metabolic cost of walking. In: 2016 IEEE International Conference on Robotics and Automation (ICRA), pp. 4628–4635. IEEE (2016)
7. Wu, Q., Wang, X., Du, F., Zhang, X.: Design and control of a powered hip exoskeleton for walking assistance. Int. J. Adv. Rob. Syst. **12**(3), 18 (2015)
8. Kawamoto, H., Kanbe, S., Sankai, Y.: Power assist method for HAL-3 estimating operator's intention based on motion information. In: Proceedings of the 12th IEEE International Workshop on Robot and Human Interactive Communication, ROMAN 2003, pp. 67–72. IEEE (2003)
9. Huysamen, K., et al.: Assessment of an active industrial exoskeleton to aid dynamic lifting and lowering manual handling tasks. Appl. Ergon. **68**, 125–131 (2018)

10. Yatsun, A., Jatsun, S.: Investigation of human cargo handling in industrial exoskeleton. In: 2018 Global Smart Industry Conference (GloSIC), pp. 1–5. IEEE, November 2018
11. Jatsun, S., Malchikov, A., Yatsun, A.: Investigation of movements of lower-limb assistive industrial device. In: Ronzhin, A., Rigoll, G., Meshcheryakov, R. (eds.) ICR 2019. LNCS (LNAI), vol. 11659, pp. 226–235. Springer, Cham (2019). https://doi.org/10.1007/978-3-030-26118-4_22
12. Jatsun, S., Malchikov, A., Yatsun, A.: Comparative analysis of the industrial exoskeleton control systems. In: Ronzhin, A., Shishlakov, V. (eds.) Proceedings of 14th International Conference on Electromechanics and Robotics "Zavalishin's Readings". SIST, vol. 154, pp. 63–74. Springer, Singapore (2020). https://doi.org/10.1007/978-981-13-9267-2_6
13. Mal'chikov, A.V., Yatsun, S.F., Yatsun, A.S.: Mathematical modeling of copying control by a robotic unit with a linear electric drive with an elastic link. J. Mach. Manuf. Reliab. **48**(5), 408–415 (2019). https://doi.org/10.3103/S1052618819050054
14. Wehner, M., Rempel, D., Kazerooni, H.: Lower extremity exoskeleton reduces back forces in lifting. In: ASME 2009 Dynamic Systems and Control Conference, pp. 49–56. American Society of Mechanical Engineers Digital Collection (2009)
15. Pratt, G.A., Williamson, M.M.: Series elastic actuators. In: Proceedings of the 1995 IEEE/RSJ International Conference on Intelligent Robots and Systems 1995. Human Robot Interaction and Cooperative Robots', vol. 1, pp. 399–406. IEEE (1995)
16. Ortega, R., Kelly, R., Loria, A.: A class of output feedback globally stabilizing controllers for flexible joints robots. IEEE Trans. Robot. Autom. **11**(5), 766–770 (1995)

Gesture-Based Intelligent User Interface for Control of an Assistive Mobile Information Robot

Ildar Kagirov[1] ⓘ, Dmitry Ryumin[1(✉)] ⓘ, and Miloš Železný[2] ⓘ

[1] St. Petersburg Institute for Informatics and Automation of the Russian Academy of Sciences,
14th Line, 39, 199178 St. Petersburg, Russia
`kagirov@iias.spb.su`, `dl_03.03.1991@mail.ru`
[2] University of West Bohemia, Pilsen, Czech Republic
`zelezny@kky.zcu.cz`

Abstract. This article presents a gesture-based user interface for a robotic shopping trolley. The trolley is designed as a mobile robotic platform helping customers in shops and supermarkets. Among the main functions are: navigating through the store, providing information on availability and location, and transporting the items bought. One of important features of the developed interface is the gestural modality, or, more precisely, Russian sign language elements recognition system. The notion of the interface design, as well as interaction strategy, are presented in flowcharts, it was made an attempt to demonstrate the gestural modality as a natural part of an assistive information robot. Besides, a short overview of mobile robots is given in the paper, and CNN-based technique of gesture recognition is provided. The Russian sign language recognition option is of high importance due to a relatively large number of native speakers (signers).

Keywords: Sign language · Gesture recognition · Computer vision · Machine learning · Intelligent interface · Assistive technology · Mobile information robot

1 Introduction

1.1 The Aim of the Paper

This article presents a gesture-based user interface designed to control a smart mobile service robot. The main tasks the authors set in this paper was to demonstrate how the interface is embedded in the overall control system, how the gesture recognition is performed and why gesture modality is important for robotics nowadays. Special attention is paid to gesture recognition technique and interaction strategy.

Before we go any further, it is important to briefly define the context that gave birth to the idea of such an interface design, i.e. give reader the notion of the mobile service robot the user interface is applied to. The robot at issue is a smart shopping cart that helps customers in supermarkets to find the goods they would like to collect. Among the main functions are: navigating through the store, providing information on availability and location, and transporting the items bought.

© Springer Nature Switzerland AG 2020
A. Ronzhin et al. (Eds.): ICR 2020, LNAI 12336, pp. 126–134, 2020.
https://doi.org/10.1007/978-3-030-60337-3_13

Needless to say, implementation of this kind of shopping carts will help to save the time and effort of the customers, because navigating through a supermarket looking for products of interest can be quite a tricky task. Being straightforward, the idea of combining a service robot with a shopping cart seems nevertheless quite reasonable.

The term "intelligent human-machine interface" is understood as interface that uses artificial intelligence technologies [1, 2]. Intelligent user interfaces allow increasing the autonomy of the device and contribute to the naturalness and ergonomics of human-machine interaction; thus, the user is free to use the ways of interaction that are convenient, or natural for certain situations. The second aspect, namely, contribution to the ergonomics and naturalness, is important when the robotic system is designed to interact with human users. A robotic shopping cart is a good example of such robotic platform, being the natural choice to implement an intelligent interface.

The presented interface makes use of deep neural networks to recognize elements of Russian sign language. Current service robots often have speech, face, facial expressions recognition systems, etc. Moreover, there are currently assistive robots which can interact with the user using sign languages [3–5]. Nevertheless, there are no robotic platforms that support Russian sign language recognition. It is worth mentioning, that the total number of Russian sign language native signers was estimated as more than 120000 in 2010 [6]. There are no recent statistics concerning the number of Russian sign language speakers. Some organizations, such as [7] estimate the overall number at 341000 (for Russia and Kazakhstan). Nowadays, Russian sign language is officially recognized as one of the languages of communication in the Russian Federation.

1.2 Overview of Mobile Service Robots

Mobile robotics is one of the most rapidly growing industries, combining information technology and artificial intelligence with cognitive science. At the current stage of development such interdisciplinary interaction makes it possible to design quite complex mechanisms for new generation mobile robot interaction of a with the environment. Mobile robots are able to move and perform certain actions autonomously without human intervention. Such opportunities allow fast development of service robotics. In particular, logistics robots [8] or exoskeletons [9] are in demand at various industries or by older people with disabilities. Automation of logistics processes can also be increased by a rather large number of various robotic platforms which previously required manual control. For example, it is possible to implement contactless control of trolley in hypermarkets by advanced computer vision and machine learning technologies.

Examples of successful application of logistics robots can be found, for example, in the hotel business. The robot courier «Jeeves» from the German company «Robotise» [10] is equipped with 3D optical vision, as well as a set of sensors. This connection allows it to move in a multistorey building and use elevators due to a wireless connection. In addition, it is modular and can be supplemented with various containers (for example, a basket for cool drinks). This approach allows a single base system to be used use, which can be supplemented or expanded for special tasks. In the near future, the company will plan to use this approach for robots in hospitals and industrial environments.

The evolution of robotic platforms is also influenced by the development of artificial intelligence. With the help of artificial intelligence technologies, it is possible to solve various cognitive, social, linguistic, and psychological problems of people. For example, with the help of natural and universal methods of exchanging information (gestures and speech), it is possible to develop interactive information systems for the tasks of human-machine interaction. The largest Japanese vehicle manufacturer Toyota has been developing mobile social robots with artificial intelligence since 2006. In July 2015, at an exhibition in Japan as part of the «Partner Robot Family» project [11], the company introduced the Human Support Robot (HSR) which focused on helping people with disabilities in everyday life and communication («assistive technologies»). The HSR is controlled by voice commands, gestures or a graphical interface based on a mobile device (smartphone, tablet) and is aimed at solving tasks such as opening doors, turning on lights, grabbing items, or delivering (for example, water bottles or tablets). In addition, the robot is equipped with telepresence and remote-control functions, which facilitates third-party care of a people with disabilities. The remaining technical details of the HSR hardware design and software architecture are described in more detail in [12, 13]. In turn, the American space agency National Aeronautics and Space Administration (NASA) is developing a gesture-controlled space robot assistant «Mars 2020 Rover» [14] as a part of the «Mars 2020» program, aimed at Mars exploration.

In recent years, the focus of world leading research centers and companies has been shifted to development of mobile information robots, which are based on multimodal human-machine interaction.

2   Robotic Trolley: Interacting with the User

The design of the interface of the robotic trolley is schematically shown in Fig. 1. The main three modalities (sensory, speech and gesture) are used to interact with the customer: sensory gestural and voice. All the input channels are functionally equivalent, and it is ultimately the choice of the user, which channel to use. The video feedback is provided via signing 3D avatar and gesture synthesis techniques [15].

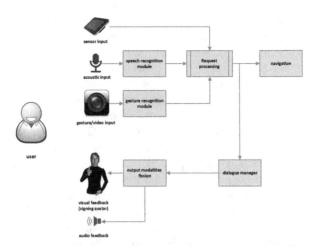

Fig. 1. A flowchart presenting the main interface modalities.

The flowchart in Fig. 2 presents the scenario tree for the actions of the robot. After processing the initial request, the shopping cart starts navigating through the store constantly determining its location based on the Monte Carlo method. On completing the full cycle, the robot comes back to the base and waits for new requests.

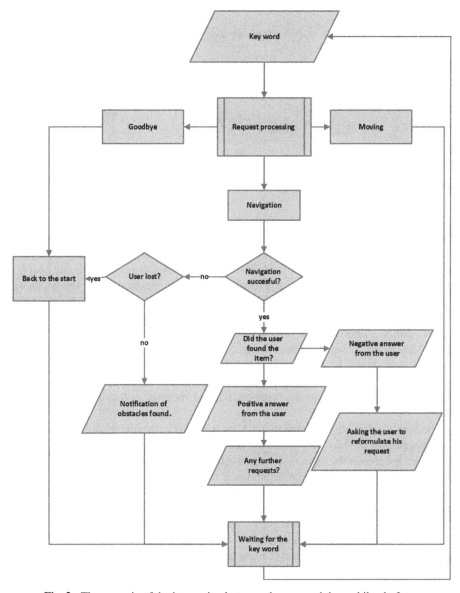

Fig. 2. The scenario of the interaction between the user and the mobile platform.

Basically, there are two ways the request is processed: either by finding out keywords from the input signal (gestural or acoustic modality) and comparing them with the elements of the dictionary, or by direct processing of sensory commands. The latter way is supported by the sensor user interface, which allows the customer choosing products or departments from a list (see Fig. 3):

Fig. 3. Examples of the touchscreen interface.

The system uses three dictionaries: the dictionary of goods, the dictionary of departments, the dictionary of commands. The dictionary of goods contains general names of goods such as "sugar", "coffee", "pasta", "bread", etc. The content of the dictionary of goods is based on the list of products defined for a particular store. The ultimate goal of the search algorithm is to determine a specific location in the shop where the goods of requested type can be found.

The dictionary of departments contains "departments" names of a given store; in fact, these are groups of goods of the same type ("confectionery", "meat", "dairy products", "drinks", etc.) In addition, the same dictionary contains such locations as checkout, exit, toilet, etc.

The third dictionary of commands is required for effective interaction with the user. It includes lexical units from the semantic field of movement, location requests and orders.

The sensory modality is implemented via a touchscreen device; the principles of voice recognition used for this device are presented in details in our work [5]. And the gesture recognition is the topic of the next section. Here one should only mention, that main tool the gesture recognition technique is based on, is the RuSLan database [16], containing 164 lexical units demonstrated by 13 signers, each with 5 iterations. The duration of the video data is about 8 h. The initial list of lexical items was built up by exporting text files from navigation menus of main Russian supermarkets websites. All the units containing specific brand names, were erased from the list. The names of goods that are not very popular among Russian consumers, as well as fingerspelled names, were removed from the vocabulary too.

Although the presented user interface is sign-language oriented, one should highlight the innovative potential of this kind of interaction with the user. The use of gesture interfaces has the following advantages:

1. Gesture control is generally more helpful in large, noisy environments, than voice control.
2. The inventory of lexical units can be changed in favor of situation-oriented, everyday gestures which are widespread and familiar to hearing users; nonverbal communication is an integral part of human communication, including body language, gestures etc.

3   Gesture Recognition

The functional diagram of video analysis of hand movements for recognition of gestures of Russian Sign Language is presented in Fig. 4.

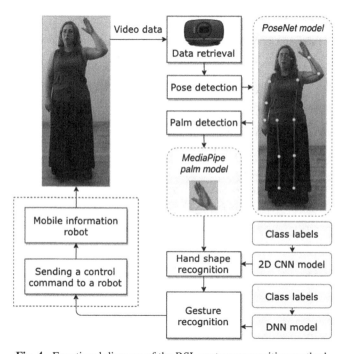

Fig. 4. Functional diagram of the RSL gesture recognition method.

The input data is a sequence of color (RGB) video frames received from an optical camera. The video stream has a RGB color rendering of 8 bits with resolution of 1920 × 1080 pixels (FullHD), and 30 frames per second. At the first stage, the PoseNet model [17] searches for people [18] and calculates their 2D 27-point models. The PoseNet model is included in an open source software library TensorFlow 2.

The next stage is aimed at forming a rectangular area with the left palm of a person. To do this, a new approach is used, which is implemented in an open source cross-platform environment MediaPipe [19]. This tool allows various architectures of deep neural networks to build with their further training and use on robotic complexes. So, in the case of tracking hands the model operates inside a system that sequentially processes the input video signal. In particular, a palm detector model accepts a rectangular area with a person as an input and returns the bounding box coordinates for the area of the hand.

The next step is to determine a hand shape using a 2D Convolutional Neural Network (CNN). To determine the optimal result, we tested various CNN architectures, which are included in the object recognition module of an open source library Keras [20]. The process of transfer learning of Deep CNNs was carried out using labeled data (see the LabelImg tool [21]) with hand shapes from TheRuSLan database (18 one-handed gestures were chosen for learning). The dataset was divided into training and testing samples in an approximate ratio of 10:3 demonstrators (80:20%). The results of a comparative analysis of trained models of CNNs that exceeded an accuracy value of 70% are presented in Table 1.

Table 1. Comparative analysis of trained models of 2D CNN.

Model	Best accuracy, %
Xception	71.17
VGG16	79.03
VGG19	81.45
ResNet50	75.32
ResNet50V2	77.94
InceptionV3	72.58
MobileNetV2	79.16
NASNetMobile	74.72
EfficientNetB0	77.14
EfficientNetB4	80.91
EfficientNetB7	82.25

Thus, during the experiments it was revealed that, the optimal option in the hand shape classification task is a convolutional neural network with the EfficientNetB7 architecture [22].

The result is Russian sign language elements recognition using a fully connected deep neural network. In a broader sense, the input parameters of the neural network are the characteristics of the gesture, in particular: the hand shape is an integer; normalized 2D Euclidean distances between skeletal points, as shown in the functional diagram (see Fig. 4). The average recognition accuracy of 18 one-handed gestures from TheRuSLan database was 85.04%. This result will be considered to be a baseline for a given selection of gestures from TheRuSLan database.

It is important to emphasize that described the automatic technology for video analysis of movements and gesture recognition using an optical camera for tasks of human-machine interaction. The considered architectures of neural networks in the future can be replaced by their more advanced analogues, which does not change the approach to recognition gestures in general.

4 Conclusions

In this paper we presented the design of a gesture-based intelligent user interface for control of an assistive mobile information robot (robotic shopping cart), that comprises gesture (Russian sign language), acoustic speech and sensory modalities, as well as developed technique for real-time gesture recognition with MediaPipe environment and deep CNNs. The gesture-based interface is shown as integral part of human-machine interaction, and the need for this modality is justified: nonverbal communication is an important part of everyday human communication, and development of gesture and body-language friendly interfaces would greatly benefit the mobile and social robotics industry. A presentation of hardware, large-scale Russian sign language dictionary, as well as gesture synthesis (such as signing avatar) are meant for further research and experiments.

Acknowledgements. This research is financially supported by the Ministry of Science and Higher Education of the Russian Federation, agreement No. 14.616.21.0095 (reference RFMEFI61618X0095) and by the Ministry of Education of the Czech Republic, project No. LTARF18017.

References

1. Antsaklis, P.J., Passino, K.M. (eds.): An Introduction to Intelligent and Autonomous Control. Kluwer Academic Publishers, Norwell (1993)
2. Shcherbatov, I.A.: Intellectual control of robotic systems in conditions of uncertainty. Vestnik Astrakhanskogo gosudarstvennogo tekhnicheskogo universiteta 1, 73–77 (2010). (in Russian)
3. Falconer, J.: Humanoid Robot Demonstrates Sign Language. https://spectrum.ieee.org/aut omaton/robotics/humanoids/ntu-taiwan-humanoid-sign-language
4. Kose, H., Yorganci, R.: Tale of a robot: humanoid robot assisted sign language tutoring. In: Proceedings of 11th IEEE-RAS International Conference on Humanoid Robots, Bled, Slovenia, 26–28 October 2011, pp. 105-111 (2011)
5. Hoshino, K. Kawabuchi, I.: A humanoid robotic hand performing the sign language motions. In: Proceedings of 2003 International Symposium on Micromechatronics and Human Science (MHS-2003), Tsukuba, Japan, pp. 89–94 (2003)
6. Ethnologue Russian Sign Language Report. https://www.ethnologue.com/language/rsl
7. Joshua Project. https://joshuaproject.net/people_groups/19007/RS
8. Ryumin, D., Ivanko, D., Axyonov, A., Kagirov, I., Karpov, A., Zelezny, M.: Human-robot interaction with smart shopping trolley using sign language: data collection. In: 2019 IEEE International Conference on Pervasive Computing and Communications Workshops (PerCom Workshops), pp. 949–954 (2019)
9. Kagirov I., et al.: Lower limbs exoskeleton control system based on intelligent human-machine interface. In: Kotenko, I., Badica, C., Desnitsky, V., El Baz, D., Ivanovic, M. (eds.) IDC 2019. SCI, vol. 868, pp. 457–466. Springer, Cham (2020). https://doi.org/10.1007/978-3-030-32258-8_54

10. The service robot for the hospitality industry has arrived: JEEVES. https://jeeves.robotise.eu. Accessed 14 June 2020
11. Toyota Global Frontier Research. https://www.toyota-global.com/innovation/partner_robot/. Accessed 14 June 2020
12. Yamamoto, T., et al.: Human support robot as research platform of domestic mobile manipulator. In: Chalup, S., Niemueller, T., Suthakorn, J., Williams, M.-A. (eds.) RoboCup 2019. LNCS (LNAI), vol. 11531, pp. 457–465. Springer, Cham (2019). https://doi.org/10.1007/978-3-030-35699-6_37
13. Yamamoto, T., et al.: Development of Human Support Robot as the research platform of a domestic mobile manipulator. ROBOMECH J. 6(1), 4 (2019). https://doi.org/10.1186/s40648-019-0132-3
14. Mars 2020 Perseverance Rover – NASA Mars. https://mars.nasa.gov/mars2020/. Accessed 14 June 2020
15. Hrúz, M., Campr, P., Krňoul, Z., Železný, M., Aran, O., Santemiz, P.: Multi-modal dialogue system with sign language capabilities. In: The Proceedings of the 13th International ACM SIGACCESS conference on Computers and Accessibility, ASSETS 2011, pp. 265–266. Association for Computing Machinery, New York (2011)
16. Kagirov, I., Ryumin, D.A., Axyonov, A.A., Karpov, A.A.: Multimedia database of russian sign language items in 3D. Voprosy Jazykoznanija 1, 104–123 (2020)
17. Pose Estimation. https://www.tensorflow.org/lite/models/pose_estimation/overview. Accessed 14 June 2020
18. Papandreou, G., Zhu, T., Chen, L.C., Gidaris, S., Tompson, J., Murphy, K.: PersonLab: person pose estimation and instance segmentation with a bottom-up, part-based, geometric embedding model. In: Ferrari, V., Hebert, M., Sminchisescu, C., Weiss, Y. (eds.) ECCV 2018. LNCS, vol. 11218, pp. 269–286. Springer, Cham (2018). https://doi.org/10.1007/978-3-030-01264-9_17
19. Lugaresi, C., et al.: MediaPipe: A Framework for Building Perception Pipelines, pp. 1–286. arXiv preprint arXiv:1906.08172 (2019)
20. Keras Applications. https://keras.io/api/applications/. Accessed 14 June 2020
21. LabelImg is a graphical image annotation tool. https://github.com/tzutalin/labelImg. Accessed 14 June 2020
22. Tan, M., Le, Q.V.: EfficientNet: rethinking model scaling for convolutional neural networks. arXiv preprint arXiv:1905.11946 (2019)

Distributed Methods for Autonomous Robot Groups Fault-Tolerant Management

Igor Kalyaev[1], Eduard Melnik[2], and Anna Klimenko[3](✉)

[1] Southern Federal University, 105/42 Bolshaya Sadovaya Street, 344006 Rostov-on-Don, Russia

[2] Federal Research Centre, the Southern Scientific Centre of the Russian Academy of Sciences, 41, Chekhov Street, 344006 Rostov-on-Don, Russian Federation

[3] Scientific Research Institute of Multiprocessor Computer Systems of Southern Federal University, 2, Chekhov Street, 347922 Taganrog, Russian Federation
anna_klimenko@mail.ru

Abstract. The current paper deals with the problem of fault tolerant failure detection in the groups of autonomous and mobile robots. To reach an efficient solution it is proposed to use fault tolerant consensus methods from the area of distributed ledger technologies, including the distributed leader and leaderless types of consensus. To use the abovementioned methods some modifications of the latter are proposed and discussed, as well as some estimations have been made from the energy consumption point of view.

Keywords: Robot groups · Distributed ledger · Fault-tolerance · Consensus

1 Introduction

A problem of fault detection and diagnosis (FDD) for groups of mobile and cooperative robots is topical and relatively new. To the best of our knowledge, only a few surveys, devoted to the problem of FDD have been presented in recent years [1, 2]. Also some new works, devoted to the problem of FDD for multi robot systems, are presented in [3, 4].

The problem of multirobot fault detection in comparison with the single robot one poses some peculiarities and challenges:

- global system knowledge depends on local beliefs of individual robots (derived from their sensors);
- the process of global decision-making and the creation of a global multi-robot plan may result in a faulty plan;
- a complete FDD mechanism is expected to diagnose the faulty components of the robot.

The essential problem of the FDD for multi robot systems is described in a comprehensive manner in the work [5]: each robot senses its local environment and generates individual beliefs. These beliefs are communicated to the global scope for global belief

A. Ronzhin et al. (Eds.): ICR 2020, LNAI 12336, pp. 135–147, 2020.
https://doi.org/10.1007/978-3-030-60337-3_14

generation. Individual robots may not know about the local beliefs of others. In addition, individual robots may not communicate all their beliefs. Global belief generation must collect the local beliefs, assess if the multirobot system has sensed all it needs to, and reason about whether the perceptions of the robots are truthful.

The global model of knowledge allows the multirobot systems to make intelligent decisions and perform global planning. Unfortunately, in the unforeseeable dynamic nature of the physical environment, it is infeasible to have the perfect knowledge and computational resources required to create globally accurate models [6].

As to possible multirobot system faults, the work [7] distinguish two major types of them:

- planning-related faults;
- coordination-related faults.

In this paper a problem of coordination faults detection is considered in terms of robot failures and the detection of these failures in the group of robots.

In our previous works some distributed ledger technologies (DLT) were investigated as an integral part of the robotics framework [8, 9]. From the monitoring and control point of view, in the area of DLT there are some very reliable and fault-tolerant solutions, which were developed for distributed computing. Yet, some peculiarities of the robot groups are not considered in the DL methods, so the application of them needs some DLT methods adaptation. Besides, the issue of energy consumption of methods developed is quite topical, so, such methods have to be explored and estimated from the energy consumption focus.

The main contribution of this paper to the robotics area is as follows:

- methods of fault-tolerant distributed dispatching for groups of robots with dynamically changing locations are presented;
- for this purpose, the methods from the DLT area were modified taking into account the dynamics of the devices location;
- the proposed methods were estimated roughly in terms of computational device energy consumption with the assumption that as more data are transferred the more energy is consumed.

The remainder of this paper is organized as follows: Sect. 2 contains an overview of related works and problem formulation; Sect. 3 considers the failure detection methods for multi robot groups with dynamically changing locations; Sect. 4 considers some abstract models to estimate the methods proposed in the previous section and contains selected simulation results; Sect. 5 contains discussion and conclusions.

2   Related Works and Problem Formulation

A problem of coordination faults detection to the best of our knowledge has been considered in the following works. A centralized architecture for the fault detection system is described in [10], but the latest research showed the inexpediency of the centralized approach due to the communication overheads and the lack of dependability. The methods for spatially distributed agents faults detection are presented in [11]. In this work the approach of clustering of agents is considered, when an agent manages a subset of agents. A novel design space for the agents failure detection is presented in [12]. It must be mentioned that it was proved that centralizing the diagnosis disambiguation process is a key factor in reducing communications, while runtime is affected mainly by the amount of reasoning about other agents. These results contradict the previous work, which proves that the distributed algorithms reduce communications. [13] presents a Casual Model Method, which concentrates on the descriptions of the possible faults of the robots. As well as some quite new works are devoted to the management in the robot groups and robot fault-tolerance [14–17].

As is mentioned above, the centralized approach to the failure detection in groups of robots seems to be unreliable and hardly scalable because of the fact of centralization, while [12], on the contrary, proposes the centralized manner of monitoring and control. Contemporary computational trends, including DLT, lay in the field of distributed systems with equal nodes and unified software. Some methods were developed to provide the consistency and integrity of the distributed systems:

- Proof-based consensus methods, for example, which include such well-known protocols as Proof of Work, Proof of Stake and many others) [18, 19].
- Vote-based consensus methods. The well-known crash-tolerant consensus algorithms use the centralized approach with the changeable leader, as is done in such well-known algorithms as Paxos, ViewStamped Replication and Raft [20–23].

The leader is elected in all methods listed above. The leader is distributed and the leader node changes through the time of system functioning.

Also, there are some systems, which use the leaderless consensus [24, 25].

The general scheme of the leaderless consensus is as follows:

1. A node sends its opinion to all network nodes.
2. A node receives opinions from the network.
3. The particular vector is formed $V = \{v_i\}$, where v_i – is the opinion of the node i.
4. The v_i is chosen by the majority.
5. A node sends the chosen v_i to the other nodes.
6. A node accepts v_i as a solution.

The methods mentioned above are interesting from the robots management point of view because of their reliability and fault-tolerance. Yet, the consensus methods were developed for the nodes with static location, while it is the unreachable condition for the groups of mobile robots. So, there must be some developed facilities to handle those cases, when groups of robots move from the data transmission coverage.

Summarizing the problem in question, the following must be declared:

- DLT area provides the robotics with reliable and fault-tolerant management methods.
- These methods must be adapted to the robotic area (to the dynamics of the devices of the group in particular).

The next section considers the proposed methods of robots failure detection.

3   Failure Detection Methods for Multi Robot Groups

In the context of this paper the dispatching process includes:

- the device failure detection;
- systems recovery by means of computational tasks relocation within the system of functioning devices;
- the distribution of information messages, including the mission knowledge updates.

In case of device dynamic location on the edge of the network, there is a parameter which describes the maximum distance of data transfer. This maximum radius of data transmission must cover a multirobot group to make the distributed dispatching efficient. So, it is important to determine if there is a constraint for inter-robot distance or there is no such a constraint but the need to delegate the leader role to one robot of the group, which data transmission radius covers all the group.

Assuming the issues listed above, we consider the inter-robot distance constraint, when every robot in the local group is reachable by the others and covered by the data transmission.

Fully distributed dispatching has some disadvantages in case of random graph topology: without the possibility to organize the data transmission between all devices at one hop, data transmission is provided by means of dedicated device (and this contradicts the decentralization concept), or by means of data transmission by some gossip-like algorithms (which are used widely in distributed systems). According to the abovementioned scheme, the time the new information covers all the network is reached in $O\ (log\ N)$ transmissions, where N is the number of robots in group. Therefore the fully distributed and decentralized dispatching is not expedient for large robot groups at least in terms of time, though it is rather applicable for some restricted number of robots, which can be combined in the local group of robots. The local group is a group where the inter-robot distance constraint works.

Consider the case, when a multirobot group, e.g., a group of UFVs, move from the initial position and distribute through the mission space according to the described functional tasks and coordinates. In the beginning, all UFVs are in one local group A_0. With the distribution through the space, UFVs, which have separate direction associated with the coordinates of the functional task, are out of the A_0 data transmission coverage. So, the problem is to prevent the efforts of the remainder of A_0 to provide the group with the tasks of A_1 (which are out of data transmission and seem to be failed). The problem for the group A_1 is the same. This is the grounding of the need to distribute the relevant data about the functional tasks and devices coordinates through the groups.

Summarizing, the following must be said:

- distributed management is efficient within the local robotic groups, when all robots are situated in the area covered by the data transmission;
- it is expedient to plan the mission in a way to divide the robot groups into the subgroups, which are the local robot groups;
- the knowledge about the mission plan and the current coordinates and its exchange allow to modify the well-known fault-tolerant consensus methods from the DLT area for usage in the robotics.

The following figures illustrate the states of the devices for the modified method with the distributed leader (see Fig. 1, 2).

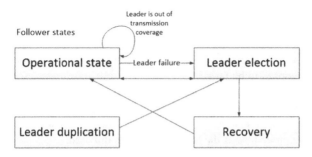

Fig. 1. The follower states.

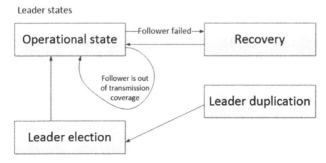

Fig. 2. The leader states.

A generic scheme of dispatching with the distributed leader is presented below.

Operational State

- The leader sends "heartbeat" message to the followers. Message contains the leader identifier and the update of the robot group state contextual information.
- Leader receives "heartbeat" messages with the followers identifiers.

The Follower Failure Detection

- The leader checks the list of identifiers received. If a timeout occurs and the identifier has not been received, the corresponding device is supposed to be failed and its identifier is added to the failed devices list.
- Having the contextual information of devices, the leader analyses, which of the followers on the list are not available due to the follower's location, which is out of the communication radius coverage. If such devices are there, they are removed from the list of failed devices. So, only devices, which are supposed to be failed must be on the list.
- The leader makes a decision about the system recovery way, i.e., how to relocate the functional tasks from the failed devices.

The Leader Failure Detection

- If a timeout occurs and the "heartbeat" message from the leader has not been received, the leader is supposed to be failed.
- The coordinates are checked: this is done to prevent the functional tasks duplicating in case when the leader is just out of the data transmission range.
- Available followers exchange the "heartbeat" messages to establish the new local group. Then the procedure of the leader election is initiated.

The Leader Duplication Detection

- If more than one "leader" "heartbeat"-messages is received by random device, then the state of leader duplication is initiated.
- Devices exchange the "heartbeat" messages to establish the new local group.
- The leader election procedure is initiated.

The Leader Election Procedure (Based on the "Wave" algorithm for the Random Network Topology)

1. Consider P as the device identifier
2. Send P to all available devices
3. Receive P from all available devices
4. If $P < P_{neighbour}$ *leader := self_id else leader := min($P_{neibour}$).*

Then consider the leaderless scheme of dispatching. The general states of the device are presented in Fig. 3.

The generic scheme, which implements fully distributed dispatching, is presented below.

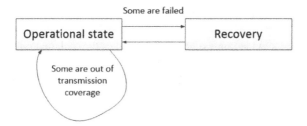

Fig. 3. The leaderless dispatching states.

Operational State

- Device sends the other available devices the "heartbeat" message, including its local mission context.
- Device receives the "heartbeat" messages from the other devices with their identifiers.

Device Failure Detection

- Device checks the list of received "heartbeat" messages and device identifiers.
- If timeout occurs, the absent identifier is supposed to be failed and is put to the list of failed devices.
- With the shared information about the goal coordinates and other contextual information of device mission the devices, which are out of communication radius are removed from the list. So only failed devices are on the list.
- The list of failed devices is sent to other available devices.
- Devices are supposed to be failed if the list is proved by the $n/2 + 1$ members of the group.

The Recovery of the Functional Tasks.

- A device checks requirements of the task I and its own resources.
- If the device meets the resource requirements, the following objective function is formed:

$$F(x_1, x_2 \ldots x_n) = \alpha_1 x_1 + \alpha_2 x_2 + \ldots + \alpha_n x_n \tag{1}$$

where x_i – device resources; α_i – a weight of parameter I, which allows to present the multiobjective function as a scalar one.

- Send the calculated $F(x_1, x_2 \ldots x_n)$ to the other devices.
- Receive calculated $F(x_1, x_2 \ldots x_n)$ from the other devices.
- Select the best value of $F(x_1, x_2 \ldots x_n)$.
- The owner of the best $F(x_1, x_2 \ldots x_n)$ value is presented as a new device for the i-task resuming.

4 Methods Estimation and Simulation Results

As was mentioned, the wide range of challenges makes the fault detection and recovery in the robotic area to be a very complex problem. In particular, the autonomous robots have the autonomous and restricted energy sources, while every monitoring and control action adds the energy consumption to the overall energy balance. In the scope of this paper we assume that the energy consumption of each device includes and depends on the data transmission activities. In other words, if a device transmits more data to the other devices, it consumes more energy.

To estimate the methods, proposed in the previous section, consider the following variables:

T – is the total time of system functioning, which consists of discrete time moments t_i, so as $T = \{t_1, t_2, \dots t_N\}$; M – is the number of devices in the group; K – is the number of failures; T-K is the number of operational steps accordingly; V_i – is a piece of contextual information, including the "heartbeat" message; V_{st} – is the size of contextual data storage, which is the analogue to the log size in the VR/Raft protocols.

Consider the case when no failure occurs in the group of robots. Then, for the leader-based method every device has to transfer the following volume of data to the network:

$$V_{l\_op} = \left\lceil \frac{T-K}{M} \right\rceil (M-1)V_i + ((T-K) - \left\lceil \frac{T-K}{M} \right\rceil)V_i. \tag{2}$$

It must be mentioned that in the equation we made an assumption of the upper bound of a device being a leader.

In case of leaderless dispatching the data transfer volumes are as follows, because every device sends the "heartbeat" message and the contextual information to the other devices in the group:

$$V_{nl\_op} = (T-K)(N-1)V_i. \tag{3}$$

Consider the case, when every t_i the failure occurs, so every t_i in case of leader-based consensus the leader change stage takes place. So, the device transmits the following data volumes to the network according with the main reconfiguration steps in the VewStamped Replication and RAFT.

$$V_{l\_r} = \left\lceil \frac{K}{M} \right\rceil ((M-1)V_{st} + (M-1)V_i) + (K - \left\lceil \frac{K}{M} \right\rceil)V_{st} + KV_i(M-1); \tag{4}$$

where $(M-1)V_{st}$ is the contextual data distribution volume; $(M-1)V$ is the contextual data request volume; $(K - \left\lceil \frac{K}{M} \right\rceil)V_{st}$ is the data volume to be transferred of the contextual data storage to the leader; $KV_i(M-1)$ is the estimation of the data transmission during the leader election procedure.

It must be mentioned that in case of leaderless method, the volumes of transferred information in case of device failure and recovery is as follows:

$$V_{nl\_r} = \alpha K(M-1)V_i. \tag{5}$$

Coefficient α includes data transfers while sending the lists of the failures devices and the voting during the failure detection and the recovery according to the major stages of the failure detection and recovery, and in this paper $\alpha = 4$.

So, the overall device activity connected with the data transmission for the leader-based method is as follows:

$$V_l^o = V_{l\_op} + V_{l\_r}; \qquad (6)$$

as well as the leaderless method is estimated by the following:

$$V_{nl}^o = V_{nl\_op} + V_{nl\_r}. \qquad (7)$$

We have estimated the leader-based and leaderless methods under the conditions of:

- constant T, K and the increase of nodes number M to check the scalability of methods in terms of communication generation;
- constant T, M and the increase of K to estimate the effect of growing failures number on the general system energy consumption.

In the pictures below the parameter V_{lo} is the overall data volume for the leader consensus, as well as V_{nlo} is the overall data volume for the non-leader consensus (Figs. 4 and 5).

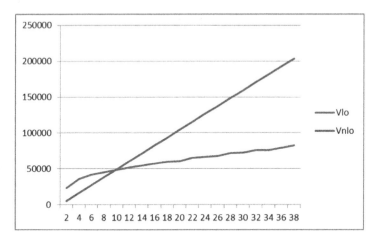

Fig. 4. $T = 50$; $K = 20$; $M = 2..38$.

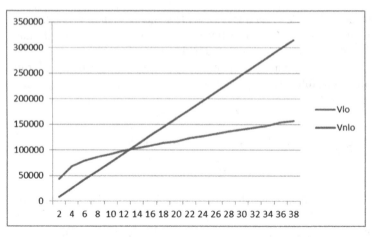

Fig. 5. T = 50; K = 40; M = 2..38.

So, one can see that the increase of the device number affects the data transmission volume of the leaderless dispatching so as doing it less efficient than the dispatching with the elected leader. Yet, till the particular nodes number, the leaderless dispatching is more efficient.

In Fig. 6 one can see that for relatively small groups the leaderless dispatching is quite efficient, yet, with the increase of node number in the group the leaderless solution is less efficient than the solution with a leader (Fig. 7).

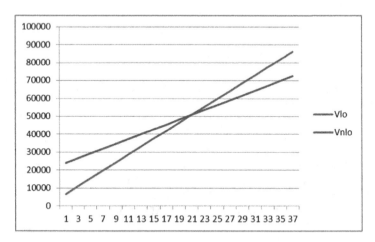

Fig. 6. T = 50; M = 10; K = 1..37

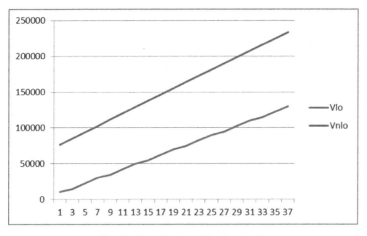

Fig. 7. T = 50; M = 30; K = 1..37

5 Discussion and Conclusion

In this paper the problem of autonomous and mobile robot groups failure detection is considered. The major directions in this field include centralized and distributed approaches to the management, yet, none of the approaches prevails: the centralized solution is not reliable, and the advantages of the distributed approach in terms of communication overheads are quite doubtful.

In this paper we have chosen a concept of distributed leader and of a leaderless interaction and modified them for the usage in robot group management, taking into account the contextual information of the robots. Also we estimated the methods proposed in terms of how much data every participant of the group must transfer to other participants, as it is an important feature in terms of energy consumption. So, some new estimates were got, which allow to propose the dispatching with the leader as more energy efficient.

Acknowledgements. This research is supported by the RFBR projects 18-29-03229 and 18-05-80092.

References

1. Pettersson, O.: Execution monitoring in robotics: a survey. Robot. Auton. Syst. **53**, 73–88 (2005)
2. Duan, Z., Cai, Z., Yu, J.: Fault diagnosis and fault tolerant control for wheeled mobile robots under unknown environments: a survey. In: IEEE International Conference on Robotics and Automation Proceedings, pp. 3428–3433. IEEE, Barcelona (2005)
3. Khalastchi, E., Kalech, M.: Fault detection and diagnosis in multi-robot systems: a survey. Sensors **19**, 4019 (2019)
4. Yan, Z., Jouandeau, N., Cherif, A.A.: A survey and analysis of multi-robot coordination. Int. J. Adv. Robot. Syst. **10**, 399 (2013)

5. Kaminka, G.A., Frenkel, I.: Flexible teamwork in behavior-based robots. In: National Conference on Artificial Intelligence Proceedings, pp. 108–113. AAAI, California (2005)
6. Parker, L.E.: ALLIANCE: an architecture for fault tolerant multirobot cooperation. IEEE Trans. Robot. Autom. **14**, 220–240 (1988)
7. Khalastchi, E., Kalech, M.: Fault detection and diagnosis in multi-robot systems: a survey. Sensors (Switzerland) **19**, 4019 (2019)
8. Kalyaev, I., Melnik, E., Klimenko, A.: Distributed ledger based workload logging in the robot swarm. In: Ronzhin, A., Rigoll, G., Meshcheryakov, R. (eds.) ICR 2019. LNCS (LNAI), vol. 11659, pp. 119–128. Springer, Cham (2019). https://doi.org/10.1007/978-3-030-26118-4_12
9. Melnik, E.V., Klimenko, A.B., Ivanov, D.Y.: A blockchain-based technique for making swarm robots distributed decision. In: Journal of Physics: Conference Series (2019)
10. Micalizio, R., Torasso, P., Torta, G.: On-line monitoring and diagnosis of multi-agent systems: a model based approach. In: 16th European Conference on Artificial Intelligence Proceedings, pp. 848–852. IOS Press, Amsterdam (2004)
11. Roos, N., Teije, A.T., Witteveen, C.: A protocol for multi-agent diagnosis with spatially distributed knowledge. In: 2nd International Joint Conference on Autonomous Agents and Multiagent Systems Proceedings, pp. 655–661. IOS Press, Amsterdam (2003)
12. Kalech, M., Kaminka, G.: On the design of coordination diagnosis algorithms for teams of situated agents. Artif. Intell. **171**, 491–513 (2007)
13. Lynne, E., Kannan, P., Kannan, B.: Adaptive causal models for fault diagnosis and recovery in multi-robot teams. In: IEEE/RSJ International Conference on Intelligent Robots and Systems, pp. 2703–2710. IEEE, China (2006)
14. Chueshev, A., Melekhova, O., Meshcheryakov, R.: Cloud robotic platform on basis of fog computing approach. In: Ronzhin, A., Rigoll, G., Meshcheryakov, R. (eds.) ICR 2018. LNCS (LNAI), vol. 11097, pp. 34–43. Springer, Cham (2018). https://doi.org/10.1007/978-3-319-99582-3_4
15. Güzey, N., Güzey, H.M.: Consensus-based localization of devices with unknown transmitting power. In: Ronzhin, A., Rigoll, G., Meshcheryakov, R. (eds.) ICR 2018. LNCS (LNAI), vol. 11097, pp. 78–84. Springer, Cham (2018). https://doi.org/10.1007/978-3-319-99582-3_9
16. Vorotnikov, S., Ermishin, K., Nazarova, A., Yuschenko, A.: Multi-agent robotic systems in collaborative robotics. In: Ronzhin, A., Rigoll, G., Meshcheryakov, R. (eds.) ICR 2018. LNCS (LNAI), vol. 11097, pp. 270–279. Springer, Cham (2018). https://doi.org/10.1007/978-3-319-99582-3_28
17. Larkin, E., Bogomolov, A., Privalov, A.: Discrete model of mobile robot assemble fault-tolerance. In: Ronzhin, A., Rigoll, G., Meshcheryakov, R. (eds.) ICR 2019. LNCS (LNAI), vol. 11659, pp. 204–215. Springer, Cham (2019). https://doi.org/10.1007/978-3-030-26118-4_20
18. Nakamoto, S.: Bitcoin: a peer-to-peer electronic cash system. https://bitcoin.org/bitcoin.pdf. Accessed 14 June 2020
19. BlockfinBFT compared to other consensus algorithms. https://storelabs.org/media/Blockf inBFT%20Compared%20to%20other%20Consensus%20Algorithms%20-%20Storecoin. pdf. Accessed 14 June 2020
20. Liskov, B., Cowling, J.: Viewstamped replication revisited. http://pmg.csail.mit.edu/papers/ vr-revisited.pdf. Accessed 14 June 2020
21. The Raft Consensus Algorithm. https://raft.github.io/. Accessed 14 June 2020
22. Understanding the raft consensus algorithm: an academic article summary. https://www.fre ecodecamp.org/news/in-search-of-an-understandable-consensus-algorithm-a-summary-4bc 294c97e0d/. Accessed 14 June 2020
23. Moshkowich, G.: Architecture of ZAB – ZooKeeper atomic broadcast protocol. https://distributedalgorithm.wordpress.com/2015/06/20/architecture-of-zab-zookeeper-atomic-broadcast-protocol/. Accessed 14 June 2020

24. 2018 could be the year of non-leader-based consensus mechanisms. https://medium.com/coinmonks/2018-could-be-the-year-of-non-leader-based-consensus-mechanisms-c06884 38034a. Accessed 14 June 2020
25. Team Rocke: Scalable and probabilistic leaderless BFT consensus through metastability. https://avalanchelabs.org/QmT1ry38PAmnhparPUmsUNHDEGHQusBLD6T5XJh4mU Un3v.pdf. Accessed 14 June 2020

Planning to Score a Goal in Robotic Football with Heuristic Search

Ivan Khokhlov[1]([✉]), Vladimir Litvinenko[1], Ilya Ryakin[1],
and Konstantin Yakovlev[1,2]

[1] Moscow Institute of Physics and Technology, Dolgoprudny, Russia
khokhlov.iyu@gmail.com, {litvinenko.vv,ryakin.is}@phystech.edu,
yakovlev@isa.ru
[2] Federal Research Center for Computer Science and Control
of Russian Academy of Sciences, Moscow, Russia

Abstract. This paper considers a problem of planning an attack in robotic football (RoboCup). The problem is reduced to finding a trajectory of the ball from its current position to the opponents goals. Heuristic search algorithm, i.e. A*, is used to find such a trajectory. For this algorithm to be applicable we introduce a discretized model of the environment, i.e. a graph, as well as the core search components: cost function and heuristic function. Both are designed to take into account all the available information of the game state. We extensively evaluate the suggested approach in simulation comparing it to a range of baselines. The result of the conducted evaluation clearly shows the benefit of utilizing heuristic search within the RoboCup context.

Keywords: RoboCup · Robotic football · Path planning · Heuristic search

1 Introduction

Robotic football competitions has been one of the prominent drivers of the robotic research since 1997. Teams of robots that play football against each other face a wide range of challenging problems: locomotion, path and motion planning, communication, localization, interaction, and many others. The idea of organizing a competition between robots playing football emerged in early 90s of XX century and since them transformed to a global initiative called *Robocup* with regular tournaments, different leagues and more than 3500 participants representing major universities, research institutes and commercial organizations involved in robotic research[1]. All RoboCup community is united by a big goal – in 2050 the champion of RoboCup Humanoid football competition should be able to play against human champions of FIFA World Cup according to FIFA rules.

---

[1] For a brief history of Robocup initiative refer to https://www.robocup.org/a_brief_history_of_robocup.

© Springer Nature Switzerland AG 2020
A. Ronzhin et al. (Eds.): ICR 2020, LNAI 12336, pp. 148–159, 2020.
https://doi.org/10.1007/978-3-030-60337-3_15

Fig. 1. Robotic football setup: humanoid-robots playing the ball on the reduced copy of a football field.

Nowadays, RoboCup Humanoid football rules is quite simpler than FIFA one. Field of the is 6×9 m, covered by 30 mm height grass and marked up with white lines. Robots must be similar to human in sensors, body structure, proportions and even center of mass position. Teams of 4 robots compete on the field each for two 10 min halves. Moreover, they can communicate via Wi-Fi network with each other and referee.

Intrinsically, robotic humanoid football is very challenging domain. The problems that arise here can be roughly decomposed into two-level hierarchy. First, one needs to ensure stable locomotion, consistent detection and localization of the key object of interest, i.e. the ball, the posts, the opponents etc., reliable peer-to-peer communication between the robots. Second, the more involved problems such as role assignment and planning to score a goal arise. In this work we are interested mainly in the latter problems and consider the first ones to be successfully solved with a desired degree of accuracy [9].

Specifically we are focused on the kick planning for attack phase of the game. This problem constantly arise within the game when our team intercepts a ball and aims to score a goal which is vital for winning. We approach this problem by boiling it down to path planning for a ball. That is, we suggest to use a graph-based heuristic search algorithm to find a shortest path for a ball from its current location to the opponent's goals. We evaluate this approach empirically in simulation and compare it to a range of the baseline strategies. We show that the suggested approach outperforms the competitors in a wide variety of different game scenarios.

2   Related Work

Initially much of the research in robotic football was concentrated around locomotion, tracking, localization etc. More recently, the teams competing in RoboCup Humanoid League have started to put more emphasis on the tactics and strategy. Meanwhile, in 2D and 3D Simulation Leagues solving them for more than 10 years. For example, noteworthy approaches with using predefined game strategies were introduced in [3] and [8]. The authors figured out that template attacks increase game quality and developed framework for fast programming such strategies. In [7] the authors consider problem similar to ours. They assume kick target to be modelled as Gaussian distribution. With such probabilistic comprehension authors calculate probability of the ball to be in one of 6 states and for each state calculated weight in predefined potential field.

Works that consider the application of heuristic search to path and motion planning for humanoid robots, not necessarily within the robotic football context, are more numerous. For example, [4] describe application of the A* algorithm to planning possible paths through uneven terrain. In [6] a more involved problem of planning steps of the humanoid robot is considered. [10] studies the combined problem of global path planning and footstep planning for legged robots. A comparison of different heuristic search algorithms applied to both of the aforementioned problems can be found in [2].

3   Problem Statement

Consider two teams of humanoid robots playing football on a plain field sized 6×9 m and covered with 30 mm artificial grass. Each team is composed of the 4 robots with body mass index in the range $[3, 30]$ and height under $1\,\mathrm{m}^2$. The ultimate aim of a team is to win the game which is achieved via scoring more goals than the opponent. The goal posts are located on the opposite sides of the field and are 2.6 m in width, the ball is 20 cm in diameter. The typical setup is depicted in Fig. 1.

Game controller that manipulates the robots of our team constantly localizes them, as well as the ball and the opponents (so we consider all these positions to be known). Assume now that the ball is close to one our robots (i.e. the distance between the ball and one of our robots is much shorter than the one between the ball and any of the opponents) and we want to start an attack. The latter is understood as a sequence of kicks made by our robots with the aim of scoring a goal. The problem now is to plan an attack and, more specifically, to estimate the direction of a first kick in such a way that *i*) the kick won't result in loosing a ball (i.e. it will be our robot that will be the first on the ball, not the opponent), *ii*) the kick results in a "winning position". The later intuitively means that the chances of scoring a goal after the kick increase.

In this work we reduce the problem of attack planning to *finding a path for a ball* from its current position to the "in-the-net" position. This path is a

---

[2] Such robots are attributed as *kid-sized* in Robocup competition.

sequence of segments. Each segment represents a ball trajectory after a kick of a predefined force performed by one of the robots of our team. The first segment of the path should not intersect the areas occupied by opponent's robots. The last segment should intersect the boundary of the field in between the opponent's poles. The criterion to be minimized is time to the goal.

4   Method

We rely on a graph search algorithm, i.e. A* [5], to solve the considered path finding problem. For this algorithm to be applied we need to *i*) define a graph; *ii*) define such search components as a cost function and a heuristic function to be used within the search. We describe these components next.

4.1   Graph

We introduce a graph by discretizing the workspace, which is a 2D rectangle sized 6×9 m, via the cell decomposition. Each cell is a square of 10×10 cm, so there is $90 \times 60 = 5400$ cells overall. The center of each cell defines a graph vertex. The current position of a ball, given to a path planner by the external localization system as a tuple (x, y), is tied to a graph vertex in the following fashion. Knowing (x, y) we identify the cell which center is the closest to the ball's position and then assume the ball to be located in the center of this cell. If there are different cells which centers are equidistantly close to the ball we choose one of these cells, as the start vertex, arbitrarily.

The edges of a graph are defined as follows. We assume that a robot can kick the ball with a predefined force, so the distance travelled by the ball, r_{kick}, is proportional to that force. When a ball is at a graph vertex v we identify all vertices v' that form a discrete approximation of a circumference of radius r_{kick} (see Fig. 2). Each tuple (v, v') defines a graph edge now. Moreover if a kick ends beyond the field but the ball travels in between the opponent's goal posts the corespondent edge is also considered to be part of the graph (a few examples of such edges are shown in red in Fig. 2).

Indeed, the overall number of edges in the introduced graph depends on the value of r_{kick} and can be very high. Moreover, different values for r_{kick} can be allowed, which contributes to increasing the number of edges. Thus we do not store it explicitly but rather implicitly construct the edges while the search.

4.2   Search

The input of the search algorithm is a graph (as defined above) as well as the positions of our robots and the robots of the opponent. The output is expected to be a least cost path in that graph that starts in the vertex associated with the current location of the ball and ends with an edge that lies in between the goal posts of the opponent. The cost of the path is the cumulative cost of the edges forming that path, thus we need to define how the cost of an individual edge is computed.

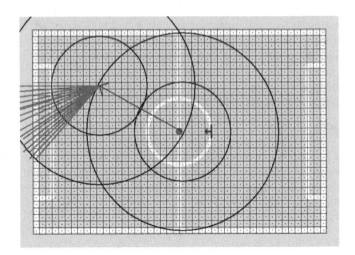

Fig. 2. Graph used for path planning. Centers of the grid cells define the vertices. Edges are defined implicitly by each pair of the vertices that (approximately) lie within the predefined kick distance from each other. (Color figure online)

Cost of an Edge. Recall, that each graph edge represents a kick performed by a robot, thus a cost of an edge is associated with the time needed for this kick to be accomplished, i.e. the time by which the ball reaches the endpoint of a kick.

In most cases we compute an edge's cost by dividing its length to the speed of the ball[3]. However, computing cost of the edges that have the start vertex as their endpoint is more involved. The rationale behind this is that we know the positions of the opponent's robots as well as the location of our robots when we start at attack, thus, it's reasonable to take this information into account.

When the first kick is performed we add to the correspondent edge cost the time that the kicking robot of our team (the one that is closest to the ball) will spend on approaching the ball. Moreover we penalize kicks that have a high risk of being intercepted by the opponent. Recall, that all positions of the opponent's robots are known. We model these robots as disks and compute whether an edge, representing the first kick, intersects any of them. If this is the case the cost of the edge is multiplied by a constant factor (we use 2 in our experiments). Thus the resultant path is less likely to contain such an edge. The reason we do not prune such edges for good is that the positions of the robots, reported by the external tracking system, are not 100% accurate in practice.

The high-level algorithm that computes the cost of an edge, associated with a kick, is presented in Algorithm 1.

---

[3] We assume a simplistic ball movement model when the ball moves with a constant speed.

Algorithm 1. Cost function

---

function COMPUTECOST(robotPos, opponentsPositions, ballFromPos, ballToPos, firstKick)

    $ballTravelTime \leftarrow getLength(toPos, fromPos)/ballSpeed$

    if firstKick **then**

        $timeToReachBall \leftarrow calcTimeToApproachBall(fromPos, robotPos)$

        if intersectOpponent(fromPos, toPos, opponentsField) **then**

            return $timeToReachBall + ballTravelTime * 2$

        else

            return $timeToReachBall + ballTravelTime$

        end if

    else

        return $ballTravelTime$

    end if

end function

Algorithm 2. Heuristic function

---

function HFUNC(teamMatesField, toPos, firstKick)

    $timeToReachGoal \leftarrow distToGoal(toPos)/ballSpeed$

    if firstKick **then**

        $timeToApproachBall \leftarrow calcTimeToApproachBall(toPos, teamMatesField)$

        return $timeToApproachBall + timeToReachGoal$

    else

        return $timeToReachGoal$

    end if

end function

Heuristic Function. Heuristic function takes as input the position of the ball, i.e. the graph vertex, and outputs the lower bound of time needed for the ball to reach the opponent's gates.

Similarly to the cost function, we compute such a heuristic estimate in most cases in a straightforward fashion. First, we calculate the distance form the ball position (vertex in the graph) to the gates by using the closed-loop formula for computing the distance between the point (ball's position) and the line segment (opponents gates). Second, we divide this distance by the ball speed.

As before, we also introduce a more involved procedure for computing heuristic for a first kick. After that kick is made it will take some time by our next kicking robot to approach the ball to continue an attack, so it's reasonable to incorporate this information into the search process and make the heuristic function more informative. To do so we identify the robot of our team that is the closest to the endpoint of an edge that represent the first kick, compute the time needed for that robot to approach the ball to perform the next (second) kick, add this time to the heuristic estimate.

The high-level algorithm that computes the cost of an edge, associated with a kick, is presented in Algorithm 2.

Heuristic Search. Having defined the cost function and the heuristic function, we employ the renowned A* algorithm to compute the least cost path in the given graph. This path corresponds to the minimal-time trajectory of the ball from its current position to the gates of the opponent. Please note, that we do not simulate the moves of our robots and the moves of the opponent when finding such a trajectory, thus it is likely to become inaccurate after the attack evolves. At the same time, the computational budget needed to accomplish the suggested search is very low, thus one can invoke re-planning after each kick to keep the plan updated.

5   Empirical Evaluation

We ran empirical evaluation of the suggested approach in a simulation of a football game, i.e. we placed our robots, enemies and the ball on the field and started the game from this layout. During the simulation we assumed perfect execution, i.e. all commands sent to robot actuators were executed perfectly. We also assume perfect localization, i.e. each robot localized itself, allies enemies and the ball perfectly. All kicks were considered to be performed precisely as well. In our evaluation we separately run test for 4 m kicks and 2 m kicks. These values were chosen based on our experience with kick controllers of real robots.

We compared four different strategies to estimating the direction of a kick during the attack:

- *Planning* Our strategy as described above. The robot closest to the ball performs the heuristic search and as a result gets the sequence of kicks from the ball's current position to the "in-the-net" position. Then the first kick from that sequence is made.
- *Reactive* This strategy chooses the most promising kick based on the one-step look-ahead planning. It can be seen as a "capped planning" when only the first kick is planned not the whole attack.
- *Forward* According to this strategy the kick is always made towards the enemy goals without taking into account any data regarding the positions of the enemies and/or allies.
- *Expert* This approach was developed by *Rhoban Team* [1]. The field is divided into the blocks sized 20 cm × 20 cm and for each block, the direction of possible kicks are specified and ranged according to the expert score. The kick with the highest score that does not intersect an opponent is chosen for an attack.

Each football game was simulated until the goal was scored by our team (*success*) or until the ball was intercepted by the opponents (*failure*). The interception may have occurred in two ways. First, an opponent might be the first to approach the ball after the kick had been made by our robot. Second, our robot might perform a kick that intersects an opponents zone, i.e. a circumference of a certain radius (we set it to be 20 cm in our experiments) centered at the position of an enemy robot (which is known from the perfect localization as described

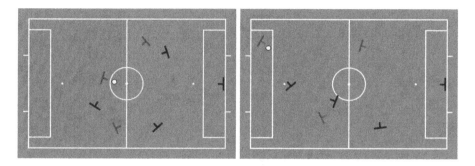

Fig. 3. Different game layouts used in the experimets: random (left), attack (right)

above). In real game, however, when the positions of the opponent robots are not precisely known, such a kick may not actually lead to an interception. To compensate for this and make the simulation more close to reality we tweaked the simulation as follows. Each time the ball passed trough an interception zone associated with some of the enemy robots we let it go through with the 0.5 probability.

We used two different types of game layouts for the experiments: *random* and *attack*. For random layout we placed 3 field robots of our team and 3 field robots of the opponent's team randomly. We also placed an enemy goal keeper appropriately (in the middle of the goals). The ball was placed at the distance of 20 cm from one of our robots. An example of this layout is shown on Fig. 3 (left).

Attack layout represents a typical phase of the game when an enemy attack has just finished and we got control over the ball and want to start an attack. One robot of our team is placed nearby our penalty zone and looks towards the enemy's goals. The ball is nearby this robot. Two other robots of our team are placed in the middle of the field, waiting for the pass. Speaking of the enemy team, we put one of its robots to our penalty zone, one to the middle of the field, and one robot was placed randomly. The enemy's goalkeeper was placed in the middle of the goals. An example of this layout is depicted on Fig. 3 (right).

Overall, we generated 100 different layouts of each type. Thus 200 football games in total were simulated.

5.1   Results

Indeed, different strategies lead to different kicks and, a result, to different game outcomes almost always. Figure 4 shows one such example comparing the most advanced strategies: *expert* and *planning*. Initially both strategies chose nearly the same kick (Fig. 4, top row). However, from then *expert* decided to kick to the goals, while *planning* opted for one extra pass (Fig. 4, middle row). As a result *expert* attack failed – the final kick was intercepted by a goal-keeper, while *planning* – did not. In general, qualitative analysis of the recorded games shows that *planning* exploits the pass option much fruitfully than other strategies.

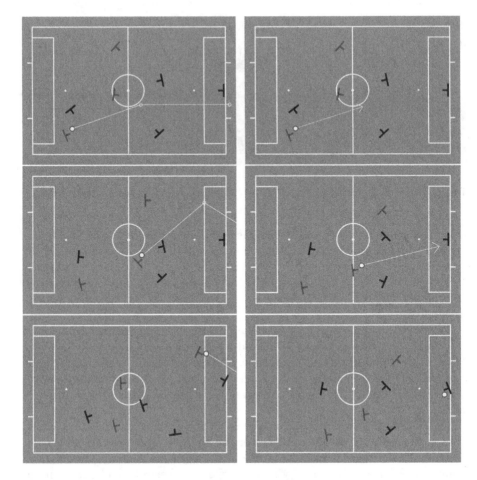

Fig. 4. Example of different behaviour resulting from different strategies: planning (left) and expert (right).

To conduct a quantitative analysis we track the following indicators. First, we tracked the number of games won by a strategy among all the games played – **success rate**. Besides, in each game won by our team we measured the following:

- **Time:** Time (simulation time) before goal
- **Kicks number:** number of kicks in our attack
- **Ball possession, %:** the ratio of the time that our robot owned the ball to the total time of the attack.

The last indicator was computed as follows. At each simulated time moment we measured the distance between the ball and the robots. If out robot was close to the ball we considered that our team possessed the ball at that time moment. When the game ended we divided the number of timesteps our team possessed the ball to the total duration of the attack. Additionally in each game

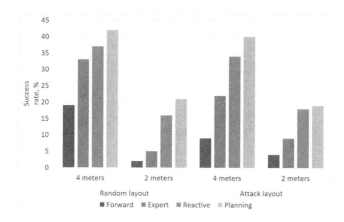

Fig. 5. Experiment results: success rate.

(not only won by our team) we measured the number of kicks that passed trough the enemy intersecting zone (recall that with 0.5 probability such a kick was considered to be successfully accomplished) – **Intersected**.

Success rates for different setups are shown in Fig. 5. As one can *planning* strategy outperformed all the competitors across all the setups. The most pronounceable difference is observed for the *attack* layout with 4 m kick length. This is the most important setup from practical point of view. The difference for 2 m is less articulated, but "short" kicks are not often used in real games.

Table 1 provides more statistics for the games when 4 m kick was used. Time, kicks number and ball possession indicators were averaged across the games successfully accomplished by expert, reactive and planning strategies. Number of intersected kicks was average across all games played.

For the random layout we see that team spend on attack slightly decreases for *planning* compared to other strategies. Kicks number is also lower, however the ball possession is better for *expert* strategy. Same holds for the number of intersections. For the attack layout we note the increased number of kicks and, correspondingly, time for the *planning* strategy. This is not an artefact but a quantitative evidence that *planning* utilized idea of pass more often. Observe that the ball possession is nearly the same for all strategies in this layout and in terms of intersections *planning* is the best.

To finalize evaluation we played several full games utilizing RoboCup Game-Controller[4] according to RoboCup rules. The results again showed the supremacy of the suggested *planning* strategy over the baselines: Game 1: Expert **1:2** Planning, Game 2: Expert **0:0** Planning), Game 3: Forward **0:1** Planning, Game 4: Forward **0:1** Planning.

Summarizing the results of the experiments one can claim that the proposed method, indeed, outperforms less advanced approaches across a large variety of game setups. Moreover, qualitative analysis shows that the suggested approach

---

[4] https://github.com/RoboCup-Humanoid-TC/GameController.

Table 1. 4 m kick strength statistics.

	Random layout				Attack layout			
	Forward	Expert	Reactive	Planning	Forward	Expert	Reactive	Planning
Time, s	-	11.9	11.4	**9.8**	-	27.3	**22.9**	28.7
Kicks number	-	2.1	2.1	**2.0**	-	**3.0**	**3.0**	3.5
Ball poss.	-	**96.85**	93.77	93.94	-	99.13	**99.49**	99.26
Intersected	33	**4**	9	9	37	12	10	**9**

extensively exploits the idea of a pass and can score goals in very complicated layouts, where straightforward approaches do not work.

6   Conclusions and Future Work

In this paper we have suggested to utilize heuristic search for planning an attack in humanoid robotic football and introduced all the necessary algorithmic components for that. We evaluated the proposed method in simulation and compared it to the baselines. The former outperformed the latter across a wide range of game scenarios. We plan to integrate the proposed method to the existing game controller software used for MIPT RoboCup team "Starkit"[5] at the official RocoCup contests.

An appealing direction of future research is designing a predictive model for robots' behavior and incorporating it to the search algorithm. An orthogonal direction is developing reinforcement learning based planners. Presented work can provide a baseline for the comparison in this case.

References

1. Allali, J.: Rhoban football club-team description paper. Technical report (2019
2. Arain, M.A., Havoutis, I., Semini, C., Buchli, J., Caldwell, D.G.: A comparison of search-based planners for a legged robot. In: 9th International Workshop on Robot Motion and Control, pp. 104–109. IEEE (2013)
3. de Koning, L., Mendoza, J.P., Veloso, M., van de Molengraft, R.: Skills, tactics and plays for distributed multi-robot control in adversarial environments. In: Akiyama, H., Obst, O., Sammut, C., Tonidandel, F. (eds.) RoboCup 2017. LNCS (LNAI), vol. 11175, pp. 277–289. Springer, Cham (2018). https://doi.org/10.1007/978-3-030-00308-1_23
4. Gutmann, J.-S., Fukuchi, M., Fujita, M.: Real-time path planning for humanoid robot navigation. In: IJCAI, pp. 1232–1237 (2005)
5. Hart, P.E., Nilsson, N.J., Raphael, B.: A formal basis for the heuristic determination of minimum cost paths. IEEE Trans. Syst. Sci. Cybern. 4(2), 100–107 (1968)
6. Hornung, A., Maier, D., Bennewitz, M.: Search-based footstep planning. In: Proceedings of the ICRA Workshop on Progress and Open Problems in Motion Planning and Navigation for Humanoids, Karlsruhe, Germany (2013)

---

[5] http://starkit.ru.

7. Mellmann, H., Schlotter, B., Blum, C.: Simulation based selection of actions for a humanoid soccer-robot. In: Behnke, S., Sheh, R., Sarıel, S., Lee, D.D. (eds.) RoboCup 2016. LNCS (LNAI), vol. 9776, pp. 193–205. Springer, Cham (2017). https://doi.org/10.1007/978-3-319-68792-6_16

8. Mendoza, J.P., et al.: CMDragons 2015: coordinated offense and defense of the SSL champions. In: Almeida, L., Ji, J., Steinbauer, G., Luke, S. (eds.) RoboCup 2015. LNCS (LNAI), vol. 9513, pp. 106–117. Springer, Cham (2015). https://doi.org/10.1007/978-3-319-29339-4_9

9. Semendyaev, S., et al.: Starkit team-team description paper. In: RoboCup 2019 Sydney (2019)

10. Wermelinger, M., Fankhauser, P., Diethelm, R., Krüsi, P., Siegwart, R., Hutter, M.: Navigation planning for legged robots in challenging terrain. In 2016 IEEE/RSJ International Conference on Intelligent Robots and Systems (IROS), pp. 1184–1189. IEEE (2016)

Q-Learning of Spatial Actions for Hierarchical Planner of Cognitive Agents

Gleb Kiselev[1]([envelope]) and Aleksandr Panov[1,2]([envelope])

[1] Artificial Intelligence Research Institute, FRC CSC RAS, Moscow, Russia
kiselev@isa.ru
[2] Moscow Institute of Physics and Technology, Moscow, Russia
panov.ai@mipt.ru

Abstract. In the paper, we consider the problem of the robotic movement inaccuracy. We suggest that clarifying the abstract actions of the behavior planner will help build more precise control of the robot. A multi-agent planner for the synthesis of the abstract actions with refinement for a two-dimensional movement task was proposed. We analyze the problem of the action execution by robots and present a way to solve navigation problems through the use of reinforcement learning and deep learning algorithms. This method made it possible to synthesize sets of atomic sub-actions for correcting the state of the robotic platform at each moment of time. We conducted a set of experiments in single and multiagent settings. The synthesis of sub-actions of several tasks formed a training set for the RL model, which was tested on a test example. All considered tasks consisted of moving robotic platforms across a map with obstacles and manipulating environmental objects.

Keywords: Cognitive agent · Sign · Sign-based world model · Human-like knowledge representation · Behavior planning · Task planning · Reinforcement learning · Q-learning · Deep reinforcement learning

1 Introduction

Behavioral planning is an important element of the decision-making cycle of cognitive architecture and often determines the purpose of creating an architecture. When considering well-known cognitive robotic architectures such as STRL [1], LIDA [2], SOAR [3], CARINA [4], it becomes obvious that there is a hierarchical structure of environmental perception and using actuators. This fact is caused by multi-level processing of data received from the sensors, the selection of information and reasoning necessary for the synthesis of the plan based on existing knowledge about the environment, also important is the process of obtaining knowledge through the received information. The presence of a behavioral planner [5–7] capable of synthesizing a multilevel plan, which includes both abstract symbolic and geometric data about the environment, contributes to the c achievement more precise control of the robotic platform.

One of the most well-known problems in Artificial Intelligence (AI) is the problem of suitable knowledge representation. In robotics, this problem can be formulated as the

© Springer Nature Switzerland AG 2020
A. Ronzhin et al. (Eds.): ICR 2020, LNAI 12336, pp. 160–169, 2020.
https://doi.org/10.1007/978-3-030-60337-3_16

task of finding, acquiring, and using the necessary information from the sensors data. In most cognitive architectures, the problem of operating with real environmental data during the synthesis of the behavior plan is not solved, and the data is represented by symbolic abstractions. Also, the non-personalization of agents' knowledge is traced, which blurs the boundaries of differences between them. One of the ways to solve these and many other problems of intellectual behavior synthesis is to use the sign psychologically plausible structure [8, 9] as a way of representing knowledge. The sign has a trapezoidal structure, which is due to the psychologically plausible way of connecting the 4 main types of information. These types of information are the scenarios of using the entity and its role or species composition, which is expressed by the component of significance m of the sign, information about the image representation of the entity in the image component p, information on the semantic description of the entity for the agent in the meaning component a, and the entity name component n. Sign components form semantic networks W_m, W_p, W_a, where a one-to-one correspondence is established between network nodes, which allows you to set the linking functions between them (see [8] for more details). A tuple of 5 elements $\langle W_p, W_m, W_a, R^n, \Theta \rangle$ is called a world model of the cognitive agent, where $R^n = \langle R^m, R^a, R^p \rangle$ are relations on the components of the sign, and Θ are operations on the set of signs.

The sign paradigm made it possible to create a multi-agent hierarchical behavior planner, in which Pospelov [10] pseudo physical spatial logic was implemented. The spatial representation of the environment displays the locations of objects on the map, describes the focus of attention of the agent, and provides the planner with information about the possibility of interaction with objects and subjects of the environment (for more details, see Sect. 2). Along with the algorithm for storing expert knowledge and the communication protocol, the behavior planner is part of the strategic level of the STRL architecture and allows the cognitive agent to increase the autonomy level.

In [11], the case of adapting the STRL cognitive architecture to the MP-RM robotic platform was considered. A multi-agent behavior planning algorithm was tested, in which agents synthesized abstract action plans for moving through a robotic training ground and manipulating environmental objects. Clarifying abstract actions were presented in the form of sub-plans, consisting of actions of moving, turning and interacting with various blocks within the extended domain «BlocksWorld». In the process of adapting the architecture to the robotic platform, several shortcomings of the existing approach were identified and partially eliminated. The main problems of adaptation were the problems of the lack of feedback from the wheelbase, which led to the accumulation of errors when moving the robot, the problem of the exact localization of the robot, and the problem of the synthesis of manipulator activity control. The solutions we used consisted of using additional equipment for reading aruko-markers (all tests were carried indoors) and creating a predefined set of scripts for the manipulator. The architecture adaptation we have presented has a module for assessing its state and, after each action, checks the state against the planned one. When an error is found after the execution of the rotation action or after the execution of the displacement action, the architecture uses the reactive state adaptation module until it reaches a predetermined neighborhood of the permissible error.

In this paper, we will consider the case of clarifying the actions of the spatial planner with reinforcement learning algorithms [12–14]. These algorithms allow us to synthesize a more detailed action plan, which is supposed to allow the architecture to track the error of movement or rotation during the action execution, and not after it, as well as to build control over the manipulator. Earlier [15], the interaction method of the on-policy reinforcement learning (RL) algorithm and the behavior planning algorithm was considered. The main problem under consideration was to obtain the object coordinates from the video stream and manipulate it. But in this paper, we performed a more detailed integration of the algorithms and used the off-policy learning algorithm. RL algorithms suggest a large volume of attempts to implement actions in the learning process, which cannot be implemented on a real robot due to technical limitations. To implement the learning, the corresponding synthetic environments «BlocksWorld» for robot movements and «Manipulator» for interaction with environmental objects were built. The interaction of the behavior planning and learning algorithms was carried out by creating parsers that search for the terminal state of the environment for each of the synthesized actions of the planner and convert them to the state of the learning environment. The result of the activity of the learning algorithm was filling the lower level of the behavior plan hierarchy of the STRL cognitive architecture with atomic actions (see Fig. 1).

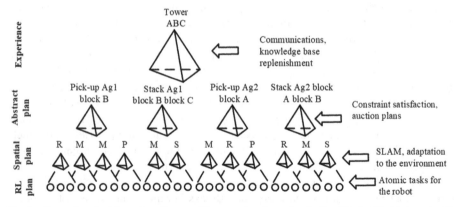

Fig. 1. Example of a hierarchy of a cognitive agent action plan in the *Blocks World* domain. R – rotate action, M – move action, P – pick-up action, S – stack action.

Further, the paper is organized as follows. Part 2 covers the process of synthesizing a dataset with a hierarchical behavior planning algorithm and the process of pre-training the RL agent. Part 3 describes the implementation process of synthesizing atomic actions by the reinforcement learning algorithm. Part 4 shows the experimental results.

2   Sign-Based Dataset Creating Tools

Based on the sign approach to cognitive agent knowledge representation, a behavior planning algorithm was created [15–17]. The version of the MAP_RL planner described in this paper represents the interconnection of the hierarchical and classical task parsers, the grounding algorithm, the behavior planning algorithm, the communication protocol, and the experience storing algorithm.

The grounding algorithm sequentially reads domain data and planning tasks, updating the agent's world model by creating new signs of objects, relationships, actions, and states. If any of the entities are in the agent's world model, it is updated by creating additional causal matrices on the networks of significances and images. In the hierarchical case, the agent clarifies the initial and target state for each of the abstract actions and remembers the possibilities of its use.

The planning algorithm is represented by the process of iterative updating of the state of the agent using the reasoning implemented by the activity propagation processes. The agent reasons which objects are included in his focus of attention and the actions that it can carry out with them. The set of all actions available at each moment is heuristically limited, which makes it possible to reduce the branching factor of the agent's arguments. Adding the selected action to the current plan entails creating the next planning situation and checking for the occurrence of the target situation in the synthesized one. If the agent cannot receive confirmation of the target situation achievement, the planning process continues. In hierarchical planning, there is no target position, but there is a sequence of abstract high-level actions that the agent must clarify. Each of the actions is iteratively clarified before constructing a plan of action for minimal abstraction. After the end of the planning process, the agent selects a plan suitable for several features [15] and optimizes the world model. The plan is saved as a sign of experience [17] and can be reused in future iterations.

The projection of the agent's activity into two-dimensional space required updating the world model with knowledge about the spatial relationships of the environment. To clarify agent knowledge, a symbolic implementation of Pospelov pseudo-physical logic was added, which made it possible to describe the relationships «Close», «Near», «Far», etc., characterizing psychologically plausible relationships. The agent's attention was clarified by 9 cells, and the medium map by 9 static regions. The focus of attention is dynamically recalculated and replenished after each action of the agent. Its size can be changed through the actions «Clarify» and «Abstract», which allow you to find the route in highly loaded places, or speed up planning in open areas.

The multi-agent component of the planner is implemented using the signs «I» and «They» in the agent's world model. The abstraction «They» describes the reflective representation of the collective by the agent, and the abstraction «I» describes abilities, experience, and external representation of oneself. Knowledge about other agents in the team is mediated by the representation of these agents from experience in interacting with them. The knowledge about their capabilities is abstract and characterizes only the logical component (Agent «X» moves only large cubes, Agent «Y» moves only inside the city), and the characteristic of geometric interpretation is present only for one's activity. Agents synthesize common plan actions using the auction plan mechanism and appoint a coordinating agent (usually the most experienced agent). The agent coordinator implements activities to describe the initial and final spatial situations for abstract actions. Further, each of the abstract actions is specified by the corresponding agent-participant using the synthesis of the spatial sub-plan. All spatial sub-plans are collected by the coordinating agent and form a common spatial plan. For each participating agent, the spatial sub-plans of the other agents are mapped to an abstract action.

To search for sub-actions of the spatial actions of the planner, a Q-learning [13, 14] reinforcement learning algorithm is used. Q-learning is a tabular learning method, the table of which describes the reward for performing various actions in environmental conditions (Q-values). The purpose of the algorithm is to form a table that will charac-terize the optimal choice of actions in each state. To describe the activity of a cognitive agent, a probability distribution that characterizes the probability of an agent choosing an action a in a state s is used. The probability distribution is called a strategy:

$$\pi(a|s) = P(a_t = a|s_t = s). \tag{1}$$

In the simplest case, a strategy can be represented greedily, complemented by random transitions. The agent, following the strategy, applies actions and moves from state to state, receiving a reward r for it, which can be either positive or negative.

In addition to the reward at the time, the action takes place, the reward for future actions is taken into account. The effect of future rewards on the choice of action is described by a discount factor $\gamma, \gamma \in [0, 1]$. The Q-values of the table are found by formula 1.

$$Q(s_t, a_t) = Q(s_t, a_t) + \alpha[r_t + \gamma \max_{a_{t+1}} Q(s_{t+1}, a_{t+1}) - Q(s_t, a_t)] \tag{2}$$

α is the learning rate, and $\max_{a_{t+1}} Q(s_{t+1}, a_{t+1})$ is the Q-value of the best action at a time $t + 1$. To describe the actions of the manipulator, the DQN representation of the

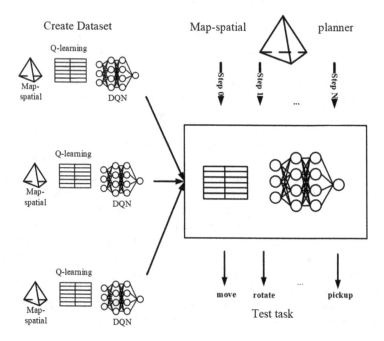

Fig. 2. Creating a dataset and solving a test task.

Q-learning algorithm with parameterization in which the table of values was replaced with a neural network, was used. The action is selected similarly to the Q-learning algorithm, then a tuple (sample) of values (s_t, s_{t+1}, a, r) is saved, random samples are selected from the memory and calculated $\max_{a_{t+1}} Q(s_{t+1}, a_{t+1})$, which is transmitted to the neural network as a reference value. The algorithm is pre-trained in tasks marked with the help of the planner and forms a strategy that used in test iterations (see Fig. 2).

The pre-trained RL agent and the planner's task enter the «input» of the platform test task, for each of the steps of the planner, is updated by the RL agent, which forms the atomic motion vector of the robot at the «output». The RL agent is trained in the synthesis sub-actions process for the planner abstract steps. On the left side of the figure, the process of training Q-learning and DQN agents is schematically shown, where for each of the spatial plans, the search for sub-actions is iteratively launched. Further, on the right side of the figure, the call of trained agents for the test problem is displayed. The better-detailed description of the whole algorithm is in Sect. 3.

3   Detailing Actions with Q-Learning and DQN Algorithms

The agent behavior plan synthesized by the MAP_RL algorithm is a list of high-level actions, which include refinement and abstraction of the focus of attention. Due to the different planned range of agent movements, the adaptation of the planner steps for the Q-learning environment was required. The adaptation process is carried out by parsing the steps of the planner and identifying subspaces of 30×30 cells, the size of which was obtained empirically. The learning process of the Q-learning agent takes place in an environment whose characteristics are set dynamically for each of the subspaces and the learning of the Q-learning agent in them is parallelized. The subspaces provided a stable synthesis of steps, which included actions for moving 1 cell in any direction, pick-up, and stack *Blocks World* environment blocks.

The *Blocks World* environment is not included in the list of base environments available for the OpenAI gym and was created by modernizing the GridWorld environment with additional actions. The environment allows the agent to evaluate the agent actions and make conclusions on whether the agent is closer to the goal. Both the environment and the agent's actions are simplified in comparison with the description of the environment and the actions of the planning algorithm, which allows to more quickly sort through all possible combinations of actions. A reward function was made in the environment that evaluated each of the agent's actions:

- -1 – to optimize the plan in length;
- -5 – to prohibit the agent from attempting to perform impossible actions, which included attempts to go beyond the map and interact with the blocks if they are absent near the agent;
- $+5$ – to motivate the agent to take actions to manipulate environmental objects if they were nearby;
- $+10$ – successful completion of the task.

Each of the actions for picking up and moving blocks is a complex action in 3D space and, decomposition it into atomic sub-actions is not trivial. To simplify the task decomposing implementation of the moving of blocks actions into atomic components, under the atomic action, we considered the actions of turning each of the joints 15° clockwise or counterclockwise. A value of 15° was obtained empirically by interacting with the design of the manipulator. The features of the MP-RM manipulator under consideration are the presence of 5 servos and an actuator in the form of a clamp or a vacuum pump. The implementation of each of the actions in the Q-learning learning environment increased the considered sets of actions and states by several times and the Q-learning algorithm ceased to converge when considering the manipulator with more than 3 servos.

A Q-learning approach based on the use of neural networks, DQN, was chosen to search for the effects of an existing manipulator. The Manipulator environment was created, within which the agent's position is considered agent-centered, each of the agent's rotation actions is performed to interact with the environment. The number of possible actions of the agent has ceased to coincide with the Q-learning environment and adaptation of the environment to the new environment was required. A parser has been created that allows you to search the generated actions of a Q-learning environment to search for actions with objects. Based on the selected actions, new subtasks were synthesized that were launched by the DQN agent.

When initializing a new task, the DQN agent receives information about the manipulator position and the target medium in 3D space. Further, the agent carries out activities based on the tolerance reward function (x, bounds, margin, value_at_margin) from Deep-Mind Control Suite [18]. This function allows the agent to receive a reward of 1 when entering the distance from the robot actuator to the desired environment object in the bound's framework. Empirically, the problem of the tolerance approach was identified, which consists in the non-optimal choice of the sequence of actions of the agent for interacting with the object, due to the increase in the agent's reward, by performing activities in the space included in the bounds, but not fulfilling the task.

4 Experiments

As part of the development of mechanisms for the interaction of reinforcement learning algorithms and a sign approach to the synthesis of a spatial plan by an agent, a series of experiments with single-agent and multi-agent tasks were carried out. The experiments differed in complexity; in the first experiments, agents needed to approach the block on the map without obstacles, pick-up it with the manipulator and move with the block to another block to stack them. Further experiments were complicated by the presence of obstacles that needed to be passed, which greatly increased the combinatorial complexity of finding the optimal plan of behavior. The first five experiments were conducted to train the RL agent and develop a strategy for interacting with the environment. The last, 6th experiment, was conducted as part of testing the result.

The planner synthesized multi-agent behavior plans using agents without shared memory. Each of the agents was separated into a separate process, agents had general knowledge about the capabilities of other agents, but did not have a detailed representation of spatial transitions. In the process of clarifying the actions by the RL agent, each of the actions was specified separately, but the weights of the neural network were formed based on the actions of all agents. There was no separation of the dataset for training by various agents, based on the mechanical uniformity of the tasks under consideration.

Out of the whole set of planner actions, steps of 30 × 30 cells that were optimal for learning algorithms were formed; actions to pick up and stack were divided into actions to move the agent to a state in which the block was in direct visibility, directly approaching and taking the block and moving to a previously planned state. A graphical representation of the experiments is shown in Fig. 3.

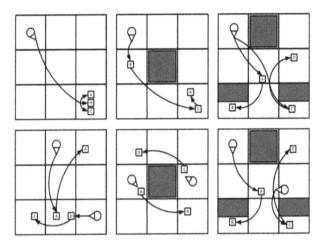

Fig. 3. Task planning problems.

The experiments were carried out on a laptop with the following characteristics: Intel Core i7-8565U CPU 1.8 GHz 199 GHz RAM 16 Gb. Evaluation of the results was carried out according to the time of the task execution, the number of planned steps, the number of sub-actions found by Q-learning, the number of sub-actions of the manipulator found by DQN. The results are shown in Table 1.

Table 1. MAP-RL results.

	Single task 1	Single task 2	Single task 3	Mul. task 1	Mul. task 2	Mul. task 3
Time (s)	22.4	112.5	263.4	283.03	526.5	617.5
Planner steps	6	12	39	11	31	35
Q-learning steps	445	412	640	430	452	608
DQN steps	400	900	700	400	900	700

Synthesized by reinforcement learning algorithms actions are described agent-centered and represent the sequence of coordinates of the agent and the block, a simplified representation of the manipulator and the action. The description of the manipulator generated by the DQN is represented by a sequence of angles of the servos, the actuator, and the relative coordinates of the block.

5 Conclusion

The paper presents a method for clarifying actions synthesized by a psychologically plausible behavior planner to the motor level. The actions of the motor level make it possible to coordinate the behavior of the robotic platform at each time moment of the execution of the planned task. In further studies, reinforcement learning algorithms will be compared as part of the search for the optimal algorithm for the tasks of moving in clattered spaces and manipulating environmental objects. We will consider options for saving the synthesized sequences of atomic actions in the form of options that allow the agent to use precedents for performing actions.

Acknowledgements. The reported study was supported by RFBR, research Project No. 17-29-07051.

References

1. Emel'yanov, S., Makarov, D., Panov, A.I., Yakovlev, K.: Multilayer cognitive architecture for UAV control. Cogn. Syst. Res. **39**, 58–72 (2016). https://doi.org/10.1016/j.cogsys.2015.12.008
2. Franklin, S., Patterson, F.G.: The LIDA architecture: adding new modes of learning to an intelligent, autonomous, software agent. Integr. Des. Process Technol. **703**, 764–1004 (2006)
3. Laird, J.E., Lebiere, C., Rosenbloom, P.S.: A standard model of the mind: toward a common computational framework across artificial intelligence, cognitive science, neuroscience, and robotics. AI Mag. (2017). https://doi.org/10.1609/aimag.v38i4.2744
4. Caro, M.F., Josvula, D.P., Gomez, A.A., Kennedy, C.M.: Introduction to the CARINA metacognitive architecture. In: Proceedings of 2018 IEEE 17th International Conference on Cognitive Informatics and Cognitive Computing, ICCI*CC 2018, pp. 530–540 (2018). https://doi.org/10.1109/ICCI-CC.2018.8482051
5. Yang, F., Lyu, D., Liu, B., Gustafson, S.: Peorl: integrating symbolic planning and hierarchical reinforcement learning for robust decision-making. In: IJCAI International Joint Conference on Artificial Intelligence, pp. 4860–4866 (2018)
6. De Silva, L.: HATP: hierarchical agent-based task planner. In: International Conference on Autonomous Agents and Multi-Agent Systems, pp. 1823–1825 (2018)
7. Kaelbling, L.P., Lozano-Pérez, T.: Integrated task and motion planning in belief space. Int. J. Robot. Res. **32**, 1194–1227 (2013). https://doi.org/10.1177/0278364913484072
8. Osipov, G.S., Panov, A.I., Chudova, N.V.: Behavior control as a function of consciousness. I. World model and goal setting. J. Comput. Syst. Sci. Int. **53**(4), 517–529 (2014)
9. Osipov, G.S., Panov, A.I., Chudova, N.V.: Behavior control as a function of consciouness. II. Synthesis of a behavior plan. J. Comput. Syst. Sci. Int. **54**, 882–896 (2015)
10. Pospelov, D.A.: Situacionnoe upravlenie. Teoria i praktika. Ph. Nauka (1986)
11. Kiselev, G.A.: Intelligent system for planning the behavior of a robotic systems coalition based on a sign world model. J. Inf. Technol. Comput. Syst. 21–37 (2020). https://doi.org/10.14357/20718632200203
12. Sutton, S.S., Barto, A.G.: Reinforcement Learning: An Introduction. MIT Press, Cambridge (1998)
13. Watkins, C.J.C.H., Dayan, P.: Q-learning. Mach. Learn. **8**, 279–292 (1992). https://doi.org/10.1007/bf00992698

14. Mnih, V., Kavukcuoglu, K., Silver, D., et al.: Human-level control through deep reinforcement learning. Nature **518**, 529–533 (2015). https://doi.org/10.1038/nature14236
15. Aitygulov, E., Kiselev, G., Panov, A.I.: Task and spatial planning by the cognitive agent with human-like knowledge representation. In: Ronzhin, A., Rigoll, G., Meshcheryakov, R. (eds.) ICR 2018. LNCS (LNAI), vol. 11097, pp. 1–12. Springer, Cham (2018). https://doi.org/10.1007/978-3-319-99582-3_1
16. Kiselev, G.A., Panov, A.I.: Sign-based approach to the task of role distribution in the coalition of cognitive agents. SPIIRAS Proc. **57**, 161–187 (2018)
17. Kiselev, G., Panov, A.: Hierarchical psychologically inspired planning for human-robot interaction tasks. In: Ronzhin, A., Rigoll, G., Meshcheryakov, R. (eds.) ICR 2019. LNCS (LNAI), vol. 11659, pp. 150–160. Springer, Cham (2019). https://doi.org/10.1007/978-3-030-26118-4_15
18. Tassa, Y., et al.: Google Deepmind 2018 DeepMind Control Suite (2018)

Modeling of Increased Rigidity of Industrial Manipulator

Eugene Larkin, Aleksey Bogomolov, and Maxim Antonov[(✉)]

Tula State University, Lenin Av. 92, 300012 Tula, Russia
elarkin@mail.ru, max0594@yandex.ru

Abstract. The main problem of using robots in industry is a providing of high precision of motions during mechanical operations. Manipulators with traditional structures include mobility modules, disposed in series, one after another, so error, occurred at the base link, amplified by the subsequent mechanical assemblies of the chain. In turn, when actuators, moving manipulator modulus, affect on it in parallel, their errors are averaged up. The manipulator, in which rigidity is provided with triangle structure and moving of rod is provided with linear actuators operated in parallel, is considered. For proposed manipulator direct and inverse kinematics tasks are solved, and dependencies, which define both space position of manipulator grip in accordance of linear actuators lengths, and needful linear actuators lengths in accordance of space position of grip, are obtained. Also functions, which determine exactness of manipulator grip positioning, are obtained. Dynamic model with a system of non-linear differential equations, which links length of linear actuators and forces on integrated actuators stems and transients as manipulator reaction on Heaviside function was constructed.

Keywords: Manipulator · Rigidity · Direct kinematics task · Inverse kinematics task · Exactness · Linear actuator

1 Introduction

Industrial robots are commonly used to perform tasks such as loading computer numerical control (CNC) machines, welding, laser and plasma cutting, painting surfaces, easy milling operations, etc. [1]. To execute of technological operations mentioned, high accuracy of manipulator grip positioning is required. Common method of increasing mechanical exactness, introducing grip position feedback, is not always possible due to the fact, that the target of grip, as a rule, is mechanically separated from manipulator. Known kinematics schemes of industrial robots include mobility modules, disposed in series, one after another, and control process is restricted with introducing local feedbacks in modules. So error, occurred at the base link, is amplified by the subsequent mechanical assemblies of the chain [2] and is not compensated with general grip position feedback. Grip positioning error arises, when it is necessary to solve step-by-step tracing problem. In this case, error of previous step increases by errors of subsequent steps and tracing in common become highly imprecise [3–5].

© Springer Nature Switzerland AG 2020
A. Ronzhin et al. (Eds.): ICR 2020, LNAI 12336, pp. 170–178, 2020.
https://doi.org/10.1007/978-3-030-60337-3_17

To solve the problem of accuracy increasing it is necessary both improve the rigidity of framework, and replace serial arrangement of mechanical modules with a parallel one [6–8]. Most rigid plane construction is the triangle. Most rigid 3D-construction is tetrahedron, which structure was laid in the basis of manipulator under investigation. Tetrahedron consists of four triangles, and all angles between edges of it are defined with their lengths only. At the same time, dependencies, which describe ratios between edges and angles of tetrahedron are rather complex, that highly restricts practical use of such type construction in engineering practice. So to overcome contradiction between needs for rigid manipulators and complexity of their kinematics and dynamics model below analytical mathematical description is worked out.

2 Task Solutions for Direct and Inverse Kinematics

The diagram of an industrial robot with increased rigidity is shown in Fig. 1.

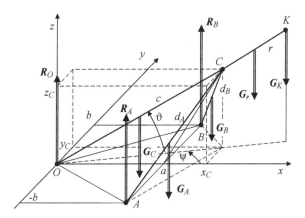

Fig. 1. The kinematic diagram of an industrial robot with increased rigidity.

The system includes the rod OC with fixed length c, on which a linear actuator is mounted, with changing stem length r, from point O to point K, in which the grip is fixed. The system is driven by linear actuators with stem lengths of d_A and d_B, respectively. Both rod c and linear actuators d_A, d_B rotate in double-hinged joints O, A, B. The rod c with rigidly linear actuator r has in the spherical coordinate system with center in the hinge O angle coordinates ψ, ϑ and linear coordinate $c + r$. Linear actuators d_A and d_B with use double-hinged joints are fasten in the point C to the rod c. The direct problem of kinematics is to determine the angles ψ, ϑ when the actuators A, and B stems lengths d_A and d_B are known. The inverse problem of kinematics [9] is to determine the required lengths of linear motors d_A and d_B from the known angles ψ and ϑ.

The lengths of segments OC, AC and BC are equal, respectively:

$$\begin{cases} c^2 = x_C^2 + y_C^2 + z_C^2; \\ d_A^2 = (a - x_C)^2 + (-b - y_C)^2 + z_C^2; \\ d_B^2 = (a - x_C)^2 + (b - y_C)^2 + z_C^2; \end{cases} \tag{1}$$

In this case, taking into account the known dependences of recalculation of Cartesian coordinates into spherical [10], a solution of the inverse kinematics problem may be obtained as follows:

$$\begin{cases} d_A^2 = (a - c \cos \vartheta \cos \psi)^2 + (b + c \cos \vartheta \sin \psi)^2 + (c \sin \vartheta)^2; \\ d_B^2 = (a - c \cos \vartheta \cos \psi)^2 + (b - c \cos \vartheta \sin \psi)^2 + (c \sin \vartheta)^2. \end{cases} \quad (2)$$

To solve the direct kinematics problem [11], the square components x_c^2, y_c^2 should be excluded from (1) by means of substitution of the first equation into the second and third ones:

$$\begin{cases} d_A^2 = a^2 + b^2 + c^2 - 2ax_C + 2by_C; \\ d_B^2 = a^2 + b^2 + c^2 - 2ax_C - 2by_C. \end{cases} \quad (3)$$

The system of Eqs. (3) is linear with respect to x_C and y_C, and have the following solution:

$$\begin{cases} x_C = \frac{2a^2 + 2b^2 + 2c^2 - d_A^2 - d_B^2}{4a}; \\ y_C = \frac{d_A^2 - d_B^2}{4b}; \\ z_C^2 = c^2 - x_C^2 - y_C^2. \end{cases} \quad (4)$$

With use (4) coordinates of the grip K are as follows:

$$\begin{cases} x_K = \frac{c+r}{c} \cdot \frac{2a^2 + 2b^2 + 2c^2 - d_A^2 - d_B^2}{4a}; \\ y_K = \frac{c+r}{c} \cdot \frac{d_A^2 - d_B^2}{4b}; \\ z_K = \frac{c+r}{c} \cdot \sqrt{c^2 - x_C^2 - y_C^2}. \end{cases} \quad (5)$$

From (5) it follows that:

$$\vartheta = \arcsin \frac{z_C}{c} = \arcsin \frac{\sqrt{c^2 - \left[\frac{2a^2 + 2b^2 + 2c^2 - d_A^2 - d_B^2}{4a}\right]^2 - \left[\frac{d_A^2 - d_B^2}{4b}\right]^2}}{c}; \quad (6)$$

$$\psi = \arctan \frac{y_C}{x_C} = \arctan \frac{a(d_A^2 - d_B^2)}{b(2a^2 + 2b^2 + 2c^2 - d_A^2 - d_B^2)}. \quad (7)$$

In (6), (7) a, b, c are parameters, d_A, d_B are arguments. Their values are restricted as follows:

$$d_{A\min} \leq d_A \leq d_{A\max}, \quad d_{B\min} \leq d_B \leq d_{B\max}; 0 \leq r \leq r_{\max}, \quad (8)$$

where $d_{A\min}$, $d_{B\min}$, $r_{\min}$ are lower bounds of values d_A, d_B, r, $d_{A\max}$, $d_{B\max}$, $r_{\max}$ are upper bounds of values d_A, d_B, r, respectively.

Dependences (5), within constraints (8) are shown in Fig. 2 (a, b, c), respectively. Figure 2 (c) represents the hemisphere of grip K movement. Modeling was carried out with use following parameters: $a = 0.2$ m, $b = 0.2$ m, $c = 0.4$ m, $0.3 \leq d_{A,B} \leq 0.6$ m.

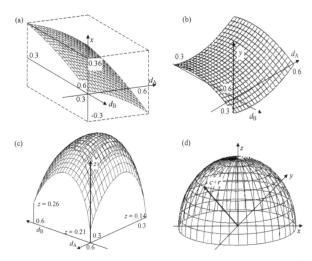

Fig. 2. The kinematic diagram of an industrial robot with increased rigidity.

3 Estimation of Positioning Accuracy

To estimate the accuracy of positioning, it is necessary to determine the influence of primary parameters a, b, c on the shifting of coordinates x_K, y_K, z_K. Degree of influence is determined by partial derivatives:

$$\frac{\partial x_K}{\partial a} = \frac{c+r}{2c}; \quad \frac{\partial x_K}{\partial b} = \frac{c+r}{c} \cdot \frac{b}{a}; \quad \frac{\partial x_K}{\partial c} = \frac{-r}{c^2} \cdot \frac{2a^2 + 2b^2 + 2c^2 - d_A^2 - d_B^2}{4a} + \frac{(c+r)c}{a^2};$$
(9)

$$\frac{\partial y_K}{\partial a} = 0; \quad \frac{\partial y_K}{\partial b} = -\frac{c+r}{c} \cdot \frac{d_A^2 - d_B^2}{4b^2}; \quad \frac{\partial y_K}{\partial c} = -\frac{r}{c^2} \cdot \frac{d_A^2 - d_B^2}{4b};$$
(10)

$$\frac{\partial z_K}{\partial a} = \frac{c+r}{c} \cdot \left(\frac{-x_C}{\sqrt{c^2 - x_C^2 - y_C^2}} \frac{\partial x_C}{\partial a} - \frac{y_C}{\sqrt{c^2 - x_C^2 - y_C^2}} \frac{\partial y_C}{\partial a} \right);$$

$$\frac{\partial z_K}{\partial b} = \frac{c+r}{c} \cdot \left(\frac{-x_C}{\sqrt{c^2 - x_C^2 - y_C^2}} \frac{\partial x_C}{\partial b} - \frac{y_C}{\sqrt{c^2 - x_C^2 - y_C^2}} \frac{\partial y_C}{\partial b} \right);$$
(11)

$$\frac{\partial z_K}{\partial c} = -\frac{r}{c^2} \sqrt{c^2 - x_C^2 - y_C^2} + \frac{c+r}{c} \cdot \left(\frac{c}{\sqrt{c^2 - x_C^2 - y_C^2}} - \frac{cx_C}{a\sqrt{c^2 - x_C^2 - y_C^2}} \right).$$

Let $\alpha \in \{a, b, c\}$. When manipulator is manufactured, parameters α are implemented with following deviations:

$$\alpha_{nom} - \Delta_\alpha^- \le \alpha \le \alpha_{nom} + \Delta_\alpha^+,$$
(12)

where α_{nom} is the nominal parameter α value; Δ_α^-, Δ_α^+ are deviations from nominal parameter, in common $\Delta_\alpha^- \ne \Delta_\alpha^+$.
Choice

$$\Delta_\alpha = \max\left(\Delta_\alpha^-, \ \Delta_\alpha^+\right)$$
(13)

gives maximum deviation of parameter $\alpha \in \{a, b, c\}$.

So, expressions

$$
\begin{aligned}
\Delta_{xK} &= \left|\frac{\partial x_K(d_A,\, d_A,\, d_r)}{\partial a}\right|\Delta_a + \left|\frac{\partial x_K(d_A,\, d_A,\, d_r)}{\partial b}\right|\Delta_b + \left|\frac{\partial x_K(d_A,\, d_A,\, d_r)}{\partial c}\right|\Delta_c; \\
\Delta_{yK} &= \left|\frac{\partial y_K(d_A,\, d_A,\, d_r)}{\partial a}\right|\Delta_a + \left|\frac{\partial y_K(d_A,\, d_A,\, d_r)}{\partial b}\right|\Delta_b + \left|\frac{\partial y_K(d_A,\, d_A,\, d_r)}{\partial c}\right|\Delta_c; \\
\Delta_{zK} &= \left|\frac{\partial z_K(d_A,\, d_A,\, d_r)}{\partial a}\right|\Delta_a + \left|\frac{\partial z_K(d_A,\, d_A,\, d_r)}{\partial b}\right|\Delta_b + \left|\frac{\partial z_K(d_A,\, d_A,\, d_r)}{\partial c}\right|\Delta_c,
\end{aligned}
$$

$$(14)$$

where d_A, d_B, d_r are restricted as (8), permits to evaluate functions $x_K(d_A, d_A, d_r)$, $y_K(d_A, d_A, d_r)$, $z_K(d_A, d_A, d_r)$, absolute deviations from nominal in the whole operational area.

4 Dynamic Model

Let us return to the scheme of the manipulation system, which is shown in Fig. 1. The entire system is driven with forces F_A, F_B, F_r, created along stems of linear actuators A, B, r, having current lengths d_A, d_B and r, respectively. In addition, the forces from the side of the rod affect on the linear actuators A, B, r, and the forces from the linear actuators affect on the rod, in accordance with Newton's third law. Linear actuators A, B affect on the rod in parallel, linear actuator r affects on it in series.

Let us assume that dissipative forces are reduced to viscous forces, affect on the stems of linear actuators, and viscous friction moments created in hinges A, B, O. Then equation systems, describing the movement of the linear actuators A, B, (the direction from the joint A, B to the joint C is considered as positive) are as follows:

$$
\begin{cases}
m_A \ddot{d}_A + \eta_l \dot{d}_A = F_A + R_{Al} - m_A g \sin\vartheta_A; \\
\frac{d(J_A \dot{\vartheta}_A)}{dt} + \eta_t \dot{\vartheta}_A = -m_A g \frac{d_A}{2} - R_{A\vartheta} d_A; \\
\frac{d(J_A \dot{\psi}_A)}{dt} + \eta_t \dot{\psi}_A = R_{A\psi} d_A,
\end{cases}
\tag{15}
$$

$$
\begin{cases}
m_B \ddot{d}_B + \eta_l \dot{d}_B = F_B + R_{Bl} - m_B g \sin\vartheta_B; \\
\frac{d(J_B \dot{\vartheta}_B)}{dt} + \eta_t \dot{\vartheta}_B = -m_B g \frac{d_B}{2} - R_{B\vartheta} d_B; \\
\frac{d(J_B \dot{\psi}_B)}{dt} + \eta_t \dot{\psi}_B = R_{B\psi} d_B,
\end{cases}
\tag{16}
$$

where m_A and m_B are masses of linear actuators A and B, respectively; F_A, F_B are forces, developed on actuators A and B stems; η_l is the coefficient of viscous friction during the movement of linear actuators stems; η_t is the coefficient of viscous friction during rotation of linear drives in hinges; F_A, F_B are forces developed along rods of linear actuators A and B, respectively; R_{Al}, R_{Bl} are longitudinal components of force vectors acting in the hinge C, on actuators A and B in the direction of axes x_A and x_B, located along actuator stems; $R_{A\psi}$, $R_{B\psi}$ are transverse components of force vectors acting in the hinge C, on actuators A and B in the direction of axes y_A and y_B, located in horizontal plane in perpendicular to actuator stems; $R_{A\vartheta}$, $R_{B\vartheta}$ are the transverse components of force vectors acting in the hinge C, on actuators A and B in the direction of axes y_A and y_B, located in vertical plane in perpendicular to actuator stems; $J_A = \frac{m_A d_A^2}{3}$ and $J_B = \frac{m_B d_B^2}{3}$ are current variable moment of inertia of the linear actuator A and B, respectively, relative to hinges A and B; g is the acceleration of the gravity [12, 13].

For modeling of payload K transfer the rod C and the linear actuator r are considered as a whole, in which actuator stem is the prolongation of the rod. In addition, we assume that the mass of the transported payload m_K is concentrated at point K. Due to such approach mathematical description includes rod rotation in the hinge O under forces $\mathbf{R}_A$, $\mathbf{R}_B$ and longitudinal movement under the force of actuator:

$$
\begin{cases}
(m_r + m_K)\ddot{d}_r + \eta_l \dot{d}_r = F_r + (m_r + m_K)g \sin\theta; \\
\frac{dJ}{dt}\dot{\vartheta} + \eta_t\,\vartheta = -m_C g\frac{c}{2} - m_r g\left(c + \frac{r}{2}\right) - m_K g(c + r) + R_{CA\vartheta}c + R_{CB\vartheta}c; \\
\frac{dJ}{dt}\dot{\psi} + \eta_t\,\psi = R_{CA\psi}c + R_{CB\psi}c,
\end{cases}
\tag{17}
$$

where m_C, m_r and m_K are masses of the rod C, the actuator r and the payload K, respectively; d_r is the linear actuator r length; $R_{CA\vartheta}$, $R_{CB\vartheta}$ are the transverse components of force vectors acting in the hinge C, on actuators A and B in the direction of axes z_A and z_B, located in vertical plane in perpendicular to actuator stems; $R_{CA\psi}$, $R_{CB\psi}$ are the transverse components of force vectors acting in the hinge C, on actuators A and B in the direction of axes y_A and z_B, located in horizontal plane; in perpendicular to actuator stems; $J = \frac{(m_C + m_r)(c+r)^2}{3} + m_K(c + r)^2$ is the current integrated variable moment of inertia of the rod C, the linear actuator r and the payload m_K [12–14].

It is necessary to admit, that longitudinal components of forces R_{CAl}, R_{CBl}, acting on the rod from actuators A and B side, are fully compensated by static reaction in the hinge O, due to the fact they are not included into (17). Also in (15), (16), (17) force vectors $\mathbf{R}_{CA}/\mathbf{R}_A$, $\mathbf{R}_{CB}/\mathbf{R}_B$ are represented in different base coordinate systems, so Newton's Third Law looks as follows:

$$
\mathbf{R}_{CA} = -\mathbf{R}_A; \ \mathbf{R}_{CB} = -\mathbf{R}_B,
\tag{18}
$$

where $\mathbf{R}_A = \left(R_{Al},\ R_{A\psi},\ R_{A\vartheta}\right)$ (explanation to (15)); $\mathbf{R}_B = \left(R_{Bl},\ R_{B\psi},\ R_{B\vartheta}\right)$ (explanation to (16)); $\mathbf{R}_{CA} = \left(R_{CAl},\ R_{CA\psi},\ R_{CA\vartheta}\right)$; $\mathbf{R}_{CB} = \left(R_{CBl},\ R_{CB\psi},\ R_{CB\vartheta}\right)$; (explanation to (17)).

Coordinate systems, linked with actuators A, B and rod C, from basic coordinate system $xOyz$ are obtained as follows:

$$
\begin{cases}
\left(i_A, j_A, k_A\right) = (i, j, k)T_{\psi A}T_{\vartheta A}; \\
\left(i_B, j_B, k_B\right) = (i, j, k)T_{\psi B}T_{\vartheta B}; \\
\left(i_C, j_C, k_C\right) = (i, j, k)T_{\psi C}T_{\vartheta C},
\end{cases}
\tag{19}
$$

where (i, j, k) are orts, linked with $xOyz$ coordinates; $\left(i_{A,B,C}, j_{A,B,C}, k_{A,B,C}\right)$ are orts, linked with $x_{A,B,C}Oy_{A,B,C}z_{A,B,C}$ $xOyz$ coordinates; $T_{\psi A,B,C}$, $T_{\vartheta A,B,C}$ are the rotation matrices;

$$
T_{\psi A,B,C} = \begin{pmatrix}
\cos\psi_{A,B,C} & \sin\psi_{A,B,C} & 0 \\
-\sin\psi_{A,B,C} & \cos\psi_{A,B,C} & 0 \\
0 & 0 & 1
\end{pmatrix};
\tag{20}
$$

$$Y_{\vartheta A,B,C} = \begin{pmatrix} \cos \vartheta_{A,B,C} & 0 & -\sin \psi_{A,B,C} \\ 0 & 1 & 0 \\ \sin \psi_{A,B,C} & 0 & \cos \psi_{A,B,C} \end{pmatrix}. \tag{21}$$

Angles $\psi_C = \psi$, $\vartheta_C = \vartheta$ were obtained above (look (7)). Angles ψ_A, ϑ_A, ψ_B, ϑ_B may be obtained from (5):

$$\psi_A = \arctan \frac{y_c + b}{x_c - a}; \quad \vartheta_A = \arctan \frac{z_c}{\sqrt{(x_c - a)^2 + (y_c + b)^2}}; \tag{22}$$

$$\psi_B = \arctan \frac{y_c - b}{x_c - a}; \quad \vartheta_B = \arctan \frac{z_c}{\sqrt{(x_c - a)^2 + (y_c - b)^2}}. \tag{23}$$

With use (19), Newton's Third Law for the case under consideration is as follows:

$$\left(R_{Al}, R_{A\psi}, R_{A\vartheta}\right)T_{\psi C}T_{\vartheta C} = \left(R_{CAl}, R_{CA\psi}, R_{CA\vartheta}\right)T_{\psi A}T_{\vartheta A}; \tag{24}$$

$$\left(R_{Al}, R_{A\psi}, R_{A\vartheta}\right)T_{\psi C}T_{\vartheta C} = \left(R_{CAl}, R_{CA\psi}, R_{CA\vartheta}\right)T_{\psi A}T_{\vartheta A}. \tag{25}$$

Dependencies (15), (16), (17), (24), (25) form full dynamic model of the industrial manipulator, and may be solved respect to coordinates d_A, d_B, d_r by one of well known method [15–17].

For clearing up a common manipulator behavior system was integrated by Euler's simplest method under forces F_A, F_B, F_r, which are performed as follows:

$$F_{A,B,r} = \eta(t), \tag{26}$$

where $\eta(t)$ is the Heaviside function.

Actual modeling was carried out based on the following design parameters of the manipulator: $a = 0.2\,\text{m}$, $b = 0.2\,\text{m}$, $c = 0.4\,\text{m}$, $m_A = 5.7\,\text{kg}$, $m_B = 5.7\,\text{kg}$, $m_C = 3\,\text{kg}$, $m_r = 1\,\text{kg}$, $0 \leq m_K \leq 2\,\text{kg}$.

Result of integration is shown in Fig. 3.

Figure 3 (a) shows the transition process, arising in actuators A and B, when control signals are applied to actuators simultaneously. Straight line 1 represents behavior of linear inertialess system, Curve 1 demonstrates reaction, when model is linear. In this case the curve tends to the asymptote 3. Curve 4 shows acceleration of stems lengths as actuator load conditions change due to changing inclination of rod C.

Figure 3 (b) shows the family of transition processes, arising in actuator r, when payload, bearing by grip K arises from 0 kg (most quick response of manipulator) till 2 kg (least quick response). Figure 3 (c) shows the family of transition processes, arising in actuator r, when rod c takes different angular ϑ positions. In this case response times under all angular rod positions are quite similar, but asymptotes, to which curves tend, are situated at different angles.

The construction of the transient families shown in Fig. 3 (b) and Fig. 3 (c) for reasons that the control signal F_r was supplied to drive r.

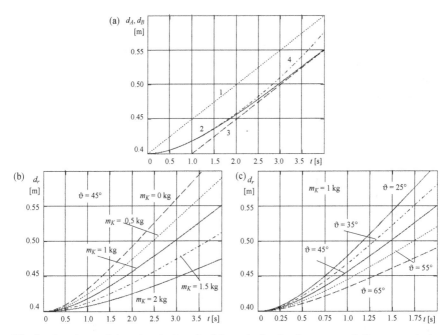

Fig. 3. Transients of changing the length of the rods d_A, d_B, d_r actuators A, B, r respectively.

5 Conclusion

The problem of increasing a rigidity of industrial manipulators was analyzed. Kinematics structure with two parallel and one serial linear actuators, which drive rod with the grip onto sphere with alterable radius, is proposed. Models, of direct and inverse kinematics tasks, exactness estimation and dynamics of actuator stems moving are worked up. Further development of the item should be directed on decreasing of weight/size characteristics and working out the engineering method of design similar construction with increased rigidity.

The research was carried out within the grant (19-38-90058\19 (C61019GRFa)) of Russian Foundation for Basic Research (RFBR).

References

1. Ji, W., Wang, L.: Industrial robotic machining: a review. Int. J. Adv. Manuf. Technol. **103**, 1239–1255 (2019)
2. Siciliano, B., Khatib, O.: Springer Handbook of Robotics, 1st edn. Springer, Heidelberg (2008). https://doi.org/10.1007/978-3-540-30301-5
3. Gong, C., Yuan, J., Ni, J.: Nongeometric error identification and compensation for robotic system by inverse calibration. Int. J. Mach. Tools Manuf **2**(14), 2119–2137 (2000)
4. Lambrechts, P., Boerlage, M., Steinbuch, M.: Trajectory planning and feedforward design for electromechanical motion systems. Control Eng. Pract. **13**(2), 145–157 (2005)
5. Swevers, J., Verdonck, W., De Schutter, J.: Dynamic model identification for industrial robots. IEEE Control Syst. **26**(5), 58–71 (2007)

6. Larkin, E., Dolgov, A., Osetrov, A., Osetrov, C.: Industrial robot module, Patent No. 103086 (RF) IPC B 25 J 9/08. Tula State University Bull, vol. 9 (2010)
7. Petrenko, V.I., Tebueva, F.B., Gurchinsky, M.M., Antonov, V.O., Pavlov, A.S.: Predictive assessment of operator's hand trajectory with the copying type of control for solution of the inverse dynamic problem. SPIIRAS Proc. **18**, 123–147 (2019). https://doi.org/10.15622/sp.18.1.123-147
8. Gorobtsov, A.S., Andreev, A.E., Markov, A.E., Skorikov, A.V., Tarasov, P.S.: Features of solving the inverse dynamic method equations for the synthesis of stable walking robots controlled motion. SPIIRAS Proc. **18**, 85–122 (2019). https://doi.org/10.15622/sp.18.1.85-122
9. Botto, D., Gola, M.: Solution of the inverse kinematic problem of a robot manipulator with Eulerian joints. IFAC Proc. Vol. **27**(14), 375–379 (1994)
10. Sciavicco, L., Siciliano, B.: Coordinate transformation: a solution algorithm for one class of robots. IEEE Trans. Syst. Man Cybern. **16**(4), 550–559 (1986)
11. Morella, A., Tarokhb, M., Acosta, L.: Solving the forward kinematics problem in parallel robots using support vector regression. Eng. Appl. Artif. Intell. **26**(7), 1698–1706 (2013)
12. Dreizler, R.M., Lüdde, C.S.: Theoretical Mechanics – Theoretical Physics 1, 1st edn. Springer, Heidelberg (2010). https://doi.org/10.1007/978-3-642-11138-9
13. Helrich, C.S.: Analytical Mechanics, 1st edn. Springer, Switzerland (2017). https://doi.org/10.1007/978-3-319-44491-8
14. Woodhouse, N.J.: Introduction to Analytical Dynamics, New edn. Springer, London (2009). https://doi.org/10.1007/978-1-84882-816-2
15. Camlibel, M.K., Julius, A.A., Pasumarthy, R., Scherpen, J.M.A.: Mathematical Control Theory I, 1st edn. Springer, Switzerland (2015). https://doi.org/10.1007/978-3-319-20988-3
16. Sontag, E.D.: Mathematical Control Theory, 2nd edn. Springer, New York (1998). https://doi.org/10.1007/978-1-4612-0577-7
17. Diederich, H., Pritchard, A.J.: Mathematical Systems Theory I, 1st edn. Springer, Heidelberg (2005)

Accurate Autonomous UAV Landing Using Vision-Based Detection of ArUco-Marker

Igor Lebedev$^{(\boxtimes)}$ ⓘ, Aleksei Erashov ⓘ, and Aleksandra Shabanova ⓘ

St. Petersburg Institute for Informatics and Automation of the Russian Academy of Sciences, 39, 14th Line, 199178 St. Petersburg, Russia
`igorlevedev@gmail.com`

Abstract. This paper presents a solution of autonomous accurate landing problem for an unmanned aerial vehicle (UAV) in the target point. The combination of two algorithms for on-image search and accurate landing on marker is presented. The UAV landing on marker includes the unit for adjustment of aerial vehicle position relative to the marker to increase the landing accuracy. Also, the paper shows the on-image marker detection algorithm, to define position and alignment of UAV camera relative to the marker. The developed algorithms were tested in the Gazebo simulation environment in real-world settings. According to the experiments, these algorithms outperform in accuracy than similar systems for automated landing, based on computer vision (5–10 cm) and GPS-based UAV control systems (2–5 m). Landing error of UAV in simulator with adjustment was 19.75 mm, in real-world settings – 21.2 mm.

Keywords: Multirotor · Automated control system · Unmanned aerial vehicles · Quadrotor · Aerial imaging · Automated landing · ArUco-marker

1 Introduction

Currently UAVs are actively used in military and civil systems for various activities: environment monitoring, search (for humans, animals and other entities in wide areas), inspection (of different constructions, power lines, wind turbines) [1, 2]. Modern systems of UAV control are insufficiently automated and assume significant human involvement to ensure device operation. Often the navigation of UAV is ensured using the global positioning system (GPS), whose accuracy is insufficient for accurate landing (2–5 m); additionally, GPS is highly susceptible to influence of magnetic fields. Therefore, developing UAV control systems, which ensure autonomous flight and landing, such problems are to be solved as increase of control accuracy and improvement of reliability of sensor systems [3]. Popular approach to control accuracy improvement in context of UAV motion consists in application of computer vision algorithms, which enable UAV landing not only on fixed platforms, but also on mobile ones [4–6]. To detect the landing platforms, various types of markers can be used: ArUco-markers, helipad etc. In this case, the position of camera in the environment is defined with marker mapping on scene image. Image preprocessing is required in this case, such as conversion to grayscale, contour detection, detection of rectangular areas and homography calculation [7]. Camera

© Springer Nature Switzerland AG 2020
A. Ronzhin et al. (Eds.): ICR 2020, LNAI 12336, pp. 179–188, 2020.
https://doi.org/10.1007/978-3-030-60337-3_18

coordinate values, obtained with ArUco library [8], further are used for calculation of required flight speed and quadrotor stabilization in hovering and landing. UAV landing error by such approach as in [7] was less than 5 cm.

UAV landing accuracy at target point depends on accuracy of on-image marker recognition. To reduce the recognition errors, several filters can be applied sequentially. So, in [9] to reduce computing load in the course of processing of noisy raw data Gaussian smoothing filter was utilized. Then the RGB-image was converted into the HSV format and further into binary image using a threshold algorithm. Further for reduction of noise, potentially troublesome because of possible marker displacement, morphological filter was utilized.

Additionally, to threshold processing of images, template matching approach is widely used for marker detection [10]. This approach consists in search of template image in the current frame; to do this, the size of the fragment under consideration is reduced to the size of the template. This is the first step; then image binarization and comparison are performed.

Image template matching can also be implemented with artificial neural network (ANN) [11]. For this, keypoints are defined on the actual image and on the template image using Speeded Up Robust Features descriptor (SURF). Template matching with the actual image is performed only in case of flight altitude change with 0.5 m interval, until the required number of matchings will be found.

In [12] authors used convolutional neural networks Region Proposal Network (RPN) and Fast R-CNN to detect markers, shaped as concentric circles and pentagon. RPN and Fast R-CNN were employed for provisional and final detection of marker-containing area, respectively. Marker position calculation was performed using the least-square method and Shi-Tomasi corner detection method. Marker detection accuracy by using this method was 97.8%.

UAV landing accuracy also depends on the flight trajectory of the vehicle while descending. Authors of [13] developed an approach, based on τ-theory (tau guidance theory), which uses the τ-function to describe the desired motion. This function describes the motion gap and takes into account the initial values of speed and acceleration of the UAV. To assess the efficiency of the proposed approach, over 60 experiments were performed indoors, which showed average accuracy of UAV landing on marker within 10 cm.

There exist some papers, in which for UAV positioning by landing multi-sensor systems and data merging algorithms are employed. Together with the cameras for visible spectrum, IMU-sensor (Inertial Measurement Unit) and infrared (IR) camera can be used [14], as well GPS-module. Though, satellite-based UAV navigation system requires near-field sensors to be used for measurement of flight altitude. Besides, for use of global positioning systems, the data on landing site coordinates is necessarily [15], whereas computer-vision systems may be applied in cases, when the landing site coordinates are unknown.

For accurate autonomous UAV landing artificial neural networks may be used, as well technical vision systems and combinations of different sensor systems. NN-based approach requires establishment of training sets and installation of additional computing hardware, what increases the cost and weight-size parameters of the UAV. Combination of several sensors provides for more accurate landing in target point, but increases efforts, needed for equipment setup and leads to overall performance decrease of the navigation system. The most promising options in this case is the technical vision because of high reliability and moderate computational complexity of algorithms for landing site detection. The purpose of this paper consists in development of algorithms for autonomous accurate landing of UAV on marker using technical vision system. In this paper ArUco-markers were considered because of their better detectability from afar compared to similar solutions (QR, Bar).

2   Algorithms for UAV Landing on ArUco-Marker

To ensure automated UAV landing on marker two algorithms were developed: 1) autonomous landing algorithm and 2) algorithm for on-image marker detection. To ensure automated multirotor landing on marker the onboard camera can be used. The surface area seen by the camera at each stage of the landing depends on the camera parameters. The flowchart of the autonomous landing algorithm is presented in Fig. 1 and includes the vehicle position adjustment relative to marker. Such adjustment assumes on-image marker centering on each iteration of UAV landing.

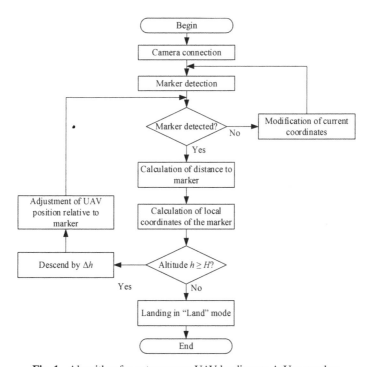

Fig. 1. Algorithm for autonomous UAV landing on ArUco-marker.

At the first step of the algorithm the connection between the vehicle and camera is established to obtain the video stream. Further marker detection is performed: if the marker was not detected, UAV moves to another position and searches for marker again. Upon successful marker detection, its coordinates are determined, as well the flight altitude of UAV relative to marker. If the obtained altitude is less than the predefined value (H), automated UAV landing is performed in «Land» mode with engines shut down. Otherwise the multirotor descends to the specified altitude (Δh) and UAV position adjustment relative to ArUco-marker in such manner, that the marker would be in the center of the image, captured with the camera. If the marker is not in the frame, it is necessary to use a control algorithm that will ensure the UAV flight near the marker. The description of this algorithm is beyond the scope of this study.

An algorithm of ArUco-marker search on image is shown in Fig. 2. This algorithm describes the unit «Marker detection» in greater details.

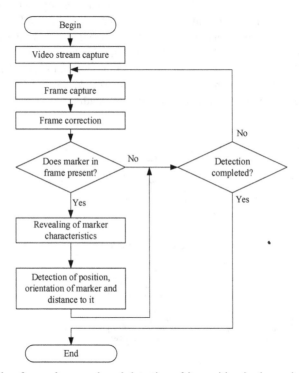

Fig. 2. Algorithm for marker search and detection of its position in the environment, as well marker orientation and distance from vehicle to marker.

The marker is generated with OpenCV library. The "aruco" module in OpenCV contains in aggregate 25 maps of predefined markers. Each marker in these maps contains the same number of blocks or bits (4×4, 5×5, 6×6 or 7×7), and each map contains a fixed number of markers (50, 100, 250 or 1000). Marker detection process assumes obtaining of video streams from cameras and processing of each frame in the video data. If no marker is present on image, to avoid infinite loops the check for completion of marker detection is performed. Having completed the detection session, the algorithm exits. Otherwise, marker shape detection and identification are performed.

As marker is detected with the aid of camera, some distortion occurs (image deformation). Because of distortion, straight lines are displayed as arcs, what causes errors in the measurement of distance from camera to marker. To reduce image distortion, correction is applied, specifically, conversion of curved lines into straight ones; thereby the similarity between the object and its geometrical image is restored. The OpenCV module, utilized here, correction for two kinds of distortions is ensured: radial and tangential ones. New pixel coordinates after radial correction are determined according to the following expressions:

$$x_c = x(1 + k_1 r^2 + k_2 r^4 + k_3 r^6);$$
$$y_c = y(1 + k_1 r^2 + k_2 r^4 + k_3 r^6), \tag{1}$$

where $r^2 = x^2 + y^2$, k_1, k_2, k_3 – radial distortion coefficients.
New pixel coordinates after correction of tangential distortion are obtained this way:

$$x_c = x + [2p_1 xy + p_2(r^2 + 2x^2)];$$
$$y_c = y + [p_1(r^2 + 2y^2) + 2p_2 xy], \tag{2}$$

where p_1, p_2 – tangential distortion coefficients.
Coefficients of tangential and radial distortion are determined on calibration data, obtained by setup of computer vision system. After that marker detection is performed. To do this, first the image binarization is fulfilled, then squared shapes are searched in the image, which will be treated as candidate markers. By outline retrieval, all polygonal shapes and shapes other than square are discarded. Then filters of OpenCV module are applied to delete shapes, which are too large or too small, as well closely adjacent shapes.

Further candidate markers are analyzed. For this, black and white pixels are detected, and marker image is segmented into cells. In each cell the pixels of both colors are counted. Based on ratios of black and white pixels, each marker is attributed to a certain map. Because several UAVs can operate simultaneously in given scene, to every of which a dedicated landing site is assigned, it is necessary to check, whether the detected marker corresponds to the assigned one. To do this, the identifier of the specified marker is compared to the identifier of the detected one. Should they match, so UAV landing is performed.

The marker orientation detection also proceeds in several steps. During this process the data of each candidate marker is retrieved: translation vector, rotation vector and coordinates of marker points on image. This problem is solved using a function, which returns the position of each marker relative to the camera. This function takes as arguments: 1) orientation of marker, detected on image, 2) actual size of the marker, as well 3) calibration data of the camera. If the landing marker was detected, then the rotational vector is transformed into rotational matrix using the Rodriguez transforms [16, 17]:

$$\theta \leftarrow norm(r),$$
$$r \leftarrow r/\theta,$$
$$R = \cos\theta \cdot I + (1 - \cos\theta)rr^T + \sin\theta \begin{bmatrix} 0 & -r_z & r_y \\ r_z & 0 & -r_x \\ -r_y & r_x & 0 \end{bmatrix}, \tag{3}$$

where θ – rotation angle of vector r.

This matrix describes the orientation of landing marker relative to camera. The position of camera relative to landing marker is calculated according to formula:

$$P_\kappa^u = -R_u^T \cdot P_u, \tag{4}$$

where R_u^T – rotational matrix of landing marker; R_u – translation vector of the landing marker. To calculate the camera orientation relative to marker, the matrix R_u^T has to be transposed.

Further the marker detection process is repeated, and the altitude is checked against the correspondence to the specified value. Step-by-step UAV descend with fixed altitude decrement proceeds, until the condition would be met, specified for landing in «Land» mode.

3   Testing of Algorithms of Automated UAV Landing on ArUco-Marker

For assessment of efficiency of the developed algorithms several experiments were performed in Gazebo simulation environment and in real-world conditions. Testing in virtual environment was performed with and without adjustment of UAV position relative to marker, whereas in real-world conditions all experiments were performed exclusively with adjustment algorithm. For each case 8 experiments were performed, every of which consisted in ascending to the specified altitude, flight from point 1 to point 2, positioned at distance of 3.5 m and landing on marker. The flight altitude of the UAV in the simulation was 4 m, and in real conditions, 1 m, so that in case of failure, equipment damage was minimal. Flight systems were controlled by a Raspberry Pi microcomputer. A Logitech 920 Full HD camera was used as a visual sensor.

During testing of the developed algorithms in simulation environment the error margin of onboard sensors was performed, but weather conditions were neglected. Examples of testing in Gazebo environment without UAV position adjustment relative to marker, as well with adjustment, are shown in Fig. 3.

The Fig. 3 demonstrates quadrotor ascent to the point 1, at altitude of 3 m. The flight is performed from point 1 to point 2, where the ArUco-marker is detected, and, finally, UAV landing on it. Absolute landing error for the UAV was determined as the distance between the actual landing and the point, where the marker sits. The average value of landing error without position adjustment was 83.75 mm.

UAV position adjustment is performed in such way, that the marker would be centered in the image by every descent step (see Fig. 3b). Landing error of UAV, when the developed algorithm is used with adjustment, is 19.75 mm. The example of testing of the developed algorithms is given in Fig. 4. UAV landing duration, utilizing algorithm without adjustment, was 21 s, with position adjustment – 13 s.

Multirotor ascended from the point 1, covered distance of 1 m to point 2 and landed in point 3. Landing process duration was 15 s. Marker detection was complicated by excessive light, because of which blind spots on ArUco-marker arised. With the UAV hardware used, the permissible height of the start of landing is 10 m. Above this height,

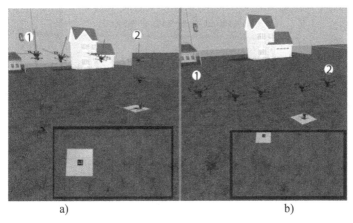

a)   b)

Fig. 3. Flight along the keypoints and UAV landing on ArUco-marker: a) without position adjustment, b) with position adjustment.

Fig. 4. Flight along points and landing on ArUco-marker in real-world settings.

the landing may not be successful. The UAV landing error on marker was 21.2 mm. The results of three test suites are given in Fig. 5.

Blue line shows landing errors during tests in simulation environment without UAV position adjustment, red line shows analogous output with correction, yellow line shows test results, obtained in real-world conditions. Accuracy of UAV landing on marker in open environment in real world conditions slightly differs from the test results, obtained in simulation environment with position adjustment. Difference of average error during tests in real-world conditions and in simulation environment using the developed algorithms was less than 1.5 mm. The presented algorithms show greater landing accuracy at target point compared to previously considered solutions.

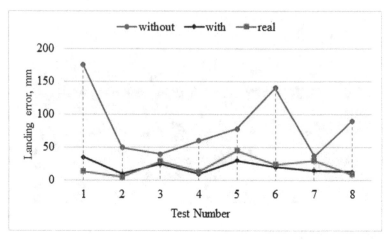

Fig. 5. Graph of UAV landing error with use of ArUco-markers. (Color figure online)

4 Conclusion

This paper presents the solution of accurate landing problem for an aerial vehicle on marker. The algorithm of autonomous UAV landing on ArUco-marker assumes adjustment of UAV position at every landing step to improve landing accuracy. Also, an algorithm for on-image marker detection was presented, allowing to determine the position and orientation of UAV camera relative to marker. The source code, implemented on the basis of the algorithm, is compatible with different assemblies of single-board computers and controllers, which support the MAVLink protocol, such as Raspberry Pi and Pixhawk, Nvidia Jetson and DJI.

Proposed algorithms were tested in Gazebo simulation environment and in real-world conditions. In simulation testing the errors of onboard sensors were taken into account, but weather conditions were neglected. In real-world testing the marker detection process was complicated by excessive lighting. The error of UAV landing on marker in simulation environment without adjustment was 83.75 mm, with adjustment – 19.75 mm. Testing of the developed algorithms in real-world conditions revealed the landing error of 21.2 mm, what is significantly less, than by utilizing GPS (2–5 m). Additionally, the proposed algorithms ensure greater accuracy, than similar systems, considered in the related work (5–10 cm) [7, 13], due to multiple landing steps and constant tracking of marker coordinates. Though, landing speed in such settings becomes less than 0.7 m/s, hence, these algorithms cannot be applied by emergency landing, such as in the case of low battery. The developed algorithms allow to automate the whole workflow, concerning motion in environment, landing and wireless battery replenishment [18, 19] of multirotor UAVs. Fully autonomous UAV systems can also interact with mobile robotic platforms [20] to perform service tasks [21–25], what is the scope of further research.

References

1. Shabanova, A.R., Tolstoy, I.M., Lebedev, I.V.: The mode of constructing safe trajectories of motion of the unmanned aerial vehicle while monitoring power lines considering the influence of their electromagnetic fields. Probl. Reg. Energy **3**(44), 17–30 (2019)
2. Ronzhin, A.L., Nguyen, V.V., Solenaya, O.: Analysis of the problems of developing unmanned aerial vehicles and the physical interaction of UAVs with ground objects. Proc. Moscow Aviat. Inst. **98**, 28 (2018)
3. Pan, C., Hu, T., Shen, L.: BRISK based target localization for fixed-wing UAV's vision-based autonomous landing. In: 2015 IEEE International Conference on Information and Automation, pp. 2499–2503. IEEE (2015)
4. Lin, S., Garratt, M.A., Lambert, A.J.: Monocular vision-based real-time target recognition and tracking for autonomously landing an UAV in a cluttered shipboard environment. Auton. Robots **41**(4), 881–901 (2016)
5. Moriarty, P., Sheehy, R., Doody, P.: Neural networks to aid the autonomous landing of a UAV on a ship. In: 2017 28th Irish Signals and Systems Conference (ISSC), pp. 1–4. IEEE (June 2017)
6. Falanga, D., Zanchettin, A., Simovic, A., Delmerico, J., Scaramuzza, D.: Vision-based autonomous quadrotor landing on a moving platform. In: 2017 IEEE International Symposium on Safety, Security and Rescue Robotics (SSRR), pp. 200–207. IEEE (2017)
7. Carreira, T.G.: Quadcopter automatic landing on a docking station. Instituto Superior Técnico (2013)
8. Aruco Library. https://github.com/synapticon/Aruco-Library. Accessed 03 Apr 2020
9. Lee, H., Jung, S., Shim, D.H.: Vision-based UAV landing on the moving vehicle. In: 2016 International Conference on Unmanned Aircraft Systems (ICUAS), pp. 1–7. IEEE (2016)
10. Nyein, E.E., Tun, H.M., Naing, Z.M., Moe, W.K.: Implementation of vision-based landing target detection for VTOL UAV using raspberry Pi. Int. J. Sci. Technol. Res. **4**(8), 184–188 (2015)
11. Sudevan, V., Shukla, A., Karki, H.: Vision based autonomous landing of an unmanned aerial vehicle on a stationary target. In: 2017 17th International Conference on Control, Automation and Systems (ICCAS), pp. 362–367. IEEE (2017)
12. Chen, J., Miao, X., Jiang, H., Chen, J., Liu, X.: Identification of autonomous landing sign for unmanned aerial vehicle based on faster regions with convolutional neural network. In: 2017 Chinese Automation Congress (CAC), pp. 2109–2114. IEEE (2017)
13. Vetrella, A.R., et al.: Improved tau-guidance and vision-aided navigation for robust autonomous landing of UAVs. In: Hutter, M., Siegwart, R. (eds.) Field and Service Robotics. SPAR, vol. 5, pp. 115–128. Springer, Cham (2018). https://doi.org/10.1007/978-3-319-673 61-5_8
14. Ivannikov, K.V., Gavrilov, A.V., Boev, A.S., Shoshin, I.S.: A method of landing an unmanned aerial vehicle of a helicopter type using an infrared camera. Bull. East Kaz. Concern Almaz-Antey **3**(18) (2016)
15. Gautam, A., Sujit, P.B., Saripalli, S.: A survey of autonomous landing techniques for UAVs. In: 2014 International Conference on Unmanned Aircraft Systems (ICUAS), pp. 1210–1218. IEEE (2014)
16. Cheng, H., Gupta, K.C.: An historical note on finite rotations (1989)
17. Sorgi, L.: Two-view geometry estimation using the rodrigues rotation formula. In: 2011 18th IEEE International Conference on Image Processing, pp. 1009–1012. IEEE (2011)
18. Saveliev, A.I., Krestovnikov, K.D., Solyony, S.V.: Development of a wireless charger for a mobile robotic platform. Intelligent Power Systems. Materials of the V International Youth Forum. In: Intelligent energy systems: proceedings of the V International Youth Forum, pp. 197–201 (2017)

19. Parshin, A.D., Krestovnikov, K.D.: The use of a wireless charger for a UAV: in the collection. Zavalishin's Readings 2018, pp. 388–391. SUAI, St. Petersburg (2018)
20. Pavliuk, N., Kharkov, I., Zimuldinov, E., Saprychev, V.: Development of multipurpose mobile platform with a modular structure. In: Ronzhin, A., Shishlakov, V. (eds.) Proceedings of 14th International Conference on Electromechanics and Robotics "Zavalishin's Readings". SIST, vol. 154, pp. 137–147. Springer, Singapore (2020). https://doi.org/10.1007/978-981-13-9267-2_12
21. Tsochev, G.R., Yoshinov, R.D., Zhukova, N.A.: Some security issues with the industrial Internet of Things and comparison to SCADA systems. SPIIRAS Proc. **19**, 358–382 (2020). https://doi.org/10.15622/sp.2020.19.2.5
22. Pyankov, O.V., Smyshnikov, D.O.: Automated search for locations of detention groups to reduce security activity risk. SPIIRAS Proc. **19**, 594–620 (2020). https://doi.org/10.15622/sp.2020.19.3.5
23. Vu, Q., Nguyen, V., Solenaya, O., Ronzhin, A., Mehmet, H.: Algorithms for joint operation of service robotic platform and set of UAVs in agriculture tasks. In: 2017 5th IEEE Workshop on Advances in Information, Electronic and Electrical Engineering (AIEEE), pp. 1–6. IEEE (2017)
24. Vu, Q., Nguyen, V., Solenaya, O., Ronzhin, A.: Group control of heterogeneous robots and unmanned aerial vehicles in agriculture tasks. In: International Conference on Interactive Collaborative Robotics, pp. 260–267 (2017)
25. Vu, Q., Raković, M., Delic, V., Ronzhin, A.: Trends in development of UAV-UGV cooperation approaches in precision agriculture. In: Ronzhin, A., Rigoll, G., Meshcheryakov, R. (eds.) ICR 2018. LNCS (LNAI), vol. 11097, pp. 213–221. Springer, Cham (2018). https://doi.org/10.1007/978-3-319-99582-3_22

Spatial Resolution-Independent CNN-Based Person Detection in Agricultural Image Data

Alexander Leipnitz$^{(\boxtimes)}$, Tilo Strutz, and Oliver Jokisch

Institute of Communications Engineering, Leipzig University of Telecommunications
(HfTL), Leipzig, Germany
{leipnitz,strutz,jokisch}@hft-leipzig.de

Abstract. Advanced object detectors based on Convolutional Neural
Networks (CNNs) offer high detection rates for many application scenarios but only within their respective training, validation and test data.
Recent studies show that such methods provide a limited generalization
ability for unknown data, even for small image modifications including
a limited scale invariance. Reliable person detection with aerial robots
(Unmanned Aerial Vehicles, UAVs) is an essential task to fulfill high
security requirements or to support robot control, communication, and
human-robot interaction. Particularly in an agricultural context, persons
need to be detected from a long distance and a high altitude to allow
the UAV an adequate and timely response. While UAVs are able to produce high resolution images that enable the detection of persons from
a longer distance, typical CNN input layer sizes are comparably small.
The inevitable scaling of images to match the input-layer size can lead
to a further reduction in person sizes. We investigate the reliability of
different YOLOv3 architectures for person detection in regard to those
input-scaling effects. The popular VisDrone data set with its varying
image resolutions and relatively small depiction of humans is used as
well as high resolution UAV images from an agricultural data set. To
overcome the scaling problem, an algorithm is presented for segmenting
high resolution images in overlapping tiles that match the input-layer
size. The number and overlap of the tiles are dynamically determined
based on the image resolution. It is shown that the detection rate of very
small persons in high resolution images can be improved using this tiling
approach.

Keywords: Convolutional neural network · Person detection ·
Resolution invariance · Input-layer scaling · Image tiling

1 Introduction

The development of high quality, lightweight camera systems enabled their
deployment on drones and therefore many new application areas. The high resolution of the captured images allows the detection of objects from long distances

© Springer Nature Switzerland AG 2020
A. Ronzhin et al. (Eds.): ICR 2020, LNAI 12336, pp. 189–199, 2020.
https://doi.org/10.1007/978-3-030-60337-3_19

and high altitudes. This is an essential safety requirement for an automated operation of flying drones for example in digital farming. In manual operation, the pilot typically analyzes the video-stream of the drone directly on his remote control, however, in an autonomous scenario this task has to be done automatically. The processing of high resolution images with advanced CNN methods requires a lot of computational power and memory and is therefore still limited to high-end hardware. Feasible CNNs, like the popular and state-of-the-art YOLOv3 architecture [1], provide a relativly small input-layer. Hence, an adjustment of the input image is required, which can be realized by (i) cropping, (ii) resizing with aspect-ratio preservation and padding or (iii) resizing by trivial 2D sub-sampling disregarding the aspect ratio. In the original YOLOv3 implementation [2] method (iv) is used, while the framework utilized for our investigations [3] sub-samples the images by method (v). Resizing with aspect-ratio preservation can lead to the smallest object sizes among the three adjustment methods if the input-layer and input-image aspect ratios differ. Using method (vi), the object-information loss is limited by using the appropriate horizontal and vertical scaling-factors. However, different scaling in horizontal and vertical direction leads to aspect-ratio distortions that can decrease the detection performance as CNNs are not robust against such image modifications [4,5]. When addressing high resolution images, scaling can even make the detection of very small objects impossible. Several solutions to this problem have already been proposed in literature.

Single-stage approaches, on the one hand, focus on special network architectures that allow the processing of the whole high resolution image at once and avoid or minimize scaling. In [6], a method is presented that reduces the memory footprint on the GPU by not storing the entire output feature maps after each layer at the same time but only the parts that are needed for the next processing step. However, this approach cannot be used for most network architectures (like YOLOv3) as the whole activation map is not present at any time and certain operations (e.g. batch normalization) are not possible. Other approaches concentrate on special network architectures that have real-time drone application [7,8] or improved scale invariance [9,10] in mind, but still rely on scaling the input image to the input-layer size.

Two-stage approaches, on the other hand, search for interesting image areas first and run the object detector only on these regions to minimize scaling of the input image. The region proposals can also be realized with neural networks [11–15]. While these methods limit the computational efforts, the risk of missing very small persons is high. All state-of-the-art methods utilize some scaling or error-prone pre-selection of interesting image areas. Our contribution investigates the capability of different YOLOv3 architectures to find very small persons in high-resolution images and proposes an image scaling-free method to improve the detection rate.

2   Methods

The processing pipeline of the proposed approach is based on the divide-and-conquer principle. At first, the input image is segmented into overlapping regions (tiles) that match the CNN input-layer size to avoid image scaling so that persons keep their size in pixels. One of three investigated CNN architectures (YOLOv3, YOLOv3-tiny, YOLOv3-spp) is then applied to every tile. The last step consists of merging the results for each tile to a global information about people positions.

2.1   Tiling

Any image with a width w and/or height h bigger than the input-layer size of the CNN can be segmented into a minimal number of overlapping tiles with a width w_t and height h_t that match the input-layer size. Figure 1 depicts the segmentation of an image in four tiles. The calculation of the necessary amount of horizontal tiles n_x with an empirically determined maximum overlap x_{max} of 80% to cover an image with arbitrary resolution is shown in Listing 1.1. The same approach can be applied vertically.

Listing 1.1. Calculating the number of horizontal tiles with a width of 416.

```
1   float x_max = 0.8;
2   float x = 0.9;
3   int w_t = 416;
4   int n_x = ceil(w / w_t);
5   while (x > x_max) {
6       x = (n_x * w_t - w) / (w_t * (n_x - 1));
7       n_x -= 1;
8   }
```

The maximum overlap x_{max} can be adjusted with respect to the person sizes to avoid splitting them between multiple tiles. If no suitable number of tiles ($n_x \geq 1$) can be found based on the minimal/maximal overlap criteria $0 \leq x \leq x_{max}$, the image has to be down-scaled slightly. For images smaller than the input-layer

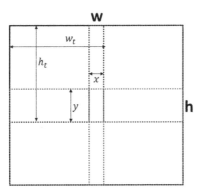

Fig. 1. Image segmentation in four overlapping tiles (red, green, blue, yellow). (Color figure online)

size zero-padding is used. Persons that are completely inside the overlap area are contained in both tiles. If the persons are larger than the overlap area or on a border between two tiles, only a part of them is represented in one tile. The smaller such a part is, the more difficult it is to derive relevant features of the person.

2.2 YOLOv3

The YOLOv3 architecture [1] is a convolutional neural network for object detection that processes the whole input image in a single pass. It predicts bounding boxes around objects in the original image on three different scales (three output paths) to allow multi-scale detection. The highest-resolution output path is able to find the smaller objects in the input image, while the smallest-resolution output path contains information about the bigger objects. The whole architecture consists of 107 layers making it rather complex. In the default configuration, the input layer has a size of 416 × 416 pixel. The horizontal and vertical dimensions of the input layer can be adjusted in steps of 32 pixels, and all the feature maps will scale accordingly. In our tests, we used a standard input-layer size of 416 × 416 pixels and also a slightly increased size of 608 × 608 pixels to address the differences for high-resolution images. Larger input-layer sizes are not feasible as the memory requirements scale linearly with the increased size. To avoid hardware limitations, other compromises would have to be made in the training process, which outweigh the advantage of the bigger input-layer size with less input-image scaling.

2.3 YOLOv3-tiny

YOLOv3-tiny is a slimmer and less complex variant of the YOLOv3 architecture due to a reduced number of layers (21 instead of 107). It lacks the branch that can detect the smallest objects but allows faster processing. The lower complexity also reduces the tendency to overfit on small data sets.

2.4 YOLOv3-spp

The spatial pyramid pooling module (spp) introduced in [10] can be integrated into the YOLOv3 architecture to obtain a more scale-invariant solution. It utilizes three different parallel max-pooling layers, which pool the input-feature map with three sliding window sizes. The resulting feature maps are then concatenated with the input-feature map before the YOLOv3 architecture continues. This allows the pooling and concatenation of multi-scale local region features.

2.5 Merging

YOLOv3 architectures output a list of bounding boxes accompanied by confidence scores per tile. This local information has to be merged into a global one by applying offsets to bounding boxes according to the tile location in the original image. In image areas with overlapping tiles, objects are often detected twice. In order to decide which bounding box to keep, the Intersection over Union (IoU) between two overlapping boxes is calculated. If $IoU > 0.7$, the two boxes get merged by using the most-outer corners, and the higher of the two confidence scores of the two boxes is kept. If $0.5 < IoU \leq 0.7$, the box with the higher confidence score is kept and the other one is deleted. For boxes with very small overlap ($IoU \leq 0.5$) the boxes are considered to contain different persons.

3 Investigations

We investigated three different variants of the YOLOv3 network architecture to identify their abilities for a detection of small persons in high-resolution images and to compare the default image-scaling with our segmentation-and-merging approach.

All models have been pre-trained on the MSCOCO trainval dataset [16], while a mini-batch size of 64 has been used for all trainings. Each of the three YOLOv3 architectures is fed with either resized (method (iii)) or segmented input images that fit the input-layer size.

3.1 VisDrone Data Set

The VisDrone object detection data set [17] is a large-scale benchmark for object detection tasks with drones. It contains various scenarios in urban and country environment. The corresponding annotation comprises ten classes (*pedestrian, person, car, van, bus, truck, motor, bicycle, awning-tricycle*, and *tricycle*). As we focus on person detection only, the classes *pedestrian* and *person* are utilized and merged into a single *person* class. The VisDrone data set consists of 8 629 images with public available annotation. This set is divided into 75.0% training, 6.4% validation and 18.6% additional data for debugging and further validation (test-dev data). The resolution of the images ranges from 480×360 up to $2\,000 \times 1\,500$ ($w \times h$) pixels. The data set contains images with many very small persons. The smallest annotated bounding box is only one pixel tall (h_b) and three pixels wide (w_b) in an image with a resolution of $1\,916 \times 1\,078$ pixels. This corresponds to a person size which is even smaller than one pixel after the image is down-scaled to $w_t \times h_t = 416 \times 416$ or 608×608 pixels depending on the CNN input-layer. The scaling factor f corresponds to

$$f = \frac{w_t \cdot h_t}{w \cdot h} \qquad (1)$$

and the resulting person size s is

$$s = w_b \cdot h_b \cdot f \ . \qquad (2)$$

When the images are segmented into tiles, the small persons are represented by an unchanged amount of pixels in the input-layer, and not one persons vanishes (s large enough) due to $f = 1$.

The characteristics of this data set when either using image-scaling or the proposed segmentation approach is summarized in Table 1. The number of boxes represents the number of annotated persons in the data set (147, 747). When scaling to the input-layer size of 416 × 416 or 608 × 608 pixels some of these person will vanish as they will be smaller than one pixel ($\min(s) < 1$).

Segmenting the image in overlapping tiles increases the total number of bounding boxes due to their multiple representation in the overlapping areas (cf. Sect. 2.1). If a bounding boxes is only partially inside a tile, it has to be cropped to the tiles dimensions. This leads to the varying person size s distribution between the two different tile sizes. However, if the new bounding box size is smaller than 20% of the original bounding box size in one of those tiles, we discard the corresponding box as it is not very likely to contain enough features for a person.

Table 1. Analysis of VisDrone data set in terms of person sizes depending on input-layer size.

	Scaling to		Tile size	
	416 × 416	608 × 608	416 × 416	608 × 608
No. of boxes	147,747	147,747	657,111	990,809
$\max(s)$	9,669.9	20,655.9	60,629.0	72,669.9
$\mathrm{mean}(s)$	75.8	161.9	488.4	550.0
$\min(s)$	0.25	0.54	2.0	3.0

3.2 AgriDrone Data Set

AgriDrone is a self-captured data set with focus on person detection in agricultural applications. All 4 586 images have been captured by two different drones: DJI Mavic2 Enterprise and DJI Mavic Pro between Spring and Winter. They share the same resolution of 3 840 × 2 160 pixels. The data set is split into 70% training 10% validation and 20% test data. The AgriDrone data set is much smaller than the VisDrone set, and the relative sizes of persons are larger. Table 2 summarizes the AgriDrone data and show the same basic findings as Table 1. In this data set, the persons are large enough to be preserved despite the scaling of the images ($\min(s) > 1$).

4 Results and Discussion

In total, 24 CNN models have been trained, validated and tested. Three architectures have been investigated in combination with two different input-layer sizes (416 × 416 and 608 × 608), with or without tiling, and both different data sets. Following measures in the style of [16] are used for the evaluation of the detection performance: the mean Average Precision (mAP) metric at a IoU threshold

Table 2. Analysis of AgriDrone data set in terms of person sizes depending on input-layer size.

	Scaling to		Tile size	
	416×416	608×608	416×416	608×608
No. of boxes	8,746	8,746	14,155	13,296
$\max(s)$	6,890.2	14,718.1	127,360.0	195,048.0
mean (s)	235.5	503.0	8,460.6	9,415.7
$\min(s)$	6.68	14.26	196.0	247.0

Table 3. Object detection results with an input-layer size of 416×416 pixels.

Data set	Seg. & Mer.	YOLOv3			YOLOv3-tiny			YOLOv3-spp		
		mAP	mAP$_{50}$	mAP$_{75}$	mAP	mAP$_{50}$	mAP$_{75}$	mAP	mAP$_{50}$	mAP$_{75}$
VisDrone training										
Validat	Off	9.56	33.04	2.19	2.53	10.84	3.21	9.57	32.98	2.12
Validat	On	19.31	55.02	8.33	8.92	31.10	2.13	18.70	**55.75**	6.89
Test-dev	Off	4.19	15.16	0.89	0.96	4.29	0.09	4.35	15.79	0.93
Test-dev	On	10.54	**32.73**	4.01	4.52	16.54	1.02	10.12	31.69	3.82
AgriDrone training										
Validat	Off	**35.55**	**89.83**	**18.32**	21.23	64.96	7.96	38.58	**91.61**	23.39
Validat	On	31.08	78.50	17.64	**31.32**	**77.86**	**17.78**	32.65	79.90	18.88
Test	Off	**34.01**	**85.66**	17.04	21.87	65.05	8.31	36.92	**88.32**	21.55
Test	On	29.25	73.74	15.38	**31.11**	**76.53**	**16.07**	32.36	78.13	18.18

of 0.5 (mAP$_{50}$) and at a IoU threshold of 0.75 (mAP$_{75}$) as well as the averaged precision over IoU thresholds $0.5 \ldots 0.95$ in steps of 0.05 (mAP).

Table 3 (input-layer size 416×416) and Table 4 (input-layer size 608×608) list the overall results of our investigations. When comparing the entries related to the original approach using scaling (Segmentation & Merging, Seg. & Mer.: Off), it can be seen that an increased input-layer size helps to detect more persons. The improvements range up to 12.92% in the mAP$_{50}$ metric on the VisDrone validation set using the YOLOv3-spp architecture. The segmentation-and-merging method always leads to an improvement in detection performance (with one exception), regardless of the architecture and input-layer size applied to the VisDrone data set, and the best results could be achieved, when the corresponding architecture was trained on the segmented images with a tile size of 416×416 pixels. These results prove that an enlarged input layer of size 608×608 pixels is still not sufficient for a reliable person detection. Instead, the person size should be kept using the proposed segmentation-and-merging approach. For the VisDrone data set, the YOLOv3-tiny architecture generally performs the worst due to its low complexity, while the two other ones are on par.

The mentioned effects can only partially be reproduced on the AgriDrone data. The YOLOv3 and YOLOv3-spp models are probably overfitting on this data, as it is smaller and has a lower variability. Only with the YOLOv3-tiny

196 A.   Leipnitz et al.

architecture, the segmentation-and-merging approach leads to an improvement in the detection performance. As the persons are larger in this data set, the best results with the YOLOv3-tiny architecture are archived with a tile size of 608×608 pixels (mAP_{50} of 85.63% and 86.25%, respectively). The improvements of the proposed segmentation-and-merging approach are not that noticeable with this data set as the input-image scaling does not lead to vanished persons (see Table 2). It can also be speculated that the very large persons that can fill up to 73.6% of a 416×416 pixel-sized tile (Table 2) are too large to be detected or spread over multiple tiles, so that the bounding boxes cannot be properly merged. Figure 2 visualizes the improvement of the segmentation-and-merging approach for the (a) VisDrone and (b) AgriDrone data sets. The magenta bounding boxes represent the ground-truth, the yellow boxes the true-positives with image-scaling and the cyan ones the true-positives with our approach (segmentation plus merging). The proposed method detects a lot more of the small humans in Fig. 2(a) while also the relatively big human on the left in Fig. 2(b) is now localized correctly.

Table 4. Object detection results with an input-layer size of 608×608 pixels.

Data set	Seg. & Mer.	YOLOv3			YOLOv3-tiny			YOLOv3-spp		
		mAP	mAP_{50}	mAP_{75}	mAP	mAP_{50}	mAP_{75}	mAP	mAP_{50}	mAP_{75}
VisDrone training										
Validat	Off	14.91	45.78	5.15	5.07	19.46	0.88	15.01	45.90	4.85
Validat	On	19.61	**53.93**	8.76	8.77	29.99	2.26	17.42	50.16	7.40
Test-dev	Off	7.04	23.40	2.12	2.14	8.83	0.27	7.64	25.44	2.19
Test-dev	On	10.79	**32.65**	4.11	4.63	16.81	1.08	9.70	30.51	3.51
AgriDrone training										
Validat	Off	43.04	**95.35**	31.11	31.61	84.15	14.93	39.83	94.47	23.41
Validat	On	38.36	85.56	24.31	37.44	85.73	23.36	38.10	85.95	24.23
Test	Off	41.72	**91.99**	29.35	31.45	81.08	15.39	39.31	91.39	23.60
Test	On	38.42	87.32	24.32	38.23	86.28	25.08	37.71	85.83	23.14

The improvement in object detection rates especially for small persons can also be seen in Fig. 3, in particular for the VisDrone data in Fig. 3(a). The relative person size ρ represents the person size in relation to the original image resolution with

$$\rho = \frac{w_b \cdot h_b}{w \cdot h} \,. \tag{3}$$

The blue bars show the number of ground-truth bounding boxes of the according relative bounding box size. Using the YOLOv3 416×416 architecture and input-image scaling shows a drop-off in detections (true-positives at $IoU = 0.5$) towards smaller person sizes (red bars). When the proposed segmentation-and-merging algorithm is applied, the detection of small persons is improved (green bars). In Figure 3(b) the improvements are not as visible due to the lack of very small persons and overfitting of the YOLOv3 architecture on this data set.

(a) VisDrone data

(b) AgriDrone data

Fig. 2. Example detections with YOLOv3 416×416. Magenta: ground-truth, yellow: true-positives at $IoU = 0.5$ (image-scaling), cyan: true-positives at $IoU = 0.5$ (image segmentation and merging). (Color figure online)

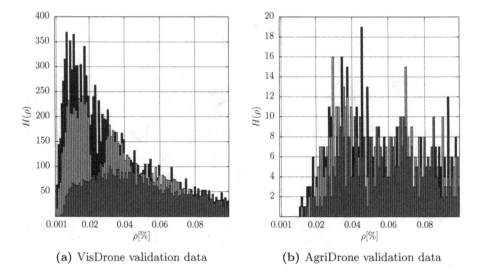

(a) VisDrone validation data   (b) AgriDrone validation data

Fig. 3. Histogram of small relative person sizes ρ: annotated (blue), correctly detected with default image scaling (red) and correctly detected with segmentation-and-merging approach (green). (Color figure online)

5 Summary

The study has shown that the detection rate of YOLOv3 architectures can be improved with the proposed method. Instead of using image-modifying pre-processing (scaling or region selection), a segmentation-and-merging approach has been investigated. All three investigated YOLOv3 architectures are able to run in real-time (more than 30 frames per second) on a NVIDIA RTX 2080TI GPU in the original version. However, the processing time scales linearly with the number of tiles. The time saved by omitting the slow scaling functions is consumed by the additional merging algorithm. Especially with very high resolution drone images with a lot of tiles (e.g. AgriDrone images) this can lead to non-real-time processing, even with optimizations like parallel processing of tiles. In long-distance image capturing scenarios with a drone, the safety requirements outweigh the real-time requirements, since the detection of humans from a greater distance gives the drone more time to react.

The proposed approach is suitable for all image resolutions bigger than the input-layer size. We proved that the detection rates of small persons in high-resolution images can be improved, which makes CNNs usable for person detection with an UAV. Future work should also include the scaled image version to avoid not detecting persons larger than the tile size. To support reproducible research, we made the software and data of our study publicly available at [18].

Acknowledgements. The authors acknowledge the financial support by the Federal Ministry of Education and Research of Germany (BMBF) within the framework of the EU Era.Net RUS+ project HARMONIC (national project number 01DJ18011).

References

1. Redmon, J., Farhadi, A.: Yolov3: An incremental improvement. arXiv preprint arXiv:1804.02767 (2018)
2. Redmon, J.: Darknet framework for object detection. https://github.com/pjreddie/darknet. Accessed 23 Jul 2020
3. Bochkovskiy, A.: Improved darknet framework for object detection. https://github.com/AlexeyAB/darknet. Accessed 23 Jul 2020
4. Rosenfeld, A., Zemel, R.S., Tsotsos, J.K.: The elephant in the room. arXiv preprint arXiv:1808.03305 (2018)
5. Azulay, A., Weiss, Y.: Why do deep convolutional networks generalize so poorly to small image transformations? J. Mach. Learn. Res. **20**(184), 1–25 (2019)
6. Pinckaers, H., Litjens, G.J.S.: Training convolutional neural networks with megapixel images. arXiv preprint arXiv:1804.05712 (2018)
7. Zhang, P., Zhong, Y., Li, X.: Slimyolov3: Narrower, faster and better for real-time UAV applications. In: The IEEE International Conference on Computer Vision (ICCV) Workshops (2019)
8. Steinmann, L., Sommer, L., Schumann, A., Beyerer, J.: Fast and lightweight person detector for unmanned aerial vehicles. In: EUSIPCO (2019)
9. Tayara, H., Chong, K.: Object detection in very high-resolution aerial images using one-stage densely connected feature pyramid network. Sensors **18**(10), 3341 (2018)
10. Huang, Z., Wang, J.: DC-SPP-YOLO: dense connection and spatial pyramid pooling based YOLO for object detection. arXiv preprint arXiv:1903.08589 (2019)
11. Yang, F., Fan, H., Chu, P., Blasch, E., Ling, H.: Clustered object detection in aerial images. In: Proceedings of the IEEE International Conference on Computer Vision, pp. 8311–8320 (2019)
12. Lu, Y., Javidi, T.: Efficient object detection for high resolution images. In: 2015 53rd Annual Allerton Conference on Communication, Control, and Computing (Allerton), pp. 1091–1098 (2015). https://doi.org/10.1109/ALLERTON.2015.7447130
13. Zhang, J., Huang, J., Chen, X., Zhang, D.: How to fully exploit the abilities of aerial image detectors. In: The IEEE International Conference on Computer Vision (ICCV) Workshops (2019)
14. Pang, J., Li, C., Shi, J., Xu, Z., Feng, H.: $\mathcal{R}^2$-CNN: Fast tiny object detection in large-scale remote sensing images. IEEE Trans. Geosci. Remote Sens. **57**(8), 5512–5524 (2019). https://doi.org/10.1109/TGRS.2019.2899955
15. Růžička, V., Franchetti, F.: Fast and accurate object detection in high resolution 4k and 8k video using gpus. In: 2018 IEEE High Performance extreme Computing Conference (HPEC), pp. 1–7 (2018). https://doi.org/10.1109/HPEC.2018.8547574
16. Lin, T.-Y., et al.: Microsoft COCO: common objects in context. In: Fleet, D., Pajdla, T., Schiele, B., Tuytelaars, T. (eds.) ECCV 2014. LNCS, vol. 8693, pp. 740–755. Springer, Cham (2014). https://doi.org/10.1007/978-3-319-10602-1_48
17. Zhu, P., Wen, L., Bian, X., Ling, H., Hu, Q.: Vision meets drones: A challenge. arXiv preprint arXiv:1804.07437 (2018)
18. Leipnitz, A.: Tile based object detection. http://www1.hft-leipzig.de/leipnitz/papers/TiledDetection-resources. Accessed 23 Jul 2020

Fast Face Features Extraction Based on Deep Neural Networks for Mobile Robotic Platforms

Maksim Letenkov$^{(\boxtimes)}$ and Dmitriy Levonevskiy

St. Petersburg Institute for Informatics and Automation of the Russian Academy of Sciences, 39, 14th Line, 199178 St. Petersburg, Russia
letenkovmaksim@yandex.ru

Abstract. The concept of Smart Environment (SE) provides a great benefit to its users: interactive informational services (corporate TV, video communication, navigation and localization services) and mobile autonomous entities: mobile robotic platforms, quadcopters, anthropomorphic robots etc. It is important to take into account all the personal details of the user's behavior so to provide him a personalized most useful data. So, the task of a person identification based on an image of his face is urgent. One of the most famous approach to recognize a client is by their face. It's important to have as huge dataset as it's conceivable to prepare an exact classifier, particularly if profound neural systems are being used. It's expensive to compose delegate dataset physically – to snap a picture of each individual from each conceivable edge with each conceivable light condition. This is the reason why generation of a synthetic data for training a classifier, utilizing least genuine information is so urgent. At this paper several face features extractors were tested based on deep learning models in order to find its advantages and disadvantages in the context of training a classifier for a facial recognition task and a clustering for a tracking unique people in SE.

Keywords: Face features · Facial recognition · Deep learning · Feature extraction

1 Introduction

Right now, the scope of human exercises where models of AI can be utilized is extending each day. One of the most encouraging regions in AI is the improvement of neural systems intended to characterize objects of various nature, since they are general approximators and can be prepared to foresee any capacity. Existing AI models can be used to improve the quality of human-machine interaction [1]. AI models are also widely used in aggressive behavior recognition cases, which can help not only improve the quality of human-machine interaction, but also increase the security of social contacts [2].

The issue of setting up a dataset for preparing AI models is particularly intense. Talking about neural systems that have practical experience in perceiving pictures of three-dimensional items from pictures, we can take note of a few genuinely voluminous information bases of commented on pictures. For instance, the ImageNet database contains in excess of 14 million pictures, which are partitioned into in excess of 21

© Springer Nature Switzerland AG 2020
A. Ronzhin et al. (Eds.): ICR 2020, LNAI 12336, pp. 200–211, 2020.
https://doi.org/10.1007/978-3-030-60337-3_20

thousand classes. However, when taking care of a particular issue, it is important to utilize a specific database. The planning of a fitting dataset can cause various specialized troubles related with a specific strategy for gathering this arrangement of information. For instance, for taking care of the issue of face acknowledgment, manual information assortment by shooting every individual isn't ideal for a few reasons on the double. Initially, it takes a ton of time. Furthermore, it is essential to gather the most representative data set, for example containing every one of the conditions wherein an individual can be identified by a video reconnaissance framework. Thus, the advancement of a computerized framework for creating engineered information is one of the most pertinent assignments in structuring any clever framework. This paper examines a few of the most encouraging strategies for producing counterfeit datasets for preparing AI models.

1.1 Synthetic Datasets

Considering the class of assignments related with computer vision, and, specifically, with pattern recognition, when working with classes of objects not beforehand represented in wide access, there emerges the issue of deciding the right for building a calculation for creating datasets for preparing a model.

In [3], the way toward getting a preparation dataset depends on the technique for generating pictures from a lot of common surfaces and three-dimensional models made in computer aided design frameworks. The way toward producing and preprocessing information for additional preparation of the model can be divided into the following steps:

- selection of three-dimensional model from the proposed set;
- generating an object mask and a set of unique images containing a 3D model in a random spatial configuration;
- for each previously obtained image of an object, a masking operation is performed, which makes it possible not to operate with information that is not related to the object;
- for each image from the resulting set, an operation of imposing a texture on a preselected image is performed.

In this manner, by utilizing sets of surfaces and three-dimensional models displayed in free access, it gets conceivable to actualize the way toward producing preparing datasets.

1.2 Qualitative Characteristics of the Generation Synthetic Dataset

The strategy proposed in [3] is one of the least demanding to actualize as far as architectural arrangements.

We have set up an examination to decide the principle subjective qualities of the generation procedure from the perspective of effective utilization of figuring force and time interims required to finish the generation cycle.

Tragically, this methodology has various disadvantages, which comprise in an elevated level of equipment necessities for the machine which register the training generations. Utilizing such free programming packages as Blender (the free-permit appropriated three-dimensional editorial manager) and AliceVision, which actualizes the execution of the specialized piece of photogrammetry forms, it gets conceivable to accomplish the accompanying results of time and equipment subordinate qualities.

This technique can be credited to a gathering of strategies that impeccably show themselves in tackling issues where the scope of classes of objects is limited. Likewise, there is the away from of the normal execution time of the full generation cycle on the creation limit of the equipment.

The Generative-adversarial system (GAN) was first presented by Jan Goodfellow [3] in 2014. The GAN depends on a mix of two neural systems and, as a first estimation, the standard of the generative-enemy system can be de-scribed as follows. The generative part (neural system G) is utilized to produce counterfeit examples of the dataset. The discriminative part (neural system D) attempts to get rid of however much as could reasonably be expected all examples that are not unique (not created by the generative part).

Using inert space factors, the generative system attempts to make new example dependent on the first genuine examples. Preparing a discriminative system closes in expanding the pointer that decides the nature of the distinction between the first and the created tests. The discriminative system learning results are nourished to the contribution of the generative system with the goal that the last can pick the most ideal arrangement of dormant parameters. Therefore, the reason for the generative system G is to build the level of blunders of the discriminative system D, and the motivation behind system D is to expand the markers of test acknowledgment exactness.

In [5], the learning procedure of the generative-adversarial system is portrayed as a non-lose-lose situation in which the generative system creates models $x = g(z; \theta(g))$, and the discriminative returns the estimation of the capacity $d(z; \theta(d))$, equivalent to the likelihood that x is a genuine instructing model. In light of the above conditions, the discriminator's installment is dictated by the capacity $v(\theta(g), \theta(d))$, and the generator acknowledges $- v(\theta(g), \theta(d))$ as its installment. As every player tries to expand his installment, the accompanying articulations will be gotten as far as possible.

While considering the instance of the working of GAN in the field of creating two-dimensional pictures, we can recognize the accompanying calculation:

- the generator gets an irregular number at the information and returns a picture air conditioning cording to the discovery standard;
- the picture got from the generator is transmitted to the contribution of the discriminator alongside a lot of pictures from the first real (genuine) dataset;
- the discriminator examines the got pictures and doles out every one of them a discrete esteem from 0 to 1, which thus is the likelihood that the pictures have a place with the counterfeit and common classes.

The schematic chart comprises of a few squares. The discriminator is spoken to by a convolutional neural system and plays out the capacity of ordering pictures utilizing a binomial classifier, characterizing them as pictures of regular beginning or fake. The generator is characterized by a switch convolutional neural system that plays out the capacity of changing over irregular clamor into a picture. The generative and discriminative pieces of the framework attempt to enhance the misfortune work in a lose-lose situation.

There are a few papers [4–8], depicting the potential outcomes and aftereffects of the down to earth utilization of generative-antagonistic neural systems, just as determining potential choices for improving the GAN engineering. Specific consideration ought to be paid to pg-GAN – the advancement of masters from Nvidia [9]. Pg-GAN permit to produce an irregular photorealistic picture of countenances of non-existent individuals and change in process the generation parameters influencing the human highlights of the created object.

Considering the undertakings that utilization the design of generative-antagonistic neural systems, it is advantageous to harp on the point of view investigation of specialists from Apple [5]. The point of the examination was to recognize the probability of making an enormous arrangement of practical pictures dependent on the generation of ridiculous examples with an ensuing increment the reasonable parameter, just as checking the parameters of the preparation nature of the model on the information got.

By adding a cradle to the schematic calculation, which contains the aftereffects of past emphases of the example generation segregation cycle, it was conceivable to accomplish top notch results for the authenticity of the produced pictures. The scientists lead ed a test wherein an extraordinarily chosen gathering of individuals attempted to survey whether the pictures they offered have a place with two classes—the class of common pictures and the class of misleadingly made ones. The exploration uncovered that lone 51.7% of individuals had the option to accurately recognize the picture.

DiscoGAN is a continuation of utilizing and improving the engineering of generative adversarial neural systems. The [6] investigates the plausibility of learning generative-adversarial neural systems to decide cross-space connections.

Throughout the examination, authorities proposed the accompanying schematic outline of the generative-antagonistic model, and furthermore led a few trials on image dependent on the meaning of cross-area associations.

DiscoGAN preparing is performed on two freely chose and non-explained datasets containing objects of various nature. For instance, the first dataset for preparing may contain shoe pictures, and the second may contain sack pictures. It won't be hard for an individual to discover signs that are normal to objects from the first and second sets. The neural system in the learning procedure attempts to discover associations between tests from the two sets. Next, the DiscoGAN input is provided with a picture from the principal set and the system, in light of the determined regularities, produces a picture that can be credited to the second dataset. Coming back to the model with datasets containing pictures of sacks and shoes, the consequence of the calculation can be represented as follows.

The design arrangements proposed in the [10] prompted the effective arrangement of the issue of creating pictures containing objects from one dataset and features of items from another.

Using this strategy, it gets conceivable to actualize the procedure of automatically expanding the measure of preparing datasets by creating tests that have various misleadingly altered parameters.

Among the upsides of utilizing generative-adversarial neural systems are the following:

- high estimations of value parameters for producing test datasets;
- impersonation of any information dissemination;
- the probability of improving the quality parameters of producing datasets by including such squares as the variational autoencoder into the schematic calculation of the calculation.

The weaknesses of utilizing generative-adversarial neural systems depend on the accompanying proposals:

- learning of the generative and discriminative parts is impossible synchronously because of the probability of inaccurate determination of weighting factors, because of which the discriminative system can return esteems near 0 or 1, and the generative to utilize the burdens of the discriminative part, returning ridiculous pictures;
- generally high prerequisites for the equipment part of the machine on which preparing is begun;
- high unpredictability settings, and, therefore, using.

In light of the above compositional varieties, a few arrangements have been proposed. For the best precision of deciding the learning procedure parameters of the quality-time attributes, just as the level of execution of the proposed models, a dataset was assembled. The proposed dataset incorporates 7 distinctive object classes and in excess of 10 thousand pictures of human faces in different spatial-light-conceal configurations. Because of the consequences of learning the DCGAN engineering model [11] on the master presented dataset, there is the clear model failure to create shading pictures of complex objects, because of the absence of summing up capacity of the pre-owned design.

In view of the standards of planning generative- adversarial systems, we discourage mined the accompanying structure. Right now, generative part is spoken to by the prepared Mobilenet model with a cut-off yield layer. Additionally, due to the integration into the generator circuit two separate info layers, it gets conceivable to simultaneously feed the turn and brightening characteristics of the three-dimensional model alongside the primary dataset spoke to by a progression of pictures. In the job of the dis-criminative part is the discriminator, characterized in the foe model from [11]. Unfortunately, under the states of the present research, the utilization of this design won't prompt any critical consequences of the learning and generation forms, separately, because of the inadequate profundity of the discriminative piece of the model. It was discovered that with the expansion in the quantity of layers in the discriminator required for demonstrating the plan of the serious model, the necessities for the figuring intensity of the gear go past the system of the examination.

During the design modernization procedure of the above-portrayed generative-adversarial model, the generative model was disconnected to examine the nature of the created tests that are not exposed to discriminator assessment. In light of the consequences of the generation acquired during the preparation of the model, it is possible to reach inferences about the nearness of a certain reliance of the AI model profundity on the degree of unpredictability of the unit of the preparation dataset, just as on the high level of having a place of this engineering structure to the arrangement of strategies for creating fake preparing datasets.

2 Synthetic Data Generation for Face Recognition System

Based on the above architectural variations, several solutions have been proposed. For the greatest accuracy of determining the learning process parameters of the quality-time characteristics, as well as the degree of performance of the proposed models, a dataset was compiled. The proposed dataset includes 7 different object classes and more than 10 thousand images of human faces in various spatial-light-shade configurations.

Because of the aftereffects of learning the DCGAN engineering model [11] on the proposed dataset, there is the obvious model failure to create shading pictures of complex objects, because of the absence of summing up capacity of the pre-owned design.

In view of the standards of structuring generative-antagonistic systems, we dissuade mined the accompanying plan. Right now, generative part is spoken to by the pre-prepared Mobilenet model with a cut-off yield layer. Likewise, due to the integration into the generator circuit two separate info layers, it gets conceivable to simultaneously feed the pivot and enlightenment signs of the three-dimensional model alongside the primary dataset spoke to by a progression of pictures. In the job of the dis-criminative part is the discriminator, characterized in the enemy model from [11]. Unfortunately, under the states of the present research, the utilization of this engineering won't prompt any noteworthy aftereffects of the learning and generation forms [12], respectively, because of the lacking profundity of the discriminative piece of the model. It was discovered that with the expansion in the quantity of layers in the discriminator required for improving the structure of the serious model, the prerequisites for the computing intensity of the gear go past the system of the examination.

During the engineering modernization procedure of the above-portrayed generative-adversarial model, the generative model was confined to research the nature of the created tests that are not exposed to discriminator assessment. In view of the aftereffects of the generation acquired during the preparation of the model, it is possible to make determinations about the nearness of a certain reliance of the AI model profundity on the degree of multifaceted nature of the unit of the preparation dataset, just as on the high level of having a place of this engineering structure to the arrangement of strategies for creating counterfeit preparing datasets.

3 Deep Face Features

In this paper we considered possible implementation of GAN approach in face recognition system. The main problems of generating synthetic photos of a human head with different rotation and lighting were revealed: insufficient training set for the classifier of the face recognition system, as well as insufficient generalizing ability of the generator and/or discriminator. The solution of the indicated problems is planned to be carried out at the next stage of the research project implementation.

Among the existing biometric methods of identification, the greatest interest for researchers in recent years is based on the use of machine vision and deep learning models. The division of the identification process into such logical blocks as an image capture block, a block for localizing objects in an image, a block for isolating feature vectors, a classification block for feature vectors, is one of the most popular approaches to implementing biometric personality identification systems. Such systems can provide a high level of object recognition, but often their use implies the presence of a high-performance hardware complex, and if it is necessary to design a distributed user identification system with a large number of agents, the hardware requirements impose wide restrictions on the design of the system. One of the most demanding logical block resources is a feature extractor.

In order to determine the possibility of classifying images of human faces based on the use of distinguished feature vectors, as well as to determine the degree of invariance of feature vectors to different positions of the human face and its lighting options, a study was conducted on Facenet [13] and VGGFace [14] (ResNet50). An artificial data set was used as a test sample (see Fig. 1), consisting of 10920 images of faces of 7 people in 13 lighting options and 120 variants of face rotation, obtained by constructing three-dimensional models based on real photographs of human faces and photogrammetry methods (Figs. 2 and 3).

Fig. 1. Test dataset.

The hypotheses put forward about the possibility of classifying users based on the analysis of feature vectors, as well as about the possibility of using artificial data for

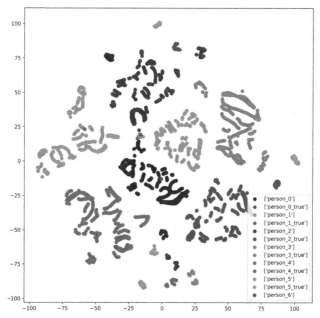

Fig. 2. Visualization of the T-SNE algorithm for feature vectors obtained using Facenet from a test dataset.

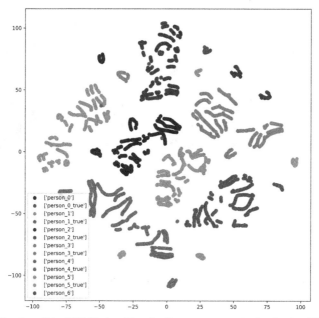

Fig. 3. Visualization of the T-SNE algorithm for feature vectors obtained using VGG-Face from a test dataset.

classification, are confirmed by the results of visualization of projections of feature space for both extractors.

To determine the degree of invariance of the obtained feature vectors to environmental conditions, it was proposed to construct heat maps for each received vector. The extractor, built on the basis of Facenet, at the output produces an array with dimension (1, 128), the elements of which are both positive and negative double precision values. Characteristic vectors at the output of the extractor built using VGGFace (ResNet50) have dimension (1, 2048), and all elements of the array are strictly positive double precision values.

When constructing heat maps in order to increase the interpretability of the data, the dimensions of feature vectors for Facenet and VGGFace (ResNet50) were changed to (8, 16) and (32, 64), respectively. The results of the visualization of the algorithm for constructing heat maps for Facenet and VGGFace (ResNet50) are shown in Fig. 4.

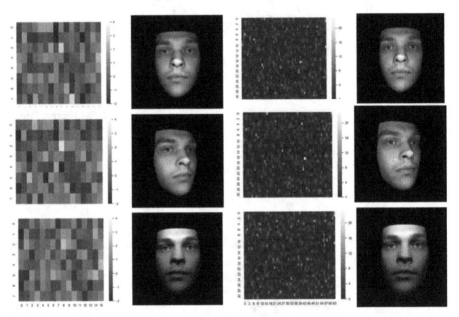

Fig. 4. Facenet and VGGFace face features representation as a heatmap for different head postures.

In the course of research, tests of the above extractors were carried out. Table 1 shows the results of the inference speed benchmark of the analyzed models.

According to the above values, the VGG_Face (ResNet50) model can process a larger number of entities per second, which can be particularly useful when developing embedded systems.

The process of classifying feature vectors can be performed using:

- Iterative calculation of Euclidean distance using programming language tools.
- Iterative calculation of the Euclidean distance on the database side.

Table 1. Inference speed benchmark.

Device	Instances per second	
	Facenet	VGG_Face (ResNet50)
Nvidia Jetson TX2	10.02	14.73
Nvidia rtx2060 (6 GB)	49.26	64.59
Nvidia gtx1080 (11 GB)	60.81	100.14
Nvidia rtx2080 super (11 GB)	70.23	126.92

- Support Vector Machine (SVM).
- CNN based classification system.

When using feature vector comparison modules based on CNN or SVM, you should take into account the time required to retrain the classifier. Figure 5 shows the time characteristics of the feature vectors classification process. Since SVM does not support working with large amounts of data, and retraining CNN-based classifiers on large amounts of data is quite resource-intensive, these characteristics were not reflected in Fig. 5.

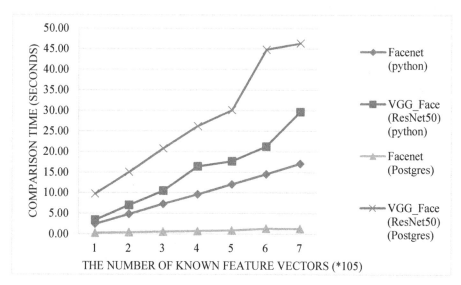

Fig. 5. Feature vectors classification process benchmark.

The choice of backend for the feature vector comparison process depends on the use case. Naturally, when the dimension of the feature space increases, the process of calculating the Euclidean distance will be more demanding to the computing resources of the computer, and it will also take more time. Figure 5 shows that the postgres database is the best solution for developing a module for classifying vectors of smaller dimensions. However, when classifying feature vectors of large dimensions, calculating the Euclidean distance using built-in language tools is more preferable.

4 Conclusion

Face features based on deep neural networks was tested, in particular Facenet and VGG (Resnet50) architectures. It's been shown that no matter what lightning condition and rotation of a head, features extracted from a photo of a face can be used as a unique digital representation of a human face. This property can make such architectures useful not only in facial recognition systems, but also in every domain where it's necessary to monitor unique person behavior [16–18]. For example, this can be particularly useful when designing software for mobile platforms [19] to interact with humans.

We can conclude that the most preferred option for classifying and developing feature vector extraction modules on embedded systems is the package from Facenet and postgres classifying backend. However, using VGG_Face (ResNet50) can be useful if you need to post-process feature vectors, for example, in order to determine not only a person's identity, but also their age.

Further research will be conducted on quantization such deep neural networks for its implementation on embedded systems on mobile robotic platforms.

Acknowledgements. This research is supported by RSF №16-19-00044П.

References

1. Kagirov, I., Tolstoy, I., Savelyev, A., Karpov, A.: Gesture control of collaborative robot. Robot. Techn. Cybern. **7**(2), 139–144 (2019)
2. Saveliev, A., Uzdiaev, M., Dmitrii, M.: Aggressive Action Recognition Using 3D CNN Architectures. In: 2019 12th International Conference on Developments in eSystems Engineering (DeSE), pp. 890–895 (2019)
3. Goodfellow, I. et al.: Generative adversarial nets. Adv. Neural Inf. Process. Syst. **56**, 2672–2680 (2014)
4. Wang, X., Gupta, A.: Generative image modeling using style and structure adversarial networks. In: Leibe, B., Matas, J., Sebe, N., Welling, M. (eds.) ECCV 2016. LNCS, vol. 9908, pp. 318–335. Springer, Cham (2016). https://doi.org/10.1007/978-3-319-46493-0_20
5. Zhu, J.Y., Krähenbühl, P., Shechtman, E., Efros, A.A.: Generative Visual Manipulation on the Natural Image Manifold. In: Leibe, B., Matas, J., Sebe, N., Welling, M. (eds.) ECCV 2016. LNCS, vol. 9909, pp. 597–613. Springer, Cham (2016). https://doi.org/10.1007/978-3-319-46454-1_36
6. Liu, M.Y., Tuzel, O.: Coupled generative adversarial networks. Adv. Neural Inf. Processing Syst. **29**, 469–477 (2016)
7. Tuzel, O., Taguchi, Y., Hershey, J. R.: Global-local face upsampling network. arXiv preprint arXiv:1603.07235 (2016)
8. Generation photorealistic celebrity faces. https://blog.insightdatascience.com/generatingcustom-photo-realistic-faces-using-ai-d170b1b59255. Accessed 10 Jan 2020, Accessed 01 July 2020

9. Kim, T., Cha, M., Kim, H., Lee, J. K., Kim, J.: Learning to discover cross-domain relations with generative adversarial networks. In: Proceedings of the 34th International Conference on Machine Learning, vol. 70, pp. 1857–1865 (2017)
10. Shrivastava, A.: Learning from simulated and unsupervised images through adversarial training. In: Proceedings of the IEEE Conference on Computer Vision and Pattern Recognition, pp. 2107–2116 (2017)
11. Goodfellow, I., Bengio, Y., Courville, A.: Deep Learning, MIT Press, Cambridge (2016)
12. Zhukovskiy, Y.L., Korolev, N.A., Babanova, I.S., Boikov, A.V.: The prediction of the residual life of electromechanical equipment based on the artificial neural network. In: IOP Conference Series: Earth and Environmental Science, vol. 87, p. 032056. IOP Publishing (2017)
13. Schroff, F., Kalenichenko, D., Philbin, J.F.: A unified embedding for face recognition and clustering. In: Proceedings of the IEEE Conference on Computer Vision and Pattern Recognition, pp. 815–823 (2015)
14. Keras-vggface. https://github.com/rcmalli/keras-vggface. Accessed 01 July 2020
15. Maaten, L.V.D., Hinton, G.: Visualizing data using t-SNE. J. Mach. Learn. Res. **9**, 2579–2605 (2008)
16. Oleinik, A.L., Kukharev, G.A.: Algorithms for Face Image Mutual Reconstruction by Means of Two-Dimensional Projection Methods. SPIIRAS Proceedings. **2**, 45–74 (2018). https://doi.org/10.15622/sp.57.3
17. Bogomolov, A.V., Gan, S.P., Zinkin, V.N., Alekhin, M.D.: Acoustic factor environmental safety monitoring information system. In: Proceedings of 2019 22nd International Conference on Soft Computing and Measurements, SCM 2019. 8903729, pp. 215–218 (2019)
18. Vasiljevic, I.S., Dragan, D., Obradovic, R., Petrović, V.B.: Analysis of compression techniques for stereoscopic images. In: SPIIRAS Proceedings. vol. 6, 197–220 (2018). https://doi.org/10.15622/sp.61.8
19. Pavliuk, N., Kharkov, I., Zimuldinov, E., Saprychev, V.: Development of multipurpose mobile platform with a modular structure. In: Ronzhin, A., Shishlakov, V. (eds.) Proceedings of 14th International Conference on Electromechanics and Robotics "Zavalishin's Readings". SIST, vol. 154, pp. 137–147. Springer, Singapore (2020). https://doi.org/10.1007/978-981-13-9267-2_12

An Estimation of Distributed Algorithms of the Fault-Tolerant Management in the Robot Groups

Eduard Melnik[1], Anna Klimenko[2(✉)], and Irina Safronenkova[1]

[1] Federal Research Centre, the Southern Scientific Centre of the Russian Academy of Sciences, 41, Chekhov Street, 344006 Rostov-on-Don, Russian Federation
[2] Scientific Research Institute of Multiprocessor Computer Systems of Southern Federal University, 2, Chekhov Street, 347922 Taganrog, Russian Federation
anna_klimenko@mail.ru

Abstract. This paper is devoted to the problem of fault-tolerant management in groups of autonomous and mobile robots. This problem is quite topical because frequent usage of robot groups and the lack of the mechanisms of the fault-tolerant robot failure detection and mission recovery. Some algorithms based on the View-Stamped Replication protocol (with a distributed leader) and on the principles of leaderless consensus have been developed and presented. The procedure of contextual information analysis and the leader election particular procedure are described. Besides, some leaderless algorithms are developed paying attention to the robot groups dynamic location. Some models for the algorithms efficiency estimation in terms of communication overheads has been developed and selected simulation results are given.

Keywords: Distributed management · Robot groups · Distributed ledger technologies

1 Introduction

Management in the robot groups, including the failure detection, is a topical problem, considering the growth of quantity of ubiquitously applied robots. The issues are related to the single-robot fault-detection coexist with the issues related to the collective management and coordination. Though some works pay attention to the multirobot management [1–4], new technologies emerged in the last decade, which provide reliable and fault-tolerant management in the large distributed computational systems. Fault-tolerance is a key issue for the management in robot groups, so it is expedient to take a look on the algorithms, which provide this for other types of systems. Yet, such algorithms were essentially developed for that technical area, where the computational nodes have the static locations (or their movements are handled by other technical facilities, e.g., roaming). Dynamically changing locations of autonomous robots play a significant role in their monitoring, because robots can cooperate in case if they are in the area of data transmission coverage of other robots transmitters.

© Springer Nature Switzerland AG 2020
A. Ronzhin et al. (Eds.): ICR 2020, LNAI 12336, pp. 212–221, 2020.
https://doi.org/10.1007/978-3-030-60337-3_21

This work considers two types of distributed consensus algorithms as applied to the fault-tolerant failure detection in the groups of robots. Yet, the algorithms considered were modified to meet the main peculiarity of the robot group – the ability to change geographic location. An assumption has been made about the "heartbeat" manner of exchanging the mission-related knowledge between the robots. The existence of this knowledge modifies the main states of distributed consensus algorithms and allows to apply the elements of such well-known algorithms as RAFT/VR to the robot fault-tolerant management.

In this paper, we do not consider in details the consensus algorithms, one can find the description in the works [5–13]. The attention is paid to the modification of the algorithms and their estimation in terms of communication workload generation.

The remainder of the paper is organized as follows. Section 2 contains the descriptions of the developed algorithms with comments. Section 3 contains some abstract models, which allow to estimate the efficiency of the developed algorithms in terms of network load. Section 4 contains some simulation results.

2 Distributed Algorithms of the Fault-Tolerant Failure Detection in the Groups of Robots

2.1 Dispatching with a Distributed Leader

This algorithm is based on the VewStamped Replication protocol, which provides the consistency and integrity of distributed database systems. It must be mentioned that the extended VR – Practical Byzantine Fault Tolerance – is used in some Cryptocurrency systems and provides the fault tolerance in cases of Byzantine malicious behavior of nodes. The algorithms of the leader and follower functioning are presented in Fig. 1. There are three main states of the system: operational, failure detection and change leader. For the follower the original algorithm has been developed:

1. If the leader identifier has not been received check if the leader is out of the data transmission coverage.
2. If the leader is failed the system state is set to "change_leader".
3. If the system state is equal to "change_leader" a group of devices is formed.
4. Leader election procedure begins:
    4.1. Send the node identifier to all devices in group.
    4.2. Receive neighbor's identifier.
    4.3. If node's identifier > neighbor's identifier Leader_id is set with self identifier. Else Leader_id is set to neighbor's identifier (leader election procedure is finished; the leader has the largest identifier).
5. System state is set to "functional" and the system returns to the operational state.
6. If Leader's identifier is equal to self identifier node state is set to the "leader".

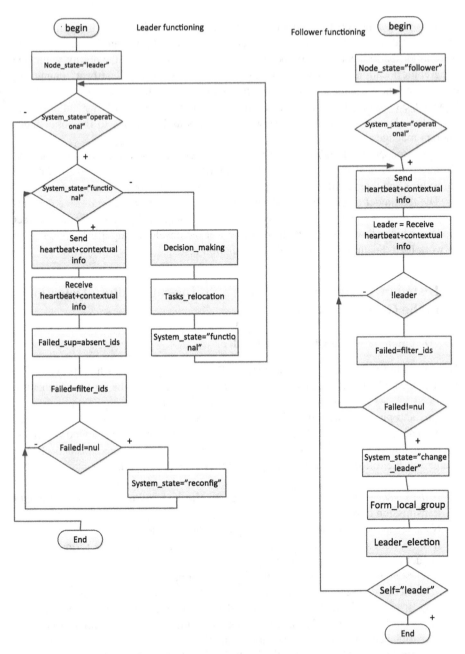

Fig. 1. Algorithms with distributed leader for the leader and the follower nodes.

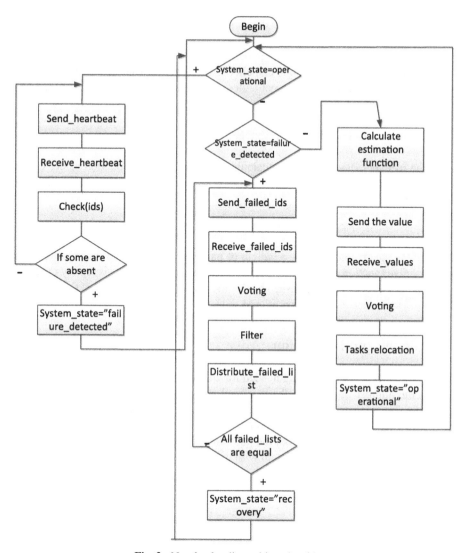

Fig. 2. Non-leader dispatching algorithm.

2.2 Non-leader Dispatching

In this case, there is no leader at all. Every device is managed by means of one unified algorithm, based on the leaderless consensus algorithms [14]. The leaderless dispatching algorithm is presented in Fig. 2.

This algorithm is listed below with comments. While the system state is operational, all nodes exchange the heartbeat. If some identifiers are lost, the system transits into the state "failure detected".

At the "failure detected" stage the nodes must to reach the consensus on the failed nodes. This can be done by means of the voting. The procedure is described below.

1. Every node has its own list of the devices supposed to be failed.
2. Every node share its knowledge about the "failed" nodes with the others, so, there must be a collection of lists for all nodes.
3. Comparing the lists, every node can choose those nodes which are supposed to be failed by more than 2/3 operational nodes.
4. -NoValue-Every node shares the improved list with the others. The final list is fair, when more than 2/3 nodes proved it.
5. The system transits to the recovery stage.

At the recovery stage every node calculates the multicriteria function value, which describes how the node meets the functional task requirements. In general, this function looks like the following:

$$F(x_1, x_2 \ldots x_n) = \alpha_1 x_1 + \alpha_2 x_2 + \ldots + \alpha_n x_n,$$

where x_i – device resources, α_i – a weight of parameter I, which allows to present the multiobjective function as a scalar one. The calculated function value is sent by the node to the others. The task is accomplished by the node with the biggest value of the function. Then the system transits to the operational state.

3   Modeling and Estimation

Consider the following parameters needed for communication workload estimation:

N is the number of nodes in the managed group; V_i is the volume of "heartbeat" information message, including some contextual data, e.g., mission information, current coordinates, etc. V_{st} is the volume of contextual data storage, which is needed for every device to store the knowledge about the mission plans, device states and so on.

The operational state of the system with distributed leader is shown in Fig. 3.

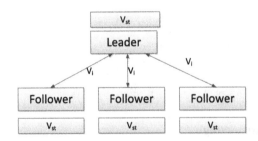

Fig. 3. Operational state of the system with distributed leader.

If the state of the system is operational, the estimation of the network load is as follows:

$$V_{op} = 2V_i(N - 1). \tag{1}$$

Then, if the failure occurs, the cases of follower failure and leader failure must be considered separately.

If the follower fails, the leader makes a decision which follower will process the functions of the failed node, so the network load will be as is shown below:

$$V_{ff} = (N - 1)V_i. \tag{2}$$

In case of the leader failure, the procedure of the leader election and the system recovery takes place, and so we deal with much more considerable data volumes transmitting through the network:

$$V_{lf} = 3N(N - 1)V_i + 2(N - 1)V_{st}. \tag{3}$$

This equation contains description of the following steps:

- group establishing;
- leader election;
- the request of contextual data storages;
- the collecting of data storages by the leader;
- the setting of the "leader" contextual data storage to the followers.

The latter three operations are inherited from the VR protocol and is needed to maintain the consistency and integrity of the contextual data of the system.

In case of leaderless management the following communication activities take place (see Fig. 4).

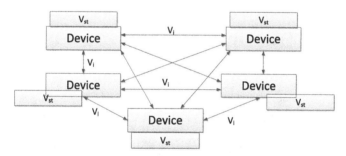

Fig. 4. The leaderless management.

In the operational state the network load is as follows:

$$V_{nlo} = N(N - 1)V_i. \tag{4}$$

Failure detection and recovery states generate the following network load:

$$V_{nlr} = 4N(N - 1)V_i. \tag{5}$$

This estimation includes the data generated by the failure detection and the consensus about the failed nodes, as well as the procedure of decision making on which node takes the functions of the failed one.

4 Simulation Results

The rough estimations were made under the following conditions: N = 5. 120 (nodes), V_i = 10 (modeling units, m.u.), V_{st} = 400 (m.u.). One can see (see Fig. 5 and 6) the trends of how the network load increases during the operational stages of leader-based and non-leader algorithms.

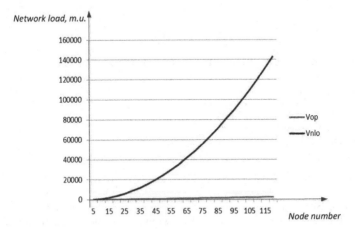

Fig. 5. Operational states of the systems with distributed leader and leaderless management (V_{op} – distributed leader case, V_{nlo} – non-leader case).

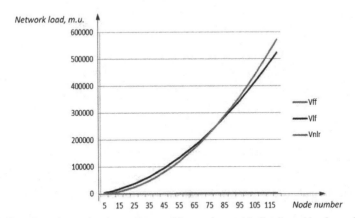

Fig. 6. Failure detection and recovery states of the systems with distributed leader and leaderless management (V_{ff} – follower failure case, V_{lf} – leader failure case, V_{nlr} – non-leader failure and recovery case).

-NoValue-One can see that with the constant contextual data storage size with the N increasing there is a threshold, when distributed leader application is more expedient. Yet, with the growing size of the contextual data storage and the fixed number of nodes the recovery state is illustrated in Fig. 7.

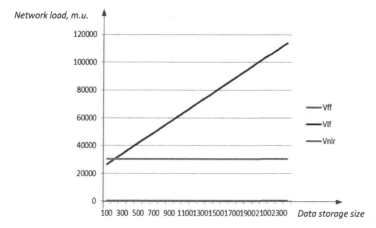

Fig. 7. The network load growth with the contextual data storage increasing (V_{ff} – follower failure case, V_{lf} – leader failure case, V_{nlr} – non-leader failure and recovery case).

-NoValue-The following graph illustrates the result of growth of the contextual data packets as a part of heartbeat message (see Fig. 8).

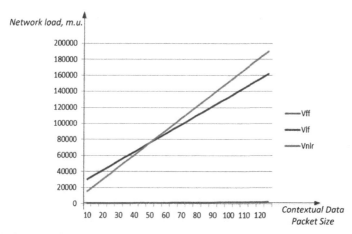

Fig. 8. The increase of the contextual data packet. (V_{ff} – follower failure case, V_{lf} – leader failure case, V_{nlr} – non-leader failure and recovery case).

One can see that when the contextual data packet size is relatively large, it is expedient to use the management with distributed leader.

5   Conclusion

Methods, provided by the DLT are reliable and fault-tolerant, and so can be efficiently applied to the management in the groups of autonomous robots. In this paper, two algorithms were presented and roughly estimated: algorithm of system dispatching with the distributed leader and the leaderless algorithm. These algorithms were designed on the basis of well-known ViewStamped Replication protocol and on the basis of leaderless consensus method. Yet, some modifications were applied: the source algorithms do not suppose the movement of the groups of nodes. This issue can be solved by the usage of contextual data storage (including mission general plans, current coordinates of the robots and so on). The need to transfer contextual data adds some additional intensity to the network load, but provides the basis for the fault-tolerance.

Estimations of the developed algorithms efficiency allow to make the following important conclusions:

- the distributed leader is efficient in the robot groups with the relatively short mission (the small size of the contextual data storage);
- the distributed leader is efficient in the groups with reliable devices, because the recovery in case of leader failure takes much time and network resource consuming;
- leaderless management is efficient under the conditions of missions with long time duration and relatively small number of robots in the group.

Besides, it is important to spotlite the situation, when the groups of robots are merged, and the leader duplicating is detected. This provides the need to initiate the leader change procedure with the considerable network load.

Summing up, the fault-tolerant algorithms based on the methods of digital economy are efficient and prospective. The following work direction lies in the area of the computational complexity and workload estimation of the robotic control systems.

Acknowledgements. This research is supported by the RFBR projects 19-07-00907 and 18-29-22086.

References

1. Pettersson, O.: Execution monitoring in robotics: a survey. Robot. Autonom. Syst. **53**, 73–88 (2005)
2. Duan, Z., Cai, Z., Yu, J.: Fault diagnosis and fault tolerant control for wheeled mobile robots under unknown environments: a survey. In: IEEE International Conference on Robotics and Automation Proceedings, pp. 3428–3433. IEEE, Barcelona, Spain (2005)
3. Khalastchi, E., Kalech, M.: Fault detection and diagnosis in multi-robot systems: a survey. Sensors **19**, 4019 (2019)
4. Parker, L.E.: ALLIANCE: An architecture for fault tolerant multirobot cooperation. IEEE Trans. Robot. Automat **14**, 220–240 (1988)
5. Liskov, B., Cowling, J.: Viewstamped replication revisited. http://www.pmg.csail.mit.edu/papers/vr-revisited.pdf. Accessed 14 June 2020
6. Oki, B.M., Liskov, B.H.: Viewstamped replication: a new primary copy method to support highly-available distributed systems. In: Annual ACM Symposium on Principles of Distributed Computing Proceedings, pp. 8–17 (1988)
7. Howard, H., Crowcroft, J.: Coracle: evaluating consensus at the internet edge. In: 2015 ACM Conference on Special Interest Group on Data Communication Proceedings, vol. 45, no. 5, pp. 85–86. ACM, USA (2015)

8. Van Renesse, R., Schiper, N., Schneider, F.B.: Paxos vs. Viewstamped Replication vs. Zab. In: IEEE Trans. Depend. Secure Comput. **12**, 472–484 (2015)

9. Li, S., Du, H., Lin, X.: Finite-time consensus algorithm for multi-agent systems with double-integrator dynamics. Automatica **47**, 1706–1712 (2011)

10. Baird, L., Harmon, M., Madsen, P.: Hedera – A Governing Council & Public Hashgraph Network. White Paper (2018)

11. Holotescu, V., Vasiu, R.: Challenges and emerging solutions for public blockchains. Brain. Broad Res. Artif. Intell. Neurosci. **11**, 58–83 (2020)

12. Gervais, A., et al.: On the security and performance of Proof of Work blockchains. In: ACM SIGSAC Conference on Computer and Communications Security Proceedings, pp. 3–16. ACM, USA (2016)

13. Leopoldo, F.: Proof of Work. In: van Tilborg, H.C.A., Jajodia, S. (eds.) Encyclopedia of Cryptography and Security. Springer, Boston (2011). https://doi.org/10.1007/978-1-4419-5906-5

14. Meng, Z., Ren, W., Cao, Y., You, Z.: Leaderless and leader-following consensus with communication and input delays under a directed network topology. IEEE Trans. Syst. Man, Cybern. Part B Cybern. 2011

Comparison of ROS-Based Monocular Visual SLAM Methods: DSO, LDSO, ORB-SLAM2 and DynaSLAM

Eldar Mingachev[1]($\boxtimes$), Roman Lavrenov[1]($\boxtimes$), Tatyana Tsoy[1]($\boxtimes$), Fumitoshi Matsuno[2], Mikhail Svinin[3], Jackrit Suthakorn[4], and Evgeni Magid[1]

[1] Laboratory of Intelligent Robotic Systems (LIRS), Intelligent Robotics Department, Higher Institute for Information Technology and Intelligent Systems, Kazan Federal University, Kazan, Russian Federation
`ermingachev@stud.kpfu.ru`, {`lavrenov,tt,magid`}`@it.kfu.ru`
[2] Department of Mechanical Engineering and Science, Kyoto University, Kyoto 615-8540, Japan
`matsuno@me.kyoto-u.ac.jp`
[3] Information Science and Engineering Department, Ritsumeikan University, 1-1-1 Noji-higashi, Kusatsu, Shiga 525-8577, Japan
`svinin@fc.ritsumei.ac.jp`
[4] Biomedical Engineering Department, Mahidol University, 4, 999 Phuttamonthon, Salaya 73170, Thailand
`jackrit.sut@mahidol.ac.th`
`http://robot.kpfu.ru/eng`

Abstract. Stable and robust path planning of a ground mobile robot requires a combination of accuracy and low latency in its state estimation. Yet, state estimation algorithms should provide these under computational and power constraints of a robot embedded hardware. The presented study offers a comparative analysis of four cutting edge publicly available within robot operating system (ROS) monocular simultaneous localization and mapping methods: DSO, LDSO, ORB-SLAM2, and DynaSLAM. The analysis considers pose estimation accuracy (alignment, absolute trajectory, and relative pose root mean square error) and trajectory precision of the four methods at TUM-Mono and EuRoC datasets.

Keywords: Simultaneous localization and mapping · Visual SLAM · Monocular SLAM · Visual odometry · State estimation · Path planning · Benchmark testing · Robot sensing systems

1 Introduction

Simultaneous localization and mapping (SLAM, [8]) is an ability of an autonomous vehicle to start in an unknown location of an unknown environment and then, using only relative observations, to incrementally construct a

© Springer Nature Switzerland AG 2020
A. Ronzhin et al. (Eds.): ICR 2020, LNAI 12336, pp. 222–233, 2020.
https://doi.org/10.1007/978-3-030-60337-3_22

map of the environment [25] while simultaneously using the map to compute a bounded estimate of the vehicle location [22]. Nowadays, SLAM is applied to state and pose estimation problems in various domains, from virtual and augmented reality to autonomous vehicles and robotics [12,15]. The field has reached a mature level [7] that causes proprietary SLAM algorithms utilizing in many commercial products as well as public availability of a number of open-source SLAM software packages [6]. Yet, due to sensor price and robot weight concerns, currently the prevailing type of SLAM is a monocular approach [5].

One of the main features of a monocular SLAM is a scale-ambiguity [10], which states that a world scale could not be observed and drifts over time, being one of the major error sources. Being both a challenge and a benefit, it allows switching seamlessly between differently scaled environments [14], while stereo or depth cameras do not allow such flexibility, having a limited range where they can provide reliable measurements [21]. This paper offers a comparative analysis in terms of a pose estimation accuracy and a trajectory precision of the most recent and popular robot operating system (ROS) based open-source monocular SLAM methods considering power constraints of mobile ground robots [18]. The four selected SLAM methods are DSO [9], LDSO [13], ORB-SLAM2 [19,20] and DynaSLAM [2]

2   Related Work

2.1   The Selected SLAM Methods

Direct Methods can estimate a completely dense reconstruction by a direct minimization of a photometric error and optical flow regularization. Some direct methods focus on high-gradient areas estimating semi-dense maps [2]. The presented study compares:

- DSO, which is a state-of-the-art pure direct method [9],
- LDSO, which is DSO's latest revision with a loop closure ability and a global map optimization [13].

Feature-Based Methods rely on matching key points and can only estimate a sparse reconstruction [3], mostly providing a good trade-off between an accuracy and a runtime. The current study presents a comparison of:

- ORB-SLAM2 [20] state-of-the-art visual SLAM method that tracks ORB features in real-time. It has a same monocular core as the original ORB-SLAM [19] but is featured with an improved and optimized workflow.
- The recently proposed DynaSLAM [2] method, which adds a front-end stage to the ORB-SLAM2 system to have a more accurate tracking and a reusable map of a scene. It outperforms the accuracy of the standard visual SLAM baselines in highly dynamic scenarios.

2.2 Benchmarks

There are several publicly available datasets for the SLAM benchmark purposes, however, some of the existing ones are not suitable to benchmark monocular SLAM algorithms due to a low precision of groundtruth data [16]. The current study considers the two most suitable datasets, TUM-Mono and EuRoC.

TUM-Mono. Schubert et al. [24], Engel, Usenko, and Cremers [11] developed a dataset for evaluating a tracking accuracy of a monocular visual odometry [17] and SLAM methods. The dataset includes 50 indoor and outdoor sequences, which start and end in the same position and contain groundtruth only for these start and end trajectory segments. All dataset sequences are photometrically calibrated and provide exposure times for each frame as reported by a sensor, a camera response function, and a dense lens attenuation factors. This allows evaluating a tracking accuracy via an accumulated drift and a reliably benchmark direct methods.

EuRoC. Burri et al. [4] proposed a visual-inertial dataset aiming at evaluation of localization and 3D environment reconstruction algorithms. The dataset consists of 11 sequences, recorded with two monocular cameras onboard a micro-aerial vehicle. The datasets range from slow flights under good visual conditions to dynamic flights with motion blur and poor illumination. Each sequence contains synchronized stereo images, extrinsic and intrinsic calibrations, an inertial unit (IMU) measurements, and an accurate groundtruth (approximately 1 mm) recorded using a laser tracker and a motion capture system. Compared to the TUM-Mono benchmark, the sequences in EuRoC are shorter and have less variety as they only contain recordings inside a single machine hall and a single laboratory room.

2.3 Metrics

TUM-Mono. To evaluate the TUM-Mono benchmark results, we used proposed by Engel, Usenko, and Cremers metrics [11], an *alignment Root Mean Square Error (RMSE)* - a combined error measure, which equally takes into account an error caused by scale, rotation and translation drifts over an entire trajectory. It is the RMSE between tracked trajectories when aligned to start and end segments.

EuRoC. The EuRoC includes entire groundtruth camera trajectories, which allows using an *absolute trajectory RMSE (ATE)*, a measure of a global trajectory accuracy, and a *relative pose RMSE (RPE)*, which is a measure of a local pose accuracy, proposed by Sturm, Engelhard, Endres, Burgard, and Cremers [26]. Overall, the RPE metric provides an elegant way to combine rotational and translational errors into a single measurement, while the ATE only considers translational errors. As a result, the RPE is always slightly larger than the ATE (or equal if there is no rotational error). However, rotational errors typically also manifest themselves in wrong translations and are thus indirectly also captured by the ATE. From a practical perspective, the ATE has an intuitive visualization, which facilitates a visual inspection. Nevertheless, as the authors noted, the two metrics are strongly correlated.

Trajectory Detail Level. In contrast to the reviewed metrics, which mainly focus on measuring a difference between corresponding frames, a trajectory detail level measures a difference between a length of trajectories, being an estimated and a groundtruth trajectories length ratio. The metric can be used to benchmark effectiveness of hardware capabilities usage and even estimate limits of a detail level of a particular SLAM algorithm while running on various hardware configurations. In addition, it could be useful in determining a suitable trade-off between an accuracy and output data detail level.

3   Comparative Analysis

Mur-Artal and Tardós [20] proposed running each sequence five times and showed median results to account for a non-deterministic nature of a system. Bescos, Fácil, Civera and Neira [2] extended this approach by increased the number of runs up to 10 times, as dynamic objects are prone to increase a non-deterministic effect. In light of the above, the current study also utilizes the extended approach.

3.1   Hardware Setup

This study focuses on SLAM methods usage with mobile ground robots that implies a restriction on energy consumption and absence of strict constraints on a mobile robot weight, which, for example, are critical for SLAM usage with a UAV. The selected hardware platform with balanced computational resources and power consumption is the *HP Omen 15-ce057ur* laptop with the technical specifications briefly described in Table 1.

Table 1. Hardware specifications.

CPU	Intel Core i7-7700 HQ, 2800 MHz
RAM	16 GB, DDR 4, 2400 MHz
Weight	2.56 kg
Battery	70 Wh Li-Ion
Power consumption	80 W (avg. load)

Fig. 1. The experimental sequence - the loop start and end (left) and the global trajectory overview (right).

3.2 TUM-Mono

To prove the effectiveness of the proposed approach [11], we expanded the TUM-Mono dataset sequences with a new real-world sequence (Fig. 1) collected with PAL Robotics TIAGo Base ground mobile robot [1] with a single monocular camera onboard [23].

The sequence presents 13 min of video and about a 100-m length trajectory in a gradually changing environment - from a narrow indoor corridor to a wide indoor corridor, which moved the robot from illuminated scenes to dark scenes. The sequence starts and ends in the same place with slow loopy motion allowing a correct initialization of the SLAM algorithms. The groundtruth for the entire trajectory was recorded with the ORB-SLAM2 [20] algorithm, in contrast to the other sequences groundtruth, which was provided by LSD-SLAM [10] only for the start and end segments.

We have evaluated the metrics over DSO, LDSO, ORB-SLAM2, and DynaSLAM methods on the expanded TUM-Mono dataset, running the dataset sequences forward and backward, with the loop closure feature being disabled, following the dataset authors' recommendations.

Figure 2 presents the cumulative error graphs – accumulated translational, rotational, and scale drifts along with the RMSE when aligning the estimated trajectory start and end segments with the provided groundtruth trajectory. The figure depicts the number of runs in which the errors are below the corresponding x-values - the closer to the top left, the better. It is important to note the difference in magnitude – the RMSE within start and end segments is about 100 times less than the alignment RMSE.

Due to the groundtruth nature and the similarity of the experimental results, Engel et al. [11] concluded that almost all of the alignment errors originate not from the noise in the groundtruth, but from the accumulated drift. Our experiments confirmed this conclusion, which means that these metrics could be used for any benchmark with a groundtruth of any accuracy as a reference, even the one collected with SLAM algorithms. Figure 3 shows the color-coded alignment RMSE ranging from 0 (blue) to 10 m (red) for each dataset sequence.

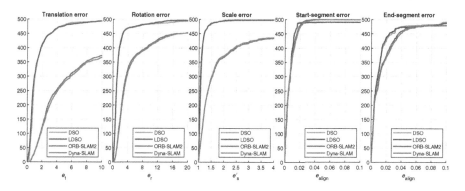

Fig. 2. Accumulated translational (e_t, m), rotational (e_r, m), and scale (e'_s, m) drifts along with the start and end segments RMSE (e_{align}, m).

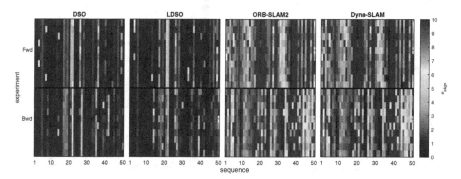

Fig. 3. Color-coded alignment RMSE (e_{align}, m) for each TUM-Mono dataset sequence. (Color figure online)

The experiments demonstrated that direct methods provide outstanding results comparing to the feature-based ones - the TUM-Mono dataset is designed especially for direct methods benchmark purposes, providing full photometric data for each frame, which greatly improves the accuracy of such methods. However, there is not that much of a difference if comparing DSO to LDSO - as we can assume, the LDSO global map optimization slightly improves the overall accuracy of the base method.

The same behaviour is observed while comparing feature-based methods - the accuracy of DynaSLAM is slightly lower comparing to ORB-SLAM2. However, the DynaSLAM initialization is always quicker than the ORB-SLAM2 initialization; in highly dynamic sequences, the ORB-SLAM2 initialization only occurs when moving objects disappear from a scene while DynaSLAM succeeds in bootstrapping the system in such dynamic scenarios.

3.3   EuRoC

We evaluated the metrics over DSO, LDSO, ORB-SLAM2, and DynaSLAM on the EuRoC dataset over all sequences for each of the two camera streams, which were interpreted as separate sequences with the same groundtruth ('.0' and '.1' notations correspond to the first and the second camera dataset respectively and are labeled on X-axis in Figs. 4 and 5). Figure 4 shows the calculated absolute trajectory RMSE (ATE, measured in metres) and the relative pose RMSE (RPE, measured in metres per second) metrics ranging from 0 (blue) to 2 (red) for all methods.

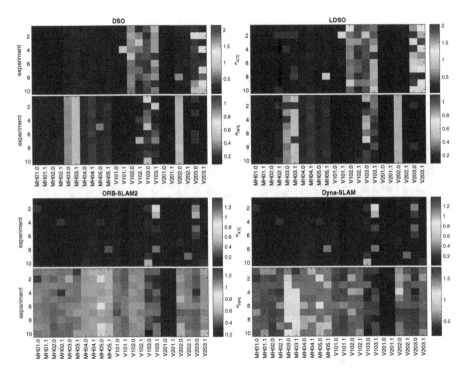

Fig. 4. Color-coded evaluation results for each EuRoC dataset sequence: absolute trajectory RMSE (ATE, m) and relative pose RMSE (RPE, m/s). (Color figure online)

As the analysis demonstrates, that in terms of the RPE, the measure of local accuracy, the direct methods generally perform significantly better than the feature-based ones, but it is still difficult for them to overcome a harsh environment with a lack of light and prevailing rotational movements (over translational movements), as shown in MH.05, V1.03, and V2.03 sequences. In terms of the ATE, the feature-based methods demonstrate a stable performance, even in the "hard" sequences. However, the accuracy of DynaSLAM is slightly lower, compared to ORB-SLAM2, since DynaSLAM succeeds in bootstrapping the system with a dynamic content and always initializes quicker than ORB-SLAM2 and thus has more frames to process (and more room for accumulating errors). Figure 5 demonstrates the calculated trajectory detail level for DSO, LDSO, ORB-SLAM2, and DynaSLAM methods for each EuRoC dataset sequence.

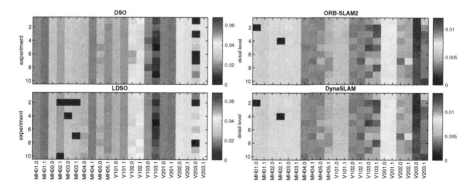

Fig. 5. Color-coded trajectory detail level for each EuRoC dataset sequence. (Color figure online)

Table 2. Median absolute trajectory RMSE (ATE, m), relative pose RMSE (RPE, m/s) & trajectory detail level (*Detail*) for each EuRoC dataset sequence.

Sequence	DSO			LDSO			ORB-SLAM2			DynaSLAM		
	ATE	RPE	Detail	ATE	RPE	Detail	ATE	RPE	Detail	ATE	RPE	Detail
MH.01	0.054	0.132	0.018	0.044	0.131	0.018	0.041	0.491	0.006	0.042	0.494	0.006
MH.02	0.063	0.134	0.025	0.044	0.139	0.025	0.035	0.458	0.006	0.036	0.465	0.007
MH.03	0.209	0.711	0.028	0.090	0.706	0.028	0.041	1.095	0.006	0.043	1.102	0.007
MH.04	0.173	0.632	0.022	0.136	0.642	0.022	0.074	0.560	0.009	0.076	0.568	0.011
MH.05	0.169	0.199	0.023	0.127	0.198	0.023	0.054	0.589	0.009	0.056	0.592	0.010
V1.01	0.104	0.088	0.023	0.099	0.089	0.023	0.054	0.454	0.005	0.054	0.459	0.006
V1.02	1.047	0.137	0.044	1.013	0.111	0.044	0.054	0.528	0.009	0.055	0.534	0.011
V1.03	0.584	0.334	0.057	0.607	0.375	0.057	0.091	0.409	0.009	0.097	0.411	0.010
V2.01	0.064	0.081	0.018	0.058	0.081	0.019	0.047	0.225	0.007	0.047	0.227	0.008
V2.02	0.162	0.306	0.037	0.106	0.281	0.038	0.051	0.508	0.009	0.053	0.552	0.009
V2.03	1.439	0.087	0.036	1.266	0.086	0.040	0.096	0.477	0.010	0.097	0.479	0.012

The obtained results suggest that the direct methods typically distinguish more keyframes and, thus, having a better trajectory detail level, show a better local (pose) accuracy, compared to feature-based methods. It is important to note the difference in the color scale of the feature-based methods plots, which is the difference in the detail level magnitude. DynaSLAM operates a slightly larger amount of frames than ORB-SLAM2 and has a slightly better trajectory detail level (due to the quicker initialization).

Table 3. Median alignment RMSE (*Align*, m), absolute trajectory RMSE (*ATE*, m), relative pose RMSE (*RPE*, m/s) & trajectory detail level (*Detail*).

Metrics	DSO	LDSO	ORB-SLAM2	DynaSLAM
Align	0.8496	0.7769	5.7571	6.1891
ATE	0.1683	0.1062	0.0507	0.0525
RPE	0.1373	0.1111	0.4765	0.4787
Detail	0.0355	0.0376	0.0086	0.0099

3.4 Summary

Tables 2 and 3 summarize the calculated metrics as a single median value for each EuRoC dataset sequence (Table 2) and the entire TUM-Mono and EuRoC datasets (Table 3).

The alignment error, accumulated drift, is in average 7.35 times lower for direct methods than for indirect:

- LDSO outperforms DSO by 8.56%
- DynaSLAM is 6.98% behind ORB-SLAM2

The absolute trajectory error, global accuracy, for direct methods is in average 2.66 times higher than for indirect:

- LDSO outperforms DSO by 36.89%
- DynaSLAM is 3.42% behind ORB-SLAM2

The relative position error, local accuracy, for direct methods is in average 3.85 times lower than for indirect:

- LDSO outperforms DSO by 19.08%
- DynaSLAM is 0.46% behind ORB-SLAM2

The level of trajectory detail for direct methods is in average 3.95 times higher than for indirect:

- LDSO outperforms DSO by 5.59%,
- DynaSLAM outperforms ORB-SLAM2 by 13.13%.

While it was expected that LDSO should outperform its original source algorithm (DSO) and experiments demonstrated its better performance with regard to all measured criteria, DynaSLAM and ORB-SLAM2 have varying benefits with respect to particular criteria, and this variety should be considered when selecting a SLAM algorithm for a specific task.

4   Conclusions and Future Work

This paper presented a comparative analysis of four publicly available ROS-based monocular SLAM algorithms in terms of the state estimation accuracy and the trajectory detail level. The analysis demonstrated that the direct methods DSO and LDSO have a better accuracy while having entire photometric data available and mainly focus on the local accuracy, which is also indirectly proven by the fact that they save and operate a relatively large amount of trajectory keyframes. For these reasons, DSO and LDSO are more suitable for tasks involving a short-range operation and requiring high accuracy in a local pose estimation, e.g.., a 3D-reconstruction of an environment. At the same time, the feature-based methods ORB-SLAM2 and DynaSLAM outperform the direct ones in terms of the global accuracy, which, combined with an average trajectory detail level, makes them a universal solution for most SLAM tasks - especially the ones that require a long-range operating with stable and reliable results throughout an entire trajectory. In tasks that involve dynamic objects the accuracy of DynaSLAM will be significantly higher than ORB-SLAM2.

The current study used HP Omen 15-ce057ur laptop hardware. However, any SLAM method performance strongly correlates with available computational resources. Our ongoing work deals with expanding the obtained results and comparing the four algorithms' performance using several different robots of the Laboratory of intelligent robotic systems [1,18]. We strongly believe that such comparison could be useful to the research community in order to have a better perspective of how each metric varies depending on availability of real robots' onboard computational resources.

Acknowledgements. The reported study was funded by the Russian Foundation for Basic Research (RFBR), according to the research project No. 19-58-70002. The second author acknowledges the support by the research grant of Kazan Federal University. The forth and the fifth authors acknowledge the support of the Japan Science and Technology Agency, the JST Strategic International Collaborative Research Program, Project No. 18065977. The sixth author acknowledges the support of the National Science and Technology Development Agency (NSTDA), Thailand, Project ID FDA-CO-2562-10058-TH. Special thanks to PAL Robotics for their kind professional support with TIAGo Base robot software and hardware related issues.

References

1. Bereznikov, D., Zakiev, A.: Network failure detection and autonomous return for PMB-2 mobile robot. In: International Conference on Artificial Life and Robotics (ICAROB), pp. 444–447 (2020)
2. Bescos, B., Fácil, J.M., Civera, J., Neira, J.: DynaSLAM: tracking, mapping, and inpainting in dynamic scenes. IEEE Robot. Autom. Lett. **3**(4), 4076–4083 (2018)
3. Bokovoy, A., Yakovlev, K.: Sparse 3D point-cloud map upsampling and noise removal as a vSLAM post-processing step: experimental evaluation. In: Ronzhin, A., Rigoll, G., Meshcheryakov, R. (eds.) ICR 2018. LNCS (LNAI), vol. 11097, pp. 23–33. Springer, Cham (2018). https://doi.org/10.1007/978-3-319-99582-3_3

4. Burri, M., et al.: The EuRoC micro aerial vehicle datasets. Int. J. Robot. Res. **35**(10), 1157–1163 (2016)
5. Buyval, A., Afanasyev, I., Magid, E.: Comparative analysis of ROS-based monocular SLAM methods for indoor navigation. Ninth International Conference on Machine Vision, ICMV, vol. 10341, p. 103411K. International Society for Optics and Photonics (2017)
6. Carballo, A., Takeuchi, E., Takeda, K.: High density ground maps using low boundary height estimation for autonomous vehicles. In: 21st International Conference on Intelligent Transportation Systems (ITSC), pp. 3811–3818. IEEE (2018)
7. Delmerico, J., Scaramuzza, D.: A benchmark comparison of monocular visual-inertial odometry algorithms for flying robots. In: IEEE 2018 International Conference on Robotics and Automation, ICRA, pp. 2502–2509. IEEE (2018)
8. Dissanayake, M.G., Newman, P., Clark, S., Durrant-Whyte, H.F., Csorba, M.: A solution to the simultaneous localization and map building (SLAM) problem. IEEE Trans. Robot. Autom. **17**(3), 229–241 (2001)
9. Engel, J., Koltun, V., Cremers, D.: Direct sparse odometry. IEEE Trans. Pattern Anal. Mach. Intell. **40**(3), 611–625 (2017)
10. Engel, J., Schöps, T., Cremers, D.: LSD-SLAM: large-scale direct monocular SLAM. In: Fleet, D., Pajdla, T., Schiele, B., Tuytelaars, T. (eds.) ECCV 2014. LNCS, vol. 8690, pp. 834–849. Springer, Cham (2014). https://doi.org/10.1007/978-3-319-10605-2_54
11. Engel, J., Usenko, V., Cremers, D.: A photometrically calibrated benchmark for monocular visual odometry. arXiv preprint arXiv:1607.02555 (2016)
12. Gabdullin, A., Shvedov, G., Ivanou, M., Afanasyev, I.: Analysis of onboard sensor-based odometry for a quadrotor UAV in outdoor environment. In: International Conference on Artificial Life and Robotics (ICAROB) (2018)
13. Gao, X., Wang, R., Demmel, N., Cremers, D.: LDSO: direct sparse odometry with loop closure. In: 2018 IEEE/RSJ International Conference on Intelligent Robots and Systems, IROS, pp. 2198–2204. IEEE (2018)
14. Ibragimov, I.Z., Afanasyev, I.M.: Comparison of ROS-based visual SLAM methods in homogeneous indoor environment. In: 2017 14th Workshop on Positioning, Navigation and Communications (WPNC), pp. 1–6. IEEE (2017)
15. Lavrenov, R., Matsuno, F., Magid, E.: Modified spline-based navigation: guaranteed safety for obstacle avoidance. In: Ronzhin, A., Rigoll, G., Meshcheryakov, R. (eds.) ICR 2017. LNCS (LNAI), vol. 10459, pp. 123–133. Springer, Cham (2017). https://doi.org/10.1007/978-3-319-66471-2_14
16. Martínez-García, E.A., Rivero-Juárez, J., Torres-Méndez, L.A., Rodas-Osollo, J.E.: Divergent trinocular vision observers design for extended Kalman filter robot state estimation. Proc. Inst. Mech. Eng. Part I J. Syst. Control Eng. **233**(5), 524–547 (2019)
17. Martinez Garcia, E.A.: 4WD robot posture estimation by radial multi-view visual odometry. Instituto de Ingeniería y Tecnología (2018)
18. Moskvin, I., Lavrenov, R., Magid, E., Svinin, M.: Modelling a crawler robot using wheels as pseudo-tracks: model complexity vs performance. In: 7th International Conference on Industrial Engineering and Applications (ICIEA), pp. 235–239. IEEE (2020)
19. Mur-Artal, R., Montiel, J.M.M., Tardos, J.D.: ORB-SLAM: a versatile and accurate monocular SLAM system. IEEE Trans. Robot. **31**(5), 1147–1163 (2015)
20. Mur-Artal, R., Tardós, J.D.: ORB-SLAM2: an open-source SLAM system for monocular, stereo, and RGB-D cameras. IEEE Trans. Robot. **33**(5), 1255–1262 (2017)

21. Nagahama, K., Nishino, T., Kojima, M., Yamazaki, K., Okada, K., Inaba, M.: End point tracking for a moving object with several attention regions by composite vision system. In: International Conference on Mechatronics and Automation, pp. 590–596. IEEE (2011)

22. Rodriguez-Telles, F.G., Mendez, L.A.T., Martinez-Garcia, E.A.: A fast floor segmentation algorithm for visual-based robot navigation. In: 2013 International Conference on Computer and Robot Vision, pp. 167–173. IEEE (2013)

23. Safin, R., Lavrenov, R., Tsoy, T., Svinin, M., Magid, E.: Real-time video server implementation for a mobile robot. In: 2018 11th International Conference on Developments in eSystems Engineering (DeSE), pp. 180–185. IEEE (2018)

24. Schubert, D., Goll, T., Demmel, N., Usenko, V., Stückler, J., Cremers, D.: The TUM-mono VI benchmark for evaluating visual-inertial odometry. In: 2018 IEEE/RSJ International Conference on Intelligent Robots and Systems, IROS, pp. 1680–1687. IEEE (2018)

25. Simakov, N., Lavrenov, R., Zakiev, A., Safin, R., Martínez-García, E.A.: Modeling USAR maps for the collection of information on the state of the environment. In: 2019 12th International Conference on Developments in eSystems Engineering (DeSE), pp. 918–923. IEEE (2019)

26. Sturm, J., Engelhard, N., Endres, F., Burgard, W., Cremers, D.: A benchmark for the evaluation of RGB-D SLAM systems. In: 2012 IEEE/RSJ International Conference on Intelligent Robots and Systems, pp. 573–580. IEEE (2012)

Cooperative Guidance for Waypoint Following of Distributed Multi-UAV System

Tagir Muslimov$^{(\boxtimes)}$ (iD) and Rustem Munasypov

Ufa State Aviation Technical University, K. Marx Street, 12, 450008 Ufa, Russian Federation
tagir.muslimov@gmail.com

Abstract. This paper proposes an algorithm for cooperative guidance of an unmanned aerial vehicle (UAV) formation following a set of waypoints. Waypoints are linked by straight lines to form a sequence, which effectively tasks the formation to cooperatively follow a rectilinear path between these points. Unlike in earlier known papers, we propose a Fermat's spiral rather than a circular arc as a fillet to smooth the trajectory. This is because a Fermat's spiral has zero curvature at its origin, which helps avoid breaks in curvature observable when using straight lines and circular arcs. To make a UAV formation and to follow the path, we propose a novel guidance vector field that is direction- and magnitude-nonuniform. This is where the novelty of this paper lies, as it proposes the vector field method for following a Fermat's spiral. Known studies used line-of-sight (LOS) guidance to that end. In that case, the UAV formation shapes itself using consensus-based coordination topology, i.e. the group has no leader. To test the algorithm for cooperative waypoint following when smoothing is provided by fillets, we utilized complete nonlinear models of two fixed-wing UAVs, each equipped with a tuned autopilot. Numerical simulation shows the proposed approach efficient.

Keywords: Vector field guidance · UAV consensus · Path following · Collective motion · Decentralized control · Path smoothing

1 Introduction

Compared to a single unit, a group of mobile robots is capable of handling more complex tasks (such as, for example, a joint transportation task [1]), which is why research in that area has been extensive as of recently. Researchers have proposed and developed a variety of basic strategies for robot formation control (including flying robots), notably leader-follower strategies [2, 3], virtual leaders [4], swarm cooperation [5], potential field method [6], unstable modes [7], consensus-based strategies [8], bioinspired behavior algorithms [9, 10], etc. At the same time, intragroup positioning methods are on the rise [11], which enables decentralized control of autonomous unmanned aerial vehicle (UAV) formations.

Formation flight may follow a variety of task-dependent scenarios. In many cases, path following is preferable to trajectory tracking. This applies especially to fixed-wing UAVs engaged in patrolling, reconnaissance, target tracking, etc. In that case, if the map

© Springer Nature Switzerland AG 2020
A. Ronzhin et al. (Eds.): ICR 2020, LNAI 12336, pp. 234–242, 2020.
https://doi.org/10.1007/978-3-030-60337-3_23

has waypoints, then the straight lines connecting them can be considered segments (legs) of rectilinear paths the UAVs must follow. However, in case of no smoothing the UAV trajectories will show overshoot when passing through a waypoint, and the trajectories themselves will not be smooth.

Spline algorithms have been well-studied for smooth path planning applicably to ground mobile robots [12] and UAVs [13]. Monograph [14] considers a possible option for a smoother waypoint passage for UAVs by inserting a fillet (a circular arc). The disadvantage of this method lies in a drastic increase in curvature that is observed where a straight line connects to an arc. A variety of alternative smoothing methods have been proposed to address the issue, including use of clothoids (Cornu spirals) [15] and Fermat's spirals [16]. Fermat's spirals are advantageous here, as they are less computationally complex since they do not require Fresnel integrals solved numerically.

Paper [17] describes following a Fermat's spiral-smoothed path by means of line-of-sight (LOS) guidance applicably to a single marine surface vehicle. With this in mind, this paper makes a twofold scientific contribution:

1) First, it applies the vector field path-following method to a inter-waypoint path smoothed by a Fermat's spiral.
2) Second, the fillet-based smoothing strategy from [14] has been tested in a cooperative guidance scenario where UAVs have not only to follow a set path, but also make and maintain a set formation, i.e. perform flight in formation. Moreover, the interaction between UAVs is consensus-based here.

2   Guidance Vector Fields for Fermat's Spiral-Smoothed Paths

2.1   Preliminary Notes

Assumption 1. This paper assumes no wind-induced disturbances that could be estimated adaptively with the guidance control laws being modified to address such disturbances.

Assumption 2. Each UAV is equipped with a standard tuned autopilot and is capable of calculating the distance to the UAVs it is interacting with.

Since UAV formation is being made and maintained by means of speed control, fixed-wing UAV airspeed constraints must be taken into account for the autopilot to operate correctly:

$$v_{min} \leq v_a \leq v_{max}, \tag{1}$$

where v_{min} is the minimum airspeed, v_{max} is the maximum airspeed.

The goal hereof is to develop a path smoothing algorithm that will use Fermat's spirals to enable UAVs to follow waypoints cooperatively, as well as to experimentally test the known fillet-based single-UAV smoothing algorithm in cooperative waypoint following.

2.2 Fermat's Spiral for Path Smoothing

Fermat's spiral dates back to the 1600 s when it was first researched by French mathematician Fermat. An important feature is its zero curvature at the origin, which further changes smoothly as the spiral grows longer. This makes Fermat's spirals similar to clothoids; however, clothoids require numerical calculation of Fresnel integrals, an additional load for the aircraft's onboard processor if the path was not calculated in advance. In polar coordinates, Fermat's spiral equation is usually written as [16]:

$$r = k\sqrt{\theta},$$

where r is the radial distance, k is the scaling constant, θ is the polar angle.

The curvature of such a spiral can be calculated as:

$$\kappa = \left(1/k\right)2\sqrt{\theta}\left(3 + 4\theta^2\right) \Big/ \left(1 + 4\theta^2\right)^{3/2}. \tag{2}$$

According to [16], the value of the polar angle $\theta_{\kappa_{max}}$ at which the curvature maxes out can be found as:

$$\theta_{\kappa_{max}} = \min\left(\theta_{end}, \sqrt{\sqrt{7}/2 - 5/4}\right),$$

where θ_{end} is the maximum value of the polar angle for this spiral in its domain $\theta \in [0; \theta_{end}]$.

Path following design must be adjusted for the fact that fixed-wing UAVs have limited turn steepness. The smallest turn radius R_{min} at constant altitude and airspeed is:

$$R_{min} = 1/\kappa_{max} = v_a^2 \Big/ \left(g\sqrt{n_{max}^2 - 1}\right), \tag{3}$$

where v_a is the airspeed, g is the freefall acceleration, n_{max} is the maximum load factor for this UAV model.

Thus, the constant k must be set correctly using the Eq. (2) to prevent following a path where the curvature radius is smaller than R_{min} (3). It should also be borne in mind that the minimum airspeed v_a in (3) should result from the constraints (1).

Paper [16] proposes the following Fermat's spiral parametrization $\mathbf{p}_{FS}$ in Cartesian coordinates that prevents singularity at $\theta = 0$:

$$\mathbf{p}_{FS}(\theta) = \begin{bmatrix} x_p(\theta) \\ y_p(\theta) \end{bmatrix} = \begin{bmatrix} x_0 + k\sqrt{\theta}\cos(\rho\theta + \chi_0) \\ y_0 + k\sqrt{\theta}\sin(\rho\theta + \chi_0) \end{bmatrix}, \qquad (4)$$

where x_0, y_0 are the initial coordinates of the spiral, χ_0 is the initial tangent angle, the parameter ρ defines the direction: counterclockwise at $\rho = 1$ and clockwise and $\rho = -1$.

To have a path with continuous curvature, paper [16] proposes using a Fermat's spiral segment and its mirrored version to smooth the inter-waypoint transition. One of the segments serves as the entrance segment for path following, while the mirrored version serves as the exit segment. In such a design, the final segment points must coincide to ensure path continuity. For details on how to calculate the parameters of Fermat's spiral-based smoothing, see [16].

3 Cooperative Guidance Algorithm for Waypoint Following

Three points can be selected from the set of waypoints $W = \{\mathbf{w}_1, \mathbf{w}_2, \ldots, \mathbf{w}_N\}$ without loss of generality: $\mathbf{w}_{i-1}, \mathbf{w}_i, \mathbf{w}_{i+1}$. This section describes a waypoint following algorithm where passage of the waypoint $\mathbf{w}_i$ is enabled by smoothing using Fermat's spiral segments. Thus, the final path must consist of rectilinear segments between the waypoints and Fermat fillets.

Further description of the algorithm uses notation from [14]. Let us use a unit vector to define the direction of the line $\overline{\mathbf{w}_i \mathbf{w}_{i+1}}$:

$$\mathbf{q}_i \triangleq (\mathbf{w}_{i+1} - \mathbf{w}_i) / \|\mathbf{w}_{i+1} - \mathbf{w}_i\|,$$

set $\mathbf{q}_{i-1}$ similarly.

To switch between the finite-state machine states from following a straight line to following a Fermat curve and back, use the half-planes $\mathcal{H}_i$ and $\mathcal{H}_{i-1}$, and define $\mathcal{H}_i$ as:

$$\mathcal{H}_i(\mathbf{z}_i, \mathbf{q}_i) \triangleq \left\{ \mathbf{p} \in \mathbb{R}^3 : (\mathbf{p} - \mathbf{z}_i)^\mathsf{T} \mathbf{q}_i \geq 0 \right\},$$

where $\mathbf{p} = (p_n, p_e, p_d)^\mathsf{T}$ are the UAV coordinates in an inertial coordinate system (ICS); $\mathbf{z}_i$ is a point on the way, where the states are switched. Define the half-plane $\mathcal{H}_{i-1}$ similarly. To switch between the entrance and exit segments of the fillets, use the half-plane:

$$\mathcal{H}_{i-1,i}(\mathbf{z}_{i-1,i}, \mathbf{n}_i) \triangleq \left\{ \mathbf{p} \in \mathbb{R}^3 : (\mathbf{p} - \mathbf{z}_{i-1,i})^\mathsf{T} \mathbf{n}_i \geq 0 \right\},$$

where $\mathbf{n}_i$ is the normal vector defined $\mathbf{n}_i \triangleq (\mathbf{q}_i + \mathbf{q}_{i-1}) / (\|\mathbf{q}_i + \mathbf{q}_{i-1}\|)$.

The coordinates of points z_{i-1}, $z_{i-1,i}$, z_i are found as follows: z_{i-1} is set as a point whose coordinates are (x_0, y_0) in (4) and is the junction of the straight line segment $\overline{w_{i-1}w_i}$ and the Fermat curve entrance segment; $z_{i-1,i}$ is the junction of entrance and exit segments of the Fermat curves; z_i is the end point of the mirrored segment of the Fermat curve, which is also the junction of that segment and the straight line $\overline{w_iw_{i+1}}$.

When following rectilinear path segments, use the standard vector field method detailed in [14, 18]. To follow segments of a Fermat's spiral, the UAV has to calculate the least distance to that curve. As noted in [17], the Newton-Raphson method is applicable here. The cross-positioning error relative to the path e_n can be found as:

$$e_n = -\left(p_e - x_p(\theta^*)\right)\sin(\gamma_p) + \left(p_n - y_p(\theta^*)\right)\cos(\gamma_p),   \tag{5}$$

where θ^* is the numerically found value of the parameter in (4), at which the point-on-path value matches the least UAV-to-path distance; γ_p is the tangential angle of the tangent to the path at that point. Thus, path following boils down to fulfill this: $\lim\limits_{t \to \infty} e_n \to 0$.

Paper [17] uses the line-of-sight method for path following. This paper uses vector fields, hence the modified control law for ith aircraft's heading angle χ_i^c from [14]:

$$\chi_i^c(t) = \gamma_p - \chi^\infty (2/\pi)\arctan\left(k_p e_n(t)\right),$$

where χ^∞ is the long-distance path approach angle, k_p is the heading angle control loop tuning factor, e_n is calculable using (5).

Let us pick the UAV airspeed control law v_i^c similarly to those presented in [8]:

$$v_i^c = v + v_f (2/\pi)\arctan\left(k_v e_i^v\right),   \tag{6}$$

where v is the final cruise speed of the UAV formation, v_f is the maximum additional speed per (1), k_v is the speed control loop tuning factor, e_i^v are the input vector elements that can be calculated by a variety of methods, e.g. by consensus as in [8, 18].

Below is a modified waypoint following algorithm based on the one proposed in [14]; compared to its earlier counterpart, it uses Fermat' spiral segments for smoothing and adds UAV formation control. In the algorithm, flag $= 1$ corresponds to following a straight line, flag $= 2$ stands for following the entrance segment of a Fermat's spiral, flag $= 3$ means following the exit segment of the same. Formation control per (6) functions in all the three states.

Algorithm 1: Cooperative waypoint following with Fermat's spiral smoothing:

Input: Waypoint path $W = \{\mathbf{w}_1, \mathbf{w}_2, \dots, \mathbf{w}_N\}$, UAV position $\mathbf{p} = (p_n, p_e, p_d)^\mathrm{T}$,

coefficients k, k_p, k_v, parameters ρ, χ^∞, v_f.

1: **if** Waypoint path W is received **then**
2:   Initialize waypoint index: $i \leftarrow 2$, and state machine: state $\leftarrow 1$.
3:   Use equation (6) as speed control law
4: **end if**
5: $\mathbf{q}_i \leftarrow (\mathbf{w}_{i+1} - \mathbf{w}_i)/\|\mathbf{w}_{i+1} - \mathbf{w}_i\|$
6: $\mathbf{q}_{i-1} \leftarrow (\mathbf{w}_i - \mathbf{w}_{i-1})/\|\mathbf{w}_i - \mathbf{w}_{i-1}\|$
7: **if** state=1 **then**
8:   flag $\leftarrow 1$
9:   Calculate parameters of line path
10:   Calculate coordinates of $\mathbf{z}_i$
11:   **if** $\mathbf{p} \in \mathcal{H}_{i-1}(\mathbf{z}_{i-1}, \mathbf{q}_{i-1})$ **then**
12:     state $\leftarrow 2$
13:   **end if**
14: **else if** state=2 **then**
15:   flag $\leftarrow 2$
16:   Calculate parameters of entering Fermat segment
17:   Calculate coordinates of $\mathbf{z}_{i-1,i}$
18:   **if** $\mathbf{p} \in \mathcal{H}_{i-1,i}(\mathbf{z}_{i-1,i}, \mathbf{n}_i)$ **then**
19:     state $\leftarrow 3$
20:   **end if**
21: **else if** state=3 **then**
22:   flag $\leftarrow 3$
23:   Calculate parameters of exiting Fermat segment
24:   Calculate coordinates of $\mathbf{z}_i$
25:   **if** $\mathbf{p} \in \mathcal{H}_i(\mathbf{z}_i, \mathbf{q}_i)$ **then**
26:: $i \leftarrow (i+1)$ until $i = N-1$
27:     state $\leftarrow 1$
28:   **end if**
29: **end if**
30: **return** flag, path parameters

4   Simulation Results

For MATLAB/Simulink modeling, we used complete nonlinear models of two flying-wing UAVs equipped with tuned autopilot models [14]. This section is dedicated to experimental verification of the waypoint following algorithm presented in [14] for a single UAV, which is modified here for cooperative dual-UAV following. The algorithm uses fillets for smoothing. Accordingly, there have been added control laws (6) for the speed controllers of each UAV, which should enable the UAVs to reach the preconfigured relative distance. Comparing the modified algorithm from [14] against the one from Sect. 3 hereof requires further research. The following parameters were used: $W = \{(0, 0, -100), (300, 0, -100), (0, 300, -100), (300, 300, -100)\}$ is the set of waypoints; $(0, 100, -100)$ – the initial conditions of the first UAV, $(20, 19, -100)$ – the initial conditions of the second UAV; 30 m – the desired relative distance between two UAVs of the formation; $v = 13$ m/s – the cruise speed of UAV formation; $\chi^{\infty} = \pi/2$; coefficients $k_p = 0.003$, $k_v = 0.02$; $\rho = -1$; additional airspeed $v_f = 3$ m/s; minimal turn radius $R_{min} = 25$ m. Figure 1 shows the results of simulating cooperative waypoint following for two UAVs.

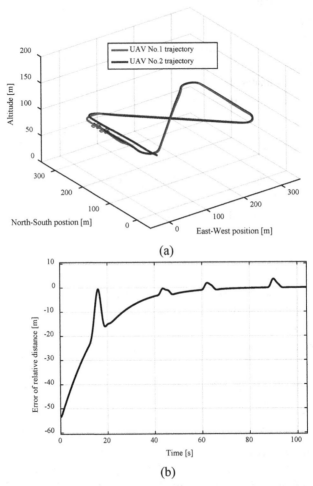

Fig. 1. Cooperative waypoint following: (a) UAV trajectories when running the cooperative waypoint following algorithm; (b) changes in relative positioning errors over time.

Simulation demonstrates that UAVs will effectively go on a given path and follow it, thus following the waypoints. At the same time, cooperative speed controllers enable the UAVs to make a formation and keep it in flight. Besides, as shown in Fig. 1b, the transient response curve for the relative distance error has spikes, which emerge due the unavoidable UAV deceleration in a coordinated turn, when UAVs follow fillets.

5   Conclusions

This paper describes an approach to cooperative UAV waypoint following using Fermat's spiral-based smoothing. The authors have modified a known single-UAV algorithm that utilizes circular arcs to smooth waypoint passage. MATLAB/Simulink modeling shows the modified algorithm functional.

This research effort could be expected to further expand to using Fermat's spirals to smooth Dubins paths. Experimental comparison between smoothing by fillets and by Fermat spirals is imperative for further research, which had better use more UAVs in a formation. This does not pose a problem as the speed control laws are decentralized. How the changing UAV speed in the process of making a formation affects the minimum curvature is also of interest.

Acknowledgements. The reported study was funded by RFBR according to the research project № 18-08-01299.

References

1. Gradetsky, V., et al.: Parameters identification in UGV group for virtual simulation of joint task. In: Ronzhin, A., Shishlakov, V. (eds.) Proceedings of 14th International Conference on Electromechanics and Robotics "Zavalishin's Readings". SIST, vol. 154, pp. 371–381. Springer, Singapore (2020). https://doi.org/10.1007/978-981-13-9267-2_30
2. Kotov, K.Y., Mal'tsev, A.S., Nesterov, A.A., Sobolev, M.A., Yan, A.P.: Decentralized control of quadrotors in a leader–follower formation. Optoelectron. Instrument. Data Process. **53**(1), 21–25 (2017). https://doi.org/10.3103/S8756699017010046
3. Kozhemyakin, I., Semenov, N., Ryzhov, V., Chemodanov, M.: Multi-agent control system of a robot group: virtual and physical experiments. In: Ronzhin, A., Rigoll, G., Meshcheryakov, R. (eds.) ICR 2019. LNCS (LNAI), vol. 11659, pp. 40–52. Springer, Cham (2019). https://doi.org/10.1007/978-3-030-26118-4_5
4. Hino, T., Tsuchiya, T.: Decentralised formation control of unmanned aerial vehicles using virtual leaders. In: Intelligent Systems, Control and Automation: Science and Engineering, pp. 133–144 (2013)
5. Ivanov, D., Kapustyan, S., Petruchuk, E.: Distribution of roles in a dynamic swarm of robots in conditions of limited communications. In: Ronzhin, A., Rigoll, G., Meshcheryakov, R. (eds.) ICR 2019. LNCS (LNAI), vol. 11659, pp. 99–108. Springer, Cham (2019). https://doi.org/10.1007/978-3-030-26118-4_10
6. Beloglazov, D.A. et al.: Group robot control in non-deterministic environments using the potential field method. In: International Conference on Control, Automation and Systems, pp. 371–376 (2016)
7. Pshikhopov, V.K., Medvedev, M.Y.: Group control of autonomous robots motion in uncertain environment via unstable modes. SPIIRAS Proc. **5**, 39–63 (2018)
8. Muslimov, T.Z., Munasypov, R.A.: Consensus-based cooperative circular formation control strategy for multi-UAV system. In: International Russian Automation Conference (RusAutoCon), pp. 1–8 (2019)

9. Luo, Q., Duan, H.: Distributed UAV flocking control based on homing pigeon hierarchical strategies. Aerosp. Sci. Technol. **70**, 257–264 (2017)

10. Zhang, T.-J.: Unmanned aerial vehicle formation inspired by bird flocking and foraging behavior. Int. J. Autom. Comput. **15**(4), 402–416 (2018). https://doi.org/10.1007/s11633-017-1111-x

11. Vasiliev, K.K., Bobkov, A.V., Korolev, L.Y.: Determination of navigation parameters of autonomous vehicles in group (In Russian). J. Inf.-Measuring Control Syst. **18**, 63–70 (2020)

12. Lavrenov, L., Magid, E., Fumitoshi, M., Svinin, M., Suthakorn, J.: Development and implementation of spline-based path planning algorithm in ROS/Gazebo environment. SPIIRAS Proc. **18**, 57–84 (2019)

13. Khachumov, M., Khachumov, V.: UAV trajectory tracking based on local interpolating splines and optimal choice of knots. In: Kuznetsov, S.O., Panov, A.I. (eds.) RCAI 2019. CCIS, vol. 1093, pp. 320–334. Springer, Cham (2019). https://doi.org/10.1007/978-3-030-30763-9_27

14. Beard, R.W., McLain, T.W.: Small unmanned aircraft: Theory and practice. Princeton University Press (2012)

15. Belokon', S.A., Zolotukhin, Y.N., Nesterov, A.A.: Aircraft path planning with the use of smooth trajectories. Optoelectron. Instrument. Data Process. **53**(1), 1–8 (2017). https://doi.org/10.3103/S8756699017010010

16. Lekkas, A.M., Dahl, A.R., Breivik, M., Fossen, T.I.: Continuous-curvature path generation using Fermat's spiral. Model. Identif. Control. **34**, 183–198 (2013)

17. Candeloro, M., Lekkas, A.M., Sørensen, A.J.: A Voronoi-diagram-based dynamic path-planning system for underactuated marine vessels. Control Eng. Pract. **61**, 41–54 (2017)

18. Muslimov, T.Z., Munasypov, R.A.: Decentralized nonlinear group control of fixed-wing UAV formation. Mekhatronika, Avtom. Upr. **21**, 43–50 (2020)

Indoor vs. Outdoor Scene Classification for Mobile Robots

Petr Neduchal$^{(\boxtimes)}$ ⓘ, Ivan Gruber ⓘ, and Miloš Železný ⓘ

Faculty of Applied Sciences, New Technologies for the Information Society,
University of West Bohemia, Univerzitní 8, 306 14 Plzeň, Czech Republic
{neduchal,grubiv,zelezny}@kky.zcu.cz
http://fav.zcu.cz/en/, http://ntis.zcu.cz/en/

Abstract. This paper deals with the task of automatic indoor vs. outdoor classification from image data with respect to future usage in mobile robotics. For the requirements of this research, we utilize the Miniplaces dataset. We compare a large number of classic machine learning approaches such as Support Vector Machine, k-Nearest Neighbor, Decision Tree, or Naive Bayes using various color and texture description methods on a single dataset. Moreover, we employ some of the most important neural network-based approaches from the last four years. The best tested approach reaches 96.17% classification accuracy. To our best knowledge, this paper presents the most extensive comparison of classification approaches in the task of indoor vs. outdoor classification ever done on a single dataset. We also address the processing time problem, and we discuss using the applied methods in real-time robotic tasks.

Keywords: Environment classification · Mobile robotics · Neural networks · Machine learning

1 Introduction

Robotics tasks are usually focused on solving problems either in an indoor or outdoor environment but not in both of them. In our previous research [9], we focused on the design of a multi-environment robot system. This kind of system can be useful, especially during the transition between indoor and outdoor environments. The major part of the design is the module for image-based environment classification. Thus, in this paper, we address the problem of indoor versus outdoor classification, which is a special case of the scene classification problem.

We can divide approaches to the indoor vs. outdoor classification into two basic categories. The first one is based on so-called classic machine learning approaches. It usually consists of image transformation to a description vector and applying the classifier such as Support Vector Machine (SVM) or Nearest Neighbors. The second one is based on the neural networks, which usually work with the whole image on their input instead of the description vector.

© Springer Nature Switzerland AG 2020
A. Ronzhin et al. (Eds.): ICR 2020, LNAI 12336, pp. 243–252, 2020.
https://doi.org/10.1007/978-3-030-60337-3_24

Both approach categories needed a lot of data to train their classifiers. Thus, it is necessary to use a sufficiently large and heterogeneous dataset.

There exist only two available datasets called IITM-SCID and IITM-SCID2, which are directly determined to be used for indoor vs. outdoor classification. They are consist of 180 and 907 images, respectively. Historically, the Kodak customer photo dataset composed of 1343 photos worth mentioning. Unfortunately, it is not available nowadays. In all three cases, the size of the mentioned datasets is small. Thus, larger datasets determined for general scene classification should be used.

There are several scene classification datasets that are suitable for solving indoor vs. outdoor classification problems. We can mention two small datasets named 15-Scene Dataset and MIT Indoor 67 dataset [8]. The first one is composed of 4485 photos collected by multiple authors. The latter consists of 15620 photos and is focused on the indoor environment, but outdoor photos can extend the dataset.

Nowadays, there are larger datasets available. In particular SUN397 [23], Places365 [26] and Miniplaces [26] datasets. They are composed of 108 754, 1 803 460, and 100 000 photos, respectively, and they are divided into several classes. In particular, it is 397, 365, and 100 classes, respectively. Thus, the file with indoor and outdoor labels for each class has to be generated.

In further text and our experiments, we will use the word dataset for the Miniplaces dataset. For exemplary images, see Fig. 1. This dataset is sufficiently large for both the classic machine learning approaches and the neural network based approaches. Besides 100k training images, it also contains 10k images in the validation set. Moreover, the authors provide a testing set, however, without any ground-truth labels. We decided to utilize the validation set as our testing data, and the original training set was split into the training and the validation set containing 90k and 10k images, respectively. All the sets contain approximately 56% of outdoor images and 44% of indoor images. All images have resolution 128 × 128 pixels.

Our paper's main contribution is an extensive comparison of various approaches from both mentioned categories on a single dataset. To our best knowledge, this is the first comparison of this size performed on a single dataset.

The paper is composed as follows. Section 2 is focused on the related work in the indoor vs. outdoor classification. In Sects. 3 and 4, all classification approaches are described. The experiments and their results are described in Sect. 5. In Sect. 6, results are discussed. Finally, the paper is summarized, and future work is mentioned in conclusion.

2   Related Work

One of the first papers addressed the problem of indoor vs. outdoor classification was paper [19]. The authors used color histogram-based description computed from two color representations of the image. They propose to use Ohta color space over the RGB because it increases classification accuracy from 69.5% to

Fig. 1. Exemplary images from Miniplaces dataset. Outdoor (top), Indoor (bottom).

73.2% on the Kodak dataset. Moreover, they combine color and texture-based Multiresolution, Simultaneous Autoregressive model (MSAR) description, and achieved 90.3%. To achieve these results, they employ a two-stage classification approach (see Sect. 3).

Using of color and texture description or their combination is an approach that appeared in multiple papers in the next years – e.g. [1,3,4,12,14,15]. These approaches differs in their approaches to classifier learning. They use either two-stage classification or Bag of Visual Words approach. Moreover, there are some papers that focused on different type of description such as image keypoints or edges – e.g. [8,11].

Some papers use neural networks as the classifier. We can mention the paper [20]. Authors use image features for semantic categorization of the scene, and the feedforward neural network is trained. The paper [21] addresses general scene classification, and it gives insight view to the Convolution Neural Networks (CNNs) based approach. This approach works with the whole image on its input instead of just a description vector. Moreover, the authors perform experiments on the Places dataset.

The problem with the mentioned papers is that it usually works with different datasets. Thus, the results are not fully comparable.

3   Classic Machine Learning Approaches

The training stage for a basic approach to scene classification is consists of two steps. The first one is the computation of description vectors for the whole dataset. The second one is to train a classifier. The example of this approach using the SVM classifier is shown in Fig. 2.

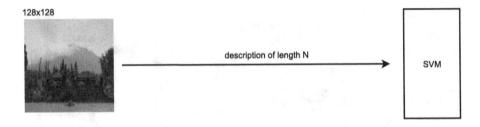

Fig. 2. Diagram of basic approach to scene classification.

This approach can be extended by dividing the input image into $n \times n$ tiles and compute vector for each tile individually. Then vectors can be concatenated into the final description vector.

A more sophisticated approach is based on the spatial pyramid generated from the input image by spatially dividing the image and the manner of levels. The next level of the pyramid is created by a decreasing image size by a half. Spatial division in levels is supposed to create tiles of the same size. The diagram of this approach for a 3 level pyramid is shown in Fig. 3. The description vector is a concatenation of $16 + 4 + 1$ vectors computed for each tile.

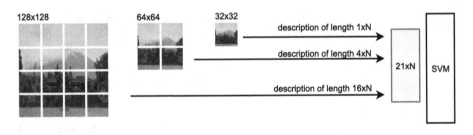

Fig. 3. Diagram of multi-scale approach to scene classification.

The most advanced classic approach is called a two-stage learning approach. It divides training images into $n \times n$ tiles and train one color and one texture classifier for each tile. In the further text, we are using $n = 4$. Thus, $2 \times 4 \times 4 = 32$ classifiers are trained in total. They usually do not have good accuracy – we got maximum 74% accuracy on such a classifier. In the second stage, classifier outputs are concatenated into vectors of length 32. Then either majority rule or an additional classifier can be used to make a final decision. In the case of majority rule, the final decision is based on the most common occurrence of class in the values from the first stage. On the other hand, the use of additional classifiers usually has better accuracy. An example of the two-stage approach using SVMs in both stages is shown in Fig. 4.

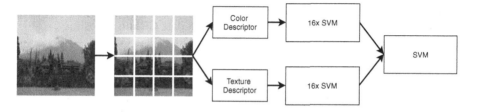

Fig. 4. Diagram of two-phase approach to scene classification.

The output of the first stage can be altered by using sum instead of concatenation. I.e., the vector for the second stage has only one bin for color classifiers and one bin for texture classifier. Another alternation – in the SVM case – is to use distance from the hyperplane instead of the classifier decision. It leads to vectors of floats instead of integers, and it contains a measure of certainty. Thus it usually has better accuracy. Both alternations can also be applied simultaneously. In our experiments, we denote these alternations by using suffix S, D, and DS.

4   Neural Network Based Approaches

Due to the improvement of the neural networks, most hand-crafted feature descriptors for image classification become obsolete. Furthermore, image classification tasks, where a sufficient amount of data is available, are nowadays dominated by neural networks based approaches.

In this paper, we decided to compare some of the most important neural network architectures designed for image classification from the last four years. Many previous works, such as [16], showed the benefits of transfer learning for similar tasks. Therefore, all the tested architectures are pretrained on ImageNet database [13]. Because the ImageNet classification task contains 1000 classes, in all models, the last fully-connected layer was replaced by the new one with only two neurons (outdoor, indoor), and its weights were randomly initialized.

As a baseline architecture, we chose VGG16 [17], which belongs to the golden standard among classification networks nowadays. The first big tested group were architectures utilizing residual skip connections, to be more specific ResNet-50 [5], ResNetWide-50 [25] and ResNeXt-50 [24]. In the second group were architectures based on inception modules, i.e. Xception [2] and InceptionNetv4 [18]. Other tested architectures are InceptionResNet [18], which combines both residual skip connections and inception modules, and DenseNet [6], which also utilize skip connections, however in the form of map concatenation instead of point-wise addition. The last big group is based on Big Transfer (BiT) [7] models provided by Google. All of them are based on ResNet. However, for their training and fine-tuning is utilized special training protocol. Specifically, we use BiT-M-R50x1 based on ResNet-50, BiT-M-R50x3 based on ResNet-50, but three times wider, and BiT-M-R101x1 based on ResNet-101.

All the architectures were implemented in Pytorch framework [10] utilizing the torchvision module or Pytorch pre-trained models Github repository.

5   Experiments and Results

In this section, we describe the performed classification experiment. It is divided into two parts on the classic and neural net approaches. Both parts use the Miniplaces dataset. Thus their results are comparable.

5.1   Classic Learning Approaches

In this experiment, we evaluated more than 280 combinations of description methods. It consists of color and texture methods mentioned in Sect. 3. We used it in basic, multi-scale, and two-stage learning approaches. It includes applying spatial division of input data on a grid in basic approaches – i.e., grids of 2 × 2, 3 × 3, and 4 × 4. We also coded description results into multiple vector lengths in order to examine its influence on classification accuracy.

To compute description vector we apply color histograms in RGB, HSV, LUV, and Ohta [19] color spaces. We also apply texture based approaches. In particular Centrist [22], Gist [4], Weighted Histogram of Gradient Orientation (WHGO) [12], Global Binary Patterns (GBP) [27], Wavelets [14] and a description based on histogram generated from the edges – i.e. texture descriptor applied on the image with detected edges.

We used all datasets to train Naive Bayes, Decision Tree, K-Nearest Neighbors, Linear SVM, and SVM with Radial Basis Function (RBF) classifiers. In all cases, a trained SVM classifier with RBF kernel had the best accuracy. Thus, results in the Table 1[1] are obtained using SVM with RBF. The table shows the TOP 3 description methods for basic (B), multi-scale (MS), and two-stage (TP) learning approach. Gist global image descriptor is the best approach for the basic learning approach with 85.44% and 85.43% with shorter description vector transformed using Principal component analysis (PCA) from 960 to 512 bins.

In the MS approach, the centrist texture descriptor had the best results. We get the best accuracy by using Centrist with a 64 bins histogram. Descriptor length sums up to 1344 bins in total. In the second place is the Centrist with 128 bins based on the original paper. Unfortunately, it has significantly more histogram bins – 3960. Thus, there is a poor ratio between accuracy value and description vector length w.r.t mentioned Centrist-64 method.

Finally, we perform the two-stage learning approach. These classifiers have better accuracy than classifiers trained by basic and multi-scale approaches. We achieved the best results using a combination of the histogram of the image transferred into HSV color space with the Centrist descriptor. Both had a length of 256 bins.

---

[1] The rest of our results can be found in public GitHub repository: https://github.com/neduchal/io_classification_experiment.

Table 1. Results of classic approaches.

Approach	Type	Des. length	Accuracy	CPU inf. time (ms)
Gist-960	B	960	85.44%	71.6
Gist-PCA-512	B	512	85.43%	54.8
Gist-PCA-256	B	256	84.65%	45.8
Centrist-64	MS	1344	85.48%	68.8
Centrist 128P	MS	3968	85.34%	189.7
Centrist-32	MS	672	84.42%	**41.7**
HSV-Centrist-256-D	TS	32 (256)	**91.87%**	1125.4
RGB-Centrist-256-D	TS	32 (256)	91.61%	1111.1
HSV-Centrist-256-DS	TS	2 (256)	91.11%	1194.5

We also focused on processing time on a single core of Intel Core i7-8750H CPU for each description and classification approach. It is visible that the TS approach, despite their accuracy, is not suitable to use in real-time tasks on weaker performance hardware. On the other hand, B and MS approaches achieved approximately similar accuracy with significantly better processing time. The method with the best result is the Centrist-32 MS approach.

5.2 Neural Networks Experiments

During the training of the neural network, we preserve original Miniplaces resolution 128 × 128 pixels. To further enrich the training set, we use data augmentations. We are generating these augmentations with a certain probability during the training process on the fly. The possible augmentations are horizontal flip, and random crop with resizing to the original resolution. All images are normalized according to the original values used during the pretraining.

All the tested architectures are trained for two-class classification (outdoor, indoor). During the training of BiT models, an unchanged BiT training protocol is used. For updating the other networks' parameters, we use the SGD optimizer with a learning rate $l = 0.001$ and the momentum $m = 0.9$ utilizing cross-entropy loss and mini-batch size 64. The training is stopped after 20 epochs.

During our experiments, we tested two training protocols. In the first, we freeze all the network's parameters except the classification layer parameters. Unfortunately, this training setup did not lead to satisfactory results. In the second protocol, we allow the optimizer to fine-tune all the parameters. In Table 2 can be found average results from 5 runs using the second training protocol on the development and the test set.

All the neural networks overcome classic machine learning approaches, some of them by a large margin. It should be noted that the usage of the BiT training protocol improved the classification accuracy of ResNet-50 by more than 1.5%, which is equal to almost 25% relative decrease of classification error. The best results were reached with the largest tested network, BiT-M-R50x3.

Table 2. Results of neural network based approaches.

Architecture	Development set	Test set
VGG16	93.98%	92.56%
ResNet-50	94.33%	93.34%
ResNetWide	94.57%	93.55%
ResNeXt	94.56%	93.49%
InceptionResNet	93.38%	92.49%
Xception	94.00%	93.17%
InceptionNetv4	93.37%	91.87%
DenseNet-161	94.65%	93.64%
BiT-M-R50x1	96.39%	94.97%
BiT-M-R101x1	96.44%	95.49%
BiT-M-R50x3	**96.70%**	**96.17%**

6 Discussion

It is worth to mention that we will be unable to utilize the largest neural network architecture available concerning the future usage of the classifier. Therefore, these architectures are completely omitted from our experiments. The size and speed of the biggest tested architecture BiT-M-R50x3 are borderline. For a more detailed comparison of the number of the parameters and selected methods' inference times, see Table 3. The listed CPU inference times are calculated using Intel Core i7-8750H CPU, while GPU inference times are using GTX 1060 GPU.

Table 3. Comparison of the # of parameters and single image average inference times.

Method	# of Param.	CPU inf. time (ms)	GPU inf. time (ms)
VGG16	134277186	258	12.4
DenseNet-161	26476418	223	21.6
BiT-M-R50x1	23504450	152	9.8
BiT-M-R101x1	42496578	1238	26.1
BiT-M-R50x3	211186370	708	15.6

Given these results, we believe, that BiT-M-R50x1 provides the best trade-off between classification accuracy and model's size and speed. It should be noted that the inference time calculation was performed without any additional optimization. We want to address this possibility in our future research.

7   Conclusion

The knowledge about the type of environment in which a robot is located is desirable considering, for example, the suitability of different SLAM methods for the different environments. In this paper, an extensive comparison of the classification method is provided. Neural network based methods reached very promising classification accuracy (approximately 96%) on the Miniplaces dataset and overcome classical approaches by a significant margin.

In our future research, we would like to test a conjunction of the environment classifier with appropriate mapping methods during real-world mapping. We believe that this combination can dramatically improve the mapping capabilities of mobile robots.

Acknowledgements. This work was supported by the Ministry of Education of the Czech Republic, project No. LTARF18017. Access to computing and storage facilities owned by parties and projects contributing to the National Grid Infrastructure Meta-Centrum provided under the programme "Projects of Large Research, Development, and Innovations Infrastructures" (CESNET LM2015042), is greatly appreciated.

References

1. Chen, C., Ren, Y., Kuo, C.-C.J.: Large-scale indoor/outdoor image classification via expert decision fusion (EDF). In: Jawahar, C.V., Shan, S. (eds.) ACCV 2014. LNCS, vol. 9008, pp. 426–442. Springer, Cham (2015). https://doi.org/10.1007/978-3-319-16628-5_31
2. Chollet, F.: Xception: deep learning with depthwise separable convolutions. In: Proceedings of the IEEE Conference on Computer Vision and Pattern Recognition, pp. 1251–1258 (2017)
3. Cvetkovic, S.S., Nikolić, S.V., Ilic, S.: Effective combining of color and texture descriptors for indoor-outdoor image classification. Facta Universitatis, Ser.: Electron. Energetics **27**(3), 399–410 (2014)
4. Ganesan, A., Balasubramanian, A.: Indoor versus outdoor scene recognition for navigation of a micro aerial vehicle using spatial color gist wavelet descriptors. Vis. Comput. Ind. Biomed. Art **2**(1), 1–13 (2019). https://doi.org/10.1186/s42492-019-0030-9
5. He, K., Zhang, X., Ren, S., Sun, J.: Deep residual learning for image recognition. In: Proceedings of the IEEE Conference on Computer Vision and Pattern Recognition, pp. 770–778 (2016)
6. Huang, G., Liu, Z., Van Der Maaten, L., Weinberger, K.Q.: Densely connected convolutional networks. In: Proceedings of the IEEE Conference on Computer Vision and Pattern Recognition, pp. 4700–4708 (2017)
7. Kolesnikov, A., et al.: Big transfer (BiT): general visual representation learning (2019)
8. Lazebnik, S., Schmid, C., Ponce, J.: Beyond bags of features: spatial pyramid matching for recognizing natural scene categories. In: 2006 IEEE Computer Society Conference on Computer Vision and Pattern Recognition, CVPR 2006, vol. 2, pp. 2169–2178. IEEE (2006)

9. Neduchal, P., Bureš, L., Železný, M.: Environment detection system for localization and mapping purposes. IFAC-PapersOnLine **52**(27), 323–328 (2019)
10. Paszke, A., et al.: PyTorch: an imperative style, high-performance deep learning library, pp. 8024–8035 (2019)
11. Payne, A., Singh, S.: Indoor vs. outdoor scene classification in digital photographs. Pattern Recogn. **38**(10), 1533–1545 (2005)
12. Raja, R., Roomi, S.M.M., Dharmalakshmi, D.: Robust indoor/outdoor scene classification. In: 2015 Eighth International Conference on Advances in Pattern Recognition (ICAPR), pp. 1–5. IEEE (2015)
13. Russakovsky, O., et al.: ImageNet large scale visual recognition challenge. Int. J. Comput. Vis. **115**(3), 211–252 (2015). https://doi.org/10.1007/s11263-015-0816-y
14. Serrano, N., Savakis, A., Luo, A.: A computationally efficient approach to indoor/outdoor scene classification. In: Object Recognition Supported by User Interaction for Service Robots, vol. 4, pp. 146–149. IEEE (2002)
15. Shahriari, M., Bergevin, R.: A two-stage outdoor-indoor scene classification framework: experimental study for the outdoor stage. In: 2016 International Conference on Digital Image Computing: Techniques and Applications (DICTA), pp. 1–8. IEEE (2016)
16. Shin, H.C., et al.: Deep convolutional neural networks for computer-aided detection: CNN architectures, dataset characteristics and transfer learning. IEEE Trans. Med. Imaging **35**(5), 1285–1298 (2016)
17. Simonyan, K., Zisserman, A.: Very deep convolutional networks for large-scale image recognition. arXiv preprint arXiv:1409.1556 (2014)
18. Szegedy, C., Ioffe, S., Vanhoucke, V., Alemi, A.A.: Inception-v4, inception-ResNet and the impact of residual connections on learning. In: Thirty-First AAAI Conference on Artificial Intelligence (2017)
19. Szummer, M., Picard, R.W.: Indoor-outdoor image classification. In: Proceedings 1998 IEEE International Workshop on Content-Based Access of Image and Video Database, pp. 42–51. IEEE (1998)
20. Tahir, W., Majeed, A., Rehman, T.: Indoor/outdoor image classification using GIST image features and neural network classifiers. In: 2015 12th International Conference on High-Capacity Optical Networks and Enabling/Emerging Technologies (HONET), pp. 1–5. IEEE (2015)
21. Wang, L., Guo, S., Huang, W., Xiong, Y., Qiao, Y.: Knowledge guided disambiguation for large-scale scene classification with multi-resolution CNNs. IEEE Trans. Image Process. **26**(4), 2055–2068 (2017)
22. Wu, J., Rehg, J.M.: CENTRIST: a visual descriptor for scene categorization. IEEE Trans. Pattern Anal. Mach. Intell. **33**(8), 1489–1501 (2010)
23. Xiao, J., Ehinger, K.A., Hays, J., Torralba, A., Oliva, A.: Sun database: exploring a large collection of scene categories. Int. J. Comput. Vis. **119**(1), 3–22 (2016). https://doi.org/10.1007/s11263-014-0748-y
24. Xie, S., Girshick, R.B., Dollár, P., Tu, Z., He, K.: Aggregated residual transformations for deep neural networks. CoRR abs/1611.05431 (2016)
25. Zagoruyko, S., Komodakis, N.: Wide residual networks. arXiv preprint arXiv:1605.07146 (2016)
26. Zhou, B., Lapedriza, A., Khosla, A., Oliva, A., Torralba, A.: Places: a 10 million image database for scene recognition. IEEE Trans. Pattern Anal. Mach. Intell. **40**, 1452–1464 (2017)
27. Zhou, L., Zhou, Z., Hu, D.: Scene classification using multi-resolution low-level feature combination. Neurocomputing **122**, 284–297 (2013)

Mathematical Modelling of Control and Simultaneous Stabilization of 3-DOF Aerial Manipulation System

Vinh Nguyen[1] ⓘ, Anton Saveliev[2] ⓘ, and Andrey Ronzhin[2](✉) ⓘ

[1] Department of Electromechanics and Robotics, SUAI, Bolshaya Morskaya Street, 67, 190000 St. Petersburg, Russia
nguyenvanvinhhvkt@gmail.com
[2] Laboratory of Autonomous Robotic Systems, St. Petersburg Federal Research Center of the Russian Academy of Sciences (SPC RAS), 14-th line of V.I., 39, 199178 St. Petersburg, Russia
ronzhin@iias.spb.su

Abstract. A robotic manipulator mounted on unmanned aerial vehicle (UAV) is called an aerial manipulation system usually. Any movements of manipulator affect the stability of the UAV. In particular, the horizontal shift of the center of mass (COM) requires of the UAV the powerful controller that change forces of the propellers of quadrotor to bring the UAV to a stable state. To make manipulations by UAV it is important to save the center of mass of the aerial manipulation system in stable state. In this study, we developed a model of a manipulator to be mounted on a quadrotor. Fuzzy PID controller has been built to control of the manipulator. Control method takes into account joint space of robotic arm and unmanned aerial vehicle. The COM stabilization issue has been solved for manipulator motion. In experiments, the horizontal shift of COM of manipulator was less than 1 mm while picked up objects up to 0.15 kg of payload.

Keywords: Unmanned aerial vehicle · UAV · Aerial manipulation system · COM · Manipulator · Fuzzy PID controller

1 Introduction

Recently, the aerial manipulation systems interacted with the ground environment are actively investigated and some real application were realized. Manipulator-mechanism design for aerial manipulation system have some additional difficulties in comparison to ground manipulator systems. Nevertheless there are three main issues during designing a manipulator should be considered: kinematics, dynamics and control [1–5]. Three controllers based on the proportional integral derivative (PID), proportional derivative (PD) and fuzzy logic (FL) for a 3-DOF robot manipulator were designed in [6]. The comparison of the obtained results showed that PID and PD perform better in terms of Rise Time and Settling Time while the FLC exhibited reduced overshoot.

PID controller for three types of modeling technique for 2-DOF manipulator: 1) model based on linearization about equilibrium point; 2) model based on Autodesk

© Springer Nature Switzerland AG 2020
A. Ronzhin et al. (Eds.): ICR 2020, LNAI 12336, pp. 253–264, 2020.
https://doi.org/10.1007/978-3-030-60337-3_25

Inventor and Matlab/Simulink software's; 3) and lastly model based on feedback linearization of the robot were designed in [7]. As a result using feedback linearization achieved the best effect. In [8] the fuzzy self-tuning PID controller was used to control of 2-DOF manipulator. In comparison to the traditional PID controller, this controller gave better results: shorter response time; small overshoot and high steady precision; good static and dynamic performance. It indicates that the conventional approach of a PID controller is not able to provide accuracy due to system nonlinearity.

In [9] a 6-DOF flexible manipulator with usage of joint spring and damper is presented. Two controllers were used for this manipulator based on fuzzy logic-tuned PID controller and RRT-tuned method. However, fuzzy logic-tuned PID controller was found to be better in comparison to the conventional PID tuned controller. In [10] four controllers were designed for 2-DOF robotic manipulator: robust PID controller; Mamdani fuzzy controller; Sugeno fuzzy controller; hybrid fuzzy controller. The most accuracy of working point was achieved with the fuzzy hybrid control. The most accuracy of working point was achieved with the fuzzy hybrid control. For two-degree freedom robotic manipulator a Fuzzy PID Controller has built to tune PID controller [11]. The Fuzzy PID has the least value of error in comparison to other controllers such as: Fuzzy PI, Fuzzy PD and PID Controller [12].

In this study, we describe the developed fuzzy PID controller for 3-DOF manipulator. Mathematical modeling of manipulator is described in Sect. 2. The design of fuzzy PID controller for the robotic arm are presented in Sect. 3. The experiment results based on usage of the proposed models are described in Sect. 4.

2   Kinematics Modelling of Manipulator Mounted to UAV

The aerial manipulation system is a complicated system consisting of an UAV and a manipulator. In order to apply it in practice, it is necessary to solve all problems related to control and stability of the system. There have been many designs presented with lots of different solutions. However, a stable model is still unavailable. Some previous studies also gave some ideas for designing manipulator for aerial manipulation systems, such as in [13] a light-weight robot manipulator consisting of 5 degrees of freedom was designed. The design is conceived to constrain the center of gravity (CoG) of the arm as close as possible to vehicle base, thus reducing the total inertia and static unbalancing of the system. In order to describe the change of CoG – the pink points are used in Figs. 1a and 1b, the COM of gripper (red points) moving along the vertical (Fig. 1b) and horizontal (Fig. 1a) axes. In another study [14] a robot manipulator consisted of 3 arms. Two consecutive arms create a 120-degree angle; each arm is configured as in the Fig. 1c. From the two studies above, a robot manipulator idea proposed for our research as shown in Fig. 1d.

The parameters of manipulator are shown in Table 1. This robot manipulator consists of 3-DOF, with three revolute joints, attached to the bottom of a quadrotor or other type of UAV. The two consecutive axes of the revolute joints are parallel to each other. The weight of the manipulator is about 0.4 kg.

Now let us to consider the structure of the manipulator during performing operation. The robotic arm moves, picks up and releases the object while maintaining its CoG

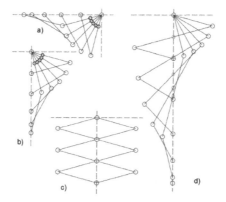

Fig. 1. Models of robot manipulator. (Color figure online)

Table 1. The parameters of manipulator links.

Link i	Mass, m (kg)	Length, L(m)
1	0.15	0.15
2	0.15	0.30
3	0.10	0.15

on the vertical axis. It is supposed that COM of each link is the midpoint of that link. According to our design, the COM of the manipulator is the midpoint of link 2 (green points) and end-effector only moves on the vertical axis (red points) in Fig. 1d.

2.1 Forward Kinematics

The manipulator consists of 3 links. The kind of joint between two consecutive links is only revolute joints such as is showed in Fig. 2. The Denavit-Hartenberg algorithm for assigning coordinate frames was used in this study. So, we have the following set of geometric parameters of the serial chain manipulator presented in Table 2, where: a_i is the distance from z_{i-1} to z_i along x_{i-1}, α_i is the angle from z_{i-1} to z_i about X_{i-1}, d_i is the distance from X_{i-1} to x_i along z_i, θ_i is the angle from X_{i-1} to x_i about z_i. The type of joint is revolute, so joint rotation matrix is [15]:

$$^{i-1}R_i = \begin{bmatrix} c_i & -s_i & 0 \\ s_i & c_i & 0 \\ 0 & 0 & 1 \end{bmatrix}, \tag{1}$$

where: $c_i = \cos\theta_i$; $s_i = \sin\theta_i$.

256   V. Nguyen et al.

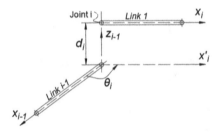

Fig. 2. Schematic of the numbering of bodies and joints of manipulator.

Table 2. Denavit–Hartenberg algorithm parameter for the manipulator chains.

i	α_i	a_i	d_i	θ_i
1	0	L_1	0	θ_1
2	0	L_2	0	θ_2
3	0	L_3	0	θ_3

Coordinate frame i can be located relative to coordinate frame $i-1$ by executing a rotation through an angle. $^{i-1}T_i$ is a homogeneous transformation matrix to determine the relative position coordinates of link i relative to link $i-1$:

$$^{i-1}T_i = \begin{bmatrix} c_i & -s_i & 0 & a_i c_i \\ s_i & c_i & 0 & a_i s_i \\ 0 & 0 & 1 & 0 \\ 0 & 0 & 0 & 1 \end{bmatrix}. \tag{2}$$

The coordinates of the link i (x_i; y_i) relative to the original coordinates are determined through Forward Kinematics:

$$^{0}T_i = \prod_1^i {}^{i-1}T_i = \begin{bmatrix} c_{1..i} & -s_{1..i} & 0 & \sum_{k=1}^{i} l_k c_{1..k} \\ s_{1..i} & c_{1..i} & 0 & \sum_{k=1}^{i} l_k s_{1..k} \\ 0 & 0 & 1 & 0 \\ 0 & 0 & 0 & 1 \end{bmatrix}. \tag{3}$$

Here $c_{1..i} = \cos(\theta_1 + .. + \theta_i)$ and $s_{1..i} = \sin(\theta_1 + .. + \theta_i)$. From (3) we have the position coordinates of the end-effector as:

$$\begin{cases} x_3 = l_1 c_1 + l_2 c_{12} + l_3 c_{123} \\ y_3 = l_1 s_1 + l_2 s_{12} + l_3 s_{123} \end{cases}.$$

The relation between the center of mass of two consecutive links is:

$$^{i-1}T_i^{COM} = \begin{bmatrix} c_i & -s_i & 0 & (l_i c_i)/2 \\ s_i & c_i & 0 & (l_i s_i)/2 \\ 0 & 0 & 1 & 0 \\ 0 & 0 & 0 & 1 \end{bmatrix}. \tag{4}$$

The matrix of COM coordinates of the link i is:

$$^{0}T_{i}^{COM} = \prod_{1}^{i}{}^{i-1}T_{i}^{COM} = \begin{bmatrix} c_{1..i} & -s_{1..i} & 0 & \sum_{k=1}^{i-1} l_{k}c_{1..k} + (l_{i}c_{1..i})/2 \\ s_{1..i} & c_{1..i} & 0 & \sum_{k=1}^{i-1} l_{k}s_{1..k} + (l_{i}s_{1..i})/2 \\ 0 & 0 & 1 & 0 \\ 0 & 0 & 0 & 1 \end{bmatrix}. \qquad (5)$$

From (5) we have Manipulators' COM coordinates:

$$\begin{cases} x_{COM} = (\sum_{1}^{i} {}^{0}T_{i}^{COM}(1,4)m_{i})/(\sum_{1}^{i} m_{i}) \\ y_{COM} = (\sum_{1}^{i} {}^{0}T_{i}^{COM}(2,4)m_{i})/(\sum_{1}^{i} m_{i}) \end{cases}. \qquad (6)$$

2.2 Inverse Kinematics

There are two approaches to solve the inverse kinematics problem: closed-form solutions and numerical methods. Closed-form solution approaches are generally divided into algebraic and geometric methods. The most common numerical methods can be divided into categories of symbolic elimination methods, continuation methods, and iterative methods. Depending on the structure of a serial-chain manipulator, a suitable method can be chosen. The working position and joint angle parameters of the robot manipulator in this study are shown in Fig. 3.

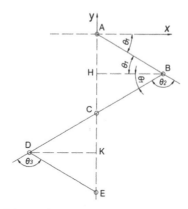

Fig. 3. Joint angle parameters of the robot manipulator.

The following notations are used: AB is the first link, BD is the 2nd link and DE is the 3rd link: AB = DE = BD/2. The angles θ_1, θ_2 and θ_3 are the deflection angles of the consecutive links. The end-effector E of the manipulator is always moving on the vertical axis y. The COM of the manipulator is the midpoint C of link 2 (BD). Therefore, the geometric method was chosen for solving the inverse kinematics problem in this study. According to the forward kinematics and the working position of the manipulator, θ_1 and θ_2 are always less than 0 and θ_3 is always more than 0. The end-effector E has coordinates of $(0, P_y)$. The angles θ_1, θ_2 and θ_3 will be determined by following steps:

- *Identify* θ_1:

Considering the triangle ABH in Fig. 2 we have:

$$\sin\theta_1 = \frac{AH}{AB},\qquad(7)$$

where: $AH = \frac{AE}{4} = \frac{P_y}{4}$; $AB = l_1$. So (7) can be rewritten as follows:

$$\sin\theta_1 = \frac{P_y}{4l_1}\qquad(8)$$

and we have:

$$\cos\theta_1 = \sqrt{1 - (\sin\theta_1)^2}.\qquad(9)$$

From (8) and (9) we also have: $\tan\theta_1 = \frac{\sin\theta_1}{\cos\theta_1}$. Then the joint position of link 1 can be found as: $\theta_1 = \text{Atan2}(\cos\theta_1, \sin\theta_1)$.

– *Identify* θ_2:

From Fig. 2 we have: $|2\theta_1| + |\theta_2| = \pi$. Due to θ_1 and θ_2 are always less than 0, then $2\theta_1 + \theta_2 = -\pi$. The angle θ_2 is obtained: $\theta_2 = -\pi - 2\theta_1$.

– *Identify* θ_3:

Also from Fig. 2 we have: $|\theta_2| = |\theta_3|$. Due to θ_2 is always less than 0 and θ_3 is always more than 0, then $\theta_3 = -\theta_2$. So, the angle θ_3 is obtained: $\theta_3 = \pi + 2\theta_1$.

2.3 Dynamics Model

There are two formulations of dynamics model most commonly used in robotics: Newton–Euler and the Lagrange. In this study we will use the Lagrange formulation. The dynamic equations of motion can then be developed using Lagrange's equation for each generalized coordinate:

$$\frac{d}{dt}\frac{\partial L}{\partial \dot{q}_i} - \frac{\partial L}{\partial q_i} = \tau_i,\qquad(10)$$

where: $L = T - U$ is the Lagrange formulation: T and U are the total kinetic and potential energy respectively; $q_i = \begin{bmatrix} \theta_1 & \theta_2 & \dots & \theta_i \end{bmatrix}^T$. The kinetic energy is given by:

$$T = \frac{1}{2}\dot{\theta}^T M \dot{\theta},\qquad(11)$$

where: $\begin{bmatrix} \dot{\theta}_1 & \dot{\theta}_2 & \dots & \dot{\theta}_i \end{bmatrix}$; M - the generalized mass matrices for the robot manipulator. And the potential energy is given by:

$$U = \sum_1^i \begin{bmatrix} 0 & m_i g & 0 \end{bmatrix} r_{0T_i^{COM}},\qquad(12)$$

where $r_{0T_i^{COM}}$ is determined as:

$$r_{0T_i^{COM}} = \begin{bmatrix} {}^0T_i^{COM}(1,4) \\ {}^0T_i^{COM}(2,4) \\ {}^0T_i^{COM}(3,4) \end{bmatrix}.\qquad(13)$$

Through (13) we get Jacobian matrix of the transitions (14):

$$J_{T_i} = \begin{bmatrix} \dot{r}_{0T_i^{COM}}(1,1)(\theta_1) & \dot{r}_{0T_i^{COM}}(1,1)(\theta_2) & \dots & \dot{r}_{0T_i^{COM}}(1,1)(\theta_i) \\ \dot{r}_{0T_i^{COM}}(2,1)(\theta_1) & \dot{r}_{0T_i^{COM}}(2,1)(\theta_2) & \dots & \dot{r}_{0T_i^{COM}}(2,1)(\theta_i) \\ \dot{r}_{0T_i^{COM}}(3,1)(\theta_1) & \dot{r}_{0T_i^{COM}}(3,1)(\theta_2) & \dots & \dot{r}_{0T_i^{COM}}(3,1)(\theta_i) \end{bmatrix}. \tag{14}$$

Direction cosine matrix is:

$$A_i = \begin{bmatrix} c_{1..i} & -s_{1..i} & 0 \\ s_{1..i} & c_{1..i} & 0 \\ 0 & 0 & 1 \end{bmatrix}. \tag{15}$$

From (15) we have the derivative of the direction cosine matrix:

$$dA_i = \begin{bmatrix} \sum_1^j \dot{A}_i(1,1)(\theta_j)\dot{\theta}_j & \sum_1^j \dot{A}_i(2,1)(\theta_j)\dot{\theta}_j & \sum_1^j \dot{A}_i(3,1)(\theta_j)\dot{\theta}_j \\ \sum_1^j \dot{A}_i(2,1)(\theta_j)\dot{\theta}_j & \sum_1^j \dot{A}_i(2,2)(\theta_j)\dot{\theta}_j & \sum_1^j \dot{A}_i(3,2)(\theta_j)\dot{\theta}_j \\ \sum_1^j \dot{A}_i(3,1)(\theta_j)\dot{\theta}_j & \sum_1^j \dot{A}_i(2,3)(\theta_j)\dot{\theta}_j & \sum_1^j \dot{A}_i(3,3)(\theta_j)\dot{\theta}_j \end{bmatrix} (j = i = 1 \div 5).$$

The angular velocity matrix of each link as follows:

$$\omega_i = \begin{bmatrix} S_{\omega_i}(3,2) \\ S_{\omega_i}(1,3) \\ S_{\omega_i}(2,1) \end{bmatrix}, \tag{16}$$

where: $S_{\omega_i} = dA_i A_i^T$. From (16) we have rotational Jacobian matrix:

$$J_{R_i} = \begin{bmatrix} \dot{S}_{\omega_i}(1,1)(\dot{\theta}_1) & \dot{S}_{\omega_i}(1,1)(\dot{\theta}_2) & \dots & \dot{S}_{\omega_i}(1,1)(\dot{\theta}_i) \\ \dot{S}_{\omega_i}(2,1)(\dot{\theta}_1) & \dot{S}_{\omega_i}(2,1)(\dot{\theta}_2) & \dots & \dot{S}_{\omega_i}(2,1)(\dot{\theta}_i) \\ \dot{S}_{\omega_i}(3,1)(\dot{\theta}_1) & \dot{S}_{\omega_i}(3,1)(\dot{\theta}_2) & \dots & \dot{S}_{\omega_i}(3,1)(\dot{\theta}_i) \end{bmatrix}, \tag{17}$$

The mass matrix of the robot manipulator is:

$$M = \sum_1^i (m_i(J_{T_i}^T J_{T_i}) + J_{R_i}^T (A_i I_i A_i^T) J_{R_i}), \tag{18}$$

where: $I_i = \begin{bmatrix} 0 & 0 & 0 \\ 0 & 0 & 0 \\ 0 & 0 & m_i l_i^2/3 \end{bmatrix}$. As a result, from Eqs. (10), (11), (12) and (18) $\begin{bmatrix} \ddot{\theta}_1 & \ddot{\theta}_2 & \dots & \ddot{\theta}_i \end{bmatrix}$ and $\begin{bmatrix} \tau_1 & \tau_2 & \dots & \tau_i \end{bmatrix}$ are determined.

3 Design of Fuzzy PID Controller

Robotic systems always have nonlinear elements. Meanwhile traditional PID controllers are designed for linear systems. If only the PID controller is used, the maximum performance cannot be achieved. Therefore, the hybrid Fuzzy PID controller will be a good choice to control a robot system. There are four main components in a Fuzzy Logic

Controller: the fuzzifier, knowledge base, inference mechanism and defuzzifier. Fuzzy PID controllers are divided into two types: the direct action fuzzy control and the fuzzy supervisory control [16]. In this study, a self-tuning fuzzy PID controller is developed to tune the three parameters K_P, K_I and K_D of PID controller. The fuzzy supervisory control was chosen. The control system diagram for each link of robot manipulator is shown in Fig. 4 including two parts: PID controller shown in Fig. 5a and Fuzzy-PID inference using Mamdani method shown in Fig. 5b. The structure of Fuzzy-PID inference includes two inputs and three outputs. The inputs are the error signal e(t) – (the error between desired velocity set point and output) and integration of error i.e.(t). Three outputs are K'_P, K'_I and K'_D respectively shown in Fig. 4b.

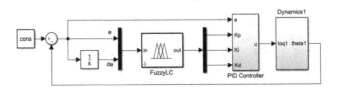

Fig. 4. Block diagram of a fuzzy self-tuning PID controller.

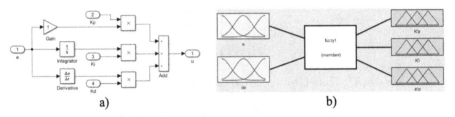

a)   b)

Fig. 5. The diagrams for: a) the PID controller; b) fuzzy PID inference.

Let the variable ranges of the parameters of PID controller are $\left[K_{Pmin}, K_{Pmax} \right]$, $\left[K_{Imin}, K_{Imax} \right]$ and $\left[K_{Dmin}, K_{Dmax} \right]$. The range of each parameters was determined based on the experimental on PID controls such as: $K_P \in \left[0, 15 \right]$, $K_I \in \left[0.001, 0.005 \right]$ and $K_D \in \left[0.1, 0.2 \right]$. The outputs K'_P, K'_I and K'_D are described as follows:

$$K'_P = \frac{K_P - K_{Pmin}}{K_{Pmax} - K_{Pmin}}, \quad K'_I = \frac{K_I - K_{Imin}}{K_{Imax} - K_{Imin}}, \quad K'_D = \frac{K_D - K_{Dmin}}{K_{Dmax} - K_{Dmin}}$$

Three triangular membership functions used for K'_I with three fuzzy set variables have the linguistic values: S (Small), M (Medium), and B (Big). K'_P and K'_D have two fuzzy sets: S-shaped and Z-shaped membership function. The fuzzy set variables are S and B. The fuzzy rule should be written according to the step response. The step response is divided into four regions, for region 1 around point (a), region 2 around point (b), region 3 around point (c) and region 4 around point (d) shown in Fig. 6.

The rule of the case 1 for region 1 is: if e is PB and Δe is ZE then K'_P is B, K'_I is S and K'_D is S. The others can be tuned at the same way as it is shown in Table 3.

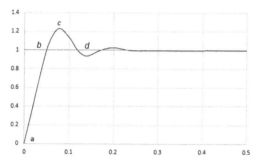

Fig. 6. Unit step response for control system.

Table 3. Fuzzy rule of K_P, K_I and K_D.

K_P, K_I, K_D		e(t)						
		NB	NM	NS	ZE	PS	PM	PB
Δe(t)	NB	BSS	SMB	SBB	SBB	SBB	SMB	BSS
	NM	BSS	BMB	SMB	SBB	SMB	BMB	BSS
	NS	BSS	BSS	BMB	SMB	BMB	BSS	BSS
	ZE	BSS	BSS	BSS	BMB	BSS	BSS	BSS
	PS	BSS	BSS	BMB	SMB	BMB	BSS	BSS
	PM	BSS	BMB	SMB	SBB	SMB	BMB	BSS
	PB	BSS	SMB	SBB	SBB	SBB	SMB	BSS

The selected fuzzy rules were used in the experiments presented below.

4 Experiment Results

During experiments, the following sequence of actions was performed for control of the robot manipulator. Its end-effector $(0, P_y)$ moves from the coordinate $(0, -0.600)$ to the coordinate $(0, -0.550)$ when not carrying payload, carrying 0.1 kg of payload and finally carrying 0.15 kg of payload. The joint angle parameters are shown in Table 4.

Table 4. Joint angle parameters.

P_y (m)	θ_1 (rad)	θ_2 (rad)	θ_3 (rad)
−0.60	−π/2	0	0
−0.55	−1.160	−0.8223	0.8223

The obtained results are presented in Table 5. The dynamic responses of the links are shown in Fig. 7. The system was stabilized after 3 s with low overshoot. The meaning of the desired angle sets is to maintain the COM of the manipulator always on the vertical axis. Therefore, in this study, it is necessary to minimize the error between the actual and desired angle value. These errors are the cause of the horizontal movements (P_x) and (X_{COM}) of the end-effector and COM respectively shown in Table 6.

Table 5. Error between the desired and actual angle.

Payload (kg)	No payload			0.10 (kg)			0.15 (kg)		
Theta (*rad*)	θ_1	θ_2	θ_3	θ_1	θ_2	θ_3	θ_1	θ_2	θ_3
Desired	−1.160	−0.822	0.822	−1.160	−0.822	0.822	−1.160	−0.822	0.822
Actual	−1.161	−0.808	0.819	−1.160	−0.801	0.817	−1.159	−0.798	0.816
Error (%)	0.086	1.732	0.305	0.000	2.544	0.599	0.086	2.942	0.772

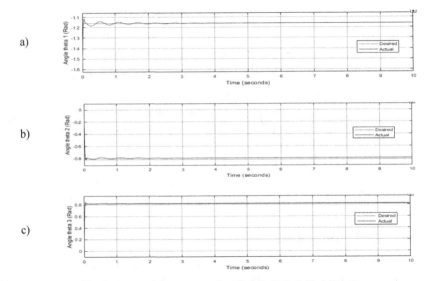

a)

b)

c)

Fig. 7. Dynamic responses of: a) link 1; b) link 2; c) link 3.

Table 6. Actual coordinates of the end-effector and COM.

Payload (kg)	P_x (*m*)	P_y (*m*)	X_{COM} (*m*)	Y_{COM} (*m*)
0	0.00469	−0.55096	0.00530	−0.24986
0.10	0.00756	−0.55144	0.00042	−0.29675
0.15	0.00923	−0.55167	−0.00087	−0.31388

The results indicate that the error is relatively small. In all case, the error between the desired and the actual angle value of link 2 is highest up to 2.942% when the robot manipulator carries 0.15 kg of payload, 2.544% with 0.1 kg of payload and 1.732% when without payload. In case of the robot manipulator carries 0.10 kg and 0.15 kg of payload, the deviation of COM horizontally less than 1 mm that acceptable in practice.

5 Conclusion

The designed 3-DOF robot manipulator for the aerial manipulation system was presented. The stability of the system is provided only if COM of the manipulator is not significantly deviated from the vertical axis. In this study, the fuzzy PID controller has been developed for robotic manipulator. The results showed that the COM of the manipulator moved horizontally less than 1 mm during operation with payload. The dynamic response of each link is sufficient that the system stabilizes quickly after only 3 s with low overshoot. Through research, we conclude that this 3-DOF robot manipulator for the aerial manipulation system is suitable for attaching to pick up objects up to 0.15 kg.

Acknowledgements. The presented work was supported by the Russian Science Foundation (grant No. 16-19-00044П).

References

1. Ermolov, I.: Industrial robotics review. In: Kravets, A.G. (ed.) Robotics: Industry 4.0 Issues & New Intelligent Control Paradigms. SSDC, vol. 272, pp. 195–204. Springer, Cham (2020). https://doi.org/10.1007/978-3-030-37841-7_16
2. Patil, A., Kulkarni, M., Aswale, A.: Analysis of the inverse kinematics for 5 DOF robot arm using D-H parameters. In: Proceedings of the 2017 IEEE International Conference on Real-time Computing and Robotics, pp. 688–693 (2017)
3. Vu, Q., Ronzhin, A.: A model of four-finger gripper with a built-in vacuum suction nozzle for harvesting tomatoes. In: Ronzhin, A., Shishlakov, V. (eds.) Proceedings of 14th International Conference on Electromechanics and Robotics "Zavalishin's Readings". SIST, vol. 154, pp. 149–160. Springer, Singapore (2020). https://doi.org/10.1007/978-981-13-9267-2_13
4. Bezruk, G.G., Martynova, L.A., Saenko, I.B.: Dynamic method of searching anthropogenic objects in use of seabed with autonomous underwater vehicles. SPIIRAS Proc. **3**, 203–226 (2018)
5. Medvedev, M.Y., Kostjukov, V.A., Pshikhopov, V.K.: Optimization of mobile robot movement on a plane with finite number of repeller sources. SPIIRAS Proc. **19**, 43–78 (2020)
6. Kabir, U., Hamza, M.F., Haruna, A., Shehu, G.S.: Performance analysis of PID, PD and fuzzy controllers for position control of 3-DOF robot manipulator. Zaria J. Electric. Eng. Technol. **8**(1), 18–25 (2019). Department of Electrical Engineering, Ahmadu Bello University, Zaria – Nigeria
7. Mustafa, A.M., Al-Saif, A.: Modeling, simulation and control of 2-R robot. Global J. Res. Eng. Robot. Nano-Tech. 14(1) (2014)
8. Nyein, T., Oo, Z.M., Hlaing, H.T.: Fuzzy based control of two links robotic manipulator. Int. J. Sci. Eng. Technol. Res. **08**, 01–07 (2019)
9. Sarkhel, P., Banerjee, N., Hui, N.B.: Fuzzy logic-based tuning of PID controller to control flexible manipulators. SN Appl. Sci. **2**(6), 1–11 (2020). https://doi.org/10.1007/s42452-020-2877-y

10. Aliabadi, M., Fard, J.M., Mohazabi, B.: Intelligent and classic control of rehabilitation robot with robust pid and fuzzy methods. Majlesi J. Mechatron. Syst. **9**(1), 31–36 (2020)
11. Meng, B.: Control of robot arm motion using trapezoid fuzzy two-degree-of-freedom PID algorithm. Symmetry **12**, 665 (2020)
12. Saxena, A., Kumar, J., Deolia, V.K.: Design a robust intelligent controller for rigid robotic manipulator system having two links and payloads. In: 2020 International Conference on Power Electronics & IoT Applications in Renewable Energy and its Control (PARC), pp. 159–163 (2020)
13. Bellicoso, C.D., Buonocore, L.R., Lippiello, V., Siciliano, B.: Design, modeling and control of a 5-DoF light-weight robot arm for aerial manipulation. In: 23rd Mediterranean Conference on Control and Automation (MED), pp. 853–858 (2015)
14. Orsag, M., Korpela, C., Oh, P.: Modeling and control of MM-UAV: mobile manipulating unmanned aerial vehicle. J. Intell. Robot. Syst. **69**, 227–240 (2013). https://doi.org/10.1007/s10846-012-9723-4
15. Siciliano, B., Khatib, O. (eds.): Springer Handbook of Robotics. Springer, Cham (2016). https://doi.org/10.1007/978-3-319-32552-1
16. Elaydi, H., Hardouss, I.A., Alassar, A.: Supervisory fuzzy control for 5 DOF robot arm. Int. J. Sci. Adv. Technol. **2**(7), 1–6 (2012)

Comparative Analysis of Approaches to Depth Map Generation for Robot Navigation

Julia Rubtsova$^{(\boxtimes)}$ ⓘ and Roman Iakovlev ⓘ

Laboratory of Autonomous Robotic Systems, St. Petersburg Federal Research Center of the Russian Academy of Sciences (SPC RAS), St. Petersburg Institute for Informatics and Automation of the Russian Academy of Sciences, 39, 14th Line, 199178 St. Petersburg, Russia
julia_rubik@mail.ru

Abstract. This paper considers approaches, which implement depth map reconstruction using stereo pair, as well deep neural network (DNN) – based approaches. Comparative evaluation of these approaches for different classes of images is performed, exampled by specific solutions; whereby the images in these classes differ in their features, distance from the camera viewport, as well scene luminosity level. Averaged frame processing time in video sequence was, in terms of NN-approach, 0.094 s, and in the stereo pair-based approach – 0.105 s. Upon the results of the performed experimental evaluation, suggestions are proposed concerning the criteria, which define preference of the approaches in question in depth map composition, depending on the conditions in the scene.

Keywords: Computer vision · Depth map · Deep learning · Deep neural networks · Stereo pair

1 Introduction

Depth map composition is one of the relevant tasks in the computer vision domain, as depth maps contain data on spatial features of the objects, observed in the scene and can also be used to obtain data on shapes of these objects. Depth maps are extensively employed in robotics and cyber-physical systems [1–4], particularly in context of robotic navigation problems [5–7], establishment of different three-dimensional representations [8], semantic segmentation [9, 10], on-image pose estimation [11] etc.

Generally, the approaches to depth map composition can be classified as follows: hardware-based approaches, NN-based approaches and approaches with stereo pairs. As a rule, depth maps are obtained using specialized hardware, such as LIDAR [12] and Kinect [13]. Scanning lidars and RGB-D cameras establish a depth map, which allows to determine positions and spatial features of the objects, captured in the scene. With all these advantages, though, such hardware is quite expensive, compared to commodity photo- and video-cameras. This paper contains analysis and practicality assessment of main approaches, which ensure solution of on-image depth map composition problem without need in specialized devices. Particularly, approaches are considered to depth map retrieval via image processing in deep neural network, as well stereo pair-based approaches.

© Springer Nature Switzerland AG 2020
A. Ronzhin et al. (Eds.): ICR 2020, LNAI 12336, pp. 265–272, 2020.
https://doi.org/10.1007/978-3-030-60337-3_26

2   Related Neural Network Approaches to Depth Map Composition

Consider some recent approaches to image-based depth map composition using neural networks (NN). So, the NN-approach, proposed in [14], includes two principal steps. At the first step, using a large-scale deep neural network, depth estimation is performed across the whole images, then the resulting map is optimized to exclude outliers, what gives at output of the neural network a depth map with sharper object outlines. In the course of experimental approbation of this method, authors obtained a mean square error value of 0.871 by depth map reconstruction.

Another NN-based approach, aimed for on-image depth map composition, is the neural network model, established in [15]. This model is based on a convolutional neural network architecture VGG [16] and trained on a dataset NYU Depth using Transfer Learning approach. Upon application of this neural network model to test dataset, authors obtained a mean square error value of 0.833 for depth map reconstruction.

In [17] a multi-scale deep convolutional neural network is presented, which ensures solving of the following problems: on-image reconstruction of a depth map, surface evaluation and semantic labeling. The said neural network model basically extends the architecture, presented in [18], but with certain optimizations: increased number of convolutional layer, as well with adjusted size of the third layer. In the course of experimental evaluation of this approach authors obtained a mean square error value of 0.641 for depth map reconstruction.

In context of depth map composition problems also models can be utilized, based on residual neural network architecture, such as ResNet-50 [19]. Authors of [20] performed experimental evaluation of performance quality of this architecture, comparing it to the AlexNet [21] and VGG [16] models, having demonstrated, that a residual neural network significantly outperforms similar solutions in depth map composition, relying on RGB image as input. These neural networks were run on test data sets NYU Depth and Make3D. SD of depth reconstruction when using ResNet-50 was 0.573.

Depth estimation problem can also be stated in terms of discrete-continuous optimization, where the continuous variables encode the depth of superpixels in the input image, whereas the discrete variables represent ratios between adjacent superpixels [22]. One of possible solutions of such problem is a conditional random field method [22], a variant of Markov random fields. Thereby, for output of graphical model the belief propagation/sum-product message passing algorithm is used. MSE of depth prediction using this method was 1.06–1.08. In a more recent study a MSE value of 0.824 was achieved [23].

Hence, the most preferable approach to on-image depth map composition is the one with residual neural network model [20], it has less training parameters and requires less data for training, compared to similar approaches [20]. Besides, the authors of the respective approach obtained the least MSE value of 0.573, what highlights better prediction accuracy of the resulting depth map within this model, compared to output of other considered solutions.

3 Review of the Existing Methods of Depth Map Composition, Based on Stereo Pairs

As a rule, depth map composition using stereo pairs includes three main steps [24, 25]: first – camera calibration to calculate the internal parameters of the camera; second – image smoothing, required primarily to get rid of distortion in such a way, that the epipolar camera lines would match; third – depth map composition. The main distinctive feature of the relevant methods of depth map composition, based on stereo pair utilization, is actually the calibration workflow. So, in [24] camera calibration is effected using the algorithm, described in [26], this algorithm assumes utilization of a flat calibration chessboard-like object. In [25] to solve a problem of stereo pair-based depth map composition, auto-calibration approach is employed. The essence of this approach consists in search of so-called feature points on image, which are necessary for correspondence analysis and revealing the interpretable information on image. Based on data of feature points, calibration parameters are calculated according to three-dimensional mappings.

Upon the performed analysis of depth map composition using a stereo pair, the approach to depth retrieval was chosen, proposed in [24], as, according to the results, presented in [24–27], this approach is characterized by the most accurate depth prediction, compared to other considered options.

Further comparative assessment of two approaches to depth map retrieval was performed: based on stereo-pair [24] and using residual neural network model [20], depending on the conditions in the scene being observed.

4 Experimental Evaluation of Approaches to Depth Map Composition

In terms of this research some experiments were performed for comparative assessment to depth map composition, based on specific solutions, given in [20, 24]. To perform relevant experiments, a dataset was prepared, consisting of 1000 images 640 × 480 pixels in size, obtained using an ELP USB-camera with resolution of 5 Mpx. This dataset includes images with different luminosity levels, containing objects of different shape and size, positioned at various distances from the camera. The images were distributed into 6 classes: scenes with small objects (up to 10 cm high), positioned close to camera (at distance maximum 50 cm from camera) (1); scenes with small objects, positioned far from camera (over 1.5 m from camera) (2); scenes with large objects (over 15 cm high), positioned close to camera (3); scenes with large objects, positioned far from camera (4); scenes with low luminosity (50% from standardized office room luminosity [28]) (5); scenes with high luminosity (100% from reference level) (6). Example images from each class are given in Fig. 1.

Comparative assessment of the approaches, considered above, was performed, based on the obtained values of depth map accuracy and the time slice, needed to process an individual video frame. To perform comparative assessment of depth map accuracy using the approaches, presented above, for every image from the test set, reference outcomes of depth map retrieval were obtained. This was achieved using the Intel RealSense Lidar Camera L515, then the results, obtained using the approaches, mentioned above, were

Fig. 1. Sample images with different conditions in the scene under consideration: a) scenes with small objects, positioned close to camera; b) with small objects, positioned far from camera; c) scenes with large objects, positioned close to camera; d) scenes with large objects, positioned far from camera; e) scenes with low luminosity; f) scenes with high luminosity.

compared to reference values. As the relevant similarity metric in terms of depth map reconstruction the structure similarity index (SSIM) was chosen [29], according to which the difference between the pixels (x, y) in two images of N × N is calculated as follows:

$$SSIM(x, y) = \frac{(2\mu_x\mu_y)(2\sigma_{xy} + c_2)}{(\mu_x^2 + \mu_y^2 + c_1)(\sigma_x^2 + \sigma_y^2 + c_1)},$$

where μ_x – average pixel intensity value for the first image; μ_y – average pixel intensity value for the second image; μ_x^2 – standard deviation for the first image; μ_y^2 – standard deviation for the second image; σ_{xy} – measure of linear dependence between two images. The obtained SSIM-index is in the range $[-1, 1]$, where value 1 is achieved only by absolute identity of the compared samples. The higher are the values of the correspondence index, the higher is the accuracy of the depth maps, retrieved using the respective solutions. Resulting index values of structure similarity between the reference and actually obtained depth maps are presented in Fig. 2.

Approach to depth retrieval using image processing with a deep neural network [20] showed the maximum accuracy of depth prediction in images, containing objects, positioned close to camera (image classes 1 and 3), as well in images with high luminosity (image class), averaged estimates of SSIM-index for these classes were {0,906; 0,751; 0,778} and {0,537; 0,550; 0,760} for the approaches [20, 24] respectively. On images with objects, positioned far from camera (image classes 2 and 4), as well in images with low luminosity (class 5), higher accuracy of depth map retrieval is achieved with the stereo-pair based approach [24]. The averaged estimates of SSIM-index for these classes were {0,766; 0,845; 0,800} and {0,681; 0,682; 0,594} for the approaches [20, 24] respectively.

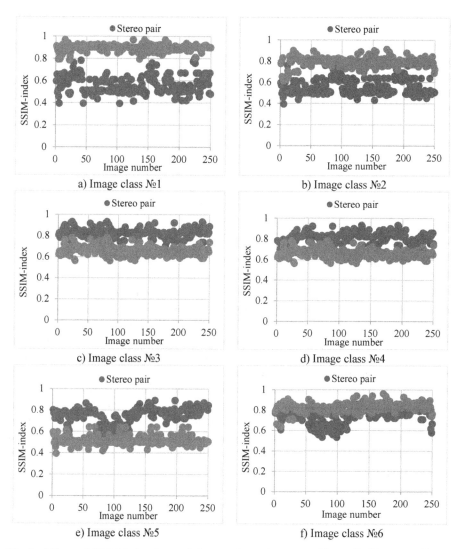

Fig. 2. Values of SSIM-index for each image class: a) scenes with small objects, positioned close to camera; b) with small objects, positioned far from camera; c) scenes with large objects, positioned close to camera; d) scenes with large objects, positioned far from camera; e) scenes with low luminosity; f) scenes with high luminosity.

Estimates of processing time for individual frames of video sequence were obtained on GTX1650 RYZEN 5 2550 h with 16 GB RAM. Respective values, obtained with the approaches, considered above, are given in Table 1.

Average time interval, required for processing of an individual frame using a deep neural network [20] was 0.094 s, whereas with the stereo-pair approach from [24] it was 0.105 s. It follows from this experiment, that both approaches require approximately

Table 1. Averaged values of time intervals, required for processing of an individual frame of video sequence in context of every class of images.

	Class 1, sec	Class 2, sec	Class 3, sec	Class 4, sec	Class 5, sec	Class 6, sec	Complete dataset, sec
Stereo pair	0.099	0.111	0.114	0.096	0.099	0.109	0.105
Neural network	0.096	0.098	0.090	0.092	0.097	0.091	0.094

equal time to process an individual frame; hence, processing speed is not a relevant criterion for preference of one of these solutions.

5 Conclusion

In this paper two main approaches to depth map retrieval are presented: via neural networks and using the stereo pair-based approach. Comparative assessment of respective implementations is performed according the criteria of accuracy and speed of their performance. This assessment showed, that both solutions ensure approximately equal speed in processing of an individual frame, but the accuracy of each specific approach depends on the conditions and features of the scene under consideration. Based on the obtained experimental results, it should be concluded that the neural network-based approach should be used when a more accurate depth prediction is required in images with objects positioned close to the camera, as well on images with high luminosity. If there is a need for more accurate depth prediction in images with low luminosity, as well as in images with objects positioned far from the camera, it is preferable to use the stereo pair-based approach.

Acknowledgements. This work was supported by RSF (project № 16-19-00044P).

References

1. Murphy, R.R.: Introduction to AI Robotics. MIT Press, Cambridge (2019)
2. Vatamaniuk, I.V., Iakovlev, R.N.: Generalized theoretical models of cyberphysical systems. Proc. Southwest State Univ. **23**(6), 161–175 (2019)
3. Levonevskiy, D., Vatamaniuk, I., Saveliev, A.: Integration of Corporate Electronic Services into a Smart Space Using Temporal Logic of actions. In: Ronzhin, A., Rigoll, G., Meshcheryakov, R. (eds.) ICR 2017. LNCS (LNAI), vol. 10459, pp. 134–143. Springer, Cham (2017). https://doi.org/10.1007/978-3-319-66471-2_15
4. Ronzhin, A., Saveliev, A., Basov, O., Solyonyj, S.: Conceptual model of cyberphysical environment based on collaborative work of distributed means and mobile robots. In: Ronzhin, A., Rigoll, G., Meshcheryakov, R. (eds.) ICR 2016. LNCS (LNAI), vol. 9812, pp. 32–39. Springer, Cham (2016). https://doi.org/10.1007/978-3-319-43955-6_5

5. Watts, K.W., Konolige, K.: U.S. Patent No. 9,886,035. Washington, DC: U.S. Patent and Trademark Office (2018)
6. Tee Kit Tsun, M., Lau, B.T., Siswoyo Jo, H.: An improved indoor robot human-following navigation model using depth camera, active IR marker and proximity sensors fusion. Robotics **7**(1), 4 (2018)
7. Gorobtsov, A.S., et al.: Features of solving the inverse dynamic method equations for the synthesis of stable walking robots controlled motion. SPIIRAS Proceedings **18**, 85–122 (2019)
8. Liang, H., et al.: An efficient hole-filling method based on depth map in 3D view generation. In: 2017 International Conference on Optical Instruments and Technology: Optoelectronic Imaging/Spectroscopy and Signal Processing Technology, vol. 10620, p. 1062018. International Society for Optics and Photonics, January 2018
9. Long, J., Shelhamer, E., Darrell, T.: Fully convolutional networks for semantic segmentation. In: Proceedings of the IEEE Conference on Computer Vision and Pattern Recognition, pp. 3431–3440 (2015)
10. Girshick, R., Donahue, J., Darrell, T., Malik, J.: Rich feature hierarchies for accurate object detection and semantic segmentation. In: Proceedings of the IEEE Conference on Computer Vision and Pattern Recognition, pp. 580–587 (2014)
11. Wickson, F., Gillund, F., Myhr, A.I.: Treating nanoparticles with precaution: recognising qualitative uncertainty in scientific risk assessment. In: Nano Meets Macro, pp. 445–472. Jenny Stanford Publishing (2019)
12. Fernald, F.G.: Analysis of atmospheric lidar observations: some comments. Appl. Optics **23**(5), 652–653 (1984)
13. Zhang, Z.: Microsoft kinect sensor and its effect. IEEE Multimedia **19**(2), 4–10 (2012)
14. Eigen, D., Puhrsch, C., Fergus, R.: Depth map prediction from a single image using a multi-scale deep network. In: Advances in Neural Information Processing Systems, pp. 2366–2374 (2014)
15. Zhu, J., Ma, R.: Real-time depth estimation from 2D images (2016)
16. Simonyan, K., Zisserman, A.: Very deep convolutional networks for large-scale image recognition. arXiv preprint arXiv:1409.1556 (2014)
17. Eigen, D., Fergus, R.: Predicting depth, surface normals and semantic labels with a common multi-scale convolutional architecture. In: Proceedings of the IEEE International Conference on Computer Vision, pp. 2650–2658 (2015)
18. Geiger, A., Lenz, P., Stiller, C., Urtasun, R.: Vision meets robotics: The kitti dataset. Int. J. Robot. Res. **32**(11), 1231–1237 (2013)
19. He, K., Zhang, X., Ren, S., Sun, J.: Deep residual learning for image recognition. In: Proceedings of the IEEE conference on computer vision and pattern recognition, pp. 770–778 (2016)
20. Laina, I. et al.: Deeper depth prediction with fully convolutional residual networks. In: 2016 Fourth International Conference on 3D Vision (3DV), pp. 239–248. IEEE (2016)
21. Iandola, F.N. et al.: SqueezeNet: AlexNet-level accuracy with 50x fewer parameters and < 0.5 MB model size. arXiv preprint arXiv:1602.07360 (2016)
22. Liu, M., Salzmann, M., He, X.: Discrete-continuous depth estimation from a single image. In: Proceedings of the IEEE Conference on Computer Vision and Pattern Recognition, pp. 716–723 (2014)
23. Liu, F., Shen, C., Lin, G.: Deep convolutional neural fields for depth estimation from a single image. In: Proceedings of the IEEE Conference on Computer Vision and Pattern Recognition, pp. 5162–5170 (2015)
24. Tolstoy, I.M., Soleny, S.V.: Building a depth map using a stereo pair and OpenCV computer vision library. In: Materials of the VI All-Russian Youth School on Robotics, Information Technologies and Engineering for Schoolchildren and Students of Roboshkola, pp. 52–57 (2017)

25. Meshchenenko, I.N.: Building a depth map of a scene by a stereo pair of images. In: International scientific and technical conference of young scientists BSTU named after VG Shukhov, pp. 4433–4440 (2017)
26. Zhang, Z.: A flexible new technique for camera calibration. IEEE Trans. Pattern Anal. Mach. Intell. **22**(11), 1330–1334 (2000)
27. Smokty, O.I.: Modeling of radiation fields of uniform anisotropically scattering slab of aarbitrary optical thickness. In: SPIIRAS Proceedings, vol. 1, pp. 214–243 (2018). https://doi. org/10.15622/sp.56.10
28. Gost, R.: 55710-2013 Lighting of workplaces inside buildings. Norms Methods Measure. **26**, 003–90 (2013)
29. Wang, Z., Bovik, A.C., Sheikh, H.R., Simoncelli, E.P.: Image quality assessment: from error visibility to structural similarity. IEEE Trans. Image Process. **13**(4), 600–612 (2004)

Approach to the State Analysis of Industry 4.0 Nodes Based on Behavioral Patterns

Viktor Semenov$^{(\boxtimes)}$ ⓘ, Mikhail Sukhoparov ⓘ, and Ilya Lebedev ⓘ

SPIIRAS, 14-th Linia, VI, No. 39, St. Petersburg 199178, Russia
v.semenov@iias.spb.su

Abstract. The state analysis of Industry 4.0 nodes and devices is an integral part of the process in order to ensure the safety of functioning. The imperfection of existing systems for monitoring and analyzing the state of hard-to-reach devices/nodes and dynamically running processes associated with them makes it necessary to analyze not just internal data, but also data sourced from side and external channels. One of the effective ways of resolving this problem is to use digitized data sequences grouped into behavioral patterns. Research objective: Development and improvement of the method of undertaking a state analysis of hard–to–reach Industry 4.0 mechatronic units and devices premised on incoming data. Methods: The use of behavioral patterns comprising of time-synchronized digitized sequences received from side and external channels for the state analysis of nodes and processes. Results: Based on the proposed method for the state analysis of Industry 4.0 nodes premised on behavioral patterns, an experiment has been carried out to obtain quantitative state estimates of the mechatronic element at any required point of time based on the analysis of existing parameter values. The underlying idea behind this experiment was to create a training sample of digitized sequences from several external channels followed by the subsequent analysis based on monitoring data. The state can be determined and monitored by quantitative estimates. The quality of the proposed approach is ascertained by making a direct comparison of results. The overall accuracy of the selected classifier for the full classification was found to be 0.90. Practical significance: The research findings allow for a significant reduction of uncertainty when making a decision on the technical state.

Keywords: State analysis · Behavioral patterns · Industry 4.0 nodes and devices

1 Introduction

Modern devices of Industry 4.0 are characterized by the explosive growth of transferred information from not only various sensors and detectors, but also by increased intelligence of automated process control systems.

In this regard, there is a certain contradiction in that the traditional, narrowly focused systems using Modbus, Profibus and Industrial Ethernet protocols have been unable to keep pace with the volume growth and quality of initial information transmitted by sensors and detectors. Widely used solutions, for example, based on Ethernet, do not have

© Springer Nature Switzerland AG 2020
A. Ronzhin et al. (Eds.): ICR 2020, LNAI 12336, pp. 273–282, 2020.
https://doi.org/10.1007/978-3-030-60337-3_27

sufficient functionality to provide effective support for real–time management services, which causes a number of problematic security issues linked to the state analysis of certain devices.

The increase in service packs, coupled with the delays in the transmission of messages between devices may critically affect the security of Industry 4.0 nodes along with the concomitant processes running in them. This underscores the importance of the state analysis of these devices, as has been proven in research studies [1].

At the same time, the decision making is complicated by the processes taking place dynamically in time because of the large number of the initial information sources, as shown in paper [2].

However, large volumes of analyzed and processed information provided in such systems are characterized by sufficiently well formalizable data, which allows for the application of various estimation methods of device states.

2   Formal Problem Statement

In most cases the analyzed device is outside the controlled area or difficult to access, as noted in paper [3]. Therefore, the ongoing processes of the devices and components of Industry 4.0 must be subject to continuous monitoring and controlling according to paper [4]. Important factors include changes in temperature, and amplitude and in the frequency of vibrations, sounds and electromagnetic spectra recorded by the sensors and detectors during the production and operation of certain components. These changes may indicate the need for process changes in order to prevent wear, failures, and defective products. This is proven in paper [5].

It is assumed that the system receives information from numerous sources D (detectors, sensors, internal monitoring elements):

$$D = \{d_n | n = 1, \ldots, N\} \tag{1}$$

The tuples of the characteristics H come from each source, determining the implementation of further actions:

$$H = \{h_m | m = 1, \ldots, M\} \tag{2}$$

In this case, the system's current state is described by the functional network Z, which identifies a set of tuples from the sources

$$Z = \{h_l | l = 1, \ldots, K\} \tag{3}$$

where K is the number of possible states to be analyzed for anomalies.

Let Z be a set of states within the system defined by the sources D and the values of the characteristics H coming from them. C is a set of state classes (for example, normal or anomalous). The function of distance between objects $r(z, z')$ is selected. There is a finite training sample of the known states $Z^k = \{z_1, \ldots, z_m\} \in Z$.

It is necessary to split the sample into subsets consisting of states close to the metric r (i.e., to find the function $a: Z \to C$).

Based on the functional network, it is determined whether the current state is normal or anomalous.

It is necessary to analyze not only the states of the devices but also those of the ongoing processes. In most cases, the internal states of both the device and the process are not available; in those cases, the analysis can be performed based on external characteristics.

Thus, the state analysis of hard–to–reach mechatronic components and devices in Industry 4.0 on the basis of incoming data from external side channels is an urgent objective.

3   Proposed Approach

Industry 4.0 is a global sphere within the information space, representing an interconnected set of infrastructures and IT platforms, including the internet, telecommunication networks, computer systems, embedded processors and controllers, and mechatronic elements according to paper [6].

Within the framework of Industry 4.0, various devices are considered, such as the sensors of manufacturing execution systems (CPCS, SCADA-systems), software and hardware nodes, elements that compose the Internet of Things, smart houses, and robotic systems for the critical application referred to in paper [7].

Despite its heterogeneity, typical devices of Industry 4.0 can be considered as separate components:

- The application software;
- The operating system;
- Hardware;
- The mechatronic part.

This division of Industry 4.0 into various components allows for the analysis of different data sets received through external channels according to papers [8–12]. The functioning of a separate part of the device is associated with the occurrence of insignificant sounds, vibrations, and radiation. Depending on the executed commands, the interactions of the nodes against one another, and the impact of the external environment, changes in the data will take place, which can be determined through both external and side channels as is proven in papers [13, 14]. To solve various tasks, grouping channels by types and sources makes it possible to consider different behavioral patterns that characterize, for example, the state, behaviour of the device or the external environment, as shown in paper [15].

Figure 1 illustrates a typical infrastructure organization.

The mechatronic devices of the Industry 4.0 infrastructure, which are located outside the controlled zone, are subject to various external and internal impacts, control commands, and technological processes, which will trigger changes in the data received through external channels as described in paper [16].

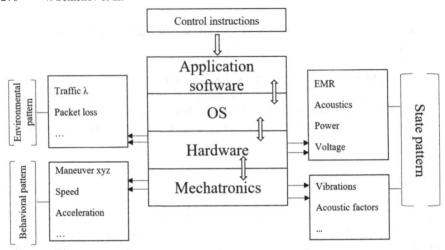

Fig. 1. The conceptual scheme of the Industry 4.0 infrastructure device with side channels of conditional behavioral patterns.

It is proposed that the analysis should consider an attribute space model for the external identification of the operational conditions of the Industry 4.0 infrastructure devices.

$$M_p = \langle H_{in}, H_{out}, H_{side} \rangle, \tag{4}$$

where:

- H_{in} are internal characteristics defined by built-in modules of network infrastructure devices (traffic intensity, packet loss probabilities, temperature, etc.)
- H_{out} are external characteristics defined by sensors and related to mechanical actions (vibrations, device coordinates, etc.)
- H_{side} are characteristics based on the signals from side channels during the operational and computational processes (electromagnetic radiation, acoustic radiation, changes in power and voltage).

To determine the state of the Industry 4.0 infrastructure nodes, a variety of indicators are used to estimate the state of the object. Amplitude, frequency, energy and many other signal parameters can be used as characteristics according to paper [17].

The approach is based on the following actions:

- selecting the elements to be analyzed;
- positioning sensors on the surface of the device;
- selecting the mode of operation, registering the received signal, and creating a training sample;
- analyzing the parameters and characteristics of the signals;
- determining the information system states.

The goal is to obtain the dependence of the quantitative performance indicators of Industry 4.0 devices and infrastructure nodes for different operating modes. For this purpose, numerous actions were performed:

- changing the system to the required operating mode by running the corresponding program;
- analyzing and digitizing the obtained data;
- analyzing the accumulated statistical data and changing the system and its remote devices to different modes with the purpose of accumulating statistics.

The information contained in the structures of received signals, grouped into behavioral patterns, is further used.

In contrast to the works presented, this research is focused on the developing an approach toward analyzing Industry 4.0 devices intended to identify the states of remote and hard–to–reach devices. This approach combines technologies of machine learning with an analysis of the heterogeneous external data of the digitized traces of the signal sequences. These sequences come from various elements and are combined in behavioral patterns.

4 Experiment

For the experiment, an acoustic side channel and an external channel were selected to record the sound and acceleration parameters of the manipulator.

The acoustic channel data were taken from microphones, one of which was on the device and another outside it. The acceleration and motion parameters were analyzed using an accelerometer mounted on the moving part of the manipulator.

The scheme of the experiment is presented in Fig. 2.

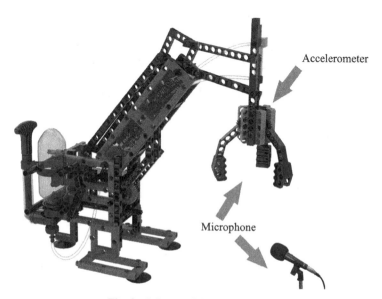

Fig. 2. Scheme of the experiment.

Digital sequences were analyzed for different states: S_1 – the resting state, S_2 – the forward movement of the manipulator, S_3 – the forward and left movement, S_4 – the forward and right movement. The duration of the states was different and ranged from 3.0 to 3.5 s.

Synchronized digital sequences from the accelerometer and microphones constitute a conventional behavioral pattern of the device state. Figure 3 shows the appearance of signals for the state S_1 as an example. The signal from the microphone, statically located in the area of the experiment, is presented at the top. The signal from the microphone located directly on the object under study is presented from the bottom. As can be seen from Fig. 3, the signals at the top are characterized by smaller amplitude and fade away with the object's distance from the microphone.

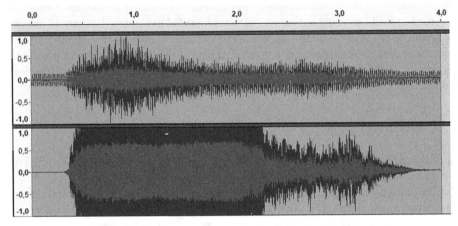

Fig. 3. Appearance of acoustic signals for the state S_2.

The second set of digitized pattern sequences is obtained by accelerometer measuring the projection of apparent acceleration (the difference between the true object acceleration and acceleration by gravity). Linear acceleration is measured with a digital three–axis accelerometer. As the Z–axis is directed vertically upwards, and the experiment for simplification was carried out on the horizontal plane (without change of the height level), the free–fall acceleration value g will always provide the greatest impact on the a_z acceleration projection onto the Z–axis (Fig. 4).

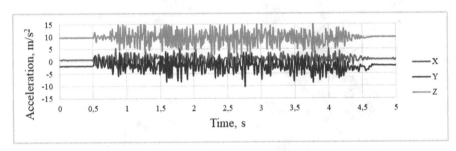

Fig. 4. Diagram of acceleration projections for the state S_2.

Different states also have different frequency spectra. Figure 5 represents a diagram of the acceleration spectrum for the state S_1 obtained using the fast–Fourier–transform algorithm. The advantage of using spectral information in classification is that there is no need to combine signal portraits over time.

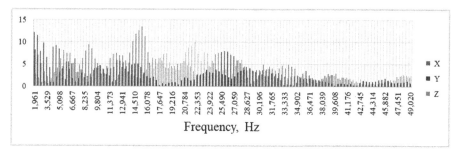

Fig. 5. Acceleration spectrum diagram for the state S_2.

The classified data array described each state at a discrete point in time using five characteristics:

$$H(t) = \{A_1(t), A_2(t), a_x(t), a_y(t), a_z(t)\}, \tag{5}$$

where H(t) is a tuple of signal values from different sensors D over time. In this case $A_1(t)$, $A_2(t)$ are values of signal amplitudes from two microphones (characteristics received based on the side channels), $a_x(t)$, $a_y(t)$, $a_z(t)$ are values of acceleration projections along x, y and z axes respectively (external characteristics).

As a classifier, we used the k–Nearest Neighbour (k–NN) method implemented in Matlab–R2020a environment. The advantages of the state identification method using the k–NN algorithm are simplicity and absence of the teaching phase. The classification is made directly in the process of applying the model over the training set and the process under study. This makes it impossible to "separate" the model from the data: to classify a new set of values, one should use examples of all known states.

For each point of spectral data of unknown state, Euclidean distances to other available points were calculated, the nearest k neighbours were selected, and conditional probabilities were calculated for each class. The spectrum point will belong to the class with the highest conditional probability. Figure 6 graphically demonstrates the assignment of an unknown point in the spectrum to one of the known states.

$$\hat{y} = \arg\min_{y=1,\dots,K} \sum_{j=1}^{K} \hat{P}(j|x)C(y|j), \tag{6}$$

where $\hat{y}$ is the predicted class, K is the number of classes, $\hat{P}(j|x)$ is a posterior probability of class j for the observation x, $C(y|j)$ is the classification coefficient of the class as y when its true class is j. $C(i|j) = 1$, if i ~= j and $C(i|j) = 0$ if $i = j$.

The set of points in the spectrum of the unknown state will belong to the class to which most of the classified points were assigned at the previous step (6).

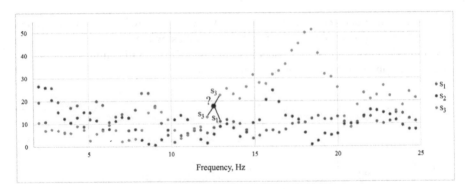

Fig. 6. Assignment of an unknown point in the spectrum at k = 3.

Thus, the k–NN algorithm according to papers [18, 19] allows the classification of all available points of the time series or spectrum of the device functioning in terms of their similarity. The results of the classification are given in Table 1.

Table 1. Classification results of the information security state by the k–NN algorithm (k = 3).

		Predicted state			
		S_1	S_2	S_3	S_4
Real state	S_1	421	10	5	1
	S_2	5	471	17	0
	S_3	1	11	473	13
	S_4	7	12	55	419

The sum of diagonal element values shows the total number of correctly classified states, and the ratio of this number to the total number of states is called the overall classification accuracy. The overall accuracy of the selected classifier for the case of the full classification was found to be 0.93.

To determine the accuracy of the classifier by test data, it is necessary to divide the number of correctly classified states of this class by the total number of states in this class according to the test data as has been proven in paper [20]. This indicator shows how well the classification result for this class matches the test data. The similar indicator is calculated for the real class by dividing the number of correctly classified states by the total number of states in this class according to the check data. Figure 7 presents the classification results in the form of the classification accuracy to classes according to the check and test data.

Thus, the type of recognition using four states demonstrates the fundamental possibility of the proposed model's application considering its acceptable accuracy of identification.

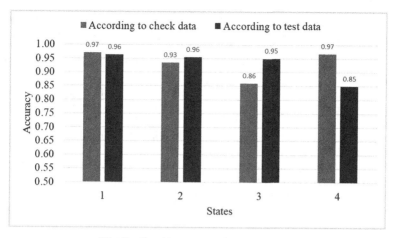

Fig. 7. Classification accuracy to classes.

5 Conclusion

The development of areas related to Industry 4.0 facilitates the presence of autonomous devices, unmanned vehicles and production without manual intervention, all of which necessitate process monitoring for mechatronic devices. The major limitations, however, are the high complexity of incoming data processing and the requirements for input data.

Current identification methods require significant resources, accuracy and credibility. Taking into account the peculiarities of the observed objects, constant changes in behavioral characteristics of time and the space of states, grouping observable symptoms for analysis and synthesis is necessary.

The proposed approach involves grouping characteristics obtained from autonomous devices into behavioral patterns. The combination of characteristics makes it possible to more accurately estimate the state of the devices.

The effectiveness of device state estimation depends upon how the received signals are processed. It is also sensitive to the training sample and the hardware–software platform under study.

References

1. Chopra, A.: Paradigm shift and challenges in IoT security. In: Journal of Physics: Conference Series, First International Conference on Emerging Electrical Energy, Electronics and Computing Technologies, vol. 1432 (2019)
2. Gorbachev, I., Glukhov, A.: Modeling of processes of information security violations of critical infrastructure. SPIIRAS Proc. 1(38), 112–135 (2015)
3. Semenov, V., Lebedev, I.: Processing of signal information in problems of monitoring information security of unmanned autonomous objects. Sci. Techn. J. Inf. Technol. Mech. Optics 19(3), 492–498 (2019)
4. Teylans, A., et al.: Assessment of cyber physical system risks with domain specific modelling and simulation. SPIIRAS Proc. 59(4), 115–139 (2018)

5. Sukhoparov, M., Semenov, V., Lebedev, I.: Information security monitoring of elements of cyber-physical systems using artificial neural networks. Meth. Techn. Means Inf. Secur. **27**, 59–60 (2018)

6. Ghobakhloo, M.: Industry 4.0, digitization, and opportunities for sustainability. J. Cleaner Prod. **252**, 16–25 (2020)

7. Devesh, M., Kant, A., Suchit, Y., Tanuja, P., Kumar, S.: Fruition of CPS and IoT in context of industry 4.0. Intelligent communication, control and devices. Adv. Intell. Syst. Comput. **989**, 367–375 (2020)

8. Buldakova, T., Mikov, D.: Matlab application for information security risk analysis. AIP Conf. Proc. **2195**, 020004 (2019)

9. Kocher, P., Jaffe, J., Jun, B. Introduction to differential power analysis and related attacks. In: Proceedings CRYPTO 1998; LNCS 1109, pp. 104–113 (1998)

10. Kuhn, M.G., Anderson, R.J.: Soft tempest: hidden data transmission using electromagnetic emanations. In: Aucsmith, D. (ed.) IH 1998. LNCS, vol. 1525, pp. 124–142. Springer, Heidelberg (1998). https://doi.org/10.1007/3-540-49380-8_10

11. Gandolfi, K., Mourte, C., Olivier, F.: Electromagnetic analysis: concrete result. CHES, LNCS **2162**, 251–261 (2001)

12. Zajić, A., Prvulovic, M.: Experimental demonstration of electromagnetic information leakage from modern processor-memory systems. IEEE Trans. Electromagn. Compatib. **56**(4), 885–893 (2014)

13. Buldakova, T.: Cybersecurity Risks Analyses at Remote Monitoring of Object's State. Cyber-Physical Systems: Industry 4.0 Challenges. Studies in Systems, Decision and Control 260 (2020)

14. Wang, M., Huang, K., Wang, Y., Wu, Z., Du, Z.: A novel side-channel analysis for physical-domain security in cyber-physical systems. Int. J. Distrib. Sensor Netw. **15**(8) 2066 (2019)

15. Lakshmanarao, A., Shashi, M.: A survey on machine learning for cyber security. Int. J. Sci. Technol. Res. **9**(1), 499–502 (2020)

16. Spatz, D., Smarra, D., Ternovskiy, I.: A review of anomaly detection techniques leveraging side-channel emissions. In: Proceedings of SPIE – The International Society for Optical Engineering, p. 11011 (2019)

17. Semenov, V., Lebedev, I., Sukhoparov, M.: Identification of information security state of unmanned vehicles using artificial neural networks. Methods Techn. Means Inf. Secur. **28**, 46–47 (2019)

18. Bishop, C.: pattern recognition and machine learning. In: Information Science and Statistics, p. 738. Springer, New York (2006)

19. Lebedev, I.: The way of formalization of connections in text constructions at creation of natural language interfaces. Inf. Manage. Syst. **3**(28), 23–26 (2007)

20. Tamrakar, P., Roy, S., Satapathy, B, Ibrahim, S.: Integration of lazy learning associative classification with kNN algorithm. In: International Conference on Vision Towards Emerging Trends in Communication and Networking (ViTECoN), pp. 1–4 (2019)

Humanoid Robot Soccer Player for RoboCup Junior League Competitions

Evgeny Shandarov$^{(\boxtimes)}$, Ilya Shabalin, Irina Prokazina, Vladimir Zhelonkin,
Egor Polyntsev, and Alina Sogomonyants

Laboratory of Robotics and Artificial Intelligence, Tomsk State University of Control, Systems
and Radioelectronics, (TUSUR University), Tomsk, Russian Federation
evgenyshandarov@gmail.com

Abstract. In this paper, we propose the concept for the new Humanoid Soccer league for RoboCupJunior, that allows juniors participate in humanoid robot
competitions. The results of developing prototype platform for a robot soccer
player based on commercially available sets are presented. The modification of
the hardware platform, software development and test results are described.

Keywords: RoboCup · Robotis Bioloid · Computer vision · Robot soccer ·
RoboCup junior · Humanoid robot

1 Introduction

RoboCup (The World Cup Robot Soccer) is an international initiative to promote AI and
robotics research by providing a task of robot soccer game for evaluation of theories,
algorithms and agent architectures. In order for the robot to play a soccer game, wide
range of technologies need to be integrated [1].

There are two big parts of RoboCup: RoboCup Major and RoboCupJunior (RCJ)
leagues. The Major is the competition for university teams while Junior for middle and
high school students teams [2].

Soccer competitions in RoboCup started in 1997 in MiddleSize, SmallSize and Simulation leagues. The Humanoid Soccer League competitions was first established in 2002
[3] and now have become ones of the most impressive in RoboCup [2, 4]. Humanoid
Soccer League teams need to solve the problems in computer vision, locomotion, navigation and robot bipedal walking [4–6]. There are three subleagues in RoboCup Humanoid
Soccer: AdultSize, TeenSize and KidSize. In Humanoid KidSize Soccer, robots from 40
to 90 cm high are allowed to participate, the game is played on a field 6 x 9 m in size
with artificial grass, and up to 5 players are allowed in each team on the field.

The rules of the Humanoid Soccer league have serious hardware requirements. This
raises the entry threshold for new teams. For example, the commercially available Kid-
Size Robotis Darwin-OP3 platform costs about $11,000 in the US market. Creating
your own platform based on available parts on the market will cost significantly more.
In addition, the participants of the "adult" soccer leagues should have high skills in

© Springer Nature Switzerland AG 2020
A. Ronzhin et al. (Eds.): ICR 2020, LNAI 12336, pp. 283–294, 2020.
https://doi.org/10.1007/978-3-030-60337-3_28

mechatronics, electronics, programming, communication systems, etc. All of this significantly complicates the participation in the competitions of this league for new teams with little or no experience, insufficient financial base and technological level.

RoboCupJunior Soccer leagues use wheeled robots; until now, juniors have not participated in humanoid robot competitions due to the high entrance threshold. Nevertheless, the juniors have an interest in this type of activity, since it is in soccer of humanoid robots that the participants solve a wide range of problems in different areas, which leads to an increase in competencies. Last years the RoboCup community has set a goal to develop a concept and rules for humanoid soccer league in Junior. Various independent university groups from Israel, Germany, and Italy work on this task. The team of the Laboratory of Robotics and Artificial Intelligence (LRAI) of Tomsk State University of Control Systems and Radio Electronics (TUSUR University) also works on Humanoid Soccer for Juniors.

2   Methods

2.1   Game Concept

From the RoboCup community point of view, junior humanoid robot soccer may become a "bridge" between RCJ Soccer Open league and Humanoind Soccer Major League. Based on our experience of participating in the RoboCup 3D Simulation Soccer and Humanoid Soccer league competitions, as well as our experience in organizing the RoboCup events in Russia, we proposed the following set of requirements.

Infrastructure Requirements. Since junior teams are based in schools, institutions of additional education, universities, the infrastructure for training and games should be affordable, inexpensive and easily placed in classrooms. We have proposed the following requirements for the field for the game (Fig. 1):

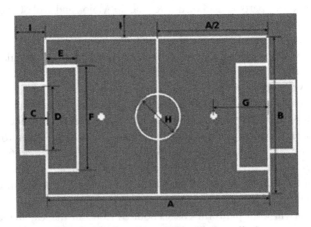

Fig. 1. Field marking. (Color figure online)

- Material: low pile carpet, green.
- Field size: external 3 x 4 m, internal (by marking) 2.6 x 3.6 m.
- The marking of the field is done in accordance with Fig. 1, the width of the line marking 5 cm, color – white.
- Gates: material plumbing PVC pipes, diameter 45 mm, mouth size (W x H x D) 90 x 65 x 40 cm, the color of the gate is white or, depending on the side of the field, blue or yellow.
- Ball: orange or red ball with a diameter of 6-7 cm, weight 50-60 g, material plastic, suitable ball for field hockey.

Gameplay. The game consists of two halves, each of 5 min, and a 5 min break between halves. The games consist of two teams of autonomous humanoid robots playing soccer against each other. Each team has two robots. If the goal difference of the opponents is 10, the game is terminated. If, as a result of the game, none of the teams hits the opponent's goal, penalti is appointed.

2.2 Robots Requirements

Based on the infrastructure parameters, the following requirements for soccer-players were proposed:

- Robots can be either made by the participants themselves, or be commercial products, in the second case, team members should modify them, re-equip robots to provide their own significant contribution.
- Robots programming must done by the participants themselves. The use of ready-made commercial code is not allowed.
- The height of the robots: from 30 to 50 cm.
- Robots weight: from 1 to 4 kg.

   The number of robots in the team: no more than two, roles: goalie, field player, can be both field players.

2.3 Team Challenges

Based on the proposed game concept, teams participating in the competition should solve the following set of tasks:

- Locomotion – movement of robots on the field on two « legs » .
- Vision – the robot's "vision" system.
- Navigation – robot orientation system on the field.
- Control – robot control system, including group control of a team of robots.

2.4   Platform Choice

The concept proposed by LRAI TUSUR implies a low entry level, it was decided to use a commercial kit to build a soccer-robot platform on its basis. After analyzing the market and the staffing of the educational institutions of the Russian Federation, the two basic platforms were chosen:

- RoboBuilder – an anthropomorphic robot platform, 28 cm in height, 16 DOF, Atmega128 controller, accelerometer, infrared distance sensor, C programming language, built-in Bluetooth module, price 35-50 thousand rubles.
- Robotis Bioloid – an anthropomorphic robot platform, 44 cm in height in the basic configuration, 18 DOF, CM-530 controller, C-like programming language, price 120 thousand rubles.

One could note the high level of prevalence of the Bioloid platform: according to the company LLC Applied Robotics, Moscow, there are at least 2000 units of such robots in Russian schools. Many educational institutions of the Russian Federation already have the experience of using this platform in the format of robo-dances at RoboFest competitions.

3   Research and Development

3.1   Locomotion

Usually, when solving robot soccer problems in the RoboCup Humanoid Soccer League, an adaptive motion model should be used. This model dynamically changes the parameters of the robot's movement depending on the current movement phase, the robot's position in space, and so on [3]. Among other things, the adaptive model should prevent the robot from falling. However, the adaptive model places high demands on the performance of the on-board computer and the implementation of mathematical models, which could be difficult for middle and high school students. So, we propose a model of non-adaptive robot movement, where complex movements (walking, turns, etc.) are implemented as a set of sequential execution of primitive movements. Such primitives can be easily created by juniors using special software that comes with robots. Thus, the team that will be able to develop more successful primitives, ensure their "seamless" gluing into complex movements will receive an advantage on the field. The requirement of robot stability on the field in this model is extremely important.

For the first stage of movement development, a simpler and cheaper model of a humanoid robot – Robobuilder was used. The movement of the robot was realized through the sequential reproduction of the primitive movements, which are called "scenes". Each scene corresponds to a certain number of frames and execution time (1 frame at a speed of 20-30 ms as optimal). Thus, there is no need to use the adaptive dynamic model to control the walking of the robot. This allows to control the gait and movements of the robot at a basic level. The following movement primitives were developed:

- step forward with the left foot;

  – step forward with the right foot;
  – turn left;
  – turn right;
  – step with the right foot to the right;
  – step with the left foot to the left;
  – stand up – lying on chest;
  – stand up – lying on back.

With such primitives of robot movements, it is possible to create complex composite movements: for example, "Walking forward" is realized as a sequence of "step forward with the left foot », « step forward with the right foot". For the demonstration, a soccer game of robots with a remote Bluetooth control was implemented.

After the positive results were obtained and it became clear that the model of movement of robots based on primitives works, we decided to apply it to the Robotis Bioloid platform, which is more preferable for humanoid robot soccer. A similar set of motion primitives has been developed for the Bioloid platform.

3.2 Vision

The technical vision system of the robot soccer player should provide recognition of objects on the field: the ball, the goal, the opponents, the mark, etc. [7]

Since the microcomputer of inexpensive humanoid robots does not have high computational power, it is possible to use specialized camera modules to organize a technical vision system, where the basic functions for recognizing predetermined objects are implemented on integrated specialized microprocessor. Examples of such cameras: PxyCam (USA), JEVOIS-A33 (USA), OpenMV Cam M7 (USA), TrackingCam (Russia).

For our concern, the TrackingCam camera was selected. This camera provides a resolution of 640 x 480 pixels, supports Dynamixel data transfer protocol, which is also used in the Bioloid platform.

TrackingCam camera technical parametrs: Omni-vision 7725 matrix, resolution 640 x 480 pixels, frame rate up to 30 frames per second, STM32f407 – ARM Cortex M4 168 MHz processor, 168 Kbytes RAM, 512 Kbytes flash memory, 5-12 V power supply voltage, I2C, UART, SPI, Dynamixel, USB interfaces.

The TrackingCam technical vision module is able to perform operations for recognizing both single-color and composite objects consisting of several color areas using the YcbCr color model [9]. The result of processing is a set of selected color areas. The camera sends a data packet about the found objects to the microcontroller with a given frequency. This data package contains information about founded color spots: the number and the type of the spot, the spot position in the frame, and the area of the spot in pixels.

To configure the camera to search for necessary objects, TrackingCamApp software for PC is used. It is recommended not to recognize more than three-color spots in the frame while configuring the camera. TrackingCamApp software allows to select the camera work protocol, its bit rate and other parameters and save the camera configuration files to the PC for subsequent quick download.

To ensure the operation of the Vision module on the Bioloid platform, we modified the robot. The working name of the modification: "Robot soccer player head".

The head of robot soccer player consists of two Dynamixel AX-12A servos mounted on the upper body of a humanoid robot, as well as a TrackingCam camera rigidly attached to the upper servo (Fig. 2). Two servos provide azimuth and tilt rotation of the robot's head relative to the horizon. However, this design has a significant drawback – when robot falls, the impact falls on the camera lens.

Fig. 2. Prototype of the football-robot.

In order to secure the camera, the robot's head case was developed. The case contains mounts for TrackingCam and for an additional microcontroller OpenCM 9.04, to expand the computing power of the robot. This whole structure is reinforced with stiffeners, for camera hits protection when the robot falls. The 3D model was developed in Autodesk Inventor 2019, and fabricated on a 3D printer from PLA plastic. The mass and overall parameters of the resulting part are: weight – 41 g., Dimensions: 94 x 77 x 74 mm.

3.3 Navigation

Navigation of the platform is provided by the software of the Navigation module, which uses the data of the subsystem "Robot soccer player head". During the game, the robot searches for a bright ball, when it is found, it points the camera at the center of mass of its color spot [8]. After centering the camera, the controller requests feedback from the servos. The robot decides to make the necessary movement, basing on the tilt and pan servos position: if the head is pointed forward and raised up – robot goes forward; if the head is directed to the left or right robot goes to the left or to the right, respectively; if the head is directed forward and lowered down at a small angle to the core – robot hits the ball.

The "Forward" movement is based on previous robot movements. If, during the previous iteration of the cycle, the robot took a step with his left foot, the next step he will take the right one. Such commands allows to increase the speed of movement of the robot with less swinging of the entire body.

Ball Seeking. The robot takes up this state if the ball is not found in the frame. In this case, the robot moves along the field along the trajectory of the cycloid, while making turns with the head around the circumference, according to:

$$Tilt = horiz + k\ sin(t);$$

$$Pan = vert + k \cdot cos(t),$$

where *Tilt* – angle of rotation of the head, relative to the horizon; *Pan* – angle of rotation of the head, relative to the vertical; *horiz* – angle of rotation of the horizontal servo equal to the horizon zero; *vert* – angle of rotation of the vertical servo is equal to the vertical zero; *k* – proportionality coefficient; *t* – variable in radians.

The robot moves around the field seeking the ball, until the ball is detected. After that, the robot switch to state of "Ball follow".

Ball Following. When the camera detects an object on the field that looks like a ball, it is centered in the frame. It is realized using the position of the ball in the frame as coordinates along the X and Y-axes; the controller sends commands to servos that rotate the camera until the ball is relatively close to the center of the frame. In addition, boundary parameters are set for centering, which do not allow the robot to turn its head at an angle that is impossible for a human. If these boundary parameters exceeded, the robot makes turns and moves with its entire body, not with its head.

Ball Centering. When the ball found and its color spot is in the center of the camera, the scenario of approaching and kicking the ball starts. The robot goes forward to the ball, using the movement primitives loaded into it (walking forward, sideways, turns, hitting the left /left foot, etc.). At the beginning of the movement, the robot tries to center the position of its body and head relative to the ball. This condition allows getting closer and hitting the ball at a right angle. After that, the robot switch on to "Ball kick" state.

3.4 Control

The robot control module defines the strategy and tactics of the game, as well as integrates and manages the operation of all the software modules described above. At the software level, the control block is an infinite loop, the first element of which checks whether the robot has fallen. If robot fell – the "stand-up" system rises up the robot.

Next, it's need to determine the current state of the game – "Find ball", "Ball follow", "Ball centering", "Ball kick", "Fallen". Finding and following the ball was discussed in detail in the Navigation module. Let's take a closer look at the "Ball kick" and "fall-stand up system" modules.

Ball Kick. The kicking occurs when the ball is in the center of the frame, and the camera tilted down, using the servos of the head, at the maximum possible angle, from the standard location. The choice of the foot for the kick depends on which side of the center of the frame is the center of the ball:

$$\begin{cases} pan > vert, RightKick(); \\ pan \geq vert, LeftKick(), \end{cases}$$

where $RightKick()$, $LeftKick()$ – functions for kicking the ball with the right or left foot.

The System Fall-stand Up. During the soccer game, robots falls are inevitable. The robot's position is tracked using an accelerometer. This sensor can detect rapid changes in the robot's position in space using two coordinates. Based on the accelerometer measurements, one can determine the robot's position: "fell on chest" or "fell on back". To bring the robot to the "standing" position, the appropriate set of motions of the Locomotion module are performed.

One of the problems when using a robot with non-adaptive motion system that moves in space using motion primitives is that it is impossible to execute parallel commands when running one of these primitives. In particular, it is not possible to get the accelerometer reading until the execution of the primitive is complete. The solution to this problem is to divide one large sample into a series of N relatively small "frames". Sequential execution each frame, allows to scan sensors between each such frame. Thus, if the robot starts to fall while playing the motion primitive, the accelerometer will have time to register this and start the "Stand up" program block.

Frame-by-frame development of movements increased the chance to recognize a sharp fall and subsequent rise up to 70-75%, which significantly increased the dynamics of the game on the field. However, there were a number of exceptions, during which the robot could fall on its back or on its chest in the absence of running movements. For example, when two robots collide. In this case, the robot could not detect rapid changes in the accelerometer reading and did not recognize the fall.

To increase the robot's fall recognition up to 100% we use a special function, which is based on the fact that the robot is in a state of absence of the ball in the frame and that the robot is unable to observe the ball when falling on its chest or back, it follows the cycloid. Since the accelerometer is located in the center of the body, when walking straight, there is always a significant permissible swing. However, in the prone position, the robot moves its legs in the air, and the cubic shape of the body contributes to the minimum swing of the accelerometer. Therefore, the average value of the sensor's frame-to-frame deviations during playback of one of the primitives could be calculated. These values differ significantly when walking straight on the field and when walking in a prone position, which confirmed by practical experience. Figure 3 shows a diagram of the evolution of the system "Fall-stand up".

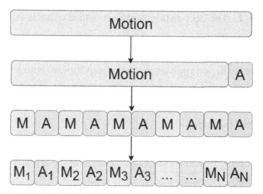

Fig. 3. Diagram of the evolution of the system "Fall-stand up". M – motions frame; A – accelerometer values.

For calculating the average value of the sensor's frame-to-frame deviations the following formula is used:

$$|S_N| = \frac{\sum_{i=1}^{N} |A_0 - A_N|}{N}$$

where N is number of frames in the primitive; A_0 is reference value of the sensor at rest; A_N is sensor value on the Nth frame.

The fall conditions are as follows:

$$\begin{cases} F = 1, |S_N| < 10; \\ F = 0, |S_N| > 10, \end{cases}$$

where F is the drop function. $F = 1$ if the robot fell, $F = 0$ if it didn't fall.

The camera determines the position of the fall. If the camera is pointing up, it detects strong external lighting, and the robot gets up from the back. Similarly, for getting up from the chest, in this case, the camera sees a black spot in the entire frame.

4   Experimental Evaluation

For evaluation of developed software and hardware the experiments were carried out. All experiments were performed in laboratory conditions. Obtained values for robot characteristics were calculated based on the average value of at least ten experiments performed.

4.1   Locomotion

Table 1 shows obtained values of the Locomotion module, which include all movement primitives of non-adaptive robot movement model. The most important parameters are: forward gait, body turns, lateral pace parameters and the parameters of fall-stand up system.

Table 1. The Locomotion module provided characteristics.

Forward gait parameters	
The distance robot covers after one movement cycle (step forward with left & right legs)	10.4 cm
Forward pace	4.03 m/min
Deviation from the initial trajectory	30–45°/m
Body turns parameters (left/right)	
The discrete value of the angle of rotation for one iteration of the primitive	42°
The time to rotate the robot's body on 90 °	4.04 s
Lateral pace parameters	
The displacement distance for one iteration of the primitive	2.2 cm
The displacement pace	2.4 cm/s
Parameters of motion primitives of fall-stand up system	
Time to stand up from a chest	2.88 s
Time to stand up from a back	3.23 s

4.2 Control

Table 2 shows obtained experimental parameters of the Control module, which include ball kick submodule and fall-stand up system. Developed fall-stand up system allows the robot to rise from a lying position on its chest or back if it falls during a soccer game.

Table 2. Numerical parameters for control module.

Fall-stand up system parameters	
Chance to detect the fall	~85–90%
Time required for fall recognition	1.87 s

4.3 Vision

The Vision module implements the technical vision of the robot based on TrackingCam. To check the operation of the Vision module, the camera was tuned to recognize the orange ball. This ball is a sports equipment designed for playing field hockey or lacrosse. The parameters of the ball are ideally suited to the requirement for the infrastructure of the game: material – plastic, weight – 53 g, diameter – 62 mm.

Ball was placed on the maximum distance from the camera, on which Vision module is able to detect the ball correctly. Figure 4a shows the ball, observed by robot. On Fig. 4b the binarized initial image is represented. Camera was tuned to recognize the orange ball. Figure 4c represents the ball, detected by Vision module. The detected are has parameters, which were discussed in Vision module (area, coordinate of the center etc).

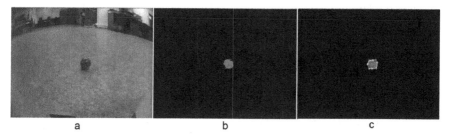

a   b   c

Fig. 4. (a) ball, observed by robot; (b) binarized initial image, observed by robot; (c) ball, detected by robot's Vision module. (Color figure online)

After the camera was tuned to detect orange ball the numerical parameters of Vision module were measured (Table 3).

Table 3. Numerical parameters for Vision module.

Maximum detection distance from the robot's body to the ball on the field	65–70 cm
Camera's arc of vision	76°
Area of the view of the camera	186.51 cm^2

According to experiments, the developed modules allow the robot to stable move across the field, track and kick the ball, stand up when it falls and generally allow robot to fully participate in the robot soccer game.

5 Discussions and Conclusions

The developed platform was demonstrated for the first time at the international robotics festival RoboFinist, St.Petersburg in October 2018. Less than a month later, LRAI students, using the developed platform, helped to form teams in two schools in Tomsk, which allowed to held the first mini-tournament at the "TUSUR Cup" in November 2018. In the spring of 2019, a new humanoid robot soccer League, Junior Humanoid Soccer, was formed at the RoboCup Russia Open 2019 competition, in which took part four teams from Tomsk, Moscow, Krasnoyarsk and Chelyabinsk. The international premier of the League was held at the RoboCup Asia-Pacific championship, which was held in Moscow in November 2019, with 5 teams participating.

Thus, in the process of work, the concept of a new soccer league of humanoid robots among junior teams was proposed, a platform prototype and software for a soccer player robot using commercially available robots were developed, the tests were conducted and the foundations for forming a team community in the Russian Federation were laid. Since the educational institutions of the Russian Federation already have a sufficiently large base of Robotis Bioloid humanoid robots, it can be assumed that this league will actively develop using the approaches described in this paper. It is important to understand that the proposed platform prototype provides ample room for modification, both in terms of equipment and in terms of software robots.

References

1. Kitano, H. (ed.): RoboCup 1997. LNCS, vol. 1395. Springer, Heidelberg (1998). https://doi.org/10.1007/3-540-64473-3
2. Ronzhin, A.L., Stankevich, L.A., Shandarov, E.S.: International robot soccer competitions robocup and prospects of Russian teams participation. Robot. Tech. Cybern. 2(7), 24–29 (2015)
3. Asada, M., Kaminka, G.A.: An overview of robocup 2002 Fukuoka/Busan. In: Kaminka, G.A., Lima, P.U., Rojas, R. (eds.) RoboCup 2002. LNCS (LNAI), vol. 2752, pp. 1–7. Springer, Heidelberg (2003). https://doi.org/10.1007/978-3-540-45135-8_1
4. Gerndt, R., Seifert, D., Baltes, J., Sadeghnejad, S., Benke, S.: Humanoid robots in soccer – robots versus humans in robocup 2050. IEEE-RAS Robot. Autom. Mag. 22(3), 147–154 (2015)
5. Gomilko, S.I., et al.: Robot footballers' team of robocup humanoid kidsize league. Robot. Tech. Cybern. 3(8), 11–15 (2015). in Russian
6. Gomilko, S., et al.: Robot soccer team for robocup humanoid kidsize league. In: Ronzhin, Andrey, Rigoll, Gerhard, Meshcheryakov, Roman (eds.) ICR 2016. LNCS (LNAI), vol. 9812, pp. 181–188. Springer, Cham (2016). https://doi.org/10.1007/978-3-319-43955-6_22
7. Shabalin, I.D., et al.: Humanoid robot for soccer based on robotics bioloid platform. In: Proceedings of the III International Conference on Cognitive Robotics, pp. 68–69 (2018)
8. Polyntsev, E.S., Klimov, A.A., Shandarov, E.S.: Ball seeking algorithm for humanoid robot soccer player. In: Proceedings of the III International Conference Cognitive Robotics, pp. 56–60 (2018)
9. Shabalin, I.D.: Trackingcam computer vision system. In: Scientific Session of TUSUR-2018: Proceedings of the International Scientific and Technical Conference of Students, Graduate Students and Young Scientists, p. 138 (2018)

A Modular Deep Learning Architecture for Anomaly Detection in HRI

Gergely Sóti[1]($\boxtimes$), Ilshat Mamaev[1], and Björn Hein[1,2]

[1] IAR-IPR, Karlsruhe Institute of Technology, Karlsruhe, Germany
{gergely.soti,ilshat.mamaev,bjoern.hein}@kit.edu
[2] Karlsruhe University of Applied Sciences, Karlsruhe, Germany

Abstract. Considering humans as a non-deterministic factor makes anomaly detection in Human-Robot Interaction scenarios rather a challenging problem. Anomalous events like unexpected user interaction or unforeseen environment changes are unknown before they happen. On the other hand, the work process or user intentions could evolve in time. To address this issue, a modular deep learning approach is presented that is able to learn normal behavior patterns in an unsupervised manner. We combined the unsupervised feature extraction learning ability of an autoencoder with a sequence modeling neural network. Both models were firstly evaluated on benchmark video datasets, revealing adequate performance comparable to the state-of-the-art methods. For HRI application, a continuous training approach for real-time anomaly detection was developed and evaluated in an HRI-experiment with a collaborative robot, ToF camera, and proximity sensors. In the user study with 10 subjects irregular interactions and misplaced objects were the most common anomalies, which system was able to detect reliably.

Keywords: Human-Robot Interaction · Anomaly detection · Unsupervised learning

1 Introduction

Since 19th-century law acts and directives were developed for safety and accident prevention at work [1]. Traditionally, work with heavy machinery or in hazardous environments should be conducted under the supervision of other people. Nowadays, technological advances facilitate new approaches for safety. In 2017, Moscow Metro has abolished the escalator attendant post, whose duty was monitoring passengers on escalators to prevent dangerous situations. Like the Moscow Metro employing remote operators for monitoring multiple escalators at once without a physical presence, in future human-robot collaboration workspaces, an artificial intelligence system could be supervising the work process by processing multi-modal sensory information in real-time and simultaneously learning new human behavior online.

© Springer Nature Switzerland AG 2020
A. Ronzhin et al. (Eds.): ICR 2020, LNAI 12336, pp. 295–307, 2020.
https://doi.org/10.1007/978-3-030-60337-3_29

Anomaly, novelty, or outlier detection all describe the problem of detecting special events that indicate a non-usual behavior, a binary classification problem. In contrast to most other binary classification problems, the availability of data is asymmetrical by nature: normal behavior events can be gathered in large amounts, while anomalous behavior is, by definition, a composite of rare or even unpredictable events. Additionally, in real-world monitoring scenarios, the properties of available data might change, or even contextual evolution is possible. Events that are considered normal might become irregular or the other way around. People starting wearing face masks in public establishments and on the streets during the COVID-19 pandemic serves as a perfect example for such a contextual change.

This paper presents a modular deep neural network architecture to learn normal behavior patterns on temporal data sequences in an unsupervised manner. The model is evaluated with different configurations on benchmark datasets. Furthermore, continuous training of the model is implemented and tested as an adaptation mechanism for contextual changes in a human-robot collaboration scenario, as detecting irregular behavior in a human-robot collaborative workspace could be a first step to a safer human-robot collaboration by e.g. limiting or stopping robot movement when required.

2   State of the Art

Recent research for anomaly detection focuses, in many cases, on deep learning techniques using neural networks to predict subsequent data frames based on previous information. In these approaches, anomalies are defined as events that are outliers with respect to a learned model: an anomaly is derived from the deviation of the predicted and the actual subsequent data frame.

Hasan et al. [2] train two autoencoders (AEs) to learn a regularity model: a fully connected AE using handcrafted features and an other fully convolutional AE that learns the features by itself. A framework introduced Del Giomo et al. [3] defines anomalies as examples that can be distinguished from other examples from the same video. Their model was trained in an unsupervised manner and detected anomalies independent from the temporal order of the anomalies. Jefferson Medel [4] trained two architectures to learn a generative model to predict subsequent video frames: in the first model multiple long short-term memorys (LSTMs) act as encoders and decoders on stacked, non-overlapping image patches; the second is an AE based model, that uses max pooling to learn the features of whole frames. An unsupervised learning method is used by Chong et al. [5], utilizing a spatiotemporal encoder - an encoder decoder architecture consisting of convolutional layers, convolutional LSTMs cells, and deconvolutional layers - to classify anomalies in video sequences based on the reconstruction error. Two independent Gaussian classifiers were trained by Sabokrou et al. [6] to differentiate normal and anomalous video patches from crowded scenes

Wang et al. [7] review multiple adaptation mechanisms for anomaly detection in their survey: probabilistic-based [8,9], neighborhood-based [10,11], density ratio-based methods [12,13] and the one-class support vector machine (SVM) [13]. They conclude, that it is still necessary to extend these approaches to handle large amounts of data in distributed resource-limited environments.

3   Concept

Anomalies can be divided into three categories [14]: 1) anomalous events have significantly different in-frame characteristics from normal events, (e.g., spatial, color); 2) anomalous events have some temporal irregularity (e.g., happen rarely, wrong order); 3) anomalous events are events that have a specific meaning.

The first two categories include anomalies that differ from normal events in certain aspects, thus by training a normal behavior model for each category, anomalies could be detected as events that do not comply with the norm. However, creating a model to detect anomalies from the third category would require some a-priori knowledge or examples of such anomalies. Hence, detecting anomalies with a specific meaning is not in the scope of the paper.

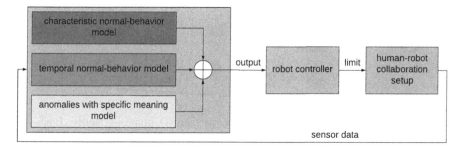

Fig. 1. Concept for using anomaly detection in an HRI setup

An anomaly detection model is obtained by combining a characteristic and a temporal normal behavior model that can be trained and adapted unsupervisedly with normal behavior data. A concept for employing such an anomaly detection system in an HRI setup is shown in Fig. 1: the anomalies are detected based on different models, and are used to limit robot movement in a human-robot collaborative task to improve safety. A key factor to this is the robot being constantly aware of the sometimes unpredictable or anomalous actions of the human co-worker and acting according to it.

To learn characteristic normal behavior, two unsupervised feature representation learning models are considered: AE and deep belief network (DBN). Both can learn to fuse multi-modal sensor data additionally to learning a feature representation [15]. The AE is chosen over the DBN as it is simpler to train and to implement since a DBN has to be trained in a greedy, layer-wise manner. The reconstruction error of the AE can also be used to calculate a characteristic regularity score, to classify characteristic anomalies.

Temporal normal behavior can be learned using a sequence model to predict the current data-frame or a sequence of data-frames using data-frames from the past and present. In this paper, both an LSTM and a generic temporal convolutional network (TCN) inspired model consisting of stacked dilated convolutional layers are tested for the task. Similarly to the characteristic regularity score, the temporal regularity score can be derived from the loss of the temporal normal behavior models.

To make the training of these models more efficient, the extracted feature representation from the characteristic normal behavior model, the bottleneck of the AE, is used as input. A conceptual architecture of a combination of the characteristic and temporal normal behavior models is shown in Fig. 2.

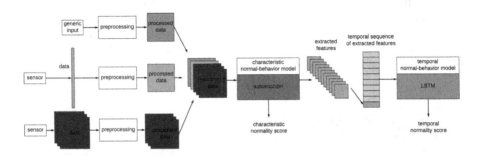

Fig. 2. Concept of the anomaly detection system

As both normal behavior models can be trained unsupervisedly, both can be trained online with real-time sensor data. Assuming that most recorded data describes normal behavior, as anomalies are rare events, each data-frame recorded while using the anomaly detection system could be used for training. This way however, anomalies would also be included in the training data, although as the concept states, only normal behavior data is intended to be used for training the model. Assuming, that anomalies make up at most around 10% of all data, their effect on the accuracy of the model would not be significant, as stated in the research of Klein et al. [17] and Khamis et al. [16]. As there is no limit to using the system, there would be enough variety in the training data, including the anomalies as occasional outliers, to prevent overfitting. This way, the model can be trained all the time, while the system is used, thus enabling adaptation to changes in the distribution of normal-behavior. Furthermore, the value of the loss function used for training can be used to compute a regularity score to distinguish anomalous from normal behavior.

4   Implementation

4.1   Neural Network Topology

Characteristic Normal Behavior Model – a stacked AE with two 2D convolutional and deconvolutional layer pairs. The AE is expected to learn a distribution of the input's characteristic normal behavior by learning the identity function. An input is considered normal if its reconstruction error is small.

Two different normalization methods for input data are considered in this paper: one that maps the data to $[0, 1]$ and one to $[-1, 1]$. Based on the normalization method, the outer activation functions of the AE are chosen to be σ (sigmoid) or tanh. The inner layers of the AE have a tanh activation function.

Figure 3 shows the architecture of the stacked convolutional AE used in our approach. This architecture is similar to the architecture of the AE from the spatiotemporal AE presented in [5], except this model has fewer kernels and optionally a sigmoid activation function at the input and output layers.

Fig. 3. The characteristic normal behavior model: a stacked convolutional AE; with an input tensor depth of $d = 6$.

Temporal Normal Behavior Model – two ANN architectures are implemented: a convolutional LSTM and a generic TCN inspired model consisting of stacked dilated convolutional layers. These two models are designed to be fully interchangeable. Both models learn a temporal normal behavior by mapping a sequence of inputs to a sequence of outputs of the same dimension. Since the input of the temporal model is the bottleneck of the AE, the output of the temporal model decoded by the AE.

The LSTM used in this paper consists of three convolutional LSTM cells. The architecture is similar to the temporal encoder-decoder model presented in [5] but with less kernels.

The convolutional temporal network used in this approach is a modified version of the generic TCN model described in [18]. Residual blocks are completely omitted since the aim of this model is to learn normal behavior by learning the identity function, which would be unnecessary if the original input was forwarded to the output, thus its main components are stacked dilated convolutional layers. Although this architecture differs from the generic TCN, it is a sequence model consisting only of convolutional layers, so the term TCN will be further used for it. A convention of the whole architecture is that the input and the output of the temporal model are in the domain $[-1, 1]$, thus the activation function of the last layer is set to tanh instead of ReLu. Additionally, an optional gating mechanism, similar to the gating mechanism of the LSTM, is added to the architecture. The TCN consists of three blocks, where each block has a dilated convolutional layer and a gate. A gate is also a dilated convolutional layer, but with σ activation function instead of tanh. The output of a block is the element-wise multiplication of the dilated convolutional layer's output and the gate. Thus the output sequence O of a block is:

$$O = \tanh(X *_d F + b) \otimes \sigma(X *_d G + c), \tag{1}$$

with F and G filters, b and c biases of the dilated convolution and gate, $*_d$ dilated convolution operation and $\otimes$ Hadamard product (Fig. 4).

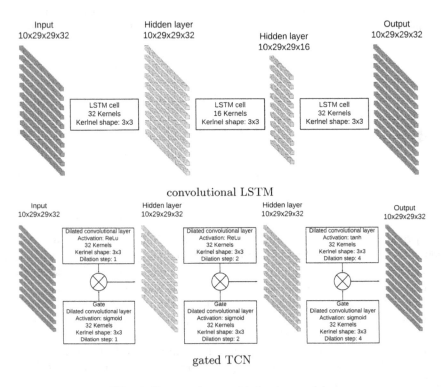

Fig. 4. Temporal normal behavior models.

4.2   Training Method

Two methods were considered for training: separate training and global training. The loss for both methods is MSE with L2 regularization.

For **separate training** the input data sequence is encoded by the AE and used as input for the decoder of the AE and for the temporal model as well. This first decoding of the AE is the characteristic reconstruction, producing the characteristic loss, which is used to update only the characteristic model. The temporal model's reconstructed sequence of features is also decoded by the AE, producing the temporal reconstruction and the temporal loss. This is used to update the temporal model only. This way, both characteristic and temporal models are trained separately ensuring that the characteristic model only learns characteristic features of the input, and the temporal model mainly learns temporal features (see Fig. 5).

For **global training** the combination of characteristic and temporal models are treated as a single neural network. Input data sequence is encoded by the AE and used as input for the temporal model. The temporal model's reconstructed

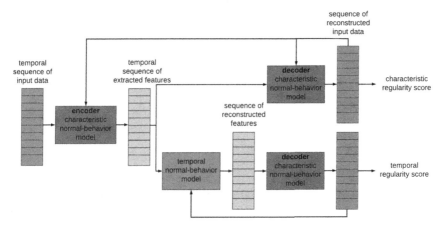

Fig. 5. Separate training of the architecture. The red arrows represent the characteristic and temporal losses. (Color figure online)

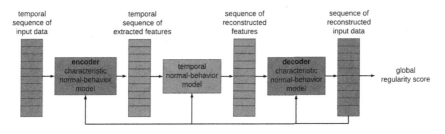

Fig. 6. Global training of the architecture. The red arrows represent the global loss. (Color figure online)

sequence of features is decoded by the AE, producing a single sequence of reconstructed inputs. This produces a global reconstruction error and loss for training both models simultaneously (see Fig. 6).

4.3 Data Preprocessing

The depth of the input tensor of the network depends on the different inputs used for the anomaly detection system; however, to be able to concatenate them, the width and height after preprocessing has to be the same. Two or more dimensional inputs e.g. RGB images or data from a sensor array are scaled to have the same dimensions, for one-dimensional inputs, a matrix of the proper shape is filled with the given value.

An additional preprocessing step is considered for inputs: by subtracting the current input from the previous one, only the changes are propagated through the network. This might enhance the learning capacity of the model as parts of the input that do not change, such as background, do not have to be learned. In this case, however, the target is sparse and has most likely many zeros and very small values and only a small amount of significant greater values. This could cause the model to learn zero mapping. To solve this, an asymmetric loss function is implemented, which penalizes the difference of a target and output element if the absolute value of the target is greater than a threshold.

4.4 Regularity Score

To evaluate the anomaly detection system, a regularity score is defined based on the reconstruction error of the network:

$$r(f) = 1 - \frac{MSE(f) - MSE_{min}}{MSE_{max} - MSE_{min}}, \tag{2}$$

where $MSE(f)$ is the mean squared error of the current frame, MSE_{min} and MSE_{max} are the minimal mean squared error and maximal mean squared error over the whole test dataset. The area under the receiver operating characteristics curve (AUC-ROC) is used to evaluate the models' performance on benchmark datasets.

The regularity score defined above can not be applied for continuous training. A similar regularity score r_{stat} is defined using the mean squared error of the model and is used to describe the regularity regarding the learned normal behavior:

$$r_{stat}(f_n) = max(min(1 - \frac{MSE(f_n) - (\mu_n - 4 \cdot \sigma_n)}{16 \cdot \sigma_n}, 1), 0), \tag{3}$$

where $MSE(f_n)$ is the mean squared error of the nth frame, μ_n and σ_n are exponentially weighted moving mean and standard deviations [23] of the MSE of preceding frames.

Additionally to r_{stat}, an other regularity score r_{stead} is used for evaluation. This measures the steadiness of the reconstruction error:

$$r_{stead}(f_n) = \frac{\sqrt{(MSE(f_n) - MSE(f_{n-w}))^2 + (s \cdot w)^2}}{\sum_{i=n-w}^{n} \sqrt{(MSE(f_i) - MSE(f_{i-1}))^2 + s^2}}, \quad (4)$$

with w observation window size and s scaling factor.

The regularity score is adapted with every new reconstruction error, as it depends on its statistics. This also means, that if an anomaly occurs frequently, it pushes the standard deviation higher, while also pushing the regularity score of the same anomaly higher. This would mean that the same anomaly would not be considered an anomaly if it occurs regularly.

5 Experiments

The implemented anomaly detection model was used in two different ways: a framework for evaluation and proof of concept on benchmark datasets and a framework for evaluation on a human-robot interaction setup.

Benchmark datasets: to check whether the method can be used for anomaly detection, it was tested on two benchmark anomaly datasets: avenue [19] and UCSD peds1 [20]. The benchmark datasets consist of training and test videos. The training videos only contain normal behavior data and the test videos contain both normal and anomalous data roughly with a proportion of 1:1.

HRI experiment: we conducted an experiment with 11 participants playing the shell-game on a human-robot collaboration table. They were asked to play the game 10 times according to the defined rules and 1 time disregarding them. During the experiment, two clusters of anomalies have emerged: irregular interactions and misplaced objects. Synchronized RGB-D images, data from the built-in 16×6 proximity sensor array [21] and game states were recorded for evaluation.

6 Evaluation

6.1 Benchmark Datasets

Models using a TCN proved to be better at detecting anomalies than using an LSTM on the benchmark datasets. Sigmoidal gates however, did not improve the performance of the TCN. Results show that using HSV encoding on images performs worse than RGB or grayscale. Although there was no significant difference when using RGB or grayscale encoding one could argue that RGB has the advantage of holding more information, while grayscale has the advantage of being smaller, thus accelerating training and evaluation.

Table 1. AUC of different models trained on the UCSD peds1 and avenue datasets.

AUC - ROC	UCSD peds1	Avenue
Discriminative framework by Del Giomo et al. [3]	N/A	0.78
Histograms of optical flow [22]	0.72	N/A
ConvAE [2]	0.81	0.70
Spatiotemporal AE [5]	0.89	0.80
Ours (TCN, difference input, global training)	0.80 (GS)	0.82 (RGB)
Ours (TCN, normal input, separate training)	0.78 (GS)	0.84 (GS)

Further investigation of the correlation between the characteristic and temporal parts of separately trained models by combining their classification result or their regularity scores shows that nearly every anomaly detected by the characteristic model is also detected by the temporal model. An additional insight is that using difference input improves performance when trained globally, but the temporal model of separate training performed better (in the case of TCNs) with normal input.

Table 1 compares the two best performing models from this paper to other published anomaly detection models based on the benchmark datasets UCSD peds1 and avenue. Both models perform similar to other models on the UCSD peds1 dataset; however, they outperform other models on the avenue dataset.

6.2 HRI Experiment

Several models with different configurations are trained and evaluated on this dataset. Data sequences of the 11 participants are sequentially processed by the anomaly detection system only once. Each model uses a TCN as temporal model. The models are different in their input channels (camera, depth camera, proximity sensor, shell-game state), image encoding (RGB, grayscale), training method (separate, global), input method (normal, difference of two consecutive frames) and gating (enabled, disabled).

Training with camera image only does not lead to significant regularity score changes even when anomalies occur. Small regularity score drops that correspond to the operator interacting with the table appear when proximity sensor data is used in the training, however irregular interactions with the table produce significantly larger score drops. This effect is slightly enhanced when depth information is also used. The proximity sensor data input channel is the most influential. One of the main reasons for this might be, that changes in sensor data are far larger than changes in other channels' data. Overall, training with more information sources still improves performance. There are no significant differences between results when using RGB or grayscale encoding.

Figure 7 shows the regularity scores of a globally and separately trained models using normal input and difference input on data sequence #1. The first misplaced object anomaly is not detected, the second irregular interaction anomaly

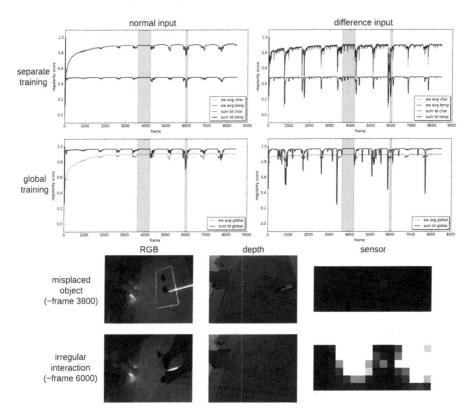

Fig. 7. Regularity scores of non-gated models trained with normal and difference input. The plots show the results on data sequence #1, trained with inputs: camera image, proximity sensor data, and depth image.

however, is indicated correctly by a large downward spike by models trained with normal input. When trained with normal input, the characteristics of the regularity scores remain the same for the separately and globally trained models. In case of training with difference input however, r_{stat} spikes remain similar and r_{stead} spikes become much larger and more frequent when training globally. All in all, training separately produces a more steady regularity score with less artifacts in case of r_{stead}, while global training has a similar effect on r_{stat}.

Using difference input results in large and frequent regularity score drops. These occur when the player regularly interacts with the collaboration table; training with normal input reduces this effect significantly. Finally, sigmoidal gates can lower the false alarm rate by suppressing regularity score drops.

The performance of the model on two Nvidia TITAN V GPUs was 20 fps for 6 input channels up to 66 fps for 1 channel.

7 Conclusion

The method described in this paper performed well on benchmark datasets while trained traditionally, especially when using stacked dilated convolutional layers as temporal model. Evaluating the continuous training approach on experiment data revealed that most irregular interaction can be detected with this method; however, misplaced objects could not be detected reliably. Nevertheless, training and evaluating different models provided valuable and interesting insights regarding preprocessing, training and using sigmoidal gates in neural networks.

Continuous training of neural networks could be important in the future, particularly in designing intelligent, general-purpose, and flexible systems. The advancement of hardware for computing neural networks makes this approach applicable in robotic systems as well. Anomaly detection, especially learning a normal behavior model, is a very well fit task to research continuous online training.

References

1. Oldenbourg, R.: Gesundheits-Ingenieur. 13, 39, 40, 163 (1890)
2. Hasan, M., et al.: Learning temporal regularity in video sequences. In: Proceedings of the IEEE Conference on Computer Vision and Pattern Recognition (2016)
3. Del Giorno, A., Bagnell, J.A., Hebert, M.: A discriminative framework for anomaly detection in large videos. In: Leibe, B., Matas, J., Sebe, N., Welling, M. (eds.) ECCV 2016. LNCS, vol. 9909, pp. 334–349. Springer, Cham (2016). https://doi.org/10.1007/978-3-319-46454-1_21
4. Medel, J.R.: Anomaly detection using predictive convolutional long short-term memory units (2016)
5. Chong, Y.S., Tay, Y.H.: Abnormal event detection in videos using spatiotemporal autoencoder. In: Cong, F., Leung, A., Wei, Q. (eds.) ISNN 2017. LNCS, vol. 10262, pp. 189–196. Springer, Cham (2017). https://doi.org/10.1007/978-3-319-59081-3_23
6. Sabokrou, M., et al.: Real-time anomaly detection and localization in crowded scenes. In: Proceedings of the IEEE Conference on Computer Vision and Pattern Recognition Workshops (2015)
7. Wang, J.H., Miao, Y.Q., Khamis, A., Karray, F., Liang, J.: Adaptation approaches in unsupervised learning: a survey of the state-of-the-art and future directions. In: Campilho, A., Karray, F. (eds.) ICIAR 2016. LNCS, vol. 9730, pp. 3–11. Springer, Cham (2016). https://doi.org/10.1007/978-3-319-41501-7_1
8. Park, C., Huang, J.Z., Ding, Y.: A computable plug-in estimator of minimum volume sets for novelty detection. Oper. Res. 58(5), 1469–1480 (2009)
9. Breaban, M., Luchian, H.: Outlier detection with nonlinear projection pursuit. Int. J. Comput. Commun. Control 8(1), 30–36 (2013)
10. Zhang, K., Hutter, M., Jin, H.: A new local distance-based outlier detection approach for scattered real-word data. Adv. Knowl. Discov. Data Min. 5476, 813–822 (2009)
11. Cabral, G.G., Oliveira, A.L.I., Cahu, C.B.G.: Combining nearest neighbor data description and structural risk minimization for one-class classification. Neural Comput. Appl. 18(2), 175–183 (2009)

12. Miao, Y.Q., Farahat, A.K., Kamel, M.S.: Locally adaptive density ratio for detecting novelty in twitter streams. In: The 6th International Workshop on Modeling Social Media (MSM) - Behavioral Analytics in Social Media, Big Data and the Web, pp. 799–804 (2015)
13. Song, L., Teo, C.H., Smola, A.J.: Relative novelty detection. In: International Conference on Artificial Intelligence and Statistics (AISTATS), pp. 536–543 (2009)
14. Sodemann, A.A., Ross, M.P., Borghetti, B.J.: A review of anomaly detection in automated surveillance. IEEE Trans. Syst. Man Cybern. Part C (Appl. Rev.) **42**(6), 1257–1272 (2012)
15. Chen, Z., Li, W.: Multisensor feature fusion for bearing fault diagnosis using sparse autoencoder and deep belief network. IEEE Trans. Instrum. Meas. **66**(7), 1693–1702 (2017)
16. Khamis, A., et al.: The effects of outliers data on neural network performance. JApSc **5**(8), 1394–1398 (2005)
17. Klein, B.D., Rossin, D.F.: Data quality in neural network models: effect of error rate and magnitude of error on predictive accuracy. Omega **27**(5), 569–582 (1999)
18. Bai, S., Kolter, J.Z., Koltun, V.: An empirical evaluation of generic convolutional and recurrent networks for sequence modeling. arXiv preprint arXiv:1803.01271 (2018)
19. Lu, C., Shi, J., Jia, J.: Abnormal event detection at 150 fps in matlab. In: Proceedings of the IEEE International Conference on Computer Vision (2013)
20. Mahadevan, V., et al.: Anomaly detection in crowded scenes. In: 2010 IEEE Computer Society Conference on Computer Vision and Pattern Recognition. IEEE (2010)
21. Alagi, H., Navarro, S.E., Mende, M., Hein, B.: A versatile and modular capacitive tactile proximity sensor. In:2016 IEEE Haptics Symposium (HAPTICS), Philadelphia, PA, pp. 290–296 (2016). https://doi.org/10.1109/HAPTICS.2016.7463192
22. Wang, T., Snoussi, H.: Histograms of optical flow orientation for abnormal events detection. In:2013 IEEE International Workshop on Performance Evaluation of Tracking and Surveillance (PETS). IEEE (2013)
23. Finch, T.: Incremental calculation of weighted mean and variance. Univ. Cambridge **4**(11–5), 41–42 (2009)

Algorithms of Posteriori Multi-objective Optimization for Robotic Gripper Design

Quyen Vu[1] and Andrey Ronzhin[2]

[1] Department of Electromechanics and Robotics, SUAI, Bolshaya Morskaya Street, 67, 190000 St. Petersburg, Russia
vuquyenntk@gmail.com

[2] Laboratory of Autonomous Robotic Systems, St. Petersburg Federal Research Center of the Russian Academy of Sciences (SPC RAS), 14-th line of V.I., 39, 199178 St. Petersburg, Russia
ronzhin@iias.spb.su

Abstract. In this paper, the posteriori methods, such as NSGA-II, MOGWO and MOPSO, are considered in solving multicriteria optimization problems. The main goal of these methods is to find set of non-dominated solutions or Pareto front using Pareto dominance. A kinematic description of the processed four-finger gripper prototype for picking tomatoes, its objective functions and constraint functions are presented. The main advantage of this prototype is that it uses the same driver to simultaneously control the movements of the fingers and the suction nozzle. Three optimization cases are considered: optimization of two objective functions, optimization of objective functions, and optimization of all objective functions simultaneously. To optimize the task of multi-objective functions, a normalized weighted objective function with weightage factors is used. The results of optimizing the kinematic gripper design using posteriori methods method performance measure are presented. Depending on the selected objective functions, we can choose a set of sizes of kinematic gripper elements.

Keywords: Multi-objective optimization · Optimal gripper design · NSGA-II · MOGWO · MOPSO

1 Introduction

The development of autonomous robotic harvesting requires the integration of several subsystems, including crop detection, path planning and manipulations. Gripper can be considered as the most important component of harvesting robots, because it directly touches and interacts with agricultural products [1, 2].

To develop a gripper mechanism, an optimization process is needed to determine the length links of the mechanism by forming a target [3]. The task of optimizing the gripper mechanism has several conflicting goals with a complex search space. Thus, solving the problem is very difficult with conventional optimization methods.

There are various methods for solving multipurpose optimization problems, but they can be divided into the following types: a priori methods, a posteriori methods and

© Springer Nature Switzerland AG 2020
A. Ronzhin et al. (Eds.): ICR 2020, LNAI 12336, pp. 308–318, 2020.
https://doi.org/10.1007/978-3-030-60337-3_30

interactive methods [4–7]. In a priori methods, multiple objectives are combined into a single objective by using a weight for each objective, which allows us to define the importance of objectives. The main drawback of this method is that the choice of weights for each objective function before the loop leads to inaccuracies and repeated calculations with different sets of weights. In the posteriori methods, all objective functions are optimized simultaneously, and the decision-making process is required only after the optimization process to select one of the solutions. In the interactive methods, decision makers are involved during the optimization process. In addition to the greater opportunity for the decision maker to adjust, adapt or adjust preferences compared to both of the above methods, the interactive methods encounter difficulties in determining information about preferences and reusing previous preferences, the general limit of interactive multipurpose optimization methods relies on the Pareto-front [5].

In this study, we describe posteriori multi-objective optimization algorithms used for the design of agriculture robotic gripper. In Sect. 2, the algorithms of the three posteriori methods are presented, including NSGA-II and MOGWO and MOPSO. Section 3 describes the kinematic scheme of gripper for picking tomatoes and the objective functions for optimizing gripper sizes. Section 4 presents the results of optimization, and finally, Sect. 5 presents conclusions and prospects of the study.

2 Posteriori Multi-objective Optimization Algorithms

All three of posteriori methods mentioned above begin with randomly initializing variable values in the search space. Solutions are compared by Pareto dominance, a set of non-dominated solutions that satisfy conditions known as the Pareto front, or a set of optimal solutions. The difference between the methods is to maintain and improve the set of optimal solutions after each loop. The flow chart of these methods is shown in Fig. 1.

The nondominated sorting genetic algorithm II (NSGA-II) is one of the most widely used algorithms for solving multi-objective optimization problems, which is based on the non-dominated sorting genetic algorithm [8]. The main features of the NSGA-II algorithm are: (1) the use of quick non-dominant sorting to reduce computational complexity, (2) the use of an elitist strategy to expand the sample space and improve the accuracy of optimization results (3) the use of crowding distance to select the best solutions.

The multi-objective grey wolf optimization (MOGWO) algorithm imitates the hierarchy of leadership and the mechanism of "hunting grey wolves in nature" [9]. Those solutions are equivalent to alpha, beta, and delta wolves. The hunting process consists of three phases: searching phase, encircling phase, and the attack phase. The mathematical model of the behavior of the encircling phase is presented in the following equations:

$$\vec{D} = \left| \vec{C} \cdot \vec{X}_p(t) - \vec{X}(t) \right|; \tag{1}$$

$$\vec{X}(t+1) = \vec{X}_p(t) - \vec{A} \cdot \vec{D}, \tag{2}$$

where: t is the current iteration, $\vec{A}$ and $\vec{C}$ are the coefficient vectors, $\vec{X}_p$ is the position vector of prey, and $\vec{X}$ indicates the position vector of the grey wolf. To simulate how the

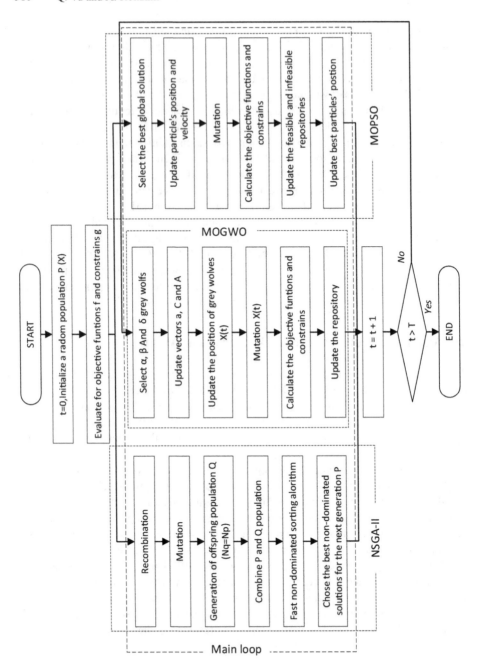

Fig. 1. Flow chart of posteriori multi-objective optimization algorithms.

position of each wolf is indicated using the alpha, beta, and delta wolves, the following equation was proposed in the original MOGWO:

$$\vec{X}(t+1) = \frac{\vec{X}_1 + \vec{X}_2 + \vec{X}_3}{3}, \tag{3}$$

where $\vec{X}_p, \vec{X}_p,$ and $\vec{X}_p$ are calculated as follows:

$$\vec{D}_\alpha = \left| \vec{C}_1 \cdot \vec{X}_\alpha - \vec{X} \right|, \vec{D}_\beta = \left| \vec{C}_1 \cdot \vec{X}_\beta - \vec{X} \right|, \vec{D}_\delta = \left| \vec{C}_1 \cdot \vec{X}_\delta - \vec{X} \right|, \tag{4}$$

$$\vec{X}_1 = \vec{X}_\alpha - \vec{A}_1 \cdot \vec{D}_\alpha, \vec{X}_2 = \vec{X}_\beta - \vec{A}_2 \cdot \vec{D}_\beta, \vec{X}_3 = \vec{X}_\delta - \vec{A}_3 \cdot \vec{D}_\delta. \tag{5}$$

The multiple objective particle swarm optimization algorithm (MOPSO) is a population-based search algorithm based on modeling the social behavior of birds within a flock [10]. In the search space, each particle is defined by a coordinate point and speed of movement. Vector $\vec{X}$ is the particle position vector, the length of which is equal to the number of task variables; $\vec{V}$ is the particle velocity vector. The mathematical model for describing the change in particle position depending on the velocity is as follows [11]:

$$\vec{X}_i(t+1) = \vec{X}_i(t) + \vec{V}_i(t+1), \tag{6}$$

where t is the iteration number, i is the index of the i-th particle.
The equation for updating the velocity in the MOPSO is as follows:

$$\vec{V}_i(t+1) = w\vec{V}_i(t) + c_1 r_1(\vec{P}_{bi}(t) - \vec{X}_i(t)) + c_2 r_2(\vec{G}_i(t) - \vec{X}_i(t)), \tag{7}$$

where w is the inertial weight, r_1 and r_2 are random number in $[0, 1]$, c_1 is the social intelligence coefficient, c_2 is the cognitive intelligence coefficient, $P_{bi}(t)$ indicates the position of the best solution obtained by the i-th particle, and $G(t)$ is the position of the best solution found by the entire swarm at t-th iteration.

3 Kinematic Description of Gripper for Harvesting Tomatoes

The kinematic description of the four-finger gripper for picking tomatoes [12, 13] is shown in Fig. 2. The vector of variables is $X = [a, b, c, e, h, \alpha]^T$, where a, b, c, e, h are grippers sizes, α is angle between links a and b; β, γ are angles of joints with horizontal lines; P is the actuation force; F is the gripping force exerted by the gripping fingers at the contact point.

The geometric dependencies of the grippers mechanisms are presented in the following formulas:

$$\gamma = 2\tan^{-1}\frac{1 - \sqrt{1 + A^2 - B^2}}{B - A}; \beta = 2\tan^{-1}\frac{1 - \sqrt{1 + A^2 - C^2}}{C + A}, \tag{8}$$

where:

$$A = \frac{z}{h - e}; B = \frac{c^2 + (h - e)^2 + z^2 - a^2}{2c(h - e)}; C = \frac{a^2 + (h - e)^2 + z^2 - c^2}{2a(h - e)}. \tag{9}$$

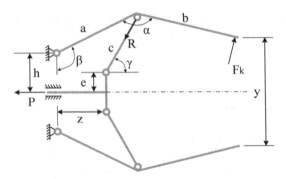

Fig. 2. Scheme of the robot gripper mechanism.

From the figure, we can write the following:

$$F_k = \frac{Pa\cos(\gamma - \beta)}{4(b - a\cos\alpha)\cos\gamma},$$ (10)

$$y(X, z) = 2(h - a\cos\beta + b\cos(\alpha + \beta)).$$ (11)

To optimize the size of this gripper, the following main objective functions are used:

1. The function, which describes the difference between the maximum and minimum gripping forces:

$$f_1(X) = \max_z F_k(X, z) - \min_z F_k(X, z),$$ (12)

where $\max_z F_k(X, z)$, $\min_z F_k(X, z)$ are the maximum and minimum gripping force respectively, where $z_{min} < z < z_{max}$.

2. The function, which describes the force transmission ratio between the gripper actuator and the gripper ends:

$$f_2(X) = \frac{P}{\min_z F_k(X, z)} = \frac{4(b - a\cos\alpha)\cos\gamma}{a\cos(\gamma - \beta)}, \text{ when } z = z_{min}.$$ (13)

3. The function, which describes the shift transmission ratio between the gripper actuator and the gripper ends:

$$f_3(X) = \left| \frac{z_{max} - z_{min}}{y(X, z_{max}) - y(X, z_{min})} \right|.$$ (14)

4. The function, which describes the lengths of all elements of the gripper:

$$f_4(X) = \sum_{i=1}^{L} l_i = a + b + c + e + h,$$ (15)

where l_i – length of the i-th element of the gripping mechanism.

5. The function that describes the force of the gripping mechanism:

$$f_5(X) = \left| \frac{\max\limits_{z} F_k(X, z)}{P} \right|. \tag{16}$$

The following main constraints that relate to geometric constraints and the limitation of the minimum gripping force are considered:

1. $g_1(X) = y(X, z_{\min}) - D_{\min} \le 0$; 2. $g_2(X) = D_{\max} - y(X, z_{\max}) \le 0$;
3. $g_3(X) = C^2 - 1 - A^2 \le 0$;   4. $g_4(X) = e - h \le 0$;   (17)
5. $g_5(X) = B^2 - 1 - A^2 \le 0$;   6. $g_6(X) = -1 - C \le 0$,

where D_{min}, D_{max} – minimum and maximum diameter of tomatoes.

4 Experiment Results of Optimization

The initial data for programming the task of optimizing the sizes of the gripper are presented in Table 1, and the parameters for multi-objective optimization are presented in the Table 2.

Table 1. Parameters of gripper.

Parameter description	Symbol	Value
Actuator force	P	10 (N)
Size of tomatoes	D_{min}	40 (mm)
	D_{max}	100 (mm)
The displacement of gripper	z_{min}	0 (mm)
	z_{MAX}	100 (mm)
Size of gripper mechanisms	a	[20, 100] (mm)
	b	[50, 100] (mm)
	c	[20, 100] (mm)
	e	[10, 50] (mm)
	h	[20, 80] (mm)
	α	[1.6, 3.0] (rad)

To optimize the task of multi-objective functions, a normalized weighted objective function is used as follows:

$$F(X) = w_1 \left[\frac{f_1(X)}{f_1^*} \right] + w_2 \left[\frac{f_2(X)}{f_2^*} \right] + w_3 \left[\frac{f_1(X)}{f_3^*} \right] + w_4 \left[\frac{f_4(X)}{f_4^*} \right] + w_4 \left[\frac{f_5(X)}{f_5^*} \right], \tag{18}$$

where $f_1^*, f_2^*, f_3^*, f_4^*, f_5^*$ are the normalizing average values of objective functions, w_1, w_2, w_3, w_4, w_5 are weightage factors for the objective functions. By combining the weightage factors, the results of optimization are presented in Tables 3, 4 and 5.

Table 2. Parameters for optimization algorithms.

Description	NSGA-II	MOGWO	MOPSO
Number of individuals in the population P	200	200	200
Number of iteration, T	500	500	500
Crossover fraction, m_c	2	–	–
Probability of mutation	0.1	0.1	0.1
Maximum speed (%)	–	–	4
Repository size	–	50	50
Inertial weight, w	–	–	0.4
Social intelligence coefficient, c_1	–	–	2
Cognitive intelligence coefficient, c_2	–	–	1

Table 3. Optimization results by NSGA-II algorithm.

w_1	w_2	w_3	w_4	w_5	F	a	b	c	e	h	α
1.000	0	–	–	–	1.252	56.47	51.24	52.77	15.45	58.55	2.971
0.750	0.250	–	–	–	2.240	55.13	51.03	54.86	15.00	59.87	2.932
0.500	0.500	–	–	–	3.256	55.09	51.02	54.98	15.00	59.93	2.930
0.250	0.750	–	–	–	4.027	55.56	51.10	54.20	15.15	59.45	2.944
0	1	–	–	–	5.197	55.80	51.13	53.82	15.22	59.21	2.951
–	–	1	0	0	5.738	55.57	51.10	54.20	15.15	59.45	2.945
–	–	0.500	0.250	0.250	1.249	56.47	51.24	52.77	15.45	58.55	2.971
–	–	0.250	0.500	0.250	2.208	55.13	51.03	54.86	15.00	59.87	2.932
–	–	0	1.000	0	3.093	55.09	51.02	54.98	15.00	59.93	2.930
–	–	0.250	0.250	0.500	3.979	55.56	51.10	54.20	15.15	59.45	2.944
–	–	0	0	1	4.860	55.80	51.13	53.82	15.22	59.21	2.951
0.250	0.125	0.125	0.250	0.250	1.249	56.47	51.24	52.77	15.45	58.55	2.971
0.125	0.125	0.250	0.250	0.250	2.208	55.13	51.03	54.86	15.00	59.87	2.932
0.125	0.250	0.125	0.250	0.250	3.093	55.09	51.02	54.98	15.00	59.93	2.930
0.125	0.250	0.250	0.250	0.125	3.979	55.56	51.10	54.20	15.15	59.45	2.944
0.250	0.250	0.250	0.125	0.125	4.860	55.80	51.13	53.82	15.22	59.21	2.951

Table 4. Optimization results by MOGWO algorithm.

w_1	w_2	w_3	w_4	w_5	F	a	b	c	e	h	α
1.000	0	–	–	–	1.286	55.60	50.92	51.57	15.84	45.28	2.660
0.750	0.250	–	–	–	2.433	55.13	51.03	54.86	15.00	59.87	2.932
0.500	0.500	–	–	–	3.522	55.09	51.02	54.98	15.00	59.93	2.930
0.250	0.750	–	–	–	4.611	55.56	51.10	54.20	15.15	59.45	2.944
0	1.000	–	–	–	5.674	55.80	51.13	53.82	15.22	59.21	2.951
–	–	1	0	0	3.282	55.21	51.51	52.51	28.50	59.79	2.669
–	–	0.500	0.250	0.250	2.499	55.96	50.03	51.75	26.66	59.65	2.807
–	–	0.250	0.500	0.250	2.242	51.13	51.15	53.18	17.46	26.69	2.862
–	–	0	1.000	0	2.310	54.20	50.60	53.55	19.52	53.16	2.716
–	–	0.250	0.250	0.500	1.816	55.62	51.39	55.47	15.18	59.99	2.809
–	–	0	0	1.000	2.571	55.65	50.95	55.01	15.22	59.61	2.830
0.250	0.125	0.125	0.250	0.250	2.295	55.94	50.17	54.08	16.27	59.36	2.841
0.125	0.125	0.250	0.250	0.250	2.623	55.36	50.51	53.84	16.39	57.71	2.838
0.125	0.250	0.125	0.250	0.250	2.862	55.84	50.03	54.15	15.34	58.63	2.831
0.125	0.250	0.250	0.250	0.125	3.288	55.96	50.03	51.75	23.66	59.65	2.806
0.250	0.250	0.250	0.125	0.125	3.160	54.744	51.20	52.65	24.71	56.73	2.710

To compare the obtained results, two quantitative measures on the performance of multi-objective optimization are: algorithm effort (AE) and ration of non-dominated individuals (RNI) [14]. The algorithm effort can be assessed as follows:

$$AE = \frac{T_{run}}{N_{eval}},\qquad(19)$$

where T_{run} is the simulation time, and N_{eval} is the total number of objective function evaluated over in T_{run}. The lower AE value, the less computational costs are required for the optimization algorithm.

The ration of non-dominated individuals can be assessed as follows:

$$RNI = \frac{N_{non\_dom}}{N_P},\qquad(20)$$

where N_{non_dom} is the number of non-dominated individuals in population P while N_P is the size of population P, $RNI \in [\,0\ 1\,]$. Figure 3 shows the simulation results of 20 independent runs and it is presented as a box plot [15].

The simulation results show that MOGWO has the smallest AE and RNI is the highest, so this is the best algorithm when judged with other two methods on the above performance measures. The NSGA-II method has the longest computation time, which can be explained by the repeated procedure for sorting the elements of a new set with a doubled number of elements. The advantage of MOPSO over MOGWO is that it

Table 5. Optimization results by MOPSO algorithm.

w_1	w_2	w_3	w_4	w_5	F	a	b	c	e	h	α
1.000	0	–	–	–	1.874	54.67	50.53	54.49	15.46	56.80	2.852
0.750	0.250	–	–	–	2.992	55.38	50.20	55.28	15.58	59.55	2.758
0.500	0.500	–	–	–	4.056	55.61	51.49	52.55	19.45	57.87	2.853
0.250	0.750	–	–	–	5.119	54..7	50.50	55.29	15.29	57.39	2.735
0	1.000	–	–	–	6.165	55.71	51.39	53.55	15.00	58.00	2.953
–	–	1.000	0	0	2.716	56.26	55.38	49.33	21.08	48.47	2.722
–	–	0.500	0.250	0.250	2.809	59.61	57.54	48.31	22.18	58.63	2.753
–	–	0.250	0.500	0.250	2.602	60.97	50.44	47.74	18.50	57.69	2.767
–	–	0	1	0	2.226	46.43	51.66	58.29	18.24	48.04	2.794
–	–	0.250	0.250	0.500	2.621	60.97	50.44	47.74	18.50	57.69	2.767
–	–	0	0	1.000	2.408	61.00	50.29	47.74	17.31	57.83	2.767
0.250	0.125	0.125	0.250	0.250	2.355	55.57	50.58	53.88	15.08	57.21	2.851
0.125	0.125	0.250	0.250	0.250	2.721	55.43	51.10	55.29	15.25	58.49	2.760
0.125	0.250	0.125	0.250	0.250	2.896	55.32	50.67	54.87	15.57	59.89	2.860
0.125	0.250	0.250	0.250	0.125	3.464	55.61	51.49	52.55	19.45	57.87	2.853
0.250	0.250	0.250	0.125	0.125	3.305	55.57	50.77	52.77	19.59	59.25	2.892

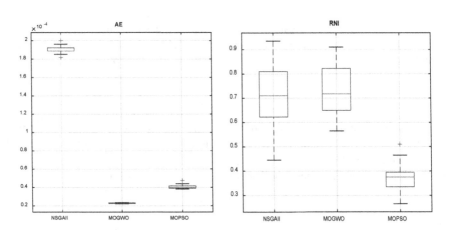

Fig. 3. Box plots for the measures of *AE* and *RNI*.

expands the search space for the global leader to an infeasible repository. However, these advantages are not shown in the above two assessment methods. The further study will be focused on implementation of the evaluated algorithms for design grippers in agriculture and industry application with using various types of sensors for accurate capturing manipulating objects [16–20].

5 Conclusion

The main goal of this study was to analyze the posteriori methods in solving multi-criteria optimization problems. Kinematic design is an important issue for improving the performance of robot modules such as grippers. However, optimization problems with many different goals and limitations become extremely difficult with conventional methods. Therefore, the use of posteriori multi-objective optimization algorithms are effective solutions and are widely used in many areas.

A kinematic description of the design of the four-finger gripper for picking tomatoes and the results of size optimization using the NSGA-II, MOGWO and MOPSO method are presented. The simulation results show that MOGWO is the algorithm with the most advantages in both estimation methods: calculation time and number of non-dominant individuals. Depending on the selected target function and their weight coefficients, we can choose a set of optimal sizes when processing the gripper for picking tomatoes.

Acknowledgments. The presented work was supported by the Russian Science Foundation (grant No. 16-19-00044П).

References

1. Nagoev, Z.V., Denisenko, V.A., Lyutikova, L.A.: System of autonomous robot machine vision for agricultural application in mountain territories based on the multi-agent cognitive architectures. Sustain. Dev. Mt. Territ. **10**(2), 289–297 (2018)
2. Pavliuk, N., Saveliev, A., Cherskikh, E., Pykhov, D.: Formation of modular structures with mobile autonomous reconfigurable system. In: Ronzhin, A., Shishlakov, V. (eds.) Proceedings of 14th International Conference on Electromechanics and Robotics "Zavalishin's Readings". SIST, vol. 154, pp. 383–395. Springer, Singapore (2020). https://doi.org/10.1007/978-981-13-9267-2_31
3. Monkman, G.J., Hesse, S., Ralf, S., Schunk, H.: Robot Grippers. Wiley-VCH, Weinheim (2007)
4. Mirjalili, S., Dong, J.S.: Multi-Objective Optimization using Artificial Intelligence Techniques. Springer, Cham (2020). https://doi.org/10.1007/978-3-030-24835-2
5. Rapoport, E.Y., Pleshivtseva, Y.E.: Method of multiobjective optimization of controlled systems with distributed parameters. SPIIRAS Proc. **5**, 64–96 (2018). https://doi.org/10.15622/sp.60.3
6. Neydorf, R.A., Aghajanyan, A.G.: Dual optimization of monochrome images tone approximation using parallel evolutionarily genetic search. SPIIRAS Proc. **5**, 156–188 (2018). https://doi.org/10.15622/sp.60.6
7. Meignan, D., Knust, S., Frayret, J.: A review and taxonomy of interactive optimization methods in operations research. ACM Trans. Interact. Intell. Syst. **5**(3), 1–43 (2015)
8. Srinivas, N., Deb, K.: Multiobjective function optimization using nondominated sorting genetic algorithms. IEEE Trans. Evol. Comput. **2**(3), 221–248 (1994)
9. Mirjalili, S., Mirjalili, S.M., Lewis, A.: Grey wolf optimizer. Adv. Eng. Softw. **69**, 46–61 (2014)
10. Poli, R., Kennedy, J., Blackwell, T.: Particle swarm optimization. Swarm Intell. **1**, 33–57 (2007)

11. Eberhart, R.C., Shi, Y.: Particle swarm optimization: developments, applications and resources. In: 2001 Congress on Evolutionary Computation, pp. 81–86. IEEE, Seoul (2001)
12. Vu, Q., Ronzhin, A.: A model of four-finger gripper with a built-in vacuum suction nozzle for harvesting tomatoes. In: Ronzhin, A., Shishlakov, V. (eds.) Proceedings of 14th International Conference on Electromechanics and Robotics "Zavalishin's Readings". SIST, vol. 154, pp. 149–160. Springer, Singapore (2020). https://doi.org/10.1007/978-981-13-9267-2_13
13. Vu, Q., Ronzhin, A.: Models and algorithms for design robotic gripper for agricultural products. Comptes Rendus de L'Academie Bulgare des Sci. **73**(1), 103–110 (2020). https://doi.org/10.7546/CRABS.2020.01.13
14. Tan, K.C., Lee, T.H., Khor, E.F.: Evolutionary algorithms for multi-objective optimization: performance assessments and comparisons. Artif. Intell. Rev. **17**, 251–290 (2002)
15. Chambers, J.M., Cleveland, W.S., Kleiner: Graphical Methods for Data Analysis. Wadsworth & Brooks, Cole (1983)
16. Pavliuk, N., Smirnov, P., Kondratkov, A., Ronzhin, A.: Connecting gripping mechanism based on iris diaphragm for modular autonomous robots. In: Ronzhin, A., Rigoll, G., Meshcheryakov, R. (eds.) ICR 2019. LNCS (LNAI), vol. 11659, pp. 260–269. Springer, Cham (2019). https://doi.org/10.1007/978-3-030-26118-4_25
17. Iakovlev, R., Denisov, A., Prakapovich, R.: Iterative method for solving the inverse kinematics problem of multi-link robotic systems with rotational joints. In: Ronzhin, A., Shishlakov, V. (eds.) Proceedings of 14th International Conference on Electromechanics and Robotics "Zavalishin's Readings". SIST, vol. 154, pp. 237–251. Springer, Singapore (2020). https://doi.org/10.1007/978-981-13-9267-2_20
18. Saveliev, A., Pshchelko, N., Krestovnikov, K.: Method of sensitivity calculation for electrete diaphragm capacitive sensors. In: International Conference on Developments in eSystems Engineering, DeSE, pp. 721–725, Springer, Cham (2019). https://doi.org/10.1109/dese.2019.00134
19. Krestovnikov, K.D., Cherskikh, E.O., Saveliev, A.I.: Investigation of the influence of the length of the intermediate magnetic circuit on the characteristics of magnetic gripper for robotic complexes of the mining industry. J. Min. Inst. **241**(1), 46–52 (2020). https://doi.org/10.31897/pmi.2020.1.46
20. Gorbach, N., Usina, E., Shabanova, A., Iakovlev, R.: Calculation methodology for power characteristics of electroadhesive contact for gripping conductive and dielectric objects. In: Ronzhin, A., Shishlakov, V. (eds.) Proceedings of 14th International Conference on Electromechanics and Robotics "Zavalishin's Readings". SIST, vol. 154, pp. 697–705. Springer, Singapore (2020). https://doi.org/10.1007/978-981-13-9267-2_58

Energy-Efficient Path Planning Algorithm on Three-Dimensional Large-Scale Terrain Maps for Mobile Robots

Konstantin Zakharov$^{(\boxtimes)}$ (ID), Anton Saveliev (ID), and Oleg Sivchenko

St. Petersburg Institute for Informatics and Automation of the Russian Academy of Sciences, 39, 14th Line, 199178 St. Petersburg, Russia
konstantizaharov@gmail.com

Abstract. This paper presents an algorithm for energy-efficient path planning for robotic systems in three-dimensional maps, called Local Roughness Local Height Difference A* (LRLHD-A*). This algorithm is an extension of A* algorithm; it uses local irregularities of the surface and local height differences to reveal static obstacles, as well as a metric for edge weight determination. Approbation of this algorithm in the Gazebo simulation environment revealed that the distance between the start and target points has no substantial effect on the duration of planning process, using this algorithm. Experimental comparison of performance efficiency of the actual algorithm with relevant alternatives showed, that the LRLHD-A* algorithm traces paths 4–15 times faster, than the most successful analogous algorithm LRLHD-Dijkstra. The path, established at output of our algorithm, outperforms similar algorithms from the A* group in energy efficiency by 1.3–6.3%. This is because the LRLHD-A* algorithm not only ensures finding of the shortest path to the target point, but also accounts for energy consumption of the robot on the route, based on the terrain features and specificity of motion within it.

Keywords: Path planning · Energy efficiency · Navigation graph · Irregular terrain · Three-dimensional reconstruction · Orthophotomap

1 Introduction

Currently the applied tasks, concerning autonomous navigation of robotic systems (RS) are of particular interest. Performing of such tasks assumes exploration of surface, in which the terrain is investigated for obstacles and other impassable areas on it. Equipment of robotic vehicles by autonomous navigation systems is relevant in various applied domains, such as: environmental conservation, agriculture, search operations, mapping. Therefore, energy efficiency depends on path length, surface features and terrain properties. In this context, robot paths should be optimized to achieve the least-cost solutions in every particular environment.

Robot path optimization in the process of servicing of large areas can be performed, particularly, using a prearranged orthophotomap of the area [1, 2]. Orthophotomap is

© Springer Nature Switzerland AG 2020
A. Ronzhin et al. (Eds.): ICR 2020, LNAI 12336, pp. 319–330, 2020.
https://doi.org/10.1007/978-3-030-60337-3_31

a kind of land maps, which enables quite realistic representation of the terrain. For orthophotomap composition, satellite images can be used, as well images, captured from an unmanned aerial vehicle (UAV) [3]. Using photogrammetry means, the orthophotomap can be transformed into a three-dimensional representation of the actual map. Such three-dimensional model provides detailed data on surface features, containing all the irregularities of the surface and local height differences [4]. Besides, in contrast to planar maps, it realistically depicts mutual positions of the objects. This type of maps is often utilized in context of RS navigation [5–7]. Further we consider existing relevant approaches to implementation of autonomous robotic navigation.

2 Related Work

The design and implementation of path finding algorithms is currently an extensive research domain. Let us consider several most important developments, described in recent papers. Paper [5] proposes a real-time navigational system for land-based robots. The system is conceptually represented as a grid. This system uses a cloud of points in the three-dimensional environment, obtained using a camera, mounted on a mobile platform, to establish a navigational grid of triangular cells in real-time mode [8, 9]. The weight of edge between two grid vertices is calculated depending on the distance between these vertices, complexity of their accessibility, average slope angle for the areas, adjacent to these vertices and maximum height differences between neighbor vertices [10]. The presented approach was successfully approbated in street environment using the VolksBot XT robot.

In [11], a novel path planning algorithm is presented for mobile robots, moving on uneven surfaces. This algorithm Bidirectional dynamic-domain transition based RRT (BiDDTRRT) is a combination of two RRT-like algorithms: Transition-based RRT (T-RRT) and Dynamic-Domain RRT (DD-RRT). The T-RRT algorithm shifts the area of path search to the areas, more favorable for motion. The DD-RRT algorithm is employed to reduce probability of selection of edge point on the map. The cost function in this algorithm is directly proportional to the least angle between the force vector, exerted on the center of mass of the robot, and the vector, directed from the center of mass of the robot to the middle of each edge among those, which establish the bottom plane of the robot. Authors compared the performance of BiDDTRRT algorithm with the performance of other RRT-like algorithms RRT, such as Bidirectional RRT (BiRRT) and Bidirectional Transition-based RRT (BiTRRT). According to the experimental results, the BiDDTRRT algorithm shows increased probability to find a low-cost path.

In [6], the authors showed a numeric approach to counting of missed/covered areas in the terrain. Utilization of this algorithm ensures full map coverage, irrespective of its geometrical features and the chosen angle of motion. The experimental results, obtained in test areas, showed, that utilization of the developed approaches ensure revealing of 2–14% passable areas on terrain map than the alternative approaches.

In [7], a path planning system in three-dimensional environment is presented. This system uses for path planning the enhanced RRT algorithm. This algorithm is called RRT* Goal Limit (RRT* GL), as it is obtained through merging of two other algorithms: RRT* Goal, which with greater probability extends the tree toward the target point, and

RRT* Limits, which, having found the possible path, increases the probability to select the point within the area, where this path has been traced. The outcomes of performance testing for algorithms from the RRT (RRT, RRT*, RRT* Goal, RRT* Limits, RRT* GL) family suggest, that the algorithm RRT* GL has the best performance and finds the optimum path in fewer iterations, than alternative algorithms.

In [12], a heuristic Z* algorithm for energy-efficient path planning is presented, where the path is traced in irregular terrain, represented as a connected graph. Energy efficiency in this case depends on the surface slope angle and distance between graph vertices, as well from local skin friction coefficient and robot weight. If the surface slope angle is too large, and the vehicle cannot reach the target point directly, the algorithm constructs jagged path to it. Experiments with different robots were performed to trace paths using D-Dopt, D-Eopt, Z* and basic Z* algorithms.

Increased demand for mobile robotic platforms for use in irregular terrains and powered from batteries, encouraged deeper research of energy efficient path planning [13–17]. When the robot moves across uneven surface, it is important to ensure robust orientation of the robot in motion [18]. Also, during ascent or descent the velocity has to be respected, which the robot has, when passing these path segments [19]. If dynamical obstacles occur in the way of the robot, the path has to be replanned [20–24].

This paper considers the problem of RS path planning in three-dimensional maps, containing over 60 thousand vertices and 120 thousand triangles. To solve it, an A*-based algorithm LRLHD-A* is proposed, which ensures energy-efficient path planning, based on local surface irregularities and local height differences as on metrics for edge weight calculation. To establish a three-dimensional representation of the terrain, an orthophotomap, stitched from UAV-captured images, is used in this paper. To reveal static obstacles and plan a path for RS motion, the three-dimensional map is presented as a connected graph.

3   Robotic Navigation in a Three-Dimensional Uneven Terrain

In our solution, the input data for path planning problem on the three-dimensional map are: connected graph, representing the real-world area, start vertex in the graph, corresponding to the current location of the robot, as well the target vertex in the graph and limit values of the parameters, describing the terrain features. The problem is formulated as follows: it is necessary to find a path from the start vertex to the target vertex, bypassing the obstacles and taking into account the terrain features. Having revealed the obstacles and calculated the edge weights, we establish an energy-efficient path from start to target, represented as an ordered set of graph vertices, sequentially connected with edges.

To reach the target vertex, the RS should sequentially pass all the vertices on the path, beginning from the start one. Thereby the robot should bypass all the obstacles on the way without collisions. In our solution, the navigation of the RS is established according to the following flowchart (see Fig. 1).

To reveal all the terrain irregularities, a three-dimensional terrain representation has to be prepared. In this paper for the establishment of a three-dimensional terrain representation an orthophotomap is used, stitched from a set of UAV-captured images

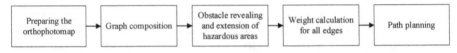

Fig. 1. Flowchart of the proposed solution for robot navigation.

[25]. Upon processing of all the images, a three-dimensional terrain model is built, represented as a set of vertices and edges, connecting them.

Before proceeding to search of impassable areas and plan path on a three-dimensional map, such a connected graph has to be composed upon this map, that the vertices of it correspond to the dots on a previously composed three-dimensional terrain model, connected by edges. The algorithm receives the established three-dimensional model as input and connects with edges those vertices, that belong to a common triangle. As result a connected graph is obtained, each vertex of which is a point, specified by coordinates x, y, z.

Before path planning, it is necessary to reveal in the terrain all areas, impassable for the robotic device: pits, steep slopes, all terrain irregularities, where the vehicle can turn over or stick. To do this, local irregularity has to be calculated and maximum local height difference for each vertex.

Local irregularity is the surface curvature, caused by the height differences. The irregularity of the area $p(v)$, adjacent to vertex v, is expressed as an average slope angle of the plane for the nearest vertices $N_l(v)$, which are positioned at distance less than l, from the vertex v. The angle between the vertex normals is calculated according to formula $c_r^{(u,v)} = acos(n(u) * n(v))$, and the average angle $a_{av}(v)$ is calculated according to (1), where $N_{d(v)}$ are all nearest neighbors of v.

$$a_{av}(v) = \frac{\sum_{u \in N_d(v)} c_r^{(u,v)}}{|N_d(v)|}, \tag{1}$$

$$p(v) = \frac{\left(a_{av}(v) + \sum_{u \in N_l(v)} a_{av}(u)\right)}{|N_l(v)| + 1}. \tag{2}$$

To reveal surface irregularities, gulleys, ravines, local height difference estimation should be employed. Local height difference $b(v)$ reflects maximum height span between the v vertex and every vertex of $N_l(v)$, and is calculated according to (3), where $v(z)$ and $u(z)$ are the coordinate values of z-component of vertices v and u, respectively.

$$b(v) = \max_{u \in N_l(v)} |v(z) - u(z)|. \tag{3}$$

The vertices, whose local irregularity or local height difference values exceeds certain limit, are labeled as obstacles and excluded from graph. Boundaries of areas, where the obstacles sit, are extended by a margin, comparable to robot size, such, that all the points of the established path would be enough spaced from the areas, which are hazardous for the robot to move. The gradual inflation algorithm smoothly decreases the weight of the vertices, positioned at distances from r_i to r_o from the area, where the obstacle is situated. The parameter $r(v)$ reflects the spacing of the v vertex from the closest obstacle and is calculated according to formula (4):

$$r(v) = c_{max} * \left(\cos\left(\frac{d_{lethal} - r_i}{r_o - r_i} * \pi \right) + 1 \right), \tag{4}$$

where c_{max} – maximum total cost, and d_{lethal} – the least distance to obstacle.

For global path planning, final edge weights have to be calculated. The final weight $c(u, v)$ for each edge $e(u, v) \in E$ is calculated according to (5)

$$C^{(u,v)} = ((k_p * \max(p(u), p(v))) + 1)^* \\ *((k_b * \max(b(u), b(v))) + 1) * d^{(u,v)} + |r(u) - r(v)|, \tag{5}$$

where k_p and k_b are used to determine effects of irregularity p and local height difference b on edge weight change, and $d(u, v)$ represents Euclidean distance between vertices u and v. The environment of the robot is represented as a connected graph $G_v = (V_v, E_v)$, where the vertices V_v, bounding triangular planes and having unique coordinates (x, y, z), are connected by edges E_v. Further we proceed to detailed consideration of developed path planning algorithm.

Figure 2 shows the flowchart of the LRLHD-A* algorithm. Path search using the LRLHD-A* algorithm is initiated from the start vertex of the graph. At the first stage the path cost to the vertices is calculated, adjacent to the start one. The cost is calculated as the aggregate weight of all edges to be traversed to reach the vertex in question. Besides the aggregate edge weight, a parent is assigned to each vertex, that is, the one, from which the current vertex has been reached. During path planning, different paths to the same vertex are considered; should the new path cost less, than already existing one, it is assigned a new cost and a new parent. Having traversed all the vertices, adjacent to current one, we add the examined vertex to an unordered set C, containing all the visited vertices. Thereby the neighbor vertices, adjacent to the current one, are added to the unordered set O, containing the vertices to be considered. Then the one vertex from the O set is considered, whose Euclidean distance to the target one would be the shortest, provided, that this vertex is not included yet in the C set. Then the algorithm proceeds to traverse the neighbors of the considered vertex. The path search finishes if the current vertex reveals to be the current one. Should the O set become empty during search, it means that the path from start to target cannot be planned. The path planning is implemented via sequential retrieval of vertex parents and addition of every of them to the start of the ordered set P. The parent retrieval process begins from the target vertex and ends with the start one.

When the algorithm LRHLD-A* finishes, if the target vertex has been reached from the start one, then the P set will be populated with the sequence of vertices, where every preceding one is connected via an edge with the next one (excluding the last one).

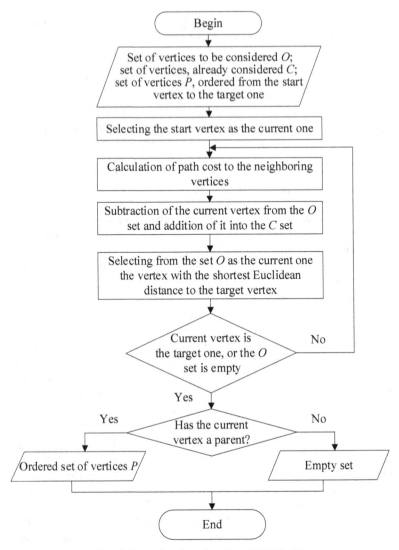

Fig. 2. Path planning algorithm LRLHD-A*.

4   Experiment Results

For approbation of the developed solution the robotic simulation environment Gazebo was chosen, into which the three-dimensional model was transferred, composed of the orthophotomap. The Fig. 3 shows the path, traced using the LRLHD-A* algorithm, where the white dots label the vertices of the traced path.

To test the passability of the path, a model of 4-wheel robotic vehicle Pioneer 3AT was used. During Gazebo experiments, the influence of physical factors of the environment on the robot was modeled. The experiments showed that the robot moves along the traced

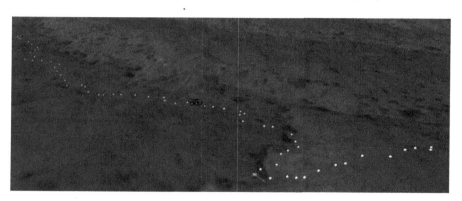

Fig. 3. Visualization of the traced path in Gazebo environment.

path without sticking and turnovers. The Fig. 4 shows visualization of a map fragment in the three-dimensional reference system, where red dots label the vertices on the path.

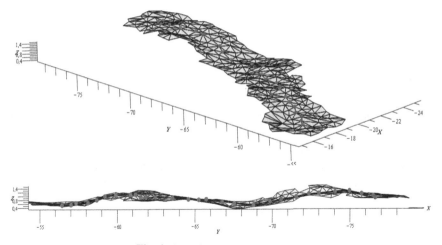

Fig. 4. Map fragment visualization.

As follows from the Fig. 4, the path composed with the LRLHD-A* algorithm, runs through the vertices with the least height differences compared to neighbor ones. The test results confirm that the paths established by this algorithm are energy-efficient indeed. The obtained path runs through the vertices with the least local irregularities and the least height differences compared to neighbor ones, as well redundant in length.

Some tests also were performed, comparing the path planning performance with the LRLHD-A* algorithm versus the algorithms from the A* family: using only local irregularity and distance (LR-A*), local height difference and distance (LHD-A*), distance only as a metric (A*) and the Dijkstra algorithm, which employs the local height difference (LRLHD-Dijkstra). The following characteristics were compared: time, spent for path planning, number of dots, examined by the algorithm, path length and cost, represented as aggregate cost of all edges, calculated according to (5). Algorithm testing was performed on a three-dimensional terrain map, containing 100082 vertices and 198580 triangles. For experiments a subset of 10 pairs of randomly chosen vertices was chosen, among which the path was traced using different algorithms. Test results are given in Figs. 5, 6, 7 and 8.

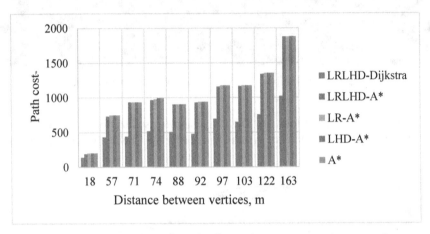

Fig. 5. Path cost dependency from the distance between start and target vertices.

As Fig. 5 shows, the path found by the LRLHD-Dijkstra algorithm, reveals to be 1.5–2 times more energy-efficient in average, compared to other tested algorithms. This is because the LRLHD-Dijkstra respects all the vertices of the graph and finds the least cost path from the start vertex to all others, including the target one. At the same time, the developed algorithm LRLHD-A* constructs the path, whose energy-efficiency is 1.3–6.3% higher, than in other algorithms of A* family, considered here. So, LRLHD-A* is less efficient than LRLHD-Dijkstra, but better than other A*-like solutions. Figure 6 shows the dependency of path planning time from the distance between the start and the target vertices for different algorithms.

As Fig. 6 shows, the algorithm LRLHD-Dijkstra requires a 10 times longer period to find the path, than the other algorithms under investigation. This is because the path planning experiments were performed in a quite big map, containing 100082 vertices and 198580 polygons. The LRLHD-Dijkstra finishes the search, having found paths to every vertex in the graph, including the target one, whereas the algorithms from the A* family utilize a heuristic function to consider first those paths, which lead to the target. Such algorithms finish the search, having found the target vertex. The developed algorithm LRLHD-A* proceeds 4–15 times faster, than the LRLHD-Dijkstra algorithm, and its execution time is comparable to those in the other algorithms of the A* family (6–11.5 s). Further compare the dependencies of path planning time from path length for the algorithms LRLHD-A* and LRLHD-Dijkstra. Figure 7 shows the dependency of path planning time from the path length for the algorithms LRLHD-A* and LRLHD-Dijkstra.

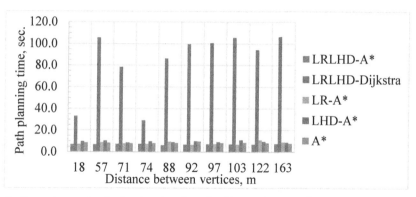

Fig. 6. Dependency of path planning time from the distance between the start and target vertices.

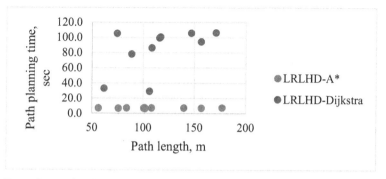

Fig. 7. Dependency of path planning time from the path length for the algorithms LRLHD-A* and LRLHD-Dijkstra.

Figure 7 shows that no direct dependency exists between path planning time and its length from vertex to vertex for both LRLHD-Dijkstra and LRLHD-A* algorithms. Despite the fact that LRLHD-Dijkstra considers all vertices, accessible from the start one, hence, the number of the vertices, traversed by the algorithm, influences its performance in greater amount, than the path length, as follows from the Fig. 8.

Points in Fig. 8 characterize the dependency of path planning time from the number of considered vertices for the algorithms LRLHD-A* and LRLHD-Dijkstra. As follows from the Fig. 8, the number of the considered vertices for the LRLHD-A* algorithm changes from 100 to 350 whereby the path planning time amounts to 7 s in average. In turn, the number of vertices considered by LRLHD-Dijkstra algorithm in every experiment changes from 20000 to 40000, where the path planning time changes from 30 to 110 s. So, by 1.7-fold increase of vertex number under consideration, the proceeding time of LRLHD-Dijkstra algorithm increases in 3–3.5 times. For this reason, with overall map growth, the path planning time on it using the LRLHD-Dijkstra algorithm will increase significantly. Compared to the LRLHD-Dijkstra for the same map, the LRLHD-A* algorithm proceeds 4–15 faster with no essential decline in quality.

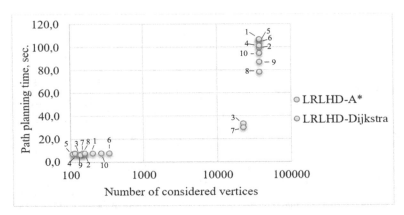

Fig. 8. Dependency of path planning time from the number of considered vertices for the algorithms LRLHD-A* and LRLHD-Dijkstra. Each dot is accompanied by the number of the test pair (formed in the course of comparison of two algorithms), to which it belongs.

Upon results of the approbation, distance between the vertices and the number of the vertices considered have virtually no influence on the path planning time, when using the LRLHD-A* algorithm. It is also revealed that the path planned with the LRLHD-A* algorithm is about 1.3–6.3% more energy-efficient, compared to the output of the other algorithms of the A* family, considered here. This is because the LRLHD-A* algorithm leverages local irregularities and local height differences as a metric for obstacle detection and edge weight calculation, whereas the LR-A* and LHD-A* algorithms rely on one of these parameters as a metric. The algorithm A* uses only the distance between the vertices.

Greater energy-efficiency of the path, established by the LRLHD-A* algorithm, established here, compared to equivalent efficiency, pertinent to the other algorithms of the A* family, enables the robotic vehicle to cover greater distances without battery recharge.

5   Conclusion

In this paper the LRLHD-A* algorithm was proposed for path planning in a three-dimensional terrain map, represented as a graph. The developed algorithm as well as other path planning algorithms (LRLHD-Dijkstra, LR-A*, LHD-A* and A*) were approbated in the Gazebo simulation environment. It was revealed that the LRLHD-A* algorithms finds the solution 4–15 times faster than the LRLHD-Dijkstra algorithm. Also, the LRLHD-A* algorithm shows greater path planning energy-efficiency by 1.3–6.3% better than the other algorithms of the A* family, considered in the paper. Further research will be aimed to boost the speed of this algorithm and accommodate it for swarm control of robotic vehicles [26–28].

References

1. Smith, M.W., Carrivick, J.L., Quincey, D.J.: Structure from motion photogrammetry in physical geography. Prog. Phys. Geogr. **40**(2), 247–275 (2016)
2. Uysal, M., Toprak, A.S., Polat, N.: DEM generation with UAV photogrammetry and accuracy analysis in Sahitler hill. Measurement **73**, 539–543 (2015)
3. Samad, A.M., Kamarulzaman, N., Hamdani, M.A., Mastor, T.A., Hashim, K.A.: The potential of unmanned aerial vehicle (UAV) for civilian and mapping application. In: 2013 IEEE 3rd International Conference on System Engineering and Technology, pp. 313–318. IEEE (2013)
4. Muchiri, N., Kimathi, S.: A review of applications and potential applications of UAV. In: Proceedings of Sustainable Research and Innovation Conference, pp. 280–283 (2016)
5. Pütz, S., Wiemann, T., Sprickerhof, J., Hertzberg, J.: 3D navigation mesh generation for path planning in uneven terrain. IFAC-PapersOnLine **49**(15), 212–217 (2016)
6. Hameed, I.A., la Cour-Harbo, A., Osen, O.L.: Side-to-side 3D coverage path planning approach for agricultural robots to minimize skip/overlap areas between swaths. Robot. Auton. Syst. **76**, 36–45 (2016)
7. Aguilar, W.G., Morales, S.G.: 3D environment mapping using the kinect V2 and path planning based on RRT algorithms. Electronics **5**(4), 70 (2016)
8. Breitenmoser, A., Siegwart, R.: Surface reconstruction and path planning for industrial inspection with a climbing robot. In: 2012 2nd International Conference on Applied Robotics for the Power Industry (CARPI), pp. 22–27. IEEE (2012)
9. Deeken, H., Puetz, S., Wiemann, T., Lingemann, K., Hertzberg, J.: Integrating semantic information in navigational planning. In: ISR/Robotik 2014; 41st International Symposium on Robotics, pp. 1–8. VDE (2014)
10. Schwarz, M., Behnke, S.: Local navigation in rough terrain using omnidirectional height. In: ISR/Robotik 2014; 41st International Symposium on Robotics, pp. 1–6. VDE (2014)
11. Jun, J.Y., Saut, J.P., Benamar, F.: Pose estimation-based path planning for a tracked mobile robot traversing uneven terrains. Robot. Auton. Syst. **75**, 325–339 (2016)
12. Ganganath, N., Cheng, C.T., Chi, K.T.: A constraint-aware heuristic path planner for finding energy-efficient paths on uneven terrains. IEEE Trans. Ind. Inform. **11**(3), 601–611 (2015)
13. Sun, Z., Reif, J.H.: On finding energy-minimizing paths on terrains. IEEE Trans. Robot. **21**(1), 102–114 (2005)
14. Krüsi, P., Furgale, P., Bosse, M., Siegwart, R.: Driving on point clouds: motion planning, trajectory optimization, and terrain assessment in generic nonplanar environments. J. Field Robot. **34**(5), 940–984 (2017)
15. Ganganath, N., Cheng, C.T., Chi, K.T.: Finding energy-efficient paths on uneven terrains. In: 2014 10th France-Japan/8th Europe-Asia Congress on Mecatronics (MECATRONICS2014-Tokyo), pp. 383–388. IEEE (2014)
16. Liu, J., Yang, J., Liu, H., Tian, X., Gao, M.: An improved ant colony algorithm for robot path planning. Soft. Comput. **21**(19), 5829–5839 (2017)
17. Yuan, Q., Lu, Q., Xi, Z.: Optimal path selection for mobile robots based on energy consumption assessment of different terrain surface. In: 2017 36th Chinese Control Conference (CCC), pp. 6755–6760. IEEE (2017)
18. Shum, A., Morris, K., Khajepour, A.: Direction-dependent optimal path planning for autonomous vehicles. Robot. Auton. Syst. **70**, 202–214 (2015)
19. Yuan, W., Ganganath, N., Cheng, C.T., Qing, G., Lau, F.C.: A consistent heuristic for efficient path planning on mobility maps. In: 2017 IEEE 18th International Symposium on a World of Wireless, Mobile and Multimedia Networks (WoWMoM), pp. 1–5. IEEE (2017)
20. Ganganath, N., Cheng, C.-T., Tse, C.K.: Rapidly replanning A*. In: International Conference on Cyber-Enabled Distributed Computing and Knowledge Discovery (2016)

21. Ganganath, N., Cheng, C.T., Tse, C.K.: An improved dynamic Z* algorithm for rapid replanning of energy-efficient paths. In: International Conference on Cyber-Enabled Distributed Computing and Knowledge Discovery (2015)
22. Ganganath, N., Cheng, C.T., Chi, K.T.: Multiobjective path planning on uneven terrains based on NAMOA. In: 2016 IEEE International Symposium on Circuits and Systems (ISCAS), pp. 1846–1849. IEEE (2016)
23. Mandow, L., De La Cruz, J.L.P.: Multiobjective A* search with consistent heuristics. J. ACM (JACM) **57**, 1–25 (2010)
24. Oral, T., Polat, F.: MOD* lite: an incremental path planning algorithm taking care of multiple objectives. IEEE Trans. Cybern. **46**(1), 245–257 (2015)
25. Aksamentov, E., Zakharov, K., Tolopilo, D., Usina, E.: Approach to robotic mobile platform path planning upon analysis of aerial imaging data. In: Ronzhin, A., Shishlakov, V. (eds.) Proceedings of 15th International Conference on Electromechanics and Robotics "Zavalishin's Readings". SIST, vol. 187, pp. 93–103. Springer, Singapore (2021). https://doi.org/10.1007/978-981-15-5580-0_7
26. Pavliuk, N., Saveliev, A., Cherskikh, E., Pykhov, D.: Formation of modular structures with mobile autonomous reconfigurable system. In: Ronzhin, A., Shishlakov, V. (eds.) Proceedings of 14th International Conference on Electromechanics and Robotics "Zavalishin's Readings". SIST, vol. 154, pp. 383–395. Springer, Singapore (2020). https://doi.org/10.1007/978-981-13-9267-2_31
27. Pavliuk, N., Smirnov, P., Kondratkov, A., Ronzhin, A.: Connecting gripping mechanism based on iris diaphragm for modular autonomous robots. In: Ronzhin, A., Rigoll, G., Meshcheryakov, R. (eds.) ICR 2019. LNCS (LNAI), vol. 11659, pp. 260–269. Springer, Cham (2019). https://doi.org/10.1007/978-3-030-26118-4_25
28. Pavliuk, N., Smirnov, P.A., Kovalev, A.D.: Functional module formation based on homogeneous units of modular autonomous reconfigurable system (MARS). Inf.-Meas. Control Syst. **17**(5), 14–20 (2019)

Author Index

Printed in the United States
By Bookmasters